THE NEW EMPIRE
OF DIOCLETIAN AND CONSTANTINE

THE NEW EMPIRE
OF DIOCLETIAN
AND CONSTANTINE

TIMOTHY D. BARNES

HARVARD UNIVERSITY PRESS

CAMBRIDGE, MASSACHUSETTS, AND LONDON, ENGLAND

1982

Library of Congress Cataloging in Publication Data

Barnes, Timothy David.
  The new empire of Diocletian and Constantine.

  "Conceived as a companion volume to Constantine
and Eusebius"—Pref.
  Bibliography: p.
  Includes indexes.
  1. Rome—Politics and government—284–476.
2. Diocletian, Emperor of Rome, 245–313.
3. Constantine I, Emperor of Rome, d. 337. I. Title.
DG313.B3   937′.08′0922   81–6569 ✓
ISBN 0-674-61126-8   AACR2

La méthode historique professe qu'aucune source d'information ne peut être negligée. Tout le monde en convient; mais trop d'historiens paraissent encore ne pas connaître l'importance des infiniment petits.

PAUL PEETERS
Recherches d'Histoire et de Philologie Orientales

PREFACE

The present work was conceived as a companion volume to *Constantine and Eusebius,* to argue in detail dates and facts which are there assumed and made the basis for historical interpretation and synthesis. It has inevitably also become an independent work of reference, for it sets out to establish the basic factual framework for a period in the history of the Roman Empire which is both obviously significant and notoriously obscure. Nevertheless, its scope continues to reflect its genesis. I have not attempted to solve all the problems posed by the imperial coinage or the legal sources, nor to draw up lists either of court and financial officials or of military commanders. The emphasis lies on emperors and imperial chronology (Part One), on the holders of the highest administrative posts and provincial governors (Part Two), and on the administration of the empire (Part Three) — and even within these restricted fields I have usually refrained from drawing general conclusions from the individual facts documented.

The work has been revised and largely rewritten several times, and I am most grateful to friends who have read one or more of the drafts, either in whole or in part, and proposed many improvements — Drs. A. K. Bowman, P. Brennan, and J. R. Rea, and Professors G. W. Bowersock, E. J. Champlin, H. A. Drake, J. F. Gilliam, C. Habicht, C. P. Jones, P. Kussmaul, F. G. B. Millar, and Sir Ronald Syme. Their comments, particularly those of Glen Bowersock, Christian Habicht, and Fergus Millar, have made the final version far more accurate than it would otherwise have been. Nonetheless, I am sure that many mistakes and omissions must remain, and I hope that readers who notice any errors or oversights will either inform me privately or publish the necessary corrections as rapidly as possible.

I must also express my gratitude to Donna Burns, Margaret von Sant, and Maria Pezzot for typing and retyping a difficult and complicated manuscript.

T. D. B.

CONTENTS

TABLES

STEMMATA

EDITIONS OF LITERARY AND
LEGAL SOURCES

The following standard editions of the most important literary and legal sources have been used in compiling the present work, and all substantive deviations from the text of these editions have (in principle) been noted.

Chr. Min. 1
: *Chronica Minora Saec. IV. V. VI. VII,* ed. T. Mommsen, 1. *Monumenta Germaniae Historica,* Auctores Antiquissimi 9 (Berlin, 1892)

Chr. Pasch.
: *Chronicon Paschale,* ed. L. Dindorf, 1 (*Corpus Scriptorum Historiae Byzantinae* 4: Bonn, 1832). (The list of consuls from 509 B.C. to A.D. 394 and some historical entries are printed by T. Mommsen in *Chr. Min.* 1.205–245.)

CJ
: *Codex Iustinianus,* ed. P. Krüger, *Corpus Iuris Civilis* 2¹⁴ (Berlin, 1967)

CJ 1.51.1ᴹ
: The superscript M indicates the acceptance of T. Mommsen's emendation of the date or place of issue (*Ges. Schr.* 2 (Berlin, 1905), 267–290)

CTh
: *Codex Theodosianus,* ed. T. Mommsen, published under the title *Theodosiani Libri XVI cum Constitutionibus Sirmondianis* 1.2³ (Berlin, 1962)

CTh 13.10.2ˢ
: The superscript S indicates the acceptance of O. Seeck's emendation of the heading and/or the subscription (*Regesten* 159–185)

Const. Sirm.	*Constitutiones Sirmondianae,* in *Codex Theodosianus,* ed. T. Mommsen, 907–921
Constantine, *Oratio*	*Eusebius Werke* 1: *Das Leben Konstantins,* ed. I. A. Heikel, *GCS* 7 (Leipzig, 1902), 149–192
Epitome	*Sexti Aurelii Victoris Liber de Caesaribus,* ed. F. Pichlmayer, reprinted with addenda and corrigenda by R. Gründel (Leipzig: Teubner, 1961), 131–176
Eusebius, *HE*	*Eusebius Werke* 2: *Die Kirchengeschichte,* ed. E. Schwartz, *GCS* 9.1 (Leipzig, 1903); 9.2 (Leipzig, 1908)
Eusebius, *Mart. Pal.* (L)	Eusebius, *The Ecclesiastical History and the Martyrs of Palestine,* translated by H. J. Lawlor and J. E. L. Oulton, 1 (London, 1927), 327–400. A translation of the ancient Syriac published by W. Cureton, *History of the Martyrs of Palestine by Eusebius, Bishop of Caesarea, discovered in a very ancient Syriac manuscript* (London, 1861), with variant readings noted from: (1) fragments of the Syriac version published by S. E. Assemani, *Acta Martyrum Orientalium et Occidentalium* 2 (Rome, 1748), 169–209; (2) the surviving fragments of the original Greek, published by H. Delehaye, *Anal. Boll.* 16 (1897), 113–139, and incorporated by E. Schwartz in his edition of the short recension (*GCS* 9.2.911–950); and (3) fragments of Latin versions collected in B. Violet, *TU* 14.4 (1896).
Eusebius, *Mart. Pal.* (S)	*Eusebius Werke* 2: *Die Kirchengeschichte,* ed. E. Schwartz, *GCS* 9.2 (Leipzig, 1908) 907–950
Eusebius, *VC*	*Eusebius Werke* 1.1: *Über das Leben des Kaisers Konstantin,* ed. F. Winkelmann (Berlin, *GCS,* 1975)
Eutropius, *Brev.*	*Eutropi Breviarium ab Urbe condita cum versionibus Graecis,* ed. H. Droysen. *Monumenta Germaniae Historica,* Auctores Antiquissimi 2 (Berlin, 1878)
Festal Index	Index to Athanasius' Festal Letters, translated by E. Payne Smith, in A. Robertson, *Select Writings and Letters of Athanasius, Bishop of Alexandria* (*Nicene and Post-Nicene Fathers,* Second Series 4 (Oxford and New York, 1892), 503–506. The Syriac original, together with an English translation, was published by W. Cureton, *The Festal Letters of Athanasius* (London, 1848).
Frag. Vat.	*Fragmenta quae dicuntur Vaticana,* in *FIRA*[2] 2.461–540
Jerome, *Chronicle*	*Eusebius Werke* 7: *Die Chronik des Hieronymus*[2], ed. R. Helm, *GCS* 47 (Berlin, 1956). References are normally given to the page of Helm's edition with the superscript letter which there precedes the relevant entry (e.g., 227[a])

Lactantius, Mort. Pers.	*Lucii Caecilii de Mortibus Persecutorum liber vulgo Lactantio tributus,* ed. S. Brandt, *CSEL* 27 (Vienna, 1897), 171–238. Two more recent editions have been published: by J. Moreau, in two volumes with a valuable commentary (*SC* 39 (Paris, 1954)), and by F. Corsaro (Catania, 1970). Both offer some improvements to Brandt's text, but Brandt's repertory of modern conjectures remains indispensable for the study of a text which depends on a single manuscript with many obvious corruptions and lacunae. (I am extremely grateful to Professor J. Rougé for allowing me to inspect the revision of Moreau's text (based on a fresh collation of the manuscript) which he has prepared for the series *Sources Chrétiennes.*)
Mos. et Rom. *legum collatio*	*Mosaicarum et Romanarum legum collatio,* in *FIRA*² 2. 541–589
Optatus	*S. Optati Milevitani libri vii,* ed. K. Ziwsa, *CSEL* 26 (Vienna, 1893)
Origo	*Excerpta Valesiana,* ed. J. Moreau (Leipzig: Teubner, 1961, with later editions revised by L. Velkov), 1–10: *Pars Prior.* I have here employed an abbreviated form of the title which appears in the manuscript: *Origo Constantini Imp(erato)ris.* (This text is cited by many modern scholars as "Anon. Val. 1" or *"Exc. Val. 1."*)
Pan. Lat.	*XII Panegyrici Latini,* ed. R. A. B. Mynors (Oxford: O.C.T., 1964). The speeches are here cited by the two numbers which appear at the head of each page in this edition.
Victor, *Caes.*	*Sexti Aurelii Victoris Liber de Caesaribus,* ed. F. Pichlmayr, reprinted with addenda and corrigenda by R. Gründel (Leipzig: Teubner, 1961), 75–129
Zosimus	*Zosimus Historia Nova,* ed. L. Mendelssohn (Leipzig: Teubner, 1887)

COLLECTIONS OF DOCUMENTS

EOMIA	C. H. Turner and others, *Ecclesiae Occidentalis Monumenta Iuris Antiquissima* (Oxford, 1899–1939)
FIRA[2]	*Fontes Iuri Romani Antejustiniani*[2] 1: *Leges,* ed. S. Riccobono (Florence, 1941); 2: *Auctores,* ed. J. Baviera; *Liber Syro-Romanus,* trans. C. Ferrini and J. Furlani (Florence, 1940); 3: *Negotia,* ed. V. Arangio-Ruiz (Florence, 1943).
Opitz, *Urkunden*	H.-G. Opitz, *Urkunden zur Geschichte des arianischen Streites 318–328. Athanasius Werke* 3.1 (Berlin and Leipzig, 1934). (I am extremely grateful to Professor W. Schneemelcher for sending me a checklist of documents to be included in his planned continuation of this collection.)
Soden, *Urkunden*	H. von Soden and H. Lietzmann, *Urkunden zur Entstehungsgeschichte des Donatismus.*[2] *Kleine Texte* 122 (Berlin, 1950)
Sotgiu 1	G. Sotgiu, *Iscrizioni latine della Sardegna* 1 (Cagliari, 1966)

MODERN WORKS

MOST FREQUENTLY CITED

BHG	F. Halkin, *Bibliotheca Hagiographica Graeca,* 3rd edition, in three volumes (*Subsidia Hagiographica* 8a, 1957), with *Auctarium* (*Subsidia Hagiographica* 47, 1969).
BHL	*Bibliotheca Hagiographica Latina antiquae et mediae aetatis,* in two volumes (*Subsidia Hagiographica* 6, 1898–1901), with *Supplementum,* 2nd edition (*Subsidia Hagiographica* 12, 1911)
BHO	P. Peeters, *Bibliotheca Hagiographica Orientalis* (*Subsidia Hagiographica* 10, 1910)
Chastagnol, *Fastes*	Chastagnol, *Les Fastes de la Préfecture de Rome au Bas-Empire. Études prosopographiques* 2 (Paris, 1962)
*Clavis*²	E. Dekkers, *Clavis Patrum Latinorum*². *Sacris Erudiri* 3 (Steenbrugge, 1961)
Comm. Mart. Rom.	H. Delehaye and others, *Propylaeum ad Acta Sanctorum Decembris. Martyrologium Romanum ad formam editionis typicae scholiis historicis instructum* (Brussels, 1940)
Jones, *LRE*	A. H. M. Jones, *The Later Roman Empire 284–602. A Social, Economic and Administrative Survey* (Oxford, 1964). (The pagination of the English edition is here employed: to convert to the American add 1070 to all page references to the third volume.)
Kolbe, *Statthalter*	H.-G. Kolbe, *Die Statthalter Numidiens von Gallien bis Constantin (268–320). Vestigia* 4 (Munich, 1962).

Lallemand, *L'administration*

J. Lallemand, *L'administration civile de l'Égypte de l'avènement de Dioclétien à la création du diocèse (284–382). Mémoires de l'Académie royale de Belgique,* Classe des Lettres 57. 2 (Brussels, 1964)

Millar, *Emperor*

F. Millar, *The Emperor in the Roman World (31 BC–AD 337)* (London, 1977)

Moreau, *Lactance*

J. Moreau, *Lactance: De la Mort des Persécuteurs. Sources Chrétiennes* 39 (Paris, 1954)

PLRE 1

A. H. M. Jones, J. R. Martindale and J. Morris, *The Prosopography of the Later Roman Empire* 1: A.D. 260–395 (Cambridge, 1971)

Seeck, *Geschichte*

O. Seeck, *Geschichte des Untergangs der antiken Welt* 1³ (Berlin, 1910); 2², 3² (Stuttgart, 1921); 4 (Berlin, 1911); 5 (Berlin, 1913); 6 (Stuttgart, 1920–21)

Seeck, *Regesten*

O. Seeck, *Regesten der Kaiser und Päpste für die Jahre 311 bis 476 n. Chr. Vorarbeit zu einer Prosopographie der christlichen Kaiserzeit* (Stuttgart, 1919)

Seston, *Dioclétien*

Dioclétien et la Tétrarchie 1: *Guerres et Réformes. Bibliothèque des Écoles françaises d'Athènes et de Rome* 162 (Paris, 1946)

Stein, *Bas-Empire* 1²

E. Stein, *Histoire du Bas-Empire,* 1, translated and revised by J.-R. Palanque (Paris/Bruges, 1959): two volumes, one of text and one of notes, with the pagination of the original *Geschichte des spätrömischen Reiches* 1 (Vienna, 1928) marked throughout

Vandersleyen, *Chronologie*

C. Vandersleyen, *Chronologie des préfets d'Égypte de 284 à 395. Collection Latomus* 55 (Brussels, 1962)

OTHER ABBREVIATIONS

The abbreviations used in citing papyri and ostraca conform in general to those proposed by J. Oates, R. Bagnall, and W. Willis, *Checklist of Editions of Greek Papyri and Ostraca*[2] (*Bulletin of the American Society of Papyrologists,* Supplement 1, 1978), while those used in citing inscriptions and periodical publications conform in general to the usage set out in the *American Journal of Archaeology* 82 (1978), 3–10. As an additional guide, the bibliography states the full title of all periodical publications cited in an abbreviated form. The names of ancient writers are not abbreviated; their works are often cited in an abbreviated form, but the full titles can easily be discovered with reference to the *Oxford Classical Dictionary*[2] (Oxford, 1970), ix–xix; H. G. Liddell, R. Scott, and W. S. Jones, *Greek-English Lexicon*[9] (Oxford, 1940), xvi–xxxviii; and G. W. H. Lampe, *A Patristic Greek Lexicon* (Oxford, 1961), ix–xliii.

PART ONE

EMPERORS

CHAPTER I

THE IMPERIAL COLLEGE

Diocletian was proclaimed Augustus on 20 November 284 and in 285 defeated the only other emperor then reigning. The following lists provide the names, rank, and order of seniority of those emperors whom the senior emperor recognized as his colleagues between 285 and 9 September 337, when the three surviving sons of Constantine were proclaimed Augusti.[1] Documentation is deliberately selective, concentrating on the evidence for the exact date at which each man entered and departed from the imperial college.[2] For the full official names, only the cases where some uncertainty exists are documented or discussed.[3]

1. For four of the eight colleges distinguished below, see the examples of the imperial titulature printed in Chapter III; for the others, see respectively *ILS* 657 (3), 663 (5), 712 (6), 724 (8).

The principles governing the order of seniority are inferred partly from the actual order of names, partly from explicit indications in ancient writers, principally Lactantius, *Mort. Pers.* 18.5, 25.5, 28.1, 32.3, cf. J. Straub, *Vom Herrscherideal in der Spätantike* (Stuttgart, 1939), 37 ff. There seem to be three main principles: (1) Augusti precede Caesars; (2) within each rank, precedence depends on the order of *dies imperii,* apparently regardless of the date at which a Caesar was promoted to Augustus; (3) seniority among two or more emperors of the same rank who have the same *dies imperii* is determined by age or antecedent seniority.

2. The Julian years are confirmed by a mass of papyrological evidence (Chapter III.3).

3. For the attestation of the names, see especially the following indexes: *RIC* 6.689–697; 7.721–727; *ILS* 3, pp. 303–310; F. Preisigke, *Wörterbuch der griechischen Papyrusurkunden* 3 (Berlin, 1931), 66–68; Supp. 1 (Amsterdam, 1971), 348–350.

1. The "First Tetrarchy"

Diocletian (C. Aurelius Valerius Diocletianus)	Augustus 20 November 284; abdicated 1 May 305[4]
Maximian (M. Aurelius Valerius Maximianus)	Caesar 21 July 285;[5] Augustus 1 April 286;[6] abdicated 1 May 305
Constantius (M. Flavius Valerius Constantius)	Caesar 1 March 293[7]
Galerius (C. Galerius Valerius Maximianus)	Caesar 1 March 293[8]

2. The "Second Tetrarchy"

Constantius	Augustus 1 May 305;[9] died 25 July 306[10]
Galerius	Augustus 1 May 305

4. *P. Beatty Panopolis* 2.162–164, 170, 187–188, 199, 260–261; Lactantius, *Mort. Pers.* 17.1 (accession), 19.1 ff. (abdication of Diocletian and Maximian). For the latter, the *Consularia Constantinopolitana* have 1 April 304 (*Chr. Min.* 1.231).

Diocletian's original *nomen* was Valerius (Victor, *Caes.* 39.1 ff.), while Maximian's was Aurelius (*Epitome* 40.10). *I. Didyma* 89, 90 (before 293) give Diocletian's *praenomen* as Marcus.

5. Maximian took the purple in 285, before his campaign against the Bagaudae (*Pan. Lat.* 10(2).3.1, 4.1), and he was a Caesar before becoming Augustus (Eutropius, *Brev.* 9.20.3). Hence the *dies festus imperatoris vestri* which the *Passio Marcelli* attests on 21 July 298 will be the anniversary of the day on which Diocletian created Maximian Caesar, as conjectured by J. Carcopino, *Le Maroc antique* (Paris, 1943), 378. (For editions of the *Passio,* see Chapter X.1; it should be observed that the *natalis imperatoris* of Recension M, 1a (H. Delehaye, *Anal. Boll.* 41 (1923), 260) occurs in a passage which is a manifest interpolation.) A. Rouselle, *Dialogues d'Histoire Ancienne* 2 (1976), 445 ff., argues that Maximian's *dies imperii* fell between 10 and 31 December 285.

6. *Chr. Min.* 1.229. A receipt dated by Maximian on 31 March 286 (*BGU* 1090, col. 4.34–39) was not necessarily written on that day, see Vandersleyen, *Chronologie* 36. The earliest indubitable attestations of Maximian as Augustus appear to be on 24 May (*BGU* 922) and 12 June 286 (*P. Oxy.* 1260). It might conceivably be relevant that there were *ludi* on 1 April (*CIL* 1[2], p. 262); they are conventionally interpreted as *ludi votivi* marking the birthday of Constantius one day late, see A. Degrassi, *Inscriptiones Italiae* 13.2 (1963), 434.

7. *Pan. Lat.* 8(5).2.2–3.1; *Chr. Min.* 1.229. For Constantius' *praenomen,* both Gaius and Marcus are attested (*PIR*[2] F 390); since Constantius was the adoptive son of Maximian, Marcus should be officially correct.

8. *Pan. Lat.* 8(5).3.1; Lactantius, *Mort. Pers.* 35.4. On the modern hypothesis that Galerius' actual investiture occurred on 21 May 293, see Chapter V, n. 73.

9. Lactantius, *Mort. Pers.* 19.1 ff. (the changes on 1 May 305); 46.8.

10. *Pan. Lat.* 6(7).8.2; Lactantius, *Mort. Pers.* 24.8; *Origo* 4; Victor, *Caes.* 40.4; *Epitome* 41.3; Zosimus 2.9.1 (Constantine proclaimed at his father's deathbed); *CIL* 1[2], pp. 268, 269; *Chr. Min.* 1.229, 234 (the day).

Severus   Caesar 1 May 305
(Flavius Valerius
Severus)

Maximinus   Caesar 1 May 305
(C. Galerius Valerius
Maximinus)[11]

3. From the death of Constantius to the Conference of Carnuntum (November 308)

Galerius	Augustus
Severus	Augustus in place of Constantius;[12] abdicated in spring 307[13]
Maximinus	Caesar
Constantine (Flavius Valerius Constantinus)	Proclaimed Augustus on 25 July 306 by his father's troops,[14] then accepted appointment as Caesar from Galerius;[15] invested as Augustus c. September 307 by Maximian,[16] and

11. The name "Daia," which Maximinus originally bore (Lactantius, *Mort. Pers.* 18.13; cf. *I. Ephesos* 311a), never formed part of his official name as emperor and is nowhere attested as such.

12. *ILS* 657 (Egypt); Lactantius, *Mort. Pers.* 25.5.

13. Lactantius, *Mort. Pers.* 26.5 ff. The date is deduced primarily from two facts: the consular date of 307 employed at Rome changed in April from *Maximiano VII et Maximino* to *post consulatum sextum* (*Chr. Min.* 1.66–67), and Galerius invaded Italy c. September 307. Severus continued to be recognized as emperor and consul in the East until his death, which was known in the Arsinoite nome of Egypt by 24 December 307 (*P. Merton* 31; *P. Col.* 138: contrast *P. Oxy.* 3192; *MPER* 1.291 = *Stud. Pal.* 20.77; *P. Mil.* 55, which include Severus' name in dating formulae on 9 May, 25 July, and 29 September). He died shortly before Galerius invaded Italy, probably on 15 or 16 September, see E. Groag, *RE* 14 (1929), 2433; W. Seston, *Carnuntina* (Graz and Cologne, 1956), 178, citing *Chr. Min.* 1.148: "Severus imp. ann. III m. IIII d. XV."

14. *CIL* 1², pp. 268, 269; *Chr. Min.* 1.231, 235 (the day); Lactantius, *Mort. Pers.* 24.8 f.; *Origo* 4; Victor, *Caes.* 40.4; *Epitome* 41.3; Zosimus 2.9.1 (the circumstances).

Constantine himself regarded 25 July 306 as his sole *dies imperii* from at least 310 (*Pan. Lat.* 6(7).9.2; Lactantius, *Mort. Pers.* 25.5), and there is no need to postulate an official *dies imperii* later than 25 July 306 in order to explain the attested examples of his imperial titulature (Table 3). That hypothesis (for which, see P. Bruun, *NC*⁷ 10 (1969), 177 ff.; *Arctos*, n.s. 9 (1975), 11 ff.) carries the corollary that at some date Constantine regarded himself as not yet an emperor in the intervening period—which is both improbable in itself and contradicted by the panegyric of 307: "cum tibi pater imperium reliquisset, Caesaris tamen appellatione contentus expectare malueris ut idem te qui illum declararet Augustum" (*Pan. Lat.* 7(6).5.3).

15. Lactantius, *Mort. Pers.* 25.3–5; *RIC* 6.128–130 (London), 207–214 (Trier), 255–259 (Lugdunum); *RIB* 1.2233, 2237, 2292, 2303, 2310. In Egypt, Constantine's *dies imperii* fell after 28 August 306 (Chapter III.3).

16. *Pan. Lat.* 7(6) celebrates both the investiture and Constantine's marriage to Fausta; hence, since the investiture was later than 25 July 307 (*RIC* 6.213, Treveri 744–746, cf. R. Strauss, *Rev. Num.*⁵ 16 (1954), 26 ff.), while the marriage coincided with Galerius' invasion of Italy (Lactantius,

subsequently (it appears) not recognized by
Galerius as a member of the imperial college[17]

4. From the Conference of Carnuntum to the death of Galerius[18]

Galerius	Augustus; died late April or early May 311[19]
Licinius (Valerius Licinianus Licinius)	Augustus 11 November 308[20]
Maximinus	Caesar; given the title *filius Augustorum* by Galerius early in 309; proclaimed Augustus by his troops in 310[21]
Constantine	a. In the East: Caesar; then *filius Augustorum;* then Augustus[22]
	b. In the West: Augustus

Mort. Pers. 27.1), the date must be c. September 307.

17. Galerius and Maximinus alone appear as emperors on *P. Cairo Isid.* 87 (29 April 308), 88 (6 May 308), 125 (6 August 308); *ILS* 658 (Aquincum, undated), and no issue of coins in Constantine's name from a mint of Galerius can be dated with certainty to the period between c. September 307 and November 308 (see C. H. V. Sutherland, *RIC* 6 (1967), 60).

18. A. Chastagnol, *Aiôn: Le Temps chez les Romains* (*Caesarodunum* 10bis, 1976), 228 f., has proposed that Galerius also proclaimed Candidianus Caesar between 29 August 310 and 10 April 311. He argues from the regnal years which appear in *P. Cairo Isid.* 51.7 (1 April 311) and *P. Princeton Roll* 2.5, 11 (17 June 312). The inference should be rejected: Lactantius is silent, there is no coinage in Candidianus' name, he is missing from the documents which attest the imperial college in 310 and 311 (Chapter III, nos. 5–7), and all other papyri and ostraca of 310–312 omit the additional and aberrant regnal year (R. S. Bagnall and K. A. Worp, *Regnal Formulas in Byzantine Egypt* (*BASP,* Supp. 2, 1979), 34–36). Its probable origin is scribal carelessness, as argued by A. E. R. Boak and H. C. Youtie, *The Archive of Aurelius Isidorus* (Ann Arbor, 1960), 225.

It should be observed that, when Maximinus and Constantine were acknowledged as Augusti, they took precedence over Licinius (*BCH* 11 (1887), 69 no. 49 (Isaura); ? *P. Rylands* 616, cf. R. S. Bagnall and K. A. Worp, *BASP* 17 (1980), 10 ff.)—although Galerius seems at first to have attempted to maintain the old order of names (Chapter III, no. 6).

19. Lactantius, *Mort. Pers.* 35.4 (the exact day in May 311 on which his death became known in Nicomedia is lost in a lacuna).

20. *Chr. Min.* 1.231, cf. Lactantius, *Mort. Pers.* 29.2.

21. Lactantius, *Mort. Pers.* 32.1–5, confirmed by *ILS* 659 (Carnuntum); *RIC* 6.514 Thessalonica 31a, 38a; 535–536, Heraclea 38, 40, 45, 46; 562–563, Nicomedia 55, 60; 586–588, Cyzicus 43, 49, 52, 55, 61; 630–634 (Antioch), 677–679 (Alexandria) (all Caesar); *RIC* 6.514–515, Thessalonica 32a, 39a (*filius Augustorum*). That Maximinus was proclaimed Augustus precisely on 1 May 310 was conjectured by C. H. V. Sutherland, *RIC* 6 (1967), 15f. Maximinus and Constantine are still *filii Augustorum* on an Egyptian census declaration dated 27 February 310 (*P. Strassburg* 42 = *P. Sakaon* 1).

22. *ILS* 659; *RIC* 6.514–515, Thessalonica 31b, 38b; 633, Antiochia 118b (Caesar); Lactantius, *Mort. Pers.* 32.5; *RIC* 6.513–515, Thessalonica 28, 32b, 39b; 562–563, Nicomedia 56, 61; 631–632, Antiochia 104, 105, 111; 678–680, Alexandria 99b, 100b, 113, 117; *P. Cairo Isid.* 47, 90,

5. From the death of Galerius to the death of Maximinus[23]

Maximinus   Augustus; died c. July 313[24]

Constantine   Augustus; declared to be the senior emperor by the Roman Senate in November 312[25]

Licinius   Augustus

6. From the death of Maximinus to the defeat of Licinius

Constantine   Augustus

Licinius   Augustus; abdicated 19 September 324[26]

Crispus (Flavius Julius Crispus)   Caesar 1 March 317

Licinius (Valerius Licinianus Licinius)   Caesar 1 March 317

Constantinus (Flavius Claudius Constantinus)   Caesar 1 March 317[27]

---

91 (*filius Augustorum*); Chapter III, nos. 4–6; *RIC* 6.537–539, Heraclea 49b, 54b, 60b; 564–565, Nicomedia 65b, 66d; 589, Cyzicus 67b; 634–640, Antiochia 126, 127b, 129, 133d, 147d, 148d, 154d; 678–679, Alexandria 104, 106, 107, 118, 120 (Augustus).

23. R. M. Grant, *Christianity, Judaism and other Greco-Roman Cults* 4 (Leiden, 1975), 144, argues that Maximinus appointed his son Maximus and Candidianus emperors in 311. Although, like Chastagnol, he adduces *P. Princeton Roll* 2.5, 11 (above, n. 18), Grant relies principally on Eusebius, *HE* 9.11.7: οἱ Μαξιμίνου παῖδες, οὓς ἤδη καὶ τῆς βασιλικῆς τιμῆς τῆς τε ἐν πίναξι καὶ γραφαῖς ἀναθέσεως πεποίητο κοινωνούς. But Eusebius knew only that Maximinus' children were depicted with the emperor on reliefs and pictures (cf. 11.2) — which by no means proves that they were formally invested with the imperial purple. Again, the silence of Lactantius (*Mort. Pers.* 50.2, 6, cf. 20.4), the vast majority of papyri from 311–313 (R. S. Bagnall and K. A. Worp, *Regnal Formulas* 35–37), and the complete absence of contemporary attestation on coins or inscriptions forbid the inference.

24. Maximinus was still recognized as emperor and consul at Oxyrhynchus on 23 July 313 (*P. Oxy.* 3144), but his death was known in Karanis by 13 September 313 (*P. Cairo Isid.* 103.20); the date of his death, therefore, is probably July or August 313, although late June cannot be excluded on present evidence.

25. Lactantius, *Mort. Pers.* 44.11: "senatus Constantino virtutis gratia primi nominis titulum decrevit, quem sibi Maximinus vindicabat." For the order Constantine, Maximinus, Licinius in Constantine's territory, *CIL* 5.8021a, 8963, 11.6667. For the order Maximinus, Constantine, Licinius, *ILS* 663 (Asia); *AE* 1963.141 (Cyrene); *ILS* 664 (Noricum).

26. *Origo* 28; *CIL* 1², p. 272; *Chr. Min.* 1.232; Praxagoras, *FGrH* 219; *Epitome* 41.8; Zosimus 2.28.1.

27. *Chr. Min.* 1.232; *Origo* 19. For Crispus the names Claudius and Valerius are also attested in place of Julius (*RIC* 7.175, Trier 138–139; *ILS* 716 (Rome)), while Constantinus is occasionally Fl. Julius Constantinus (*AE* 1889. 34 (Sbrangatu, Sardinia); *AE* 1938. 85 = *I. Ephesos* 312, where the published supplement *Con*[*stantio*] is impossible, since the date is before 19 September 324).

7. Constantine as sole Augustus[28]

Constantine	Augustus; died 22 May 337[29]
Crispus	Caesar; executed c. May 326[30]
Constantinus	Caesar
Constantius (Flavius Julius Constantius)	Caesar 8 November 324[31]
Constans (Flavius Julius Constans)	Caesar 25 December 333[32]
Dalmatius (Flavius Julius Dalmatius)	Caesar 18 September 335;[33] killed between 2 August and 9 September 337[34]

8. The sons of Constantine

Constantinus	Augustus 9 September 337;[35] killed spring 340
Constantius	Augustus 9 September 337; died 3 November 361
Constans	Augustus 9 September 337; killed shortly after 18 January 350

28. Hannibalianus, whom Constantine proclaimed king over territory outside the Roman Empire (*Origo* 35; Ammianus 14.1.2; *Epitome* 41.20), was not technically a member of the imperial college; he was *nobilissimus,* but not a Caesar (Zosimus 2.39.2).

29. Festal Index 10; *Chr. Min.* 1.235; Eusebius, *VC* 4.64; Socrates, *HE* 1.39.2, 40.3.

30. Crispus disappears from the imperial coinage in the course of 326, see P. Bruun, *RIC* 7 (1966), 71f. His death is dated to late March by O. Seeck, *Regesten* 63, 176, to May/June by A. Piganiol, *L'Empire chrétien* (Paris, 1947), 35, and to September or October by P. Bruun, *RIC* 7 (1966), 71. *Epitome* 41.12; Zosimus 2.29.2 imply a date not long before Constantine arrived in Rome in mid-July 326.

31. *CIL* 1², p. 276; *Chr. Min.* 1.232; *AE* 1937.119 (with plain *idibus Nob.* in error); Ammianus 14.5.1 (with *Oct.* for *Nov.*).

32. *Chr. Min.* 1.234.

33. *Chr. Min.* 1.235. Both Dalmatius and Delmatius are attested. It may be relevant that the antiquarian Varro had insisted on calling the province Delmatia (*De Gramm.* frag. 73 Goetz-Schoell).

34. On the date of his death, A. Olivetti, *Riv. Fil.* 43 (1915), 67 ff. *CTh* 13.4.2 shows Valerius Maximus, who appears to be Dalmatius' praetorian prefect, still in office on 2 August 337 (Chapter VIII.4).

35. *Chr. Min.* 1.235.

APPENDIX: AUGUSTAE

On the strictest definition, Augustae are not members of the imperial college, since their names never appear among those of the emperors who jointly issue imperial pronouncements.[36] Nevertheless, an Augusta did possess at least some of the privileges of an Augustus: her name might appear in the nominative case on the imperial coinage, and at least one Augusta released prisoners from exile and the mines and had unfettered access to imperial funds (Eusebius, *VC* 3.44; 47.3).[37] Between 284 and 337, the following Augustae are attested:

1. Galeria Valeria, the wife of Galerius.
   Proclaimed Augusta, apparently at the Conference of Carnuntum in November 308 (*RIC* 6.498–500, 559–562, 583–590, 625–639, 671–680),[38] exiled in 311 and put to death c. September 314 (Lactantius, *Mort. Pers.* 39.5, 41.1, 51).
2. Flavia Julia Helena, wife of Constantius and mother of Constantine.
3. Flavia Maxima Fausta, wife of Constantine.
   Helena and Fausta both appear as Augustae on the coinage of Constantine immediately after the defeat of Licinius (*RIC* 7.116, 137, 203, 263–264, 325–326, 383, 447, 475, 514–515, 551, 612–613, 647, 709), and it is an attractive conjecture that both were proclaimed Augustae when Constantius became Caesar, i.e. on 8 November 324.[39] Fausta died in the summer of 326 (*Epitome* 41.12; Philostorgius, *HE* 2.4; Zosimus 2.29.2), Helena in the summer or autumn of 327 (Eusebius, *VC* 3.46.2).[40]

36. E.g., Chapter III, nos. 5–7, issued while Galeria Valeria was an Augusta; *P. Oxy.* 889 (re-edited below, Chapter XIV.3), probably issued when Helena and Fausta were Augustae.

37. On the legal status of an empress in both the Roman and Byzantine periods, cf. S. Maslev, *Byzantinoslavica* 27 (1966), 308 ff.

38. P. Bruun, *Numismatica e Antichità Classiche* 8 (1979), 255 ff.

39. P. Bruun, *RIC* 7 (1966), 26, 77.

40. Helena made a pilgrimage to the Holy Land after encountering Constantine in Rome c. August 326 (Zosimus 2.29.2) and died in his presence (Eusebius, *VC* 3.46.2). Her death must fall before 7 January 328, when Constantine refounded Drepanum as Helenopolis in her memory (*Chr. Pasch.* 527, cf. Chapter V: Constantine).

CHAPTER II

OTHER EMPERORS AND USURPERS

Between 20 November 284 and 9 September 337, more than a dozen men assumed the imperial purple without the agreement (previous or subsequent) of the senior emperor then ruling. The following list (which is in the chronological order of their proclamations) states and documents succinctly (1) the names of the usurpers, (2) the dates of their proclamation and suppression, and (3) the territory which they controlled. Where ascertainable, their careers as private citizens are also noted.

Amandus
Leader of the Bagaudae in Gaul, defeated by Maximian in 285 (Victor, *Caes.* 39.17; Eutropius, *Brev.* 9.20.3). Coins are known with the legends *Imp. C. C. Amandus p. f. Aug.* and *Imp. S. Amandus p. f. Aug.* (*RIC* 5.2.595).

?Aelianus
Named with Amandus as if both were joint leaders of the Bagaudae (Victor, *Caes.* 39.17; Eutropius, *Brev.* 9.20.3).

M. Aur(elius) Maus. Carausius
Carausius' full nomenclature is imperfectly attested, the penultimate name always being abbreviated to the letter *M* (*RIC* 5.2.483 ff.: Colchester) or to *Maus.* (*ILS* 8928 = *RIB* 2291: near Carlisle).[1] He was commissioned by Maxim-

---

1. Presumably *Mausaeus,* or *Mausaius,* as proposed by R. Mowat, *BSNAF* 1895.148; *Rev. Num.*[3] 13 (1895), 129 ff.

ian to build a fleet and suppress German pirates, but rebelled against him (Victor, *Caes.* 39.19 ff.; Eutropius, *Brev.* 9.21). The date of his rebellion is only indirectly attested. Carausius was killed when Constantius attacked Boulogne shortly after his appointment as Caesar on 1 March 293 (*Pan. Lat.* 8(5).6.1, 12.2). Since later sources give the length of Carausius' reign as either six or seven years (Victor, *Caes.* 39.40 (*sexennium*); Eutropius, *Brev.* 9.22.2 (*septennium*); Orosius, *Hist. Adv. Pag.* 7.25.5 (*septem annos*)), while a hoard of coins found in Sussex appears to establish that he was consul for the fourth time in 290 (*RIC* 5.2.497 no. 393),[2] it may be deduced that he proclaimed himself Augustus during the course of 286 and had styled himself consul in 287, 288, and 289.

Carausius was recognized as Augustus in Britain and over a large part of northwestern Gaul: he minted coins, not only in Britain (*RIC* 5.2.463 ff.: London and Colchester), but also in Gaul, apparently at Rouen (*RIC* 5.2.516 ff.) and perhaps at Boulogne (*RIC* 5.2.523, nos. 702–705).[3]

Allectus

After Constantius recovered northwestern Gaul for the central imperial government in 293, Allectus murdered Carausius and replaced him as Augustus in Britain (*Pan. Lat.* 8(5).12.2; *RIC* 5.2.558 ff.). He was defeated and killed in 296 (*Pan. Lat.* 8(5).14–19; Victor, *Caes.* 39.40–42; Eutropius, *Brev.* 9.22; Orosius, *Hist. Adv. Pag.* 7.25.6).

Before 293 Allectus had served under Carausius, perhaps with the title *rationalis summae rei:* the speech of 297 styles him a *satelles* of the *archipirata* (*Pan. Lat.* 8(5).12.2), Victor describes him as having charge of the *summa res* by Carausius' permission (*Caes.* 39.41), and the puzzling mint-mark *RSR* on coins of Carausius (*RIC* 5.2.508–516) has been interpreted as an abbreviation of some such title.[4]

L. Domitius Domitianus

Papyri and ostraca from lower Egypt register L. Domitius Domitianus as Augustus from late August to early December of a single Julian year (*P. Cairo Isid.* 139 (year 1, 24–28 August); 38, 39, 104 (November); *P. Michael.* 24.34 (2 December), etc.).[5] The only two possibilities for the year are 296 and 297, and

2. For the date, P. H. Webb, *NC*[5] 5 (1925), 173 ff.

3. On Carausius and Allectus, see N. Shiel, *The Episode of Carausius and Allectus* (*BAR* 40, 1977). R. A. G. Carson, *JBAA*[3] 22 (1959), 33 ff., and P. J. Casey, *Britannia* 8 (1977), 283 ff., have shown that Carausius controlled the ports of northwestern Gaul from 286 to 293, not merely from 289 (as assumed, e.g., by H. G. Pflaum, *Rev. Num.*[6] 2 (1959-60), 53).

4. P. H. Webb, *NC*[4] 7 (1907), 48 ff.; *RIC* 5.2 (1933), 434. However, O. Seeck, *RE* 1 (1894), 1584, held that Allectus was Carausius' praetorian prefect — which might appear preferable on a priori grounds (cf. Chapter VIII).

5. For a full list, R. S. Bagnall and K. A. Worp, *Regnal Formulas in Byzantine Egypt* (*BASP*, Supp. 2, 1979), 28 f.

the later year can be firmly established from close examination of contemporary Egyptian documents,[6] and from the varied evidence for the movements of Diocletian.[7] Domitianus minted both coins on the Roman imperial standard (*RIC* 6.661, 663, Alexandria 5, 6, 19, 20) and Alexandrian tetradrachms (J. Lallemand, *Revue Belge de Numismatique* 97 (1951), 94–99).[8]

Aurelius Achilleus

Attested as *corrector* under the regime of Domitianus in September 297 (*P. Cairo Isid.* 62: Karanis; *P. Michigan* 220 = *Sammelbuch* 7252: Philadelphia), but named in all the literary sources as leader of the rebellion (Eusebius, *Chronicle* p. 227 Karst; Jerome, *Chronicle* 226[a]; Victor, *Caes.* 39.23, 39.38; Eutropius, *Brev.* 9.22–23; *Epitome* 39.3; Orosius, *Hist. Adv. Pag.* 7.25.4, 8; John of Antioch, frag. 164; Jordanes, *Get.* 110; Zonaras 12.31). The contradiction can be removed by the hypothesis that Domitianus died in December 297 and that Achilleus was in command during the siege of Alexandria (which lasted until at least March 298).[9]

Anonymous

Eusebius alludes to an attempted usurpation near Melitene in 303 (*HE* 8.6.8), of which nothing further appears to be known.

Eugenius

Commander of a company of five hundred infantry at Seleucia in 303: saluted emperor by his men, he marched on Antioch and was defeated (Libanius, *Orat.* 11.158–162, 19.45–46, 20.18–20, cf. *Orat.* 1.3; Eusebius, *HE* 8.6.8).

M. Aur(elius) Val(erius) Maxentius[10]

Maxentius, the son of Maximian, was invested with the purple at Rome on 28 October 306 and drowned in the River Tiber on 28 October 312 (*Pan. Lat.* 12(9).16.2; Lactantius, *Mort. Pers.* 26.1 ff., 44.3 ff.; *CIL* 1², p. 274).

---

6. J. D. Thomas, *ZPE* 22 (1976), 253 ff.; 24 (1977), 233 ff. The earlier date has often been argued, most fully and most recently by J. Schwartz, *L. Domitius Domitianus: Étude numismatique et papyrologique* (*Papyrologica Bruxellensia* 12, 1975), 94 ff.; *ZPE* 25 (1977), 217 ff. In refutation, it suffices to observe that Schwartz is compelled to date the deaths of Carausius and Allectus to 292 and 295 (*Domitianus* 102).

7. Chapter V: Diocletian. An allusion to an imperial victory in the speech of 297 provides a strong additional argument in favor of 297: "dent veniam trophaea Niliaca sub quibus Aethiops et Indus intremuit" (*Pan. Lat.* 8(5).5.2: delivered on 1 March 297). Only if the revolt of Domitianus had not yet begun could the orator use the phrase *trophaea Niliaca* without risk of ambiguity to refer to Galerius in Egypt before 296.

8. On the coinage of Domitianus, see A. Giessen, *ZPE* 22 (1976), 280 ff., Tafeln XVI, XVII.

9. *PLRE* 1.263.

10. Before his proclamation, M. Val(erius) Maxentius, *vir claris(simus)* (*ILS* 666: Rome). He was residing at Rome in 306 (Zosimus 2.9.2).

At first Maxentius avoided the title Augustus: his earliest issues of coins from the Roman mint bear the legends *d. n. Maxentius princ(eps)* and *Maxentius princ(eps) invict(us)* (*RIC* 6.367–370). The title *princ(eps) invict(us)* also occurs on coins minted in Africa (*RIC* 6.432, Carthago 53), but the first issues in Maxentius' name there give him a title which he never officially assumed: *nobilissimus Caesar* (*RIC* 6.430–431, Carthago 47, 48a, 51a).[11] Maxentius soon proclaimed himself Augustus, probably in the early months of 307, and his official style was then *imp. Caes. M. Aurelius Maxentius pius felix invictus Augustus* (*ILS* 669, 670, 672; *IRT* 464). Now an inscription from Mauretania, which refers to Galerius as *divus Maximianus,* styles Maxentius *pius felix invictus et gloriosissimus semper Augustus* (*ILS* 671: Caesarea). That might reflect an official modification of his titles after the suppression of Domitius Alexander in 309.

Proclaimed at Rome, Maxentius was rapidly acknowledged as ruler in southern Italy, Sicily, Africa, Sardinia, and Corsica (cf. *Pan. Lat.* 12(9).25.2–3). He gained control of northern Italy early in 307, but lost control of the African provinces to Domitius Alexander for a period (probably 308–309). There is no reason to believe that Maxentius ever ruled Spain: the evidence indicates that in 305 Constantius added Spain to his portion of the empire, and that in 306 it passed peacefully under the sway of Constantine.[12]

Maximian

Maximian abdicated on 1 May 305 and retired to private life, taking up residence in Campania (Lactantius, *Mort. Pers.* 26.7) or Lucania (Eutropius, *Brev.* 9.27.2, 10.2.3).[13] Not long after 28 October 306 Maxentius "sent him the purple and named him 'Augustus for the second time'" (Lactantius, *Mort. Pers.* 26.7). In this capacity, Maximian helped Maxentius to defeat Severus (spring 307) and to secure an alliance with Constantine by giving him his daughter Fausta in marriage and investing him as Augustus (c. September 307). The following April he attempted to depose Maxentius (Lactantius, *Mort. Pers.* 28.1 ff.; cf. *Chr. Min.* 1.66, 231), then fled to Constantine and attended the Conference of Carnuntum in November 308 (Lactantius, *Mort. Pers.* 29.1 ff.), where he was forced to retire a second time (*Pan. Lat.* 6(7).14.6). He betook himself to Constantine in Gaul, against whom he rebelled and assumed the purple yet again (*Pan. Lat.* 6(7).14–20; Lactantius, *Mort. Pers.* 29.3 ff.). He was quickly suppressed and allowed (or encouraged) to commit suicide, probably c. July 310.[14]

11. Maxentius could also be the *Herculi Caes(ar)* invoked on a brooch manufactured, or at least inscribed, in 306/7 (*ILS* 681, cf. Chapter III, n. 11).

12. Chapter XI.

13. Presumably, therefore, near Salerno, cf. S. Mazzarino, *Rendiconti Lincei*[8] 8 (1953), 417 ff. On Maximian's career after 305, see still E. A. Sydenham, *NC*[5] 14 (1934), 141 ff.

14. The date is inferred from *Pan. Lat.* 6(7), cf. Chapter V, n. 105.

L. Domitius Alexander

Inscriptions give the usurper's name and titles as L. Domitius Alexander *invictus pius felix Augustus* (*ILS* 674 = *ILAlg*. 2.580, etc.).[15] Before his proclamation, Alexander had been *vicarius* of Africa (Victor, *Caes.* 40.17; Zosimus 2.12.2). He should probably, therefore, be identified with the Val(erius) Alexander attested as *vicarius* in 303 (*AE* 1942/3.81: Aqua Viva, in Numidia) and again under Maxentius (*IRT* 464: Lepcis).[16]

Neither the beginning nor the end of Alexander's rebellion against Maxentius can be dated from explicit evidence; nevertheless, it almost certainly began between May and autumn 308,[17] and had almost certainly been suppressed by the end of 309.[18] Although African milestones indicate that Alexander recognized Constantine (*ILS* 8936: *impp. dd. nn. L. Domitio Alexandro et Fl. Constantino Augg.* — a peculiar order), it is neither attested nor probable that Constantine ever recognized Alexander as a colleague.[19] Nor is there any ex-

15. P. Salama, *Bulletin van de Vereeniging tot Bevordering der Kennis van de Antieke Beschaving* 29 (1954), 73–74, conveniently prints the eight inscriptions of Alexander known to him, viz. *CIL* 8.7004 (= *ILS* 674); 21959, 22183 (= *ILS* 8936); *ILAlg*. 1.3921; *BCTH* 1901, ccvii, no. 3; *Revue Africaine* 95 (1951), 250; and two unpublished, one of which was subsequently published by E. Marec, *BCTH 1955-56* (1958), 106, no. 3. Since then there has been the important discovery of a milestone of Alexander from the road between Caralis and Sulci in Sardinia: Sotgiu 1.372 = *AE* 1966, 169, cf. G. Sotgiu, *Archivio Storico Sardo* 29 (1964), 149 ff.

16. For the *nomen* Valerius as a status designation, J. Keenan, *ZPE* 11 (1973), 44 ff. Identity is, however, denied by L. Leschi, *Études d'épigraphie, d'archéologie et d'histoire africaines* (Paris, 1957), 52; Kolbe, *Statthalter* 67 n. 4. *PLRE* 1.43/4, Alexander 17,20, has separate entries for usurper and *vicarius*, with implicit appeal to G. M. Bersannetti, *Epigraphica* 5-6 (1943-44), 127 ff., who mistakenly dated *IRT* 465 (a parallel dedication to *IRT* 464) after the fall of the usurper.

17. An inscription from Numidia (*ILS* 668: "domino nostro Maxentio Augusto nobilissimo viro consuli") appears to show that Maxentius was still recognized in Africa in May 308 or later, while Zosimus connects the proclamation of Alexander with Maxentius' falling out with his father in April 308 (2.12). The precise date of the proclamation has been argued to be June or 28 October 308 (respectively, J. Maurice, *MSNAF* 61 (1902), 1 ff.; E. Groag, *RE* 14 (1930), 2440 f.). On the other hand, R. Andreotti interprets the revolt as a result of the Conference of Carnuntum in November 308 and hence adopts a date in 309 (*Epigraphica* 31 (1969), 158 ff.).

18. For modern estimates of the date, see especially G. Laffranchi, *Aquileia nostra* 9 (1938), 123 ff. = *Numismatica* 13 (1947), 17 ff. (309); Chastagnol, *Fastes* 55 (late 309 or early 310); P. Salama, *Numario Hispánico* 9 (1960), 176 (between 25 July and 28 October 310); J. Maurice, *MSNAF* 61 (1902), 9 ff. (spring 311); R. Andreotti, *Epigraphica* 31 (1969), 169 ff. (311); H. Schoenebeck, *Klio,* Beifheft 43 (1939), 74 (late 311 or early 312). The date 309 is here adopted on the following grounds. Alexander was defeated by Rufius Volusianus as praetorian prefect of Maxentius (Victor, *Caes.* 40.18; Zosimus 2.14.2). Hence the expedition to suppress Alexander should be dated either before or after Volusianus' urban prefecture, which he held from 28 October 310 to 28 October 311 (*Chr. Min.* 1.67). By late 311, however, Maxentius was already embroiled in conflict with Constantine, while the coinage of Rome and Ostia seems strongly to imply that Maxentius won a victory during the course of 309 (G. Laffranchi, *Numismatica* 13 (1947), 17 ff.). Moreover, African coin hoards appear to confirm a date no later than the beginning of 310 (P. Salama, *Libya Antiqua* 3/4 (1966/7), 21 ff.).

19. R. Andreotti, *Epigraphica* 31 (1969), 163. Collusion and an alliance were argued by H. G. Pflaum, *Bulletin d'Archéologie Algérienne* 1 (1962-65, publ. 1967), 159 ff.

plicit evidence that Alexander controlled the Mauretanias as well as Tripolitania, Africa proper, and Numidia, though a milestone now attests his control of Sardinia, for however brief a period (Sotgiu 1.372 = *AE* 1966.169).[20]

Aur(elius) Val(erius) Valens

Valens was *dux limitis* in Dacia when Licinius made him emperor after his defeat at Cibalae on 8 October 316 (*Origo* 16–17). He was deposed and executed before Licinius negotiated a peace settlement with Constantine in January/February 317 (*Origo* 18; *Epitome* 40.9; Zosimus 2.20.1; Petrus Patricius, frag. 15).

Although the literary sources describe Valens as a Caesar (*Origo* 17; Zosimus 2.19.2), what seem to be the only two genuine coins of Valens both style him Augustus (*RIC* 7.644, Cyzicus 7; 706, Alexandria 19).[21]

Mar. Martinianus

Martinianus was *magister officiorum* of Licinius (*Epitome* 41.6; Zosimus 2.25.2; Johannes Lydus, *De Mag.* 2.25).[22] Licinius put him up as emperor after the battle of Adrianople on 3 July 324, but Constantine deposed him and soon ordered his execution (Victor, *Caes.* 41.9; *Epitome* 41.7; Zosimus 2.26.2, 28.2). About his rank, the evidence diverges as it does for Valens: the majority of the literary sources explicitly style him Caesar, the coins Augustus (*RIC* 7.608, Nicomedia 45–47; 645, Cyzicus 16).

Calocaerus

There appear to be only three independent items of evidence concerning Calocaerus:

1. Victor, *Caes.* 41.11–12: Calocaerus *magister pecoris camelorum* seized Cyprus *specie regni,* and was rightly executed in a manner appropriate to a slave or brigand. Victor expressly dates the revolt immediately after the execution of Crispus in 326.
2. Jerome, *Chronicle* 233[g]: "Calocaerus in Cypro res novas molitus opprimitur," under 28 Constantine = 333/4.[23]
3. Theophanes, a. 5825, p. 29.28–31 de Boor = Philostorgius, p. 207.22–25 Bidez: (a) Dalmatius was proclaimed Caesar; (b) "Calocaerus who usurped power in the island of Cyprus succumbed to the Roman attack"; (c) "and

---

20. On the significance of this inscription, see especially G. Sotgiu, *Archivio Storico Sardo* 29 (1964), 154 ff.

21. For the many forgeries of coins of Valens, see R. A. G. Carson, *NC*[6] 18 (1958), 55 ff.

22. Conceivably identical with the military officer Martinianus who visited the hermit Antony in 313 (Athanasius, *Vita Antonii* 48).

23. Jerome is the source of Orosius, *Hist. Adv. Pag.* 7.28.30, whence the interpolation in *Origo* 35.

after his defeat he was executed with his accomplices at Tarsus in Cilicia, being burnt alive by the Caesar Dalmatius."[24]

The discrepancy over the date must be resolved by the hypothesis that Victor is mistaken or misinformed: Theophanes (or his source) has clearly confused the Caesar Dalmatius, proclaimed on 18 September 335, with his father, Dalmatius the *censor,* who was residing in Antioch in 334, apparently with wide executive authority (Athanasius, *Apol. Sec.* 65.1 ff., whence Socrates, *HE* 1.27.19 ff.).[25] The insurrection occurred c. 334, and was presumably connected with the earthquake, registered by Theophanes under the preceding year, which destroyed Salamis (Theophanes, a.m. 5824, p. 29.23–25 de Boor = Philostorgius, p. 207.19–21 Bidez, cf. Malalas 313 Bonn).

24. Theophanes is the source of Cedrenus 1.519 Bonn.
25. W. Ensslin, *Rh. Mus.,* n.f. 78 (1929), 203 ff.

CHAPTER III

THE IMPERIAL TITULATURE

The names and titles of the emperors between 284 and 337 are attested in their fullest and most official form in a small number of surviving documents, viz. in the headings of six imperial edicts or letters and two military diplomas, some of which are preserved only in a very fragmentary state.[1] These documents emanate from the senior emperor, and may be regarded as authoritative statements of the emperors' titles in a way in which inscriptions and papyri of a less official nature cannot.[2] Hence an exposition of the rules governing the imperial titulature should begin by presenting the evidence of this select group of edicts, letters, and diplomas. Printed below are the emperors' names and titles as they appear in each of the eight.

1. THE PRINCIPAL DOCUMENTS

1. Currency Edict of 301 (before 1 September) (Aphrodisias). Text: K. T. Erim, J. Reynolds, and M. Crawford, *JRS* 61 (1971), 172, frag. a = *AE* 1973.

---

1. For some examples of less complete titulature, N. Lewis, *Greek Papyri in the Collection of New York University* (Leiden, 1967), 46.
2. For example, Diocletian's possession of the titles *Brittanicus maximus* in 285 (*ILS* 615: Rome) and *Persicus maximus* in 290 (*ILS* 618: a dedication by the governor of Raetia) is chronologically incompatible with the official order of his victory titles in nos. 1 and 2. A rigid distinction must be drawn between the unofficial attribution of a victory title to an emperor by his subjects and his own adoption of it as part of his official titulature. Once this is done, there is no need to argue that Diocletian took a victory title like *Brittanicus maximus* and later dropped it (e.g., Seston, *Dioclétien* 75 n. 9).

526 a, which incorporates *CIL* 3, p. 2208, Aphrodisias I = K. T. Erim and J. Reynolds, *JRS* 60 (1970), 121 no. 1. Photograph: *JRS* 61 (1971), Plate XII.1, + *JRS* 60 (1970), Plate IX.1.

2   Imperator Caesar Gai. Aur. Val. Diocletianus p. f. Aug. p[ont.
m. Germ. m. vi Sarm. m.]
IIII Pers. m. II Brit. m. Carp. m. Aram. m. Med. m. Adiab.
m. trib. [pot. vxiii cons. vii p. p. procs. et]
4   Imperator Caesar M. Aur. Val. Maximianus p. f. Aug. pont. m.
[Germ. m. v Sarm. m. iii Pers. m. ii Brit. m.]
Part. m. Arab. m. Med. m. Adiab. m. tri[b. pot.] VXI[i cons.
vi p. p. procs. et]
6   Flabius Valerius Constantius [et G. Val. Maximianu]s Ge[rmm.
Sarmm. Perss. Britt. Carpp. Aramm.]
Medd. Adiabb. III conss. nob[b. Caess. dicunt]

The restorations are those printed in *JRS* 61 (1971), 172 (where a bracket seems to be omitted in line 7), with question marks and dots removed. Although the number of Maximian's *tribunicia potestas* should be XVII (as in no. 2), the traces in line 5 impose the order VX. *Aram.* in line 3 and *Arab.* in line 5 are both errors for *Arm(enicus)*; *Part.* in line 5 is an error for *Carp(icus)*. Both in this inscription and in the Aphrodisias copy of no. 2, the stonecutter appears to be a Greek imperfectly familiar with Latin.

The date is deduced from the fact that the edict took effect "ex kal. Se[pte]mbribus Titiano et Nepotiano cons.," i.e. from 1 September 301 (*JRS* 61 (1971), 173, frag. b. = *AE* 1973.526 b).

2. Price Edict of 301 (between 20 November and 9 December).[3] Only three of the many known copies preserve the heading: (1) from Egypt, now in Aix-en-Provence, transcribed by T. Mommsen, *CIL* 3, pp. 802–803; photograph in M. Giacchero, *Edictum Diocletiani* 2 (1974), Tav. IV; (2) from Aphrodisias, published by K. T. Erim and J. Reynolds, *JRS* 63 (1973), 100, with photograph (Plate X); (3) from Ptolemais, published by G. Caputo and R. G. Goodchild, *JRS* 45 (1955), 112, fragment (N) = *AE* 1956.113. It should be observed that the edition of the heading in S. Lauffer, *Diokletians Preisedikt* (Berlin, 1971), 90, uses a fragment from Aphrodisias now known to belong to the Currency Edict (*CIL* 3, p. 2208, Aphrodisias I).

The text printed here reproduces the readings and abbreviations of the Egyptian copy, supplementing from the Aphrodisias copy, but disregards the lineation of both. Where these two copies overlap and present divergent

3. Most recently edited by M. Giacchero, *Edictum Diocletiani et Collegarum de pretiis rerum venalium in integrum fere restitutum e Latinis Graecisque fragmentis* (Genoa, 1974).

readings, I print the reading of the Egyptian copy (except in line 10) and note that of the Aphrodisias copy below the text. (Differing abbreviations for the same word are disregarded.) The copy from Ptolemais preserves only PF INV and ET IM[P] in lines 1 and 4–5 of the present text.

[Imp. Caesar C. Aurel. Val. Diocletian]us p. f. inv. Aug. pont. max.
2   Germ. max. VI Sarm. max. IIII Persic. max. II Britt. max.
Carpic. max. Armen. max. Medic. max. Adiabenic. max.
4   trib. p. XVIII coss. VII imp. XVIII p. p. procoss. et
Imp. Caesa[r] M. Aurel. Val. Maximianus p. f. inv. Aug. pont. max.
6   Germ. max. V Sarm. max. III Persic. max. II [Britt. max.]
[Carpic. max. Armen. max. Medic. max. Adiabenic. max.]
8   [tri]b. p. XVII coss. VI imp. XVII p. p. procoss. et
Fla. Val. Constantius Germ. max. II Sarm. max. II Persic. max. II
10   Britt. max. Carpic. max. Armenic. max. Medic. max.
Adiaben. max. trib. p. VIIII coss. III nobil. Caes. et
12   G. Val. Maximianus Germ. max. II Sarm. [max. ii] Persic. max. [ii]
[Britt. max.] Carpic. max. Armenic. max. Medic. max.
14   [Adia]b. max. trib. p. VIIII coss. III nobil. Caes. dicunt

1, 5   Aph. omits INV.
4   t]RIB POT VX CONS VII PP Aph.
8   trib. pot.] VX CONS VI PP Aph.
9–14   Aph. combines the titles of Constantius and Galerius and ne-
glects their iterations.
9, 12   Aph. omits the title *Sarmatici maximi* for the Caesars.
10   Aph. also omits *Brittanici maximi*.
10   CCPP Aph., SARM Eg.: all editors before 1973 emended to
Carpic.
10, 13   ARAM Aph.

The date of the edict is established by the titles of Diocletian and the Caesars: Diocletian became *imperator XVIII* on 20 November 301, and entered on his nineteenth *tribunicia potestas* on 10 December 301, after which day the Caesars would have been *tribunicia potestate X*.

3. Military diploma of 7 January 305 (or possibly 304) (Aeclanum, now in Naples). Text: A. de Franciscis, *Rendiconti della Accademia di Archeologia, Lettere e Belle Arti, Napoli*, n.s. 32 (1957), 181–182 (whence *AE* 1958.190); G. Forni, *Bulletino dell'Istituto di Diritto Romano*[3] 1 (1959), 264–265. Photograph: *Rendiconti* etc., Tav. 1 (facing p. 180). (The text was discovered in 1823, then lost: hence it was printed in *CIL* 3, p. 900; 10.1113 and 16.157 from R. Guarini, *Novelli monumenti eclanesi* (Naples, 1824), 16.)

[Sar. m. v Per. m. ii Br. m. Car. m. v] Ar.m. II Med. m.
[Ad. m.---et]
2 [Imp. Caes.] M. Aur. Val. Maximian. Ger. [m. viii Sarm. m. iv
Pers. m. ii]
[Br.] m. Car. m. V Ar. m. II Med. m. Ad. m. [---]
4 [et Fl.] Val Constantiu. et G. Val. Max[imianus Ger. m. v Sar.
m. iii]
[Pe]r. m. Br. m. Car. m. V Ar. m. Med. m. A[d. m. nobb.
Caess.]

The text printed here comprises lines 1–5 of the exterior face of the diploma, with the emperors' victory titles supplemented from nos. 2 and 4. I reject G. Forni's reading of "[cos. i]III" before the clear "nomin(a) milit(um) qui militaver(unt)" in line 6. The portion of the emperors' names and titles on the interior face (*Rendiconti*, etc., Tav. 2) shows Maximian as "[cos. v]III."

The date can be deduced from the title *Car(picus) m(aximus) V:* since the emperors had only taken this title once before November/December 301, the date is more likely to be 7 January 305 than 7 January 304. This titulature differs from nos. 1 and 2 in that Diocletian and Maximian are each *Ar(menicus) m(aximus) II:* the position of the title, between *Carpicus maximus* (taken for the first time in 296) and *Medicus maximus* (298), is incompatible with the fact that Constantius and Galerius are *Ar(menici) m(aximi)* without iteration. The iteration, therefore, should be dismissed as erroneous.

4. Military diploma dated 7 January 306 (found at Campagnatico in Tuscany, now in Florence). Text: M. Bizzarri, *Notizie degli Scavi*[8] 13 (1959), 59–61; *Athenaeum,* n.s. 38 (1960), 7–8, whence *AE* 1961.240.[4] Photographs: *Athenaeum,* n.s. 38 (1960), Tav. 1–IV. I print the emperors' names as they appear on the outside of the bronze diptych; the same formula appears inside, with different lineation.

Impp. Caess. Fl. Val. Constantius G. Val. Ma-
2 ximian. p. f. in. Aug. p. m. Germ. m. V Sar. m. III Per. m. II Br.
m. II Car. m. V Ar. m. Med. m. Ad. m. tr. p. XVI cos. VI p. p. p.
4 dd. nn. Diocletian. et Maximian. patr. Augg. et Caess.
dd. nn. Severi [*sic*] et Maximin. nob. Caess.

The text is perfectly and doubly preserved, but TRP XVI must be an error for TR P XIV (cf. Table 2).

4. Also M. M. Roxan, *Roman Military Diplomas 1954–1977* (London, 1978), 100 no. 78, cf. 27 (no. 3).

5. Fragment of an imperial edict or letter of late 310 (Sinope). Published by T. Mommsen from a report by Constantine Lanaras, *Ephemeris Epigraphica* 4 (1881), 31 no. 44. Mommsen reports "ectypum ut acciperem frustra laboravi": the publications in *CIL* 3.6979 and *ILS* 660 depend on the same report alone.

2   Imperator Caesa[r] Galeri[us
      invictus Augustus pontif[ex max.
4   quint. Persic. max. tert. Brett.
      Med. max. Adiab. max. trib. pot.
6   pater patriae procons.
      ////////////////////////////////
8   [Caes]ar Flavius Va[l]erius Cons[tantinus

In view of the poor attestation of the text, I print it largely without restorations. Galerius' names and titles (lines 2–6) can be supplied from comparison with nos. 6 and 7. If the erasure in line 7 effaced the name of Maximinus (as seems likely on general grounds), then the name of Licinius must have stood either before the erasure (as in no. 6) or after Constantine (as in no. 7).

6. Fragment of an edict or letter of late 310 (Tlos in Lycia). Text: *CIL* 3. 12133 (right side), with the supplements proposed by T. D. Barnes, *ZPE* 21 (1976), 277.

      Imp. Ca[es. Gal. Val. Maximianus p. f. invict. Aug.]
2   po[nt. max. Germ. max. vii Aegypt. max. Theb. max.]
      Sar[m. max. v Persic. max. iii Britt. max. ii Carp.]
4   ma[x. vi Arm. max. Med. max. Adiab. max. trib. pot.]
      XV[iiii cons. vii imp. xviiii p. p. procons. et]
6   Imp. Ca[es. Val. Lic. Licinius p. f. inv. Aug. pont. max.]
      tr[ib. pot. iii cons. imp.- p. p. procons. et]
8   *Imp. Ca[es. Gal. Val. Maximinus p. f. inv. Aug. pont.]*
      ma[x. trib. pot. vi cons. imp. vi p. p. procons. et]
10   Imp. Ca[es. Flav. Val. Constantinus p. f. inv. Aug.]
      po[nt. max. trib. pot. v cons. imp. v p. p. procons.]
12   pii[ssimi et fortissimi principes]

The form of the restorations is of course conjectural: nothing on the stone indicates how the titles in lines 1–11 were in fact abbreviated or how line 12 continued after *pii[ssimi]*. The substance of these conjectural supplements is, however, guaranteed by comparison with no. 7. The fragment, though exiguous, it important. The position of *Sar[m(aticus) max(imus)]* in line 3 confirms the attribution to Galerius of the titles *Aegyptiacus maximus Thebaicus maxi-*

mus in no. 7. Lines 8–9 have been erased; the erasure indicates that the name of Maximinus, who suffered *damnatio memoriae* in 313, occurred in third place, and hence implies that Galerius continued for a time to treat Maximinus and Constantine as junior to Licinius even after he acknowledged them as Augusti.

7. Proclamation ending the persecution of Christians, issued by Galerius in April 311.[5] Text: Eusebius, *HE* 8.17.3–5 (emended).

Αὐτοκράτωρ Καῖσαρ Γαλέριος Οὐαλέριος Μαξιμιανὸς ⟨εὐσε-
βὴς εὐτυχὴς⟩ ἀνίκητος Σεβαστός, ἀρχιερεὺς μέγιστος, Γερμα-
νικὸς μέγιστος ⟨ἑπτάκις⟩, Αἰγυπτιακὸς μέγιστος, Θηβαϊκὸς μέγιστος, Σαρματικὸς μέγιστος πεντάκις, Περσῶν μέγιστος ⟨τρίς,
5   Βρεττανῶν μέγιστος⟩ δίς, Κάρπων μέγιστος ἑξάκις, Ἀρμενίων
μέγιστος, Μήδων μέγιστος, Ἀδιαβηνῶν μέγιστος, δημαρχικῆς
ἐξουσίας τὸ εἰκοστόν, αὐτοκράτωρ τὸ ἐννεακαιδέκατον, ὕπατος
τὸ ὄγδοον, πατὴρ πατρίδος, ἀνθύπατος, καὶ Αὐτοκράτωρ Καῖσαρ
Φλάυιος Οὐαλέριος Κωνσταντῖνος εὐσεβὴς εὐτυχὴς ἀνίκητος
10   Σεβαστός, ἀρχιερεὺς μέγιστος, δημαρχικῆς ἐξουσίας ⟨τὸ ἕκτον⟩,
αὐτοκράτωρ τὸ πέμπτον, ὕπατος, πατὴρ πατρίδος, ἀνθύπατος,
καὶ Αὐτοκράτωρ Καῖσαρ Οὐαλέριος Λικιννιανὸς Λικίννιος εὐσεβὴς εὐτυχὴς ἀνίκητος Σεβαστός, ἀρχιερεὺς μέγιστος, δημαρχικῆς
ἐξουσίας τὸ τέταρτον, αὐτοκράτωρ τὸ τρίτον, ὕπατος, πατὴρ πατ-
15   ρίδος, ἀνθύπατος, ἐπαρχιώταις ἰδίοις χαίρειν.

The text printed here differs from the edition of E. Schwartz, *GCS* 9.2 (1908), 790–792, in four places. In Galerius' titles, I have supplied εὐσεβὴς εὐτυχὴς and ἑπτάκις,[6] while H. Dessau, *ILS* 1, p. 151, proposed the necessary supplement of his victory titles (cf. no. 5). In Constantine's titles, I have supplied the number of his *tribunicia potestas* which harmonizes with *imp. V.* Licinius' name and titles, together with the following three words, are missing in some manuscripts, and were clearly deleted by Eusebius after Licinius' defeat by Constantine in 324.

It is not certain who deleted the name of Maximinus from the imperial col-

5. The proclamation has the form of a letter ("greetings to their provincials") and implicitly describes itself as one (*Mort. Pers.* 34.5 = *HE* 8.17.9), but Lactantius, who omits the protocol, twice styles it an *edictum* when recording its publication at Nicomedia on 30 April 311 (*Mort. Pers.* 33.11, 35.1). R. M. Grant, *TU* 115 (1975), 417, has recently emitted the strange theory that the emperor whose name stands first is Maximinus and that the date of the document is December 311. The titles of Galerius, Constantine, and Licinius are all consistent with the date attested by Lactantius and Eusebius (Tables 2–7).

6. Representing the five German victories attested in 306 (no. 4) plus the two which Constantine won between 306 and 310 (no. 8, cf. Table 8).

lege.[7] Although Galerius issued the proclamation in the name of both himself and his three imperial colleagues (Lactantius, *Mort. Pers.* 36.3), Maximinus did not in 311 officially publish it in his provinces (Eusebius, *HE* 9.1.1). Moreover, since Maximinus suffered *damnatio memoriae* in 313, his name may already have been removed from any copy which Eusebius was able subsequently to procure. Eusebius implies that he translated the Latin original into Greek himself (*HE* 8.17.11), so that the peculiar genitives in Galerius' victory titles may derive from his mistaken Greek expansion of an abbreviated Latin original which read "Pers. max. III, Britt. max. II, Carp. max. VI, Armen. max., Med. max. Adiab. max." (cf. nos. 1–5, 8).

8. Letter of Constantine to the Senate of Rome, c. February 337. Text: R. Paribeni, *Notizie degli Scavi*[6] 9 (1933), 489 no. 165 (whence *AE* 1934.158); T. D. Barnes, *ZPE* 20 (1976), 150. Photograph: *Notizie degli Scavi*[6] 9 (1933), Tav. XIV.

> Imp. Caes. Fl. Constantinus
> 2   p. f. vict. ac triumfat. August.
>   pont. max. Germ. max. IIII [Sa]rm. max. II
> 4   Gothic. max. II Dac. max. trib. potest. XXXIII
>   consul{i} VIII imp. XXXII p. p. p. et
> 6   Fl. Cl. Constantinus Alaman. et
>   Fl. Iul. Constantius et Fl. Iul.
> 8   Constans *et Fl. Iul. Dalmatius*
>   nobb. Caess.

In line 5 Paribeni printed PP for the PPP which is clear on the photograph. In line 8 the erased name is totally illegible, but certain — see J. Gascou, *MEFR* 79 (1967), 620.

2. ELEMENTS IN THE IMPERIAL TITULATURE

The fullest form of the imperial titles in these eight authoritative documents is perhaps best exemplified in the Price Edict of 301, where the names and titles of Diocletian read as follows:

> Imp(erator) Caesar C. Aurel(ius) Val(erius) Diocletianus P(ius) F(elix) Inv(ictus) Aug(ustus) pont(ifex) max(imus) Germ(anicus) max(imus) VI Sarm(aticus) max(imus) IV Pers(icus) max(imus) II Britt(anicus) max(imus) Carpic(us) max(imus) Armen(icus) max(imus) Medic(us) max(imus) Adiabenic(us) max(imus), trib(u-nicia) p(otestate) XVIII, coss. [i.e. consul] VII, imp(erator) XVIII, p(ater) p(atriae), procoss. [i.e. proconsul].   [no. 1]

---

7. Millar, *Emperor* 579, assumes that the heading never named Maximinus.

Apart from the name, which is unique to each emperor, there are four different categories of title: (1) standard epithets, (2) imperial consulates, (3) *tribunicia potestas* and the title *imperator,* which are both renewed annually, (4) victory titles taken and renewed on the occasion of actual victories in the field. Each category must be considered separately.

Standard Epithets[8]

The full official name of an Augustus includes a series of titles which normally do not change at either regular or irregular intervals: *imperator Caesar* before the proper name, *pius felix invictus Augustus* and *pontifex maximus* after, and *pater patriae proconsul* at the very end. A Caesar, in contrast, lacks the *praenomina imperatoris* and the honorific epithets, he is neither *pontifex maximus* nor *pater patriae* nor *proconsul;* usually he is simply *nobilissimus Caesar,* though other epithets may be added (e.g. *nobilissimus ac beatissimus Caesar, nobilissimus et fortissimus Caesar, nobilissimus et invictus Caesar).*[9]

Many minor variations are attested, and some epithets not yet noted are significant. Diocletian, Galerius, Maximinus, and Licinius and his son are all Iovii,[10] Maximian, Constantius, Severus, and Constantine all Herculii,[11] while after their abdication in 305 Diocletian and Maximian became *seniores Augusti* and "fathers of the Augusti and Caesars."[12] Further, two changes in Constantine's titulature reflect specific political events. The title *maximus* advertises Constantine's standing as senior emperor: the *primi nominis titulus* was voted by the Roman Senate shortly after 28 October 312 and the epithet assumed in consequence (Lactantius, *Mort. Pers.* 44.11).[13] Similarly, in 324, after defeating Licinius, Constantine took the title *victor* or *triumphator* (Eusebius, *VC* 2.19.2, naturally using the Greek equivalent νικητής).[14]

8. On the earlier use of descriptive epithets such as *felix* and *invictus,* see L. Berlinger, *Beiträge zur inoffiziellen Titulatur der römischen Kaiser* (Diss. Breslau, 1935), 1 ff.

9. For examples of these and other phrases, see *ILS* 3, pp. 304 (Constantius), 305 (Galerius), 306 (Severus and Maximinus), 309-310 (the sons of Constantine). In the following three footnotes, the documentation is deliberately selective.

10. *ILS* 634 (the "First Tetrarchy"); 621, 623, 659, 8930 (Diocletian); 661, 8931 (Galerius); *RIC* 6.636, Antiochia 134 (Maximinus); *RIC* 7.600-608 (Nicomedia), 676-682 (Antioch: the two Licinii).

11. *ILS* 622, 623, 659 (Maximian); *Pan. Lat.* 9(4).8.1 (Constantius); *RIC* 6.287, Ticinum 54a, b; 317, Aquileia 47a, b (Severus); *Pan. Lat.* 7(6).2.5, 8.2 (Constantine). In his attempts to present himself as a legitimate emperor, Maxentius too may have styled himself Herculius, see *RIC* 6.367-368, Roma 137-139; 369, Roma 147; 373, Roma 171; 374, Roma 181-184. Hence "Herculi Caes. vincas!" on a brooch now in Turin (*ILS* 681, republished by R. Noll, *Bonner Jahrbücher* 174 (1974), 235/6) may refer to Maxentius rather than to Constantine.

12. *ILS* 645 (*seniores Aug.*); no. 4 (*patres impp. et Caess.*); *ILS* 646 (*seniores Augg., patres impp. et Caess.*).

13. E. Babelon, *Mélanges Boissier* (Paris, 1903), 53.

14. For the inscriptions which prove Eusebius correct, A Chastagnol, *Latomus* 25 (1966), 543 ff.; E. Guadagno, *Rendiconti Lincei*[8] 25 (1970), 111 ff.; G. Camodeca, *Atti dell'Accademia di Scienze Morali e Politiche, Napoli* 82 (1971), 30 ff.

Imperial Consulates

The identity of the *consules ordinarii* for any year normally admitted of no uncertainty and complete lists have survived from antiquity. At times of political conflict, however, different consuls were sometimes recognized in different jurisdictions. Such was the case in 284, 285, 307–313, and 321–324, but only in two cases between 284 and 337 is the actual date of an imperial consulate subject to any doubt. Galerius was *cos. VII* in 308, except in the territory of Maxentius where this consulate was not recognized, but where Galerius had been regarded as *cos. VII* from 1 January to April 307; Constantine was consul for the first time in 307, but this consulate was not recognized outside his own domains, while he refused ever to acknowledge the consulate with Licinius which Galerius, Licinius, and Maximinus attributed to him in 309.[15]

Tribunicia Potestas *and* Imperator

Both Augusti and Caesars received the tribunician power on the day of their proclamation as emperor and they renewed it on each subsequent 10 December. Diocletian, for example, who received the tribunician power on 20 November 284, renewed it for the first time on 10 December 284, and thus became *trib. pot. II* on that day, *trib. pot. III* on 10 December 285, and so on. The full titulature of an Augustus contains the word *imperator* twice: once at the beginning in the unvarying phrase *imperator Caesar,* once as an attributive title which follows the proper name and is renewed annually on the anniversary of his *dies imperii,* i.e. the day on which he took or was officially deemed to have taken the purple.[16] Hence the titles of Diocletian, which show no irregularities, are numbered as follows:

trib. pot. imp.	20 November–9 December 284
trib. pot. II imp.	20 December 284–19 November 285
trib. pot. II imp. II	20 November 285–9 December 285
trib. pot. III imp. II	10 December 285–19 November 286, etc.[17]

The titles of Licinius, who was appointed to the imperial college as an Augustus, without holding the rank of Caesar, are equally straightforward: he took the purple and received *tribunicia potestas* on 11 November 308, became *trib. pot. II imp.* on 10 December 308, *trib. pot. II imp. II* on 11 November 309, and so on.

The titles of Augusti who had previously been Caesars exhibit complexities, and even confusion. On the strictest definition, since a Caesar lacked the title

15. For consulates from 284 to 337, Chapter VI.1; Table 1.

16. H. Dessau, *EE* 7 (1892), 429 ff. No one has seriously challenged Dessau's explanation of how the titles behave (though some have ignored it). The earliest apparent example of *imperator* renewed annually which I can find is a series of boundary stones in Rome where Hadrian in 121 is *trib. potest. V imp. IIII cos. III* (*ILS* 5931).

17. Hence the edict on prices (no. 2) was issued after 20 November 301, when Diocletian became *imp. XVII,* but before 10 December 301, when his nineteenth *tribunicia potestas* began.

imperator (which well-informed contemporary writers use as a synonym for Augustus),[18] an Augustus who had previously been a Caesar should reckon his possession of the title only from his promotion to the higher rank. Some inscriptions do indeed employ this computation. Two datable to 306 style Constantius *imp. II;* since he became Caesar on 1 March 293, Augustus on 1 May 305, this implies that he assumed the title *imperator* in 305 and renewed it on 1 May 306 (*ILS* 651; *AE* 1895.80: both Thibilis). On a broader definition, however, an Augustus may be counted as having possessed the title, not from his promotion to that rank, but from his earlier proclamation as Caesar. Thus in the letter or edict which Galerius promulgated in April 311 (no. 7), Constantine is *imp. V,* which seems to presuppose that he became *imperator* on 25 July 306, *imp. II* on 25 July 307, and so on.

The observable phenomena, however, cannot be explained in terms of the preceding rules alone. For three Augusti who had previously been Caesars are attested as possessing both one more *tribunicia potestas* and one more imperatorial salutation than a straightforward reckoning from their *dies imperii* would provide. The first case is Maximian, who was *trib. pot. X imp. VIIII* in 294 (*ILS* 640: near Vitudurum) and *trib. pot. XVII* in late November or early December 301 (no. 2). Since Diocletian in both 294 and 301 regarded the *dies imperii* of Maximian as being 1 April 286,[19] Maximian must have received an irregular renewal of both titles in or before 294; hence it is a plausible conjecture that both titles were augmented on 1 March 293, when Maximian invested Constantius as Caesar.[20] (Even before 293, however, Maximian himself appears to have regarded his reign as beginning with his appointment as Caesar on 21 July 285 (*Pan. Lat.*10(2).3/4); and an inscription from Rome has *imp. VIII cos. III* (*CIL* 6.1124), i.e. seven renewals of the title *imperator* before 1 January 293.)[21] The titles of Galerius and Constantine also exhibit the same apparent anomaly. Galerius was *trib pot. XX imp. XIX* in April 311 (no. 7); Constantine *trib. pot. VII imp. VI* on 9 June 311 (*FIRA*² 1.93), and *trib pot. XXXIII imp. XXXII* c. February 337 (no. 8). In both cases the numbers are correct if they are calculated from the initial *dies imperii* (respectively, 1 March 293 and 25 July 306), with an additional renewal of both titles on the promotion of the Caesar to Augustus in 305 and 307 (Table 2).[22]

18. E.g., *Pan. Lat.* 7(6).1.1: "Caesari additum nomen imperii"; Lactantius, *Mort. Pers.* 25.5: "non imperatorem, sicut erat factus, sed Caesarem." Also *ILS* 657 (Heroonpolis: 306/7).

19. Chapter I, n. 6; below, section 3.

20. J. B. Mispoulet, *CRAI* 1908.455 ff., cf. A. Rousselle, *Dialogues d'Histoire Ancienne* 2 (1976), 445 ff. For other explanations of the change, see R. E. Smith, *Latomus* 31 (1972), 1058 ff.

21. Observe, however, that coins of Lugdunum with the reverse legend "P M TR P VIII COS IIII PP" seem to imply accession after 10 December 285, i.e. the official chronology (P. Bastien, *Le monnayage de l'atelier de Lyon* (Paris, 1972), 57 f., 198–202, nos. 462–466, 478–481).

22. As proposed by W. Seston, *REA* 39 (1937), 203 (Galerius); T. D. Barnes, *Phoenix* 30 (1976), 190 n. 61.

Some examples of Constantine's titulature cannot be accommodated within the patterns described here, and the evidence appears to compel the hypothesis that his *tribunicia potestas* and imperatorial acclamations were reckoned in at least four different ways (Table 3).

Victory Titles

The rules which govern the assumption, order, and iteration of victory titles like Diocletian's *Germanicus maximus VI* in 301 must be inferred from observation and by an inductive argument.[23] When the authoritative examples of the imperial titulature are analyzed, and unofficial documents disregarded, two rules can be seen to be paramount and invariable. No emperor between 284 and 337 officially assumed a victory title except for a victory which a member of the imperial college won on active campaign; and victory titles always appear in the order in which they were assumed for the first time, regardless of iterations.[24] In some documents, however, the criteria for inclusion are stricter than others. At the one extreme, the titulature of the two edicts of 301 observes the principle of full collegiality, whereby all four emperors take and renew the titles pertaining to victories won after their *dies imperii* by any number of the imperial college; hence Diocletian is *Germanicus maximus VI,* while Maximian is *Germanicus maximus V* and the Caesars are *Germanici maximi II* (nos. 1, 2). At the other extreme, the letter of Constantine to the Roman Senate early in 337 records victory titles only for those victories which the emperor won himself: Constantine has four victory titles, the Caesar Constantinus one which his father lacks and the other three Caesars none at all (no. 8). An intermediate criterion for inclusion was also sometimes adopted. Some less authoritative examples of the titulature of Constantine exhibit a combination of titles which seems explicable only on the hypothesis that they reflect victories won by Constantine himself and by some, but not all, of his imperial colleagues (*ILS* 696 (near Sitifis); 8942 (Semta): Constantine and Licinius; *ILAlg.* 1.3956 (between Theveste and Thelepte): Constantine, Licinius, and Maximinus).[25]

For reconstructing the military history of the period, three sets of victory titles are of central importance: those of Diocletian and his colleagues in late 301 (Table 4), those of Galerius in 301, 306, and 311 (Table 6), and those of Constantine c. February 337 (no. 8). When all the available evidence is collated and analyzed, the approximate chronology can be deduced (Tables 5, 7, and 8).[26]

23. The collection of material in P. Kneissl, *Die Siegestitulatur der römischen Kaiser* (*Hypomnemata* 23, 1969), 238–240, is incomplete: of the eight examples of the full imperial titulature printed above, Kneissl omits nos. 3 and 5–7. On individual titles, see O. Seeck, *RE* 1 (1894), 1280, s.v. Alamannicus; A. Stein, *RE* 3 (1899), 1610, s.v. Carpicus; *RE* 7 (1912), 1251–57, s.v. Germanicus; 1683–85, s.v. Gothicus; *RE* 2A (1921), 15–23, s.v. Sarmaticus.

24. A. Arnaldi, *Rendiconti dell'Istituto Lombardo,* Classe di Lettere, Scienze morali e storiche 106 (1972), 28 ff.

25. *ZPE* 20 (1976), 153 ff.

26. *Phoenix* 30 (1976), 174 ff.; *ZPE* 20 (1976), 149 ff., cf. A. Arnaldi, *Rendiconti dell'Istituto*

3. EGYPTIAN REGNAL YEARS

Egyptian regnal years observe principles of their own. The official year begins on 1 Thoth, which corresponds to 29 August (except in the Julian year preceding a leap year, when it corresponds to 30 August), so that an emperor's first year is the period (however short) between his *dies imperii* and the following 29 (or 30) August.[27] On the latter day the emperor's second year begins, regardless of whether news of his accession had reached Egypt before 29 (or 30) August. Hence the following well-attested equations:

1 Diocletian = 20 November 284–28 August 285
2 Diocletian = 29 August 285–28 August 286, etc.
1 Constantius = 1 Galerius = 1 March 293–28 August 293, etc.
1 Severus = 1 Maximinus = 1 May 305–28 August 305, etc.
1 Licinius = 11 November 308–28 August 309, etc.
1 Crispus = 1 Licinius Caesar = 1 Constantinus Caesar
= 1 March 317–28 August 317, etc.
1 Constantius = 8 November 324–28 August 325, etc.
1 Constans = 25 December 333–28 August 334, etc.
1 Dalmatius = 18 September 335–28 August 336, etc.[28]

The regnal years of Maximian and Constantine as attested in contemporary documents import a complication. The dating formulae in papyri from spring 286 to late 303 consistently state the regnal years of Maximian as one fewer in number than those of Diocletian, which implies a *dies imperii* on or after 29 August 285; but papyri from the end of 303 consistently give Maximian exactly the same number of regnal years as Diocletian, which implies a *dies imperii* on or before 28 August 285.[29] For Constantine, there is a formal and simple contradiction: his *dies imperii* was 25 July 306, but his first regnal year was equated with 15 Galerius and 3 Severus and Maximinus (*P. Cairo Isid.* 45, 46, 52, 116, etc.), i.e., with the Egyptian year which began on 29 August 306. Both cases can readily be explained. Until 20 November 303 Maximian's *dies imperii* was deemed to be his proclamation as Augustus on 1 April 286, but from 20 November 303 it was deemed to be his prior appointment as Caesar on 21 July 285. Although Constantine was proclaimed Augustus in Britain on 25 July 306, he then sought recognition from Galerius as the senior reigning emperor.

Lombardo 106 (1972), 28 ff.; *Contributi di Storia antica in onore di A. Garzetti* (Genoa, 1976), 175 ff.

27. U. Wilcken, *Griechische Ostraka* 1 (Leipzig and Berlin, 1899), 789; *Grundzüge und Chrestomathie der Papyruskunde* 1.1 (Leipzig and Berlin, 1912), lvi.

28. R. S. Bagnall and K. A. Worp, *Regnal Formulas in Byzantine Egypt* (*BASP*, Supp. 2, 1979), 2 ff.

29. A. Chastagnol, *Rev. Num.*[6] 9 (1967), 69 ff.; J. D. Thomas, *CE* 46 (1971), 173 ff.

The latter deliberated long before he recognized Constantine as Caesar, and, instead of acknowledging the proclamation of 25 July, he sent Constantine the imperial purple himself (Lactantius, *Mort. Pers.* 25.1–5).[30] Hence, in Galerius' eyes, the *dies imperii* of Constantine was not 25 July 306, but subsequent to 29 August 306 — presumably the day on which Galerius dispatched the purple, or, possibly, the day on which Constantine received it.[31] Under the circumstances, it is perhaps surprising that Constantine did not revise the official computation of his regnal years when he gained political control of Egypt.

30. *Mort. Pers.* 25.3; "suscepit itaque imaginem admodum invitus atque ipse purpuram misit" (with my emendation *ipse* for the ms. *ipsi*).

31. News of Constantine's appointment had not reached Karanis by 17 November 306 (*P. Cairo Isid.* 115), but it was known at Oxyrhynchus by 30 November (*P. Oxy.* 1750).

THE CAREERS AND FAMILIES
OF EMPERORS

The present chapter discusses the principal evidence for the families and private careers of the legitimate emperors from Diocletian to the Caesars whom Constantine created. Each emperor will be treated separately, in order of seniority in the imperial college, and each discussion will have approximately the same format: (1) date of birth and parentage, (2) career before accession, (3) marriages and progeny, (4) where relevant, details of life after abdicating the imperial power. Where the facts are clear and well attested, a summary statement with references will be given, extended discussion being reserved for matters of real doubt or obscurity.

Diocletian

Born on 22 December (*P. Beatty Panopolis* 2.164, 173, 181/2, 193/4, 262). Two sources give Diocletian's age: one written shortly after 395 implies that he died in the early months of 313 and states that he lived sixty-eight years (*Epitome* 39.7); another of the late sixth century estimates his age at death as seventy-two (Malalas 311 Bonn). Their testimony is normally rejected and Diocletian's birth has been dated as early as c. 225.[1] But no positive reason exists for rejecting the explicit evidence, and of the two witnesses the earlier presum-

1. Seeck, *Geschichte* 1³.437. Less extreme hypotheses are adopted by W. Ensslin, *RE* 7A (1948), 2421, who wished to emend *LXVIII annos* to *LXXVIII* (which implies birth c. 234), and in *PLRE* 1.253–254, Diocletianus 2, which argues that "the *Epitome* has perhaps confused his age on abdicating with his age at death."

ably deserves preference:[2] it indicates (depending on the base date and method of computation) that Diocletian was born on 22 December 243, 244, or 245.

Diocletian originally bore the name Diocles (Lactantius, *Mort. Pers.* 9.11, 19.5, 52.3; Libanius, *Orat.* 19.45 ff.; *Epitome* 39.1), which he changed after he became emperor, though not immediately on his proclamation (*P. Oxy.* 3055 (7 March 285)).[3]

About Diocletian's parentage and origins, the ancient sources exhibit vagueness or uncertainty: he came from Illyricum (Victor, *Caes.* 39.26) or, better, Dalmatia (Eutropius, *Brev.* 9.19.2; *Epitome* 39.1), his mother and birthplace were both called Dioclea (*Epitome* 39.1), and some thought that his father was a scribe, others that he himself was a freedman of the senator Anullinus (Eutropius, *Brev.* 9.19.2). How much of this rests on secure knowledge? Perhaps only Dalmatia as the province of origin.[4] As for Diocletian's precise origin, Lactantius perhaps implies, and two late writers state, that he hailed from Salonae, close to Spalato where he built a palace and passed his years of retirement.[5]

No valid evidence attests Diocletian's career before 284, when he was *domesticos regens* (Victor, *Caes.* 39.1; *HA, Carus* 13.1) or κόμης δομεστικῶν (Zonaras 12.31), i.e., commander of a special corps which always attended the emperor.[6]

Diocletian's wife was Prisca, whose origin is unknown, and their daughter was Valeria, who married Galerius (Lactantius, *Mort. Pers.* 7.9, 15.1, 39.5, 51).

On 1 May 305 Diocletian abdicated at Nicomedia and retired to the palace which he had built at Spalato on the Dalmatian coast (Lactantius, *Mort. Pers.* 19.6; Eutropius, *Brev.* 9.27.2; *Epitome* 39.6).[7] Only one subsequent political act is known: he attended the Conference of Carnuntum in November 308, but refused to emerge from retirement (Lactantius, *Mort. Pers.* 29.2, 43.5–6; *Epitome* 39.6). About the date and manner of his death, the ancient testimony is

2. T. C. Skeat, *Papyri from Panopolis* (Dublin, 1964), 146. E. Stein, *Hermes* 52 (1917), 576, preferred Malalas, and deduced that Diocletian was born in 244 on the grounds that he died on 3 December 316 (not 311, as argued here).

3. "Diocles" is the form which appears in Egyptian demotic, see J. Baines, *Oxyrhynchus Papyri* 47 (London, 1980), xviii.

4. R. Syme, *Emperors and Biography: Studies in the Historia Augusta* (Oxford, 1971), 211 f., 233. The present chapter (it may be noted here) discounts all inferences from *HA, Probus* 22.3 for the careers of Diocletian or any of his colleagues (cf. ibid. 213 f.).

5. Lactantius, *Mort. Pers.* 19.6: "veteranus rex foras exportatur in patriamque dimittitur"; Constantinus Porphyrogenitus, *De Thematibus* p. 58.1–2 Bonn; Zonaras 12.32, cf. F. Bulić, *L'imperatore Diocleziano* (Split, 1916), 14 ff.

6. Jones, *LRE* 53, 636; R. I. Frank, *Scholae Palatinae: The Palace Guards of the Later Roman Empire* (*Papers of the American Academy in Rome* 23, 1969), 42 f.

7. For the surviving remains of the palace, J. and T. Marasović, *Diocletian Palace* (Zagreb, 1968); J. and T. Marasović, S. McNally, and J. Wilkes, *Diocletian's Palace: Report on Joint Excavations in Southeast Quarter* 1 (Split, 1972).

contradictory.[8] Whether he killed himself deliberately (Lactantius, *Mort. Pers.* 42) or died of illness alone (Eusebius, *HE* 8, app. 3) was clearly a matter of uncertainty even to contemporaries. More serious, different dates are stated or implied:

1. Lactantius, *Mort. Pers.* 42: Diocletian starved himself when he heard that his name had become involved in the *damnatio memoriae* of Maximian. Since the latter belongs to the time of Constantine's war against Maxentius,[9] a date in 311 or 312 is implied.
2. *Epitome* 39.7; Socrates, *HE* 1.2.10: Diocletian's death is linked to the marriage of Licinius and Constantia in February 313.[10]
3. A date of 315 or 316 is stated by Jerome *Chronicle* 230[d] (from which derive Prosper Tiro (*Chr. Min.* 1.448) and a later Gallic chronicle (*Chr. Min.* 1.643)); Zosimus 2.8.1; *Chr. Pasch.* 523.
4. *Consularia Constantinopolitana* a. 316 (*Chr. Min.* 1.231); *P. Berol.* 13296:[11] 3 December 316.

Lactantius' chronology should be preferred to the others, and, if the *Consularia Constantinopolitana* may be supposed to have confused the consular dates of 311 (*Volusiano et Rufino*) and 316 (*Sabino et Rufino*), then the day on which Diocletian died was 3 December 311.[12]

Maximian

Stated to be *sexagenarius* at the time of his death (*Epitome* 40.11): therefore, born c. 250. A speech survives which was delivered on Maximian's birthday in 291, but it does not disclose the day and month (*Pan. Lat.* 11(3)).[13]

The only precise statement about Maximian's parents asserts that they were shopkeepers near Sirmium (*Epitome* 40.10: "exercebant opera mercenaria"). Otherwise there are vague allusions to Illyricum as his *patria* (Victor, *Caes.* 39.26), to his *Pannonia virtus* and upbringing "in illo limite, illa fortissimarum sede legionum" (*Pan. Lat.* 10(2).2.2 ff., cf. 11(3).3.9).

Nor is Maximian's career any better documented. He served in the army together with Diocletian, rising gradually through promotion (*Pan. Lat.*

---

8. See especially J. Moreau, *Lactance* 421 ff.; T. D. Barnes, *JRS* 63 (1973), 32 ff.

9. *JRS* 63 (1973), 34 f., 41 ff.

10. Both writers are probably dependent on Eunapius, see *CP* 71 (1976), 267.

11. Published by H. Lietzmann, *Quantulacumque: Studies presented to K. Lake* (London, 1937), 339 ff.

12. *JRS* 63 (1973), 35. Consecration of Diocletian as *divus* is alleged by Eutropius, *Brev.* 9.28; Jerome, *Chronicle* 230[d], probably by confusion with Maximian.

13. *P. Beatty Panopolis* 2.164, etc., shows that Diocletian and Maximian had different birthdays (T. C. Skeat, *Papyri from Panopolis* 145 f.); the occasion of *Pan. Lat.* 11(3), therefore, is the *genuinus natalis* of Maximian alone, not a *geminus natalis* shared by both Augusti (Chapter V, n. 52).

11(3).5/6). The areas where he served can perhaps be deduced from an allusion to his military service before 285: "ibo scilicet virtutis tuae vestigiis colligendis per totum Histri limitem perque omnem qua tendit Euphraten et ripas peragrabo Rheni et litus Oceani?" (*Pan. Lat.* 10(2).2.6). Even without such testimony, however, it could reasonably be conjectured that Maximian was with Carus when he invaded Mesopotamia in 283 and present when Diocletian was proclaimed emperor at Nicomedia on 20 November 284.[14]

For Maximian, one wife is attested, and another must probably be postulated. The Syrian Eutropia, who was still alive after 324 (Eusebius, *VC* 3.52, cf. Sozomenus, *HE* 2.4.6), bore him both Maxentius and Fausta (*Origo* 12; Julian, *Orat.* 1, 6a; *Epitome* 40.12; Sozomenus, *HE* 2.4.6). It is normally believed that Eutropia had previously been married to someone else (often identified as Afranius Hannibalianus, cos. 292) and that Theodora, the wife of Constantius, was her daughter by her first husband, and thus the stepdaughter of Maximian.[15] This view should be rejected. The writers who call Theodora the stepdaughter of Maximian (Victor, *Caes.* 39.25; Eutropius, *Brev.* 9.22; Jerome, *Chronicle* 225[g]; *Epitome* 39.2, 40.12) all derive their information from a single lost source written c. 337, whose testimony is not necessarily reliable.[16] Other extant writers make Theodora the full daughter of Maximian; though fewer in number, they are superior in authority (*Origo* 2; Philostorgius, *HE* 2.16[a]).[17] Their evidence should be preferred on the general ground that, when no decisive evidence exists, normally reliable sources deserve credit over those whose inaccuracy can be detected on other matters. Moreover, if Theodora was the full daughter of Maximian, then a more natural meaning can be assigned to the panegyrist of 289, when he declares that Maximian has bound his praetorian prefect to him by a marriage which produces "non timoris obsequia sed vota pietatis" (*Pan. Lat.* 10(2).11.4): the allusion is to Constantius as his son-in-law, not to Hannibalianus as the first husband of Eutropia.[18] Hence Theodora was born no later than c. 275.

If Theodora was not the daughter of Eutropia, then she must be Maximian's daughter by a previous wife, whose name, origin, and existence are nowhere directly attested. It may be relevant, therefore that one of the sons of Constantius and Theodora was called Hannibalianus. That might indicate that

14. For discussion of Maximian's career before 285, W. Ensslin, *RE* 14 (1930), 2486 ff.

15. E.g., O. Seeck, *RE* 4 (1901), 1041; *Geschichte* 1³.27 ff.; Stein, *Bas-Empire* 1².68, 435; W. Ensslin, *RE* 5A (1934), 1773-74, Theodora 2; *PLRE* 1.895, Theodora 1.

16. Viz. the lost "Kaisergeschichte," postulated by A. Enmann, *Philologus,* Supp. 4 (1884), 335 ff. For some of its errors concerning the reign of Diocletian, see *Phoenix* 30 (1976), 174; *The Sources of the Historia Augusta* (Collection Latomus 155, 1978), 92 f.

17. On their value, see, respectively, D. J. A. Westerhuis, *Origo Constantini Imperatoris sive Anonymi Valesiani pars prior* (Diss. Groningen, 1906); J. Bidez, in the introduction to his edition of Philostorgius, *GCS* 21 (1913), cvi ff. In *BHAC 1968/69* (1970), 25, I mistakenly followed the *communis opinio,* to the detriment of my own argument.

18. The passage is quoted and discussed more fully in Chapter VIII.1.

Maximian married a daughter of Afranius Hannibalianus (cos. 292), one of whose ancestors appears to derive from Tralles.[19]

The ages of Maxentius and Fausta are nowhere explicitly attested. Modern estimates for the date of Maxentius' birth have diverged widely, from c. 277 to c. 287,[20] while the birth of Fausta has often been dated c. 298.[21] But the latter date depends on the supposition that it was only in 298 or 299 that Maximian first visited Rome, where Fausta was born, according to Julian (*Orat.* 1, 5d). That premise is vulnerable.[22] Probability, and the evidence of contemporaries, appear to indicate that Maximian's son and daughter were born c. 283 and in 289 or 290. The panegyric of 289, when interpreted strictly, seems to indicate that Maxentius has not yet reached his seventh birthday (*Pan. Lat.* 10(2).14.1: "felix aliquis praeceptor expectat"),[23] while by 305 he was both married and a candidate for the purple (Lactantius, *Mort. Pers.* 18.9. ff.). Maxentius' mother, in November 312, swore that she had conceived him in adultery with a Syrian (*Origo* 12); that might imply that Maxentius was born, or at least conceived, in Syria—where Maximian would have been c. 283, serving under the emperors Carus and then Numerianus.[24] As for Fausta, a mosaic in the palace of Aquileia, whose dramatic date was no later than 296 (and may have been 293) depicted her as a girl (*Pan. Lat.* 7(6).6.2), and the panegyric delivered at her wedding in 307 appears to assume that she is already of child-bearing age (*Pan. Lat.* 7(6).2.1 ff.; cf. 6.2: "sed adhuc [i.e. in the 290s] impar oneri suo"). Moreover, if Fausta was indeed born in Rome while her father was there, then the evidence for Maximian's movements appears to render it probable that she was born in 289 or 290.[25]

When Maximian abdicated on 1 May 305, he retired to Campania (Lactantius, *Mort. Pers.* 26.7) or Lucania (Eutropius, *Brev.* 9.27.2, 10.2.3), whence he issued forth late in 306 to help his son, again an Augustus, but never again recognized as such by the senior emperor.[26]

Maximian's posthumous reputation requires discussion. He suffered *damnatio memoriae,* not immediately after his death c. July 310 (cf. *Pan. Lat.* 6(7).14.3 ff.; 20.3 ff.), but probably in late 311, when Constantine was at war with Maxentius, who had proclaimed his father Divus Maximianus and professed to be avenging his death (Lactantius, *Mort. Pers.* 42.1 ff.; *RIC* 6.382,

19. E. Groag, *JÖAI* 10 (1907), 288 f., cf. *PIR*[2] H 14.

20. Respectively, E. Groag, *RE* 14 (1930), 2419 f.; *PLRE* 1.571 ("probably born c.a. 287").

21. E.g., Seeck, *Geschichte* 1[3].462; I. König, *Chiron* 4 (1974), 576. Against, see X. Lucien-Brun, *BAGB* 1970, 393.

22. Chapter V, n. 49.

23. D. de Decker, *Byzantion* 38 (1968), 490 n. 1.

24. Numerianus was at Emesa in April 284 (*CJ* 5.52.2).

25. Chapter V: Maximian.

26. Chapter II. *P. Cairo Isid.* 8, however, dated 14 June 309, implies that Maximian was recognized as a member of the imperial college by Maximinus, cf. A. E. R. Boak and H. C. Youtie, *The Archive of Aurelius Isidorus* (Ann Arbor, 1960), 72 f.

Roma 243/4, 250/1; 404, Ostia 24-26).[27] When Maxentius was dead, however, his mother swore on oath that he was not Maximian's son (*Origo* 12, cf. *Pan. Lat.* 12(9).3.4, 4.3), and the memory of Maximian was rehabilitated: by 318 he was being commemorated as *divus* on Constantine's coinage, together with Constantius and Claudius, from whom Constantine had begun to claim descent in 310 (*RIC* 7.180, Trier 200-207; 252, Arles 173-178; 310-312, Rome 104-128; 395, Aquileia 21-26; 429/30, Siscia 41-46; 503, Tessalonica 24-26).[28]

Two pieces of evidence may be argued to refer to the consecration of Maximian, which technically required a formal decree of the Roman Senate.[29] First, Eutropius (*Brev.* 9.28) and Jerome (*Chronicle* 230ᵈ), both probably dependent on the same lost source,[30] report that Diocletian was consecrated. That is not only unattested, but highly improbable[31] — presumably, therefore, a confusion with Maximian. Second, Athanasius refers vaguely to recent consecrations of dead emperors: οὐ πολλῷ πρότερον, ἢ τάχα καὶ μέχρι νῦν ἡ Ῥωμαίων σύγκλητος τοὺς πώποτε αὐτῶν ἐξ ἀρχῆς ἄρξαντας βασιλέας, ἢ πάντας, ἢ οὓς ἂν αὐτοὶ βούλωνται καὶ κρίνωσι, δογματίζουσιν ἐν θεοῖς εἶναι καὶ θρησκεύεσθαι θεοὺς γράφουσι (*Contra Gentes* 9.50-53 Thomson). The only emperors whom the Roman Senate consecrated as *divi* between 284 and 337 were Constantius in 306 (*Pan. Lat.* 6(7).3.3, 14.3; *RIC* 6.256, Lugdunum 202), Maximian and Galerius in 311 (*RIC* 6.382, Roma 243-255; 404, Ostia 24-31; *ILS* 671: Caesarea; 673: Rome), and Maximian again at some date after 28 October 312, if the apotheosis under Maxentius was regarded as null and void. It can be demonstrated, on philosophical grounds, that Athanasius wrote the *Contra Gentes* some years before 324.[32] Hence an allusion to reports of the consecration of Maximian c. 317 seems probable.

Constantius

Born on 31 March (*CIL* 1², p. 255); the year is unknown, but Constantius' career and the age of his eldest son entail a date no later than c. 250. Constan-

27. On the date, *JRS* 63 (1973), 34 f., 41 f. C. H. V. Sutherland, *RIC* 6 (1967), 33, had proposed early 312.

28. On the fictitious descent from Claudius, R. Syme, *BHAC 1971* (1974), 237 ff.

29. For the Senate's role, E. Bickermann, *Archiv für Religionsgeschichte* 13 (1926), 1 ff.; *AJP* 94 (1973), 362 ff.

30. Viz. the lost "Kaisergeschichte" (above, n. 16).

31. Consecration cannot be inferred from Maximinus' words in May 313: ὑπὸ τῶν θειοτάτων Διοκλητιανοῦ καὶ Μαξιμιανοῦ τῶν γονέων τῶν ἡμετέρων (Eusebius, *HE* 9.10.8). Although Constantine showed respect toward Diocletian during his lifetime (*Pan. Lat.* 6.(7).15.4), the *damnatio memoriae* of Maximian involved the destruction of Diocletian's pictures too (Lactantius, *Mort. Pers.* 42.1), and after 28 October 312 Constantine was bound to disapprove officially of Diocletian because of his legislation against the Christians (*Oratio* 25; *VC* 2.50).

32. E. P. Meijering, *Orthodoxy and Platonism in Athanasius: Synthesis or Antithesis?*² (Leiden, 1974), 108 ff.; J. M. Rist, *Basil of Caesarea: Christian, Humanist, Ascetic,* ed. P. J. Fedwick (Toronto, 1981), 175 ff.

tius' family appears to derive from the later Dacia Ripensis (Julian, *Misopogon* 348d),[33] and his parents (so it has been conjectured) were perhaps a Flavius Dalmatius and a Julia Constantia.[34]

A reliable source gives the outline of his career: "protector primum, inde tribunus, postea praeses Dalmatiarum" (*Origo* 2).[35] The *Historia Augusta* dates the governorship in Dalmatia to the reign of Carinus (*HA, Carus* 17.6), which must be at least approximately correct. By 288 Constantius was praetorian prefect to Maximian in Gaul (*Pan. Lat.* 10(2).11.4, 8(5).1.5 ff.).[36]

Constantius married twice. His first wife was Helena, the mother of Constantine. She is reported to have been of humble origin (*Origo* 2; Ambrose, *De Obitu Theodosii* 42 (*CSEL* 73.393); Zosimus 2.8.2, 9.2), and she was a native of Drepanum in Bithynia, which Constantine renamed in her honor (Jerome, *Chronicle* 231[h]; Philostorgius, *HE* 2.12; Procopius, *De Aedificiis* 5.2.1; *Chr. Pasch.* 527). Several writers allege that Helena was merely the mistress or concubine of Constantius (Jerome, *Chronicle* 228[g], whence Orosius, *Hist. Adv. Pag.* 7.25.16; *Chronica Gallica a. DXI* 445 (*Chr. Min.* 1.643); Zosimus 2.8.2; *Chr. Pasch.* 516/7). But more and better evidence states that she was in fact Constantius' wife (*ILS* 708: Salernum; *CIL* 10.1483: Naples; *Origo* 1; Victor, *Caes.* 39.25; Eutropius, *Brev.* 10.2.2; Jerome, *Chronicle* 225[g]; *Epitome* 39.2). Since Helena was about eighty when she died in 327 (Eusebius, *VC* 3.46–47), while Constantine was born in 272 or 273, she must have married Constantius before c. 270, i.e., before he rose to the rank of *tribunus* in the Roman army.[37]

An allusion in the panegyric of 310 may now be considered. The vital name is obscured by textual corruption: "te enim tantus ille et imperator in terris et in caelo deus in primo aetatis suae flore generavit toto adhuc corpore vigens, illa praeditus alacritate ac fortitudine quam bella plurima, praecipue campi †videris idonei†" (*Pan. Lat.* 6(7).4.2, retaining the reading of the lost archetype in the last two words). Emendation is unavoidable. Recent editors have printed *videre Vindonii,* which produces an allusion to fighting near Vindonissa.[38] But

---

33. R. Syme, *BHAC 1971* (1974), 237 ff.

34. A. Piganiol, *L'Empereur Constantin* (Paris, 1932), 32—who also suggested that Constantius' original name was Flavius Julius Constantius.

35. The inscription *CIL* 3.9860 (Grabavo), reported from "una memoria del defunto Stephano Petković di Knin" by X. Alačević, *Bullettino di Archeologia e Storia Dalmata* 5 (1882), 136, is a forgery: see T. Mommsen and O. Hirschfeld, *CIL* 3, Supp. 2 (1902), p. 43*; G. Morin, *Rev. Ben.* 38 (1926), 217 f.; E. Stein, *PIR*[2] F 390.

36. Chapter VIII.1.

37. Hence, presumably, the discrepancy or doubts concerning Helena's status: a *stabularia,* as she was believed to have been (Ambrose, *De Obitu Theodosii* 42), could not contract a valid marriage with a senator or *vir perfectissimus* (*CTh* 4.6.3 (336), cf. *Dig.* 23.2.41–47). Observe also that the epitaph of a *protector Aureliani Augusti* at Nicomedia (*ILS* 2775) may imply that emperor's presence in Bithynia shortly after 270.

J. Vogt, *Saeculum* 27 (1976), 211 ff. = *Classical Folia* 31 (1977), 135 ff., argues that Helena was Jewish.

38. Thus E. Baehrens (1874), W. Baehrens (1911), E. Galletier (1952), and R. A. B. Mynors

the orator is speaking of the time when Constantius sired Constantine, i.e. the early 270s. He ought, therefore, on general grounds, to allude to the campaign in which Aurelian defeated Zenobia. It was presumably to produce such an allusion that scholars of the fifteenth century who corrected two manuscripts of the speech conjectured *videre Sydonii*.[39] Even though Zenobia fought near Antioch and at Palmyra itself, not near Sidon or in Phoenicia (Zosimus 1.50 ff.), *campi videre Sidonii* will supply exactly what the sense of the passage requires.[40]

If these conjectures are well founded, the following career can be established for Constantius:

born	c. 250
protector with Aurelian in Syria	271/2
tribunus	
praeses of Dalmatia	284/5
praetorian prefect of Maximian	288–293

Constantius' second wife was Theodora, the daughter of Maximian, whom he had married before 21 April 289 (*Pan. Lat.* 10(2).11.4).[41] They had six children, whose ages are in no case directly attested:

1. Flavius Dalmatius, cos. 333
2. Julius Constantius, cos. 335
3. Hannibalianus, who presumably died before c. 335 (Philostorgius, *HE* 2.16[a]; *Chr. Pasch.* 516; Zonaras 12.33, cf. Eutropius, *Brev.* 9.22.1)
4. Constantia, who married Licinius in February 313 (Lactantius, *Mort. Pers.* 43.2, 45.1)
5. Anastasia, married by 316 to the senator Bassianus (*Origo* 14)
6. Eutropia, mother of Nepotianus, who was proclaimed Augustus in 350 (Eutropius, *Brev.* 10.11; *Epitome* 42.3; Zosimus 2.43.2)[42]

Galerius

Galerius' date of birth is unknown; it might fall as late as c. 260.[43] He was born (and subsequently buried) at Romulianum on the Danube, whose name

---

(1964) — all following the conjecture of his father reported by H. J. Arntzen, *Panegyrici veteres* 1 (Utrecht, 1790), 358.

39. Reported by Mynors in his critical apparatus (p. 188.19).

40. G. W. Bowersock has suggested to me that the correct reading might be *videre Eoi,* which would avoid the apparent geographical imprecision.

41. Chapter VIII.1.

42. *PLRE* 1.316, Eutropia 2.

43. An inference (admittedly uncertain) from his long-standing friendship with Licinius (Lactantius, *Mort. Pers.* 20.3; Eutropius, *Brev.* 10.4.1). It is impermissible to deduce that Galerius

allegedly derived from his mother Romula, and his parents are said to have been peasants, Galerius himself once a shepherd (*Epitome* 40.15-16, cf. Lactantius, *Mort. Pers.* 9.9; Victor, *Caes.* 39.24, 40.1, 40.6; Eutropius, *Brev.* 9.22.1; Jerome, *Chronicle* 225⁸). His father's name is unknown, but Galerius himself originally bore the name Maximinus (Lactantius, *Mort. Pers.* 18.13).

Galerius' career before 293 is also unknown; but he certainly served in the army, and it is a permissible conjecture that he was praetorian prefect to Diocletian.[44]

Galerius' marriages and children present a problem, and much depends on Lactantius' statement that Valeria, the daughter of Diocletian and wife of Galerius, had adopted Candidianus, her husband's son by a concubine, *ob sterilitatem* (*Mort. Pers.* 50.2). Lactantius is normally taken to say that Valeria bore no children at all;[45] hence Valeria Maximilla, who married Maxentius (*ILS* 667: near Rome, cf. *ILS* 671: Caesarea in Mauretania; Lactantius, *Mort. Pers.* 18.9), is deduced to be Galerius' daughter by an earlier, otherwise unattested marriage.[46] Lactantius, however, could be taken to mean that Valeria was unable to conceive any children except a single daughter. If so, then Valeria Maximilla may (as her names perhaps imply) be the daughter of Galerius and Valeria, whose marriage consequently occurred before Galerius became Caesar.[47]

Candidianus was born c. 296 and executed in 313 (Lactantius, *Mort. Pers.* 20.4, 35.3, 50.2 ff.).[48]

Severus

From Illyricum (Victor, *Caes.* 40.1), of humble birth (*Origo* 9). No ancient source reveals anything about Severus' career before 305 except that he commanded soldiers and was a friend of Galerius (Lactantius, *Mort. Pers.* 18.12; *Origo* 9). Nor is anything known of Severus' family except that his son Severianus was *aetate robustus* in 313, when he fought under Maximinus and was executed by Licinius (Lactantius, *Mort. Pers.* 50.4). Nevertheless, a conjecture may be advanced, based on the phrase with which Lactantius makes Galerius

---

"served under Aurelian and Probus" (*PLRE* 1.574) from Victor's remark that the concord of all four Tetrarchs showed how virtue could be attained by "ingenium usumque bonae militiae, quanta his Aureliani Probique instituto fuit" (*Caes.* 39.28). Besides being plural, the statement derives from Victor's ratiocination rather than from precise information.

44. Chapter VIII.5.

45. W. Ensslin, *RE* 7A (1948), 2282; *PLRE* 1.937.

46. E.g., *PLRE* 1.575; Stemma 1.

47. The ancient statements that Galerius (like Constantius) divorced his first wife in 293 are of no weight, since they all derive from the lost "Kaisergeschichte" (Victor, *Caes.* 39.25; Eutropius, *Brev.* 9.22.1; Jerome, *Chronicle* 225⁸).

48. On the recent theory that Candidianus was proclaimed Caesar, Chapter I, n. 18.

commend him to Diocletian as a candidate for empire in 305: "militibus fideliter praefuit" (*Mort. Pers.* 18.12). Severus was perhaps the praetorian prefect of Galerius — or conceivably of Maximian.[49]

Severus surrendered his imperial insignia to Maximian in spring 307 at Ravenna; he was then taken to Rome, where he was either forced to commit suicide or executed (Lactantius, *Mort. Pers.* 26.9–11; *Origo* 9–10; *Chr. Min.* 1.148, 231; Victor, *Caes.* 40.7; Eutropius, *Brev.* 10.2.4; *Epitome* 40.3; Zosimus 2.10.2).

Maximinus

Son of Galerius' sister and originally called Daia (Lacantius, *Mort. Pers.* 18.13–14; *Epitome* 40.1, 40.18; Zosimus 2.8.1). Lactantius provides the only evidence for his career before 305: "sublatus nuper a pecoribus et silvis, statim scutarius, continuo protector, mox tribunus, postridie Caesar" (*Mort. Pers.* 19.6). When he died in 313, Maximinus left a widow, a son of seven or eight named Maximus, and a daughter aged six or seven who was betrothed to Candidianus (Lactantius, *Mort. Pers.* 50.6; Zonaras 13.1).[50]

Maximinus' birthday fell on 20 November (Eusebius, *Mart. Pal.* 6.1). The year is unknown. It has been argued, mainly from his iconography, that Maximinus was born c. 285;[51] if the inference were sound, then it would be an attractive conjecture that he was born on the very day on which Diocletian became emperor (20 November 284). However, the fact that Maximinus entered the army as a *scutarius* (i.e., an ordinary recruit in the ranks) suggests that his uncle did not yet hold high office; hence the hypothesis of birth c. 270, enrollment c. 285, may be closer to the truth.

Constantine

The son of Constantius and Helena, Constantine was born at Naissus (Firmicus Maternus, *Math.* 1.10.13; *Origo* 2) on 27 February (*CIL* 1², pp. 255, 258, 259) in 272 or 273. Although none states the exact year, the ancient sources do not diverge greatly on the date of Constantine's birth. Eusebius assumes a date of birth c. 273 when he asserts that Constantine began to reign at the age at which Alexander died, that he lived twice as long as Alexander (*VC* 1.8), and that his life was about twice as long as his reign (*VC* 4.53). Later writers state Constantine's age at his death (22 May 337) as follows:

49. Chapter VIII.5.
50. For the correct interpretation of Lactantius, *Mort. Pers.* 50.6 (*filium suum Maximum,* not *maximum*), H. J. Lawlor and J. E. L. Oulton, *Eusebius: Ecclesiastical History* 2 (London, 1928), 304; R. M. Grant, *Christianity, Judaism and other Greco-Roman Cults* 4 (Leiden, 1975), 144 n. 6. On the hypothesis that Maximinus proclaimed his son Caesar, Chapter I, n. 23.
51. T. Christensen, *C. Galerius Valerius Maximinus: Studier over Politik og Religion i Romerriget 305–313* (Copenhagen, 1974), 16 f.

65   Eutropius, *Brev.* 10.8.2; Jerome, *Chronicle* 234[b]; Socrates, *HE* 1.39.1, 40.3; Photius, *Bibliotheca* 234[52]

c. 64 Sozomenus, *HE* 2.34.3; Zonaras 13.4

63   *Epitome* 41.15

62   Victor, *Caes.* 41.16

60   Malalas 324.10/11 Bonn

Despite this approximate unanimity among the sources, modern scholars have often dated Constantine's birth between 280 and 288.[53] But such a late date renders Constantine's career incomprehensible, and it has been deduced from evidence which is both imprecise and tendentious. Three categories of evidence are normally adduced: (1) Descriptions of Constantine as *imperator adulescens* in speeches delivered in 307 and 310 (*Pan. Lat.* 7(6).5.3, 6(7).17.1) and as *adulescens* and *iuvenis* by Lactantius when writing in 313/4 of events in 305/6 and 310 (*Mort. Pers.* 18.10, 24.4, 29.5). (2) Retrospective statements in panegyrical contexts to the effect that Constantine was very young at his accession in 306 (*Pan. Lat.* 4(10).16.4, drawing a comparison with the infant Hercules (321); Lactantius, *Div. Inst.* 1.1.14 (324); Firmicus Maternus, *Math.* 1.10.13 (337)) or shortly before his accession (Eusebius, *VC* 1.19 (337 or 338, referring to 301/2). (3) The words of Constantine himself, who many years later alleged that he was "still a mere child" in 303 when Diocletian decreed the persecution of Christians (Eusebius, *VC* 2.51: τότε κομιδῇ παῖς ἔτι ὑπάρχων— translating a Latin original whose precise wording is unknown).

All of these statements may be discounted. The clear contradiction which exists between most of the contemporary and all the narrative sources should be resolved at the expense of the former, not of the latter. Since Constantine's official propaganda emphasized and exaggerated his youthfulness,[54] the contemporary writers who stress his youth are merely reflecting what the emperor wished to be believed. Nor can Constantine's own statement legitimately be regarded as decisive, for it occurs in a damaging context, where the victor over Licinius is reviewing the origins of the "Great Persecution" (*VC* 2.50/51). Although at the court of Diocletian in 303, the young Constantine had done

52. Summarizing the *Vita Metrophanis et Alexandri* (*BHG* 1279).

53. A. Piganiol, *L'Empereur Constantin* (Paris, 1932), 37; N. H. Baynes, *CAH* 12 (1939), 678; R. MacMullen, *Constantine* (New York, 1969), 21; R. Syme, *BHAC 1971* (1974), 237; H. A. Drake, *In Praise of Constantine: A Historical Study and New Translation of Eusebius' Tricennial Orations* (Berkeley, 1976), 15 (c. 280); J.-R. Palanque, *REA* 40 (1938), 241 ff. (282); A. H. M. Jones, *JEH* 5 (1954), 196 (283 or 284); J. Vogt, *Röm. Mitt.* 58 (1943), 190 ff.; H. Kraft, *Kaiser Konstantins religiöse Entwicklung* (*Beiträge zur historischen Theologie* 20, 1955), 1; H. Dörries, *Konstantin der Grosse* (Stuttgart, 1958), 19 (c. 285); O. Seeck, *Geschichte* 1³.434 ff. (288). The last date is alleged to be confirmed by the surviving portraits of Constantine by B. Berenson, *The Arch of Constantine, or The Decline of Form* (London, 1954), 57 ff.

54. Thus his first issue of coins at Trier salutes PRINCIPI IUVENTUTIS (*RIC* 5.204 Treveri 607).

nothing to defend or protect those whose champion he proclaimed himself in 324; misrepresentation of his true age helps to dissociate him from the emperors who persecuted the Christians.[55] It would, accordingly, be imprudent to trust such evidence completely, even if its accuracy were not belied by facts on independent attestation.

Constantine's career before 306 is known from a number of precise, though partial, allusions which complement one another very neatly:[56]

1. *Pan. Lat.* 7(6).5.3: "cum per maximos tribunatus stipendia prima conficeres"; 6(7).3.3: "stipendiis in ordinem meritis et militiae gradibus emensis"; Lactantius, *Mort. Pers.* 18.10: "eratque tunc praesens [at Nicomedia, in spring 305] iam pridem a Diocletiano factus tribunus ordinis primi."[57]

2. *Origo* 2: "obses apud Diocletianum et Galerium, sub iisdem fortiter in Asia militavit."

3. *Pan. Lat.* 7(6).6.2: a mosaic in the palace at Aquileia depicted Fausta offering to Constantine ("etiam tum puero") a plumed helmet gleaming with gold and jewels.[58]

4. Constantine, *Oratio* 16.2: Constantine claims to have seen with his own eyes "the pitiable fate of the cities" of Memphis in Egypt and Babylon in Mesopotamia.[59]

5. *Origo* 3, cf. Lactantius, *Mort. Pers.* 24.4: Constantine helped Galerius to win a victory over the Sarmatians. The context in the *Origo* seems to imply a date of 305/6, but it would not be prudent to assume that the author in-

---

55. J. Vogt, *Röm. Mitt.* 58 (1943), 194. For examples of *puer* used of full-grown men, P. Franchi de' Cavalieri, *Constantiniana* (*Studi e Testi* 171, 1953), 62 — to which add *Eleg. in Maecenatem* 2.5 (*Appendix Vergiliana* (O.C.T.), p. 94) (Augustus' stepson Drusus at the time of his death); *HA, Clod. Alb.* 2.5 (a man over thirty); Rutilius Namatianus, *De reditu* 1.170, 470 (a proconsul of Africa and a *praefectus urbi*).

56. *Phoenix* 30 (1976), 184; *HSCP* 80 (1976), 250 ff.

57. Moreau, *Lactance* 313 f., argues that Lactantius has conflated Constantine's army rank of *tribunus* with his rank at court as *comes primi ordinis*. But Eusebius attributes the creation of three ranks of *comites* to Constantine (*VC* 4.1.2).

58. It is necessary to distinguish between the mosaic, which presumably did depict the scene described, and the interpretation of that scene as representing a betrothal — which need be no more than a happy invention of the orator of 307, see E. Galletier, *Panégyriques latins* 2 (Paris, 1952), 71.

59. Constantine clearly claims to have seen the ruins of both cities; after claiming that Memphis and Babylon were destroyed because of their idolatry, he affirms: καὶ ταῦτα οὐκ ἐξ ἀκοῆς λέγω, ἀλλ᾽ αὐτός τε παρὼν καὶ ἱστορήσας ἐπόπτης τε γενόμενος τῆς οἰκτρᾶς τῶν πόλεων τύχης (16.2, p. 177.3–4 Heikel). He then discusses Memphis, with mention of Moses and Pythagoras (16–17, p. 177.5–23), before turning to Babylon, whose fate he describes at some length, though without uttering the name of the city again (17, pp. 177.23–179.3). Constantine's argument would be clearer if modern editors divided the text logically, instead of slavishly following the ancient division into chapters which Eusebius or his literary executor has provided (on the origin of the chapter division and chapter headings, see *JTS*, n.s. 27 (1976), 418 ff.). New paragraphs ought to begin at p. 177.5 (Μέμφις ἔρημος) and at p. 177.23 (Δανιὴλ δὲ ὁ θεσπίσας τὰ μέλλοντα).

tended to do more than situate the episode before Constantine's journey to Britain to join his father (cf. *Origo* 2).

6. Eusebius, *VC* 1.19: Eusebius saw him traveling across Palestine with Diocletian, and at the emperor's right hand.

7. Constantine, *Oratio* 25: in Nicomedia in spring 303.

8. Lactantius, *Mort. Pers.* 18.10, 19.1 ff.: in Nicomedia in April 305 and on 1 May 305.

9. Lactantius, *Mort. Pers.* 24.1 ff.; Eusebius, *VC* 1.21; *Origo* 4; Victor, *Caes.* 40.2–4; *Epitome* 41.2/3; Zosimus 2.8.2 ff.: Constantine fled the court of Galerius and joined his father in Britain.

10. *Pan. Lat.* 6(7).7.1 ff.; *Origo* 4: with Constantius on a campaign against the Picts in 305.[60]

All these partial allusions can be combined as follows:

Leaves the West to serve as a *tribunus* in the East (1, 2, 3)	?293
Serves under Diocletian and Galerius in Syria (2)	296/7
Accompanies Galerius on his invasion of Mesopotamia (4)	298/9
Accompanies Galerius to the Danubian frontier (5)	299
Accompanies Diocletian to Egypt (4, 6)	301/2
Is with Diocletian in Nicomedia (7)	303
Presumably accompanies Diocletian during his visit to Rome	303/4
Is with Diocletian in Nicomedia (8)	spring 305
Goes to Britain (10, 11)	summer 305

This reconstruction of Constantine's career precludes a date of birth as late as 280, but is perfectly consistent with the explicit testimony for his age, which, with only three exceptions (Victor, the *Epitome,* and Malalas), indicates that Constantine was sixty-four or sixty-five when he died. It may be concluded, therefore, that Constantine was born on 27 February in either 272 or 273.[61]

Constantine married twice. His first wife was Minervina, whose origin and parentage are unknown, and she bore him the Caesar Crispus. The ancient sources who name Minervina call her a concubine (*Epitome* 41.4; Zosimus 2.20.2; Zonaras 13.2), and many modern scholars have concurred.[62] These

60. For the date, Chapter V: Constantius.

61. Burckhardt and Schwartz, it may be recalled, adopted the dates of 274 and c. 275: J. Burckhardt, *Die Zeit Constantin's des Grossen*[2] (Leipzig, 1880; often reprinted), Chapter VIII; E. Schwartz, *Charakterköpfe aus der Antike*[2] (Leipzig, 1943), 235. E. Galletier, *Panégyriques latins* 2 (Paris, 1952), 45, implied that Constantine was born in 270; more recently, *PLRE* 1.223 states his date of birth as "perhaps 272."

62. E.g., O. Seeck, *Geschichte* 1[3].477 f.; W. Ensslin, *RE* 15 (1932), 1807; J. Vogt, *The Conflict between Paganism and Christianity in the Fourth Century* (ed. A. Momigliano, 1963), 46; X. Lucien-Brun, *BAGB* 1970. 401 ff.

sources, however, depend on the hostile and inaccurate Eunapius.[63] The panegyric recited at the wedding of Constantine and Fausta is quite explicit in the opposite sense: "Quomodo enim magis continentiam patris aequare potuisti quam quod te ab ipso fine pueritiae ilico matrimonii legibus tradidisti, ut primo ingressu adulescentiae formares animum maritalem, nihil de vagis cupiditatibus, nihil de concessis aetati voluptatibus in hoc sacrum pectus admitteres, novum iam tum miraculum, iuvenis uxorius? sed, ut res est, mente praesaga omnibus te verecundiae observationibus imbuebas, talem postea ducturus uxorem" (*Pan. Lat.* 7(6).4.1). The past tenses (with *iam tum*), the contrast with Fausta ("talem . . . uxorem"), and Constantine's age in 307 render an allusion to an earlier marriage certain. Further, the nature of the reference should indicate that Minervina had died without losing her husband's affection.[64]

Constantine's second wife was Flavia Maxima Fausta, the daughter of Maximian and Eutropia. He married her c. September 307 (*Pan. Lat.* 7(6)), and they had five children whose names are known:

1. Constantinus, born 7 August 316
2. Constantius, born 7 August 317
3. Constantina, who married Gallus (Caesar 351–354)
4. Constans, born in 323 (or possibly 320)
5. Helena, who married the emperor Julian[65]

The ages of Constantina and Helena are nowhere exactly stated. But Constantina was the elder (Philostorgius, *HE* 3.22), and she married Hannibalianus, the son of Flavius Dalmatius (cos. 333) and brother of the Caesar Dalmatius, before 337. Helena was not married in the reign of her father, presumably because she was too young.[66] It may be suggested, therefore, that Constantina was probably born in 318 or 319, Helena after 320.

Licinius

Born c. 265 (*Epitome* 41.8, cf. Eusebius, *HE* 10.8.13). A native of the new Dacia, south of the Danube, and of peasant stock (*Origo* 13; Eutropius, *Brev.* 10.4.1; *Epitome* 41.9; Socrates, *HE* 1.2.1).

63. *CP* 71 (1976), 267. Eunapius seems to have denied that any of Constantine's sons were born in wedlock (Zosimus 2.29.1).

64. J.-R. Palanque, *REA* 40 (1938), 247. *PLRE* 1.603 dates the marriage c. 290, citing only *Pan. Lat.* 7(6).4.1.

65. There may, of course, have been other children who died in infancy, as Seeck argued, *ZfN* 21 (1898), 40 ff. He adduced coins of c. 325 which show Fausta as Salus or Spes holding two babies in her arms (*RIC* 7.753, s.v. SPES REIPUBLICAE) and *Pan. Lat.* 4(10).36.1: "Roma . . . haurit insuper ingentis spei fructum, quam propositam sibi ex Caesaribus nobilissimis habet eorumque fratribus" (in 321).

66. For the two daughters, *PLRE* 1.222, Constantina 2; 409–410, Helena 2.

Lactantius describes his relationship to Galerius as "veteris contubernii amicum et a prima militia familiarem" (*Mort. Pers.* 20.3). Eutropius is more specific: "notus ei antiqua consuetudine et in bello, quod adversus Narseum gesserat, strenuus laboribus et officiis acceptus" (*Brev.* 10.4.1). Other sources also have his friendship with Galerius (Victor, *Caes.* 40.8; Zosimus 2.11; Socrates, *HE* 1.2.1). In 307, Galerius sent him to negotiate with Maxentius (*Origo* 7) — which prompts a conjecture that he was his praetorian prefect.[67]

Licinius married Constantia, the sister of Constantine, in February 313; their son Licinius Caesar was born c. August 315 (*Epitome* 41.4; Zosimus 2.20.2). Licinius also appears to have had a bastard son by a slave woman, who was legitimized and given high rank by imperial rescript, but later (in 336) reduced to slavery (*CTh* 4.6.2/3).

After his defeat in 324, Licinius abdicated, and was sent to Thessalonica, where he was later put to death in the spring of 325 (*Origo* 28–29; Victor, *Caes.* 41.8-9; Eutropius, *Brev.* 10.6.1; *Epitome* 41.7/8; *Chr. Min.* 1.232; Socrates, *HE* 1.4.6; Sozomenus, *HE* 1.7.5; Zosimus 2.28.1; Jordanes, *Getica* 111).

Crispus

Son of Constantine and Minervina. Cripus' date of birth is unknown, though it is usually assumed to be some years after 300.[68] But if Constantine was born in 272 or 273, then Crispus could easily have been born as early as c. 295, and since he was already a young man ($\nu\varepsilon\alpha\nu\acute{\iota}\alpha\varsigma$) in 316/7 (Zosimus 2.20), he was certainly born no later than c. 300.[69] His wife was called Helena (parentage unknown); they produced a child shortly before 30 October 322 (*CTh* 9.38.1) and were perhaps expecting another in 324 (Publilius Optatianus Porfyrius, *Carm.* 10, *versus intexti*).[70] Now Justina, the wife of Valentinian, appears to belong to the Constantinian dynasty;[71] it is legitimate to conjecture that her mother was the daughter of Crispus and Helena, her father Justus (Socrates, *HE* 4.31.11; John of Antioch, frag. 187) a son of Vettius Justus, cos. 328.

Constantinus

Born in summer 316 (*Epitome* 41.4; Zosimus 2.20.2), probably on 7 August (*CIL* 1², p. 271). The son of Constantine and Fausta (*CIL* 12.688 = *AE* 1952.107: Arles; ?*ILS* 723: from Noricum; Julian, *Orat.* 1, 9d; J. A. Cramer,

---

67. Chapter VIII.5.

68. J.-R. Palanque, *REA* 40 (1938), 245 ff. (303); J. Vogt, *Constantin der Grosse und sein Jahrhundert* (Munich, 1949), 143 (305); *PLRE* 1.233, Crispus 4 (c. 305); O. Seeck, *RE* 4 (1901), 1723 (307).

69. X. Lucien-Brun, *BAGB* 1970. 395.

70. On the date, *AJP* 96 (1975), 181.

71. J. Rougé, *Cahiers d'Histoire* 3 (1958), 11; *Latomus* 33 (1974), 676 ff.

Anecdota Graeca e codd. manuscriptis Bibliothecae Regiae Parisiensis 2 (Oxford, 1839), 111.32–112.3; Theophanes, pp. 5, 19 de Boor).[72] Proclaimed Caesar in infancy. Married before 336 to a wife whose identity is unknown (Eusebius, *VC* 4.49). No known issue.

Licinius Caesar

Born c. August 315 (*Epitome* 41.4; Zosimus 2.20.2). The son of Licinius and Constantia. At Sirmium in October 316 (*Origo* 17). Proclaimed Caesar on 1 March 317; deposed in autumn 324 (*Origo* 29), then executed (Eutropius, *Brev.* 10.6.3), presumably at the same time as his father.

Constantius

Born on 7 August 317 (*CTh* 6.4.10; *CIL* 1², p. 270; Eutropius, *Brev.* 10.15.2; *Epitome* 42.17; Socrates, *HE* 2.47). Son of Constantine and Fausta (*ILS* 730; Athanasius, *Hist. Ar.* 44, 64; *De Syn.* 18; Julian, *Orat.* 1, 9b; 2, 51c). Married in 336 to a daughter of Julius Constantius (Eusebius, *VC* 4.49; Julian, *Ep. ad Ath.* 272d; Athanasius, *Hist. Ar.* 69).[73]

Constans

Son of Constantine and Fausta (*ILS* 725, etc.). About his date of birth, the evidence diverges; his age at death (shortly after 18 January 350) is given as either twenty-seven (*Epitome* 41.23; Malalas 325 Bonn) or thirty (Eutropius, *Brev.* 10.9; Zonaras 13.6). However, a medallion which clearly celebrates his proclamation as Caesar depicts Constans as significantly younger than his brothers (*RIC* 7.580, Constantinople 67), so that 323 should be preferred over 320 for the date of his birth.[74] No known marriage or issue, though before 337 Constans was betrothed to Olympias, the daughter of Fl. Ablabius, cos. 331 (Athanasius, *Hist. Ar.* 69; Ammianus 20.11.3).

Dalmatius

Son of Fl. Dalmatius, cos. 333, the son of Constantius and Theodora. Date of birth unknown. Educated by the rhetor Exsuperius at Narbo (Ausonius, *Professores* 18(17).8 ff.). No known marriage or issue.

---

72. On the legitimacy of Constantinus' birth (often doubted needlessly or on the basis of false premises), P. Guthrie, *Phoenix* 20 (1966), 330 f.; T. D. Barnes, *JRS* 63 (1973), 36 n. 71, 38 n. 110.

73. It is not known how or when the marriage ended: Constantius' other attested marriages are to Eusebia c. 353, and to Faustina in 361 (*PLRE* 1.300–301, Eusebia; 326, Faustina). His only known child was posthumous—Constantia, the wife of Gratian (*PLRE* 1.221, Constantia 2).

74. O. Seeck, *ZfN* 21 (1898), 38 ff.

APPENDIX: MALALAS ON THE AGES OF EMPERORS

Johannes Malalas, writing in the late sixth century, states the age at death of nine of the emperors discussed in the present chapter. His testimony has usually been disregarded, for it is late and of dubious provenance, and in some cases disproved outright by earlier and better evidence.[75] Nevertheless, it deserves to be reported, on the chance that Malalas might sometimes be close to the truth where no decisive evidence exists. His evidence may be tabulated as follows:

Emperor	Alleged age at death	Implied birth date	Actual or probable birth date
Diocletian (311.1/2)	72	c. 240	c. 244
Maximian (312.5/6)	57	254	c. 250
Constantius (313.21)	60	247	c. 250
Galerius (313.3)	53	249	c. 260
Licinius (315.10/11)	46	280	c. 265
Constantine (324.10/11)	60 years, 3 months	278	272 or 273
Constantinus (325.4)	20	321	316
Constantius (326.12)	40	322	317
Constans (325.7)	27	323	323 (or 320)

75. For the age of Constantine, Malalas appeals to Nestorianus, who wrote in the late fifth century (324.11–13, cf. 376.19; *Chron. Pasch.* 599). It is flatly impossible that Galerius could have been older than Maximian (Lactantius, *Mort. Pers.* 18.1, 18.7).

CHAPTER V

IMPERIAL RESIDENCES

AND JOURNEYS

The city of Rome ceased to be the normal abode of Roman emperors during the third century. Diocletian and his colleagues and successors visited the former capital only on rare and special occasions; they normally resided in cities nearer the frontiers, where they were free from the restraints which the survival of Republican forms still imposed on them in Rome itself.[1] They were, moreover, often forced to undertake journeys through the provinces and along the frontiers in order to protect themselves and their subjects from internal rebellion and foreign invasion.

Imperial residences and journeys, therefore, are an important theme in the history of the Roman Empire.[2] Yet the full evidence for the period of Diocletian and Constantine has never been gathered or deployed. In some areas, it is true, much has been done, and the present chapter is heavily indebted to two classic studies: Theodor Mommsen on the legislation of Diocletian and his colleagues between 284 and 305,[3] and Otto Seeck's register of dates and dated documents from 311 to 476.[4] But these two studies, though of superb accuracy and acumen, need to be supplemented by a similar study of the years between 305

---

1. On this aspect of the emperors' relationship to Rome, see J. Straub, *Vom Herrscherideal in der Spätantike* (Stuttgart, 1939), 175 ff.

2. R. MacMullen, *Athenaeum,* n.s. 54 (1976), 26 ff.; Millar, *Emperor,* chap. II.

3. *Abh. Berlin* 1862. 417 ff. = *Ges. Schr.* 2 (Berlin, 1905), 262 ff.

4. For the years 311–37, *Regesten* 159–185. Seeck's first attempt at the chronology of Constantine's laws, thirty years earlier (*ZSS,* Rom. Abt. 10 (1889), 1 ff., 177 ff.), was not so methodical, and drew heavy criticism from Mommsen (*Ges. Schr.* 2 (1905), 397 ff.). The principal types of error in the headings and subscriptions of the *Codex Theodosianus* are briefly summarized by P. Krüger, *ZSS,* Rom. Abt. 42 (1921), 58 ff.

and 311, and to be revised throughout in the light of new evidence and subsequent research.[5] Presented below is a reconstruction of the movements of Diocletian and his recognized colleagues and successors from 20 November 284 to 9 September 337. For residences, a simple statement is given, based on the emperor's attested movements, and with references to other evidence and to modern discussions.[6] For an emperor's attested activities or attested presence in a particular place at a particular time, the full evidence is normally adduced, but annotation and bibliography are deliberately brief and selective.

One matter requires prior discussion. Since imperial pronouncements were normally issued in the name of the whole imperial college,[7] neither the original protocol nor the heading preserved in later compilations such as the *Codex Theodosianus* and *Codex Justinianus* shows which emperor actually uttered a document.[8] That must be deduced from the date and place of issue, and from the identity of the recipient. Hence there is room for debate over which emperors were entitled to issue laws. Mommsen peremptorily denied that the Caesars Constantius and Galerius could issue even rescripts, and it has been argued that Licinius lost the right to legislate in February 317.[9] This chapter, in contrast, does not exclude a priori the possibility that any emperor could issue any type of administrative or legal pronouncement. Legislation by an Augustus other than the senior emperor can be documented in the cases both of Galerius and Licinius,[10] as well as for later emperors.[11] As for Caesars, they issued at

5. Of especial importance are the excellent catalogues of imperial coins, *RIC* 6 (1967), by C. H. V. Sutherland, covering the years 294 to 313, and *RIC* 7 (1966), by P. Bruun (313–337). Too many modern scholars have drawn mistaken conclusions from the unreliable catalogue of J. Maurice, *Numismatique constantinienne* (Paris, 1908–12) or even from the inaccurate and negligent compilation of H. Cohen, *Description historique des monnaies frappées sous l'empire romain* 6–7 (Paris, 1886 and 1888).

For the years 314–317, Seeck's chronology was unfortunately constructed on an insecure basis, see P. Bruun, *The Constantinian Coinage of Arelate* (*Finska Fornminnesföreningens Tidskrift* 52.2, 1953), 17 ff.; C. Habicht, *Hermes* 86 (1958), 360 ff.; P. Bruun, *Studies in Constantinian Chronology* (*NNM* 146, 1961), 10 ff.

6. For a survey of imperial residences between 284 and 337, Millar, *Emperor* 40 ff.

7. Chapters III, XI.

8. On the evidence of the Codes, see Seeck, *Regesten* 111 ff. Rescripts of Diocletian and his colleagues suffered different fates in different compilations: although the *Codex Justinianus* normally registers four emperors, the so-called *Fragmenta Vaticana* omit Maximian and Galerius (22; 41; 270; 275; 297; 312; 338), while the *Mosaicarum et Romanarum legum collatio* on one occasion omits both Caesars (6.4, of 295), on another Constantius alone (15.3, of 302). For the relevance of such facts to the genesis of these collections, E. Volterra, *Mélanges W. Seston* (Paris, 1974), 500 ff.

9. Mommsen, *Ges. Schr.* 2.265; C. Habicht, *Hermes* 86 (1958), 370.

10. Lactantius, *Mort. Pers.* 21.7 (*datis legibus*); *CIL* 3.12134 (Tlos in Lycia) = *IG* 2/3².1121 (Athens), cf. E. Steinwenter, *Studi in onore di E. Betti* 4 (Milan, 1962), 137 ff. (Galerius in 305/6); *FIRA*² 1.93, 94; *CTh* 8.4.3, 10.7.1, 10.20.1, 12.1.5, cf. Seeck, *Regesten* 53 f. (Licinius: 9 June 311, 1 January 314, 21 July 317).

11. *Phoenix* 34 (1980), 164 f. (Constans, 338–350); Seeck, *Regesten* 217 ff. (Valens, 364–375); 251 ff. (Theodosius, 379–392).

least some types of document on their own authority. Eumenius quotes a letter written by Constantius, in the name of the whole imperial college, which appointed him to teach rhetoric at Autun (*Pan. Lat.* 9(4).13-15), and it was by letters to officials that Maximinus in 306 ordained that everyone in his domains should sacrifice to the gods (Eusebius, *Mart. Pal.* 4.8: both recensions).[12] Hence it is unwise to emend the date or place of issue of a law solely on the grounds that the emperor who is implied as its author lacked the legal power to issue it.[13] Similarly, and again contrary to conventional doctrine, this chapter attributes some Diocletianic rescripts in the *Codex Justinianus* to western emperors.[14]

DIOCLETIAN[15]

Principal Residences

285-296	Sirmium[16] and Nicomedia[17]
296-299	In Syria and Egypt
299-302	Antioch[18]
302-305	Nicomedia[19]

Attested Movements

284, Nov. 20	Proclaimed emperor at Nicomedia	*P. Beatty Panopolis* 2.162, etc.; Lactantius, *Mort. Pers.* 17.1 (day);[20]

12. Eusebius also records similar letters directed against the Christians c. November 309 (*HE* 8.14.9/10; *Mart. Pal.* (S) 9.2).

13. Libanius, *Orat.* 59.46, seems to imply that even the Caesars of Constantine, who were completely dominated by their father, possessed the legal power to legislate.

14. E.g., *CJ* 6.8.1, 4.24.9, 6.59.2, 9.16.5(6) (Maximian), 5.12.21 (Constantius). For the standard opinion, see P. Krüger, *Geschichte der Quellen und Litteratur des römischen Rechts* (Leipzig, 1888), 282 f.

15. For previous attempts to establish Diocletian's movements, Mommsen, *Ges. Schr.* 2 (1905), 262 ff.; G. Costa, *Diz. ep.* 2 (1912), 1794 ff.; Seston, *Dioclétien* 129 ff.; W. Ensslin, *RE* 7A (1948), 2423 ff.; P. Bastien, *Le monnayage de l'atelier de Lyon* (Paris, 1972), 11 f. (284-294 only); T. D. Barnes, *Phoenix* 30 (1976), 176 ff., 180 ff.

16. For archaeological traces of the palace at Sirmium, see E. L. Ochsenschlager and V. Popović, *Archaeology* 26 (1973), 85; D. Bosković, N. Duval, P. Gros, and V. Popović, *MEFR (A)* 86 (1974), 616 ff.

17. On Nicomedia as Diocletian's residence, J. Sölch, *Kilo* 19 (1925), 177 ff.

18. An imperial palace existed at Antioch in 303 (Libanius, *Orat.* 11.161), built by Diocletian (Malalas 306 Bonn, cf. Ammianus 25.10.2): for discussion, see G. Downey, *A History of Antioch in Syria* (Princeton, 1961), 318 ff.

19. Lactantius, *Mort. Pers.* 7.9-10, 10.6, 17.4-19.6.

20. Indirectly confirmed by Eusebius, *Mart. Pal.* 1.5 + 2.4. The Paschal Chronicle has 17 September (510), which many scholars preferred (e.g., Seston, *Dioclétien* 51) until Lactantius was vindicated by the papyrus from Panopolis (publlished in 1964).

		Zosimus 1.73.2 = John of Antioch, frag. 163 (place)[21]
285, spring	Campaign against Carinus, ending in a battle near Viminacium	Victor, *Caes.* 39.11 ff.; Eutropius, *Brev.* 9.20.1/2; *Itinerarium Burdigalense* p. 564.9 Wesseling
285, summer	Visit to Italy	*RIC* 5.2.241 no. 203 (Ticinum: ADVENTUS AUG); Zonaras 12.31 (alleges a visit to Rome)
285, Nov. 2	At Civitas Iovia (otherwise known as Botivo) and Sonista (on the road between Poetovio and Mursa)	*CJ* 4.48.5 (*Atubino*); *Frag. Vat.* 297 (*Suneata*)[22]
?285, autumn	Campaign against the Sarmatians[23]	
286, Jan. 20–March 3	At Nicomedia	*CJ* 4.21.6; 3.28.18 (Feb. 14); 7.35.2 (Feb. 15); *Frag. Vat.* 275 (March 3);[24] *Chr. Pasch.* 510/11 = *Chr. Min.* 1.229/30 (winter at Nicomedia)
286, March 22	At Byzantium	*Frag. Vat.* 281
286, May 31–	At Tiberias[25]	*CJ* 4.10.3 (May 31: one ms.); ?*CJ*

21. Also Lactantius, *Mort. Pers.* 19.2, as emended below, n. 73.

22. The two places are nine miles apart (*Itinerarium Burdigalense* p. 561.10–11). A. Mócsy, *RE,* Supp. 9 (1962), 570; 11 (1968), 1258, prefers to postulate an otherwise unknown Suneate.

23. The date depends on the Aphrodisias copy of the price edict, which styles Maximian *Sarmaticus maximus III* (Chapter III, no. 2; Tables 3, 4). Before its discovery, it was assumed that Diocletian and Maximian were both *Sarmatici maximi IV* in 301 (Mommsen's supplement in *CIL* 3, pp. 824/5), and hence the victory was dated to 289, as by A. Arnaldi, *Rendiconti dell' Istituto Lombardo,* Classe di Lettere 106 (1972), 40.

24. *Frag. Vat.* 280 = *CJ* 3.29.7 may also have been issued on 3 March 286, sinc its date is transmitted as "⟨Data⟩ Nicomediae V non. Mart. Augustis III et II conss." (*Frag. Vat.* 280) and "pp. V id. Mai. Maximo II et Aquilino conss." (*CJ* 3.29.7). Mommsen, *Ges. Schr.* 2.268 f., dated the rescript to 11 May 286 and questioned *Nicomediae* (also *Byzantio* in *Frag. Vat.* 281).

25. For discussion of Jewish evidence relating to Diocletian in Palestine, see H. Graetz, *Monatschrift für Geschichte und Wissenschaft des Judentums* 28 (1878), 5 ff.; A. Marmorstein, *REJ* 98 (1934), 26 ff. None of it is precisely dated, but it refers to Diocletian's arrival in the province, either in 286 or between 296 and 302, and to his presence at Tyre in Phoenicia and at Paneas: Jerusalem Talmud, *Aboda Zara* 5.4, 1.3; *Berakot* 3.1; *Shebiith* 9.2; *Terumot* 8.12 (translated into French by M. Schwab (Paris, 1871–90), 6.238, 185; 1.57; 2.415; 3.108). The second passage quotes an inscription recording that Diocletian dedicated the market of Tyre to the tutelary deity of his brother Herculius—which implies a date before rather than after 293, see M. Avi-Jonah, *RE,* Supp. 13 (1973), 408.

Aug. 31		1.51.1ᴹ (July 14); 5.17.3ᴹ (Aug. 31)[26]
286, Oct. 13	At Heraclea in Thrace	*Frag. Vat.* 284
287	Negotiates with Persian ambassadors, presumably in Syria, and installs Tiridates as ruler in Armenia	*Pan. Lat.* 10(2).7.5, 9.2, 10.6 f., 8(5).3.3, cf. *ILS* 618 (*Pers(icus) maximus)* in 290)[27]
?287	Fortifies Circesium and reorganizes the Syrian frontier	Ammianus 23.5.2
288	Campaign on the frontier of Raetia, and conference with Maximian	*Pan. Lat.* 10(2).9.1
?289, summer	Sarmatian campaign, defense of Dacia	*Pan. Lat.* 11(3).5.4, 7.1, 8(5).3.3
290, Jan. 11	At Sirmium	*CJ* 10.3.4
290, Feb. 27	At Adrianople	*CJ* 6.55.2
290, April 3	At Byzantium	*CJ* 2.4.13
290, May 6	At Antioch	*Frag. Vat.* 276ᴹ
290, May 10	At Emesa	*CJ* 9.41.9
290, ?May/ June	Campaign against Saraceni	*Pan. Lat.* 11(3).5.4; 7.1
290, May 25	At Laodicea	*CJ* 6.15.2[28]
290, summer	Returns from Syria to Pannonia	*Pan. Lat.* 11(3).4.2

A dedication by a procurator could imply Diocletian's presence at Caesarea in 286 (*AE* 1966.494, reread by B. Lifshitz, *Hommages à M. Renard* 2 (*Collection Latomus* 102, 1969), 467; M. Christol, *ZPE* 22 (1976), 169 f.).

26. A. Honoré, *Emperors and Lawyers* (London, 1980), 111 n. 60, argues that the consular date of *CJ* 1.51.1 ought to be *Tiberiano et Dione conss.,* i.e. 291. The mss. of *CJ* 4.10.3 also attest the diurnal date *prid. k. Ian.,* i.e. 31 December 286.

27. For other evidence, and full discussion, see M.-L. Chaumont, *Recherches sur l'histoire d'Arménie de l'avènement des Sassanides à la conversion du royaume* (Paris, 1969), 93 ff. Observe also the possible occurrence of *Armeniaci maximi* before *Persici maximi* in the victory titles in *P. Theadelphia* 2.2 ff. = *P. Sakaon* 59.2 ff. (305).

28. The mss. have *d. vii k. Iun. Laodiceae AA. conss.* Mommsen construed the date intended as 293 and emended the place to *Serdicae* (*Ges. Schr.* 2.275), but he also considered emending the consular date to *ipsis IIII et III AA. conss.* (*Ges. Schr.* 2.232) — which P. Krüger, ad loc., rightly prefers.

290, July 1–Dec. 18	At Sirmium	*CJ* 6.30.6; 8.54(55).3 = *Frag. Vat.* 286 (Sept. 21); *CJ* 2.3.19 (Nov. 19), 2.28.1 (Nov. 22); 9.16.4(5) (Nov. 30); 3.28.19ᴹ
290, late Dec., or 291, Jan.	Confers with Maximian in Milan	*Pan. Lat.* 11(3).8.1 ff.
291, May 13	At Sirmium	*CJ* 9.41.12
291, Dec. 4	At Oescus (mss. have *Triballis*)	*CJ* 8.47(48).5
293, Jan. 1–Feb. 26	At Sirmium	*CJ*, p. 495
293, March 1	Invests Galerius with the purple, probably at Sirmium[29]	
293, April 1	At Heraclea	*CJ* 8.55(56).4
293, April 2–13	At Byzantium	*CJ*, p. 495
293, April 15	At Melantias	*CJ* 4.49.7
293, April 17–May 1	At Heraclea	*CJ*, p. 495
293, May 1	At Tzirallum (Tzurulon), near Heraclea	*CJ* 2.3.21, 5.3.8, 6.30.7, 6.53.6ᴹ, 8.35(36).5ᴹ
293, May 10–13	At Adrianople	*CJ* 7.16.16, 10.32(31).7ᴹ, 8.13(14).16 (May 12), 8.50(51).10ᴹ
293, May 17	At Beroea	*CJ* 5.24.1ᴹ
293, May 25–June 17	At Philippopolis	*CJ* 2.17(18).3ᴹ, 2.52(53).4ᴹ (May 25), 2.12(13).17 (June 5), 4.49.9ᴹ, 7.67.1
293, June 21–28	At Serdica	*CJ* 8.44(45).21; *Mos. et Rom. legum collatio* 10.3 (June 24); *CJ* 5.16.18
293, July 2–15	At Philippopolis	*CJ* 9.33.5; 5.12.14ᴹ (July 4), 5.34.7, 6.23.12 (July 6), 6.49.4 (July 10), 8.15(16).6 (July 11), 5.16.19ᴹ, 7.16.18
293, Aug. 8–Sept. 1	At Viminacium	*CJ*, p. 495

29. Below, n. 73.

293, Sept. 11– 294, May 1	At Sirmium	*CJ,* pp. 495/6
294, May 3	Near Sirmium	*CJ* 6.21.14[30]
294, May 18– Aug. 20	At Sirmium	*CJ* 6.59.1,[31] 9.12.4 (June 15: year emended from 293), 4.18.1 (June 25), 6.58.8[M] (July 7), 5.16.22 (Aug. 1), 6.24.10 (Aug. 17), 9.18.2
294, Sept. 8– 12	At Singidunum	*CJ* 4.19.21[M], 9.20.12
294, Sept. 22	*Demesso* (mss.): not yet identified	*CJ* 2.12(13).20[32]
294, Sept. 26– Oct. 1	At Viminacium	*CJ,* pp. 496/7
294, Oct. 5	At Cuppae	*CJ* 8.44(45).28[M]
294, Oct. 8–10	At Ratiaria	*CJ* 4.33.5(4)[M], 6.59.8[M], 7.60.3[M], 8.13(14).21[M]
294, Oct. 11	At Cebrum	*CJ* 2.4.30[M]
294, Oct. 13	At Varianae	*CJ* 2.3.6, 8.37(38).9[M]
294, Oct. 17	At Appiaria	*Mos. et Rom. legum collatio* 10.5[M]
294, Oct. 18	At Transmarisca	*CJ* 6.42.28[M]
294, Oct. 21– 22	At Durostorum	*CJ* 8.41(42).6, 9.22.20
294, Oct. 25	*Reginassi* (mss.): not yet identified	*CJ* 4.20.8[M], 4.21.10
294, Oct. 26	At Marcianopolis	*Consultatio* 6.17

30. The mss. have *Aurris,* which Mommsen thought might conceal Turris Ferrata (*Ges. Schr.* 2.286). It might be better to consider emending to *Fossis* or *Bassianis,* places which the *Itinerarium Burdigalense,* p. 563.10–11, registers as the first two stopping points on the road from Sirmium to Singidunum (respectively, nine and nineteen miles from Sirmium).

31. The fact that *CJ* 6.59.2–4 bear earlier dates than 6.59.1 may indicate that the compilers dated 6.59.1 to 293: P. Krüger, ad loc., suggests that its original date may have been 18 December 293.

32. The geographical sources register only six stations between Singidunum and Viminacium, viz. Ad Sextum, Tricornia Castra, Ad Sextum Miliarem, Aureus Mons, Vinceia, and Margus. *PLRE* 1.950, Verinus 1, construes the date as 305.

It should be noted that Diocletian won a victory over the Sarmatians during the autumn of 294: *Pan. Lat.* 8(5).5.1; *Chr. Min.* 1.230; *RIC* 6.175–178, 281–282, 352–354, 459–461, 529–530, 555–556, 579, 616, cf. A. Alföldi, *Arch. Ért.* 2³ (1941), 49 ff.

294, Oct. 28	At Anchialos	*CJ* 5.12.24[M], 5.51.11[M], 6.50.17, 8.31(32).2[M], 8.47(48).9
294, Oct. 29	At Develtus	*CJ* 6.36.5[M], 8.50(51).17[M]
294, Oct. 31	At Adrianople	*CJ* 8.42(43).20
294, Nov. 1–3	At Burtudizum	*CJ* 5.16.23[M], 2.3.28[M], 8.35(36).9
294, Nov. 5–8	At Heraclea	*CJ* 7.48.3, 5.18.10 (Nov. 7), 2.3.27, 7.35.6[M], 8.27(28).19[M]; *Frag. Vat.* 325[M]
294, Nov. 9	At Melantias	*CJ* 2.4.33(34); *Frag. Vat.* 314
294, Nov. 10	At Byzantium	*CJ* 2.4.31[M], 8.27(28).20[M]
294, Nov. 11	At Pantichium	*CJ* 4.29.18[M], 5.12.25[M], 6.22.4
294, Nov. 15– Dec. 30	At Nicomedia	*CJ*, p. 497[33]
295, March 18	At Nicomedia	*CJ* 5.72.3[34]
296, summer/ autumn	Campaign against the Carpi	*Pan. Lat.* 8(5).5.2
296, late	Goes to Syrian frontier and campaigns against the Persians	*P. Argent.* 480, 1 verso 1 ff.[35]
297, autumn– 298, spring	Suppresses revolt in Egypt; long siege of Alexandria	Jerome, *Chronicle* 226[e]; Eutropius, *Brev.* 9.22–23[36]

33. A law dated 23 February 295 states its place of issue as *Trimontii* (*CJ* 6.20.14). Mommsen construed this as indicating Philippopolis and rejected the date (*Ges. Schr.* 2.288, cf. 285). But *Trimontii* might conceal the name of a place close to Nicomedia.

34. *Mos. et Rom. legum collatio* 6.4 = *CJ* 5.4.17, issued at Damascus on 1 May 295, is here attributed to Galerius (below, n. 76).

35. Best edited by E. Heitsch, *Die griechischen Dichterfragmente der römischen Kaiserzeit* 1[2] (*Abh. Göttingen, Phil.-hist. Klasse*[3] 49, 1963), 79–81, no. XXII. The fragment is normally assumed to come from an epic poem (e.g., *Phoenix* 30 (1976), 182); perhaps rather from a panegyric composed for recitation before Diocletian while he was in Egypt in 298, as *Corpus Hermeticum* 18 may also have been, see R. Reitzenstein, *Zwei religionsgeschichtliche Fragen nach ungedruckten griechieschen Texten* (Strassburg, 1901), 51; *Poimandres: Studien zur griechisch-ägyptischen und frühchristlichen Literatur* (Leipzig, 1904), 199; A. D. Nock and A.-J. Festugière, *Hermès Trismégiste* 2 (Paris: Budé, 1960), 244.

36. On Diocletian's presence in Egypt in 297–298, J. D. Thomas, *ZPE* 22 (1976), 273 ff.; A. K. Bowman, *BASP* 15 (1978), 28 ff. Both, however, follow Seston, *Dioclétien* 153 f., in adducing the metaphrastic *Passio Procopii* (*BHG* 1578) as proof that Diocletian approached Egypt by way of Pelusium. Even if he did so, the passion is not good evidence, see H. Delehaye, *Les légendes hagiographiques*[3] (*Subsidia Hagiographica* 18, 1927), 131 ff.

298, May or June	Visits Oxyrhynchus and travels up the Nile	*P. Oxy.* 1416; *P. Beatty Panopolis* 1.375[37]
298, summer	Reaches Elephantine and negotiates with Nobatae	Procopius, *Bella* 1.19.27 ff.; *IGRR* 1.1291 = *Sammelbuch* 8393[38]
298, Sept.	Return northward expected at Panopolis	*P. Beatty Panopolis* 1, cf. *Pan. Lat.* 9(4).21.2
299, Feb. 5	At Antioch	*CJ* 8.53(54).24M
?299, late winter	Goes to Mesopotamia	Eutropius, *Brev.* 9.25.2
?299, spring	Meets Galerius at Nisibis	Petrus Patricius, frag. 14
300, Feb. 12– 301, July 4	At Antioch	*CJ* 9.21.1M, 3.3.3M (25 March), 7.22.2 (June 25), Malalas 310.7 ff. Bonn (300, July/August);[39] *CJ* 3.28.25 (301, July 4)
301/2	Visits Egypt	*Chr. Min.* 1.290; *Chr. Pasch.* 514 Bonn; Eusebius, *VC* 1.19 (journey through Palestine)[40]
302, March 31	At Alexandria	*Mos. et Rom. legum collatio* 15.3 (year not given)[41]
302, ?autumn	At Antioch	Eusebius, *Mart. Pal.* (L) 2.2 ff.
302, late	Goes to Bithynia for for winter	Lactantius, *Mort. Pers.* 10.6

---

37. C. Vandersleyen, *CE* 33 (1958), 113 ff.; A. K. Bowman, *JRS* 66 (1976), 159. Diocletian's presence in Oxyrhynchus in 298 may also be alluded to in *P. Flor.* 33.7 ff., as re-edited by J. R. Rea, *CE* 46 (1971), 144.

38. Also apparently alluded to in O. Spengel, *Rhetores Graeci* 3 (1856), 387.23–27.

39. On the date, G. Downey, *History of Antioch* 326.

40. Observe also the corrupt subscription to *CJ* 3.3.4: "d. X k. dec. dec hioppe diocl. VIII et cerio max. VII AA." The law might have been issued at Joppa on 22 November 301. The edict on maximum prices may imply that Diocletian reached Alexandria before 9 December (Chapter III, no. 2), since it calculates the prices of sea transport from Nicomedia and Alexandria alone, see J. Rougé, *Recherches sur l'organisation du commerce maritime en Méditerranée sous l'Empire romain* (Paris, 1966), 370.

41. The year must be 302, see L. Poinssot, *MSNAF* 76 (1919–23), 313 ff.; T. D. Barnes, *HSCP* 80 (1976), 246 ff. H. Chadwick, *Early Christian Literature and the Classical Intellectual Tradition* (Paris, 1979), 138 ff., essays a characteristically judicious defense of the date of 297 argued by W. Seston, *Mélanges Ernout* (Paris, 1940), 345 ff.

303, Jan. 6– March 12	At Nicomedia	*CJ* 2.30(31).4; Lactantius, *Mort. Pers.* 10.6 ff.; Constantine, *Oratio* 25 (late Feb.); Eusebius, *HE* 8.5 (Feb. 23), 8.6.2, cf. *PO* 10.14 (March 12)
303, June 8	At Durostorum	*CJ* 5.73.4
303, summer/ autumn	?Visits Sirmium	*Passio Quattuor Coronatorum* 21 f.[42]
303, before Nov. 20–Dec.	At Rome	Lactantius, *Mort. Pers.* 17.1 ff.
303, Dec. 20	Leaves Rome	Lactantius, *Mort. Pers.* 17.3
304, Jan. 1	At Ravenna	Lactantius, *Mort. Pers.* 17.3
304, summer	On the Danube; per- haps defeats the Carpi	Lactantius, *Mort. Pers.* 17.4; Tables 6, 7[43]
304, Aug. 28– 305, May 1	At Nicomedia	*CJ* 3.28.26; Lactantius, *Mort. Pers.* 17.4 ff.; Eutropius, *Brev.* 9.27.2; Jerome, *Chronicle* 228[d]; *Epitome* 39.5

MAXIMIAN[44]

Principal Residences

285–286	On campaign
286–?293	Trier[45]
?293–296	Milan and Aquileia[46]
296–299	On campaign and at Carthage
299–305	Milan and Aquileia

42. Edited by H. Delehaye, *Acta Sanctorum,* Nov. 3 (Brussels, 1910), 765 ff. On the cult of these martyrs, see J. Guyon, *MEFR (A)* 87 (1975), 505 ff. Their *Passio* also states that Diocletian reached Rome by 8 November 303 (22). Both items are plausible—and may be true without being based on authentic information.

43. This may be the occasion on which Diocletian settled Carpi in Pannonia (Ammianus 28.1.6, cf. Lactantius, *Mort. Pers.* 38.6). The date of 295 given in *Chr. Min.* 1.230; Jerome, *Chronicle* 226[b], appears to be too early, see P. Brennan, *Chiron* 10 (1980), 565. For what it is worth, Eutropius puts the settlement of Carpi and Basternae after the Persian war (*Brev.* 9.25.2).

44. For previous attempts to establish Maximian's movements, W. Ensslin, *RE* 14 (1930), 2489 ff.; T. D. Barnes, *Phoenix* 30 (1976), 176 ff.

45. On Trier as an imperial residence, see E. M. Wightman, *Roman Trier and the Treveri* (London, 1970), 58 ff., 98 ff.

46. *Pan. Lat.* 7(6).6.2 attests an imperial palace at Aquileia in the 290s. Victor names no city, but notes the resumption of imperial residence in north Italy in a difficult passage: "hinc denique parti Italiae invectum tributorum ingens malum. nam cum omnis eadem functione moderateque

Attested Movements

285, July 21	Proclaimed Caesar, probably in Milan	Eutropius, *Brev.* 9.20.3 (Caesar); *RIC* 5.2.241 no. 203 (Ticinum: AD-VENTUS AUG); *Passio Marcelli* 2 (day)
285, late summer	Campaign against the Bagaudae	*Pan. Lat.* 10(2).4.2 ff.
285, c. Sept.	?At Boulogne	Eutropius, *Brev.* 9.21 (which strictly attests only Carausius' presence at Bononia)
285, autumn	Repels a German invasion of Gaul	*Pan. Lat.* 10(2).5.1 ff.
286, Feb. 10	At Milan	*CJ* 8.53(54).6 + 3.29.4 = *Frag. Vat.* 282[47]
286, June 21	At Mainz	*Frag. Vat.* 271
287, Jan. 1	At Trier (or possibly Cologne or Mainz)	*Pan. Lat.* 10(2).6.2 ff.
287	Expedition across the Rhine	*Pan. Lat.* 10(2).7.1 ff.
288	Conference with Diocletian	*Pan. Lat.* 10(2).9.1
288, late	Receives Gennoboudes and his Franci, presumably in northwestern Gaul	*Pan. Lat.* 10(2).10.3 f.
289, April 21	At Trier (or possibly Cologne or Mainz)	*Pan. Lat.* 10(2)[48]

---

ageret, quo exercitus atque imperator, qui semper aut maxima parte aderant, ali possent, pensionibus inducta lex nova" (*Caes.* 39.31). On the interpretation of *parti Italiae,* conventionally but erroneously taken to denote the whole of Italy, see L. Ruggini, *Economia e società nell'Italia annonaria: Rapporti fra agricoltura e commercio dal IV al VI sec. d. C.* (Milan, 1961), 36.

On the literary, legal, and archaeological evidence for imperial palaces in Milan and Aquileia, see N. Duval, *Aquileia e Milano* (*Antichità Altoadriatiche* 4, 1973), 158 ff. In the same volume, M. Bonfioli chronicles imperial visits and periods of residence from Diocletian onward (*Aquileia e Milano* 125 ff.).

47. Mommsen emended *Mediolani* in all three places to *Nicomediae* (*Ges. Schr.* 2.268 f.). The emendation is defended by H. J. Wolff, *ZSS,* Rom. Abt. 69 (1952), 141.

48. The speech was delivered on the *natalis Romae dies* (1.4). As for the year, Mamertinus alludes to a barbarian raid which disrupted Maximian's consular ceremonies in a year which cannot be earlier than 287, followed by an expedition across the Rhine (6.2 ff.) and almost a whole year building a fleet to attack Carausius (12.3 ff.), yet there is no reference to the *quinquennalia* — which would have been obligatory in 290. The place of delivery might not be Trier (as is universally

?289 or 290	?Visits Rome	Julian, *Orat.* 1, 5d[49]
290, early	Visits Lugdunum	*RIC* 5.2.222 no. 13, 261 no. 347 (ADVENTUS AUGG)[50]
290	Tours Gaul	*Pan. Lat.* 11(3).4.2
290, c. Dec. 22	Crosses the Alps	*Pan. Lat.* 11(3).2.4
290, late Dec., or 291, Jan.	Confers with Diocletian in Milan	*Pan. Lat.* 11(3).8.1 ff.
291, Feb. 18	At Durocortorum (Reims)	*Frag. Vat.* 315[51]
291, summer	At Trier	*Pan. Lat.* 11(3)[52]
293, March 1	Invests Constantius with the purple, presumably at Milan	*Pan. Lat.* 8(5).2.2 ff.; *Chr. Min.* 1.229 (day)[53]

assumed), but could be Cologne or Mainz (cf. 6.4, 12.6).

49. Julian states that Fausta was born in Rome: if true, that should imply that Maximian visited the city no later than 290 (Chapter IV, at n. 25).

A passage in the panegyric of 310 appears to imply that Maximian never visited Rome before c. 299: "tu ferocissimos Mauretaniae populos...expugnasti recepisti transtulisti. te primo ingressu tuo tanta laetitia tanta frequentia populus Romanus excepit ut etc." (*Pan. Lat.* 6(7).8.6 f.). But *ingressus* perhaps here means specifically "triumphal entry," with the orator deliberately ignoring earlier visits without a triumph.

50. On the date, P. Bastien, *Le monnayage de l'atelier de Lyon* (Paris, 1972), 48 f.

51. The place of issue is emended from *Durocortoro* to *Durostoro* by V. Velkov, *Charisteria F. Novotný octogenario oblata* (Prague, 1962), 151 ff. His motive was to attribute the law to Diocletian. W. Ensslin had proposed *Durotinco* (*RE* 14 (1930), 2501), which lies between Grenoble and Briançon.

52. Although the approximate date of *Pan. Lat.* 11(3) seems clear from its references to Diocletian's movements, the exact date and occasion have occasioned some perplexity: see especially O. Schäfer, *Die beiden Panegyrici des Mamertinus und die Geschichte des Kaisers Maximianus Herculius* (Diss. Strassburg, 1914), 34 ff.; A. Passerini, *Acme* 1 (1948), 184 ff.; S. d'Elia, *Annali Napoli* 9 (1960/1), 256 ff.

Mamertinus makes it clear that he is speaking on Maximian's birthday (2.1: "dies...qui te primus protulit in lucem"; 19.1 ff., especially 3: "nascentes vos...bona sidera et amica viderunt"), not on his *dies imperii* or on the anniversary of his assumption of the title Herculius (as argued by W. Seston, *Historia* 1 (1950), 257 ff.). In 1.1, 2.2, 19.1, and 19.3 the text printed by modern editors describes the occasion as a *geminus natalis,* which would be a joint birthday of Diocletian and Maximian and imply a date of 22 December 291 (*Phoenix* 30 (1976), 177 n. 15). However, Dr. C. E. V. Nixon informs me that the British Museum manuscript Harleianus 2480 (H) has *genuinus* or *genui nus* (divided) in all four passages. This reading is stemmatically of equal value to the *geminus* of the other manuscripts, and deserves preference on historial grounds (E. Wistrand, *Eranos* 62 (1964), 137 ff.; T. C. Skeat, *Papyri from Panopolis* (Dublin, 1964), 145 f.). Mamertinus also reveals that he delivered the speech after Maximian's *quinquennalia* (1.1) and apparently shortly after his *dies imperii* (2.1); unfortunately, it is not clear whether Maximian calculated his reign as beginning with his appointment as Caesar in the summer of 285 or with his proclamation as Augustus on 1 April 286 (Chapter I; Chapter III.2, 3).

53. The place seems not to be explicitly attested.

?293, March 18	At Ravenna	*CJ* 6.8.1[54]
293, May 2	At Milan	*CJ* 4.24.9[55]
293, May 19	At Verona	*CJ* 6.59.2[56]
293, autumn	Visits Lugdunum	P. Bastien, *Le monnayage de l'atelier de Lyon* (Paris, 1972), 218 nos. 560–561
294, Oct. 27	?At Rome	*CJ* 9.16.5(6)[57]
295, March 21	At Milan	*Consultatio* 5.7
295, Dec. 21	At Milan	*Frag. Vat.* 292
296, March 31	At Aquileia	*Frag. Vat.* 313
296, summer	On the Rhine	*Pan. Lat.* 8(5).13.3
296, autumn	Fighting in Spain	*P. Argent.* 480, 1 verso 3[58]
297, March 1	On campaign in Mauretania	*Pan. Lat.* 8(5).5.2, cf. *ILS* 645 (Tubusuctu)
298, March 10	At Carthage	*Frag. Vat.* 41, cf. *RIC* 6.422–426, Carthago 1, 2, 10–28 (FELIX ADVENT AUGG NN)
?298	Expedition to Tripolitania	Corippus, *Joh.* 1.478 ff., 5.175 ff., 7.530, cf. *Pan. Lat.* 9(4).21.2[59]
?299	Goes from Africa to Italy	*ILS* 646 (Rome)
?299	Enters Rome in triumph	*Pan. Lat.* 7(6).8.7
303, Nov.–Dec.	With Diocletian in Rome	*Pan. Lat.* 6(7).15.4 ff.; *Chr. Min.* 1.148; Eutropius, *Brev.* 9.27.2; Jerome, *Chronicle* 227[m] (joint triumph)[60]

54. The date is transmitted as *ipsis AA. cons.*, which could also signify 290. Mommsen pronounced *Ravennae* corrupt rather than attribute the law to Maximian (*Ges. Schr.* 2.279).

55. O. Seeck, *Geschichte* 1³.454, proposed to emend the day to 2 March.

56. Mommsen perforce emended *Veronae* to *Beroeae* (*Ges. Schr.* 2.275).

57. Mommsen emended *Romae* to *Soatrae* or *Scatrae,* a place between Marcianopolis and Durostorum (*Ges. Schr.* 2.287).

58. Observe also that the confused version of the imperial titles of Diocletian in *IGRR* 1.1291 = *Sammelbuch* 8398 (Elephantine) includes the sobriquet Ἰβηρικὸς μέγιστος.

59. On the Ilaguas or Laguantan named by Corippus, see J. Desanges, *Catalogue des tribus africaines de l'antiquité classique à l'ouest du Nil* (Dakar, 1962), 101 f.

60. On the joint triumph, W. Ensslin, *RE* 7A (1948), 2487 ff.

304, ?after April 21	Leaves Rome	*Pan. Lat.* 7(6).8.8, cf. *Passio Sabini* (*BHL* 7451–54)[61]
304/5, winter	Meets Galerius at an unknown location	Lactantius, *Mort. Pers.* 18.1.
305, May 1	Resigns the imperial power at Milan	Eutropius, *Brev.* 9.27.2; Jerome, *Chronicle* 228[d]; Zonaras 12.32

CONSTANTIUS

Principal Residence

293–306   Trier[62]

Attested Movements

293, March 1	Proclaimed Caesar, probably in Milan	*Pan. Lat.* 8(5).2.2 ff.; *Chr. Min.* 1.229 (day)[63]
293, early summer	Expels troops of Carausius from north-western Gaul	*Pan. Lat.* 8(5).6–7
293	Repels invasion of Batavia	*Pan. Lat.* 8(5).8–9, 7(6).4.2, 6(7).5.3
294, Aug. 5	At Cologne	*CJ* 5.12.21[64]
?295	Visits Italy, passing through Autun on his return to Gaul	*Pan. Lat.* 9(4).14.1 (letter of Constantius)[65]
296	Recovery of Britain	*Pan. Lat.* 8(5).11 ff.
297, March 1	At Trier	*Pan. Lat.* 8(5), especially 2.2 ff., 4.1 f.[66]

61. The relevant passages of three versions of the *passio* are printed in parallel by D. Liebs, *Hermogenians Iuri Epitomae* (*Abh. Göttingen,* Phil-hist. Klasse³ 57.3, 1964), 32 f. F. Lanzoni, *RQ* 17 (1903), 1 ff., damned the *Passio Sabini* as historically worthless: I am grateful to Mr. W. Turpin for showing me the draft of an article which argues that that verdict may be premature.

62. E. Wightman, *Roman Trier and the Treveri* (London, 1970), 58 ff.; 98 ff.

63. The place is nowhere explicitly attested, but *Pan. Lat.* 8(5).6.1 implies that it was outside Gaul.

64. Mommsen attributed the law to Diocletian and asserted that *Agrippinae* designated a place near Sirmium (*Ges. Schr.* 2.286).

65. Constantius speaks of "meum Constanti Caesaris ex Italia revertentis...comitatum," which suits an occasion c. 295 better than his initial arrival as Caesar in Gaul in 293 (the date assumed by E. Galletier, *Panégyriques latins* 1 (Paris, 1949), 114).

66. D. Kienast, *JNG* 10 (1959/60), 71 ff., dates the recovery of Britain to 297 — which entails a date of 1 March 298 for the speech.

300 or 301	Victory over the Franci	*Pan. Lat.* 6(7).6.2[67]
302	Victory over German invaders in the territory of the Lingones	*Pan. Lat.* 6(7).6.2; *CIL* 10.3343 (date)
303	German victory near Vindonissa	*Pan. Lat.* 6(7).6.3
304, late winter	Victory over German raiders who had crossed the frozen Rhine	*Pan. Lat.* 6(7).6.4[68]
305	Crosses from Boulogne to Britain, and campaigns against the Picts	*Pan. Lat.* 6(7).7.1 ff.; *Origo* 4; *AE* 1961.240 (before 7 Jan. 306)[69]
306, July 25	Dies at York	*CIL* 1², pp. 268, 269; *Chr. Min.* 1.231; Socrates, *HE* 1.2.1 (day); Eutropius, *Brev.* 10.1.3; Jerome, *Chronicle* 228ᵍ (place)

GALERIUS[70]

Principal Residences

293–296	?Antioch
296–299	On campaign
299–c. 303	Thessalonica[71]

67. On Constantius' campaigns between 300 and 306, see *Phoenix* 30 (1976), 179, 191; Tables 4–7.

68. The titulature of Maximinus in an edict of 313 as quoted by Eusebius (*HE* 9.10.7: Αὐτοκράτωρ Καῖσαρ Γάϊος Οὐαλέριος Μαξιμῖνος, Γερμανικός, Σαρματικός, εὐσεβὴς εὐτυχής, ἀνίκητος Σεβαστός) implies that Constantius' last German victory was won, or at least celebrated, after 1 May 305. But this abbreviated titulature cannot be regarded as authoritative, and *Sarmaticus* precedes *Germanicus* in Maximinus' victory titles as they appear on *ILAlg.* 1.3956 (near Thelepte), cf. *ZPE* 20 (1976), 155.

69. The presence of Constantius' army in Dumfriesshire is indirectly attested by a brooch with an inscription commemorating the *vicennalia* of Diocletian: J. Curle, *Proceedings of the Society of Antiquaries of Scotland* 66 (1931/2), 370 f.; M. W. Hassall, *Aspects of the Notitia Dignitatum* (*BAR*, Supp. 15, 1976), 107 f.

70. For earlier attempts to establish Galerius' movements, W. Ensslin, *RE* 14 (1930), 2518 ff.; T. D. Barnes, *Phoenix* 30 (1976), 180 ff. The latter article argues more fully the view adopted here and in Chapter XI, that in 293 Galerius was assigned the East, not the Danube as alleged by Aurelius Victor, *Caes.* 39.30, and Praxagoras (*FGrH* 219).

71. The dates of Galerius' residence at Thessalonica and Serdica are inferred from the trans-

c. 303–winter 308/9   Serdica[72]

winter 308/9–311   Thessalonica

Attested Movements

293, March 1	Invested with the purple by Diocletian, probably at Sirmium	*Pan. Lat.* 8(5).3.1; Lactantius, *Mort. Pers.* 35.4 (day)[73]
293, Dec.	?In Egypt	*P. Grenfell* 2.110[74]
?294	Expedition to Upper Egypt	Eusebius, *Chronicle* 227 Karst; Jerome, *Chronicle* 226[a]; *Pan. Lat.* 8(5).5.2
295, Jan.	?In Upper Egypt	*P. Oxy.* 43 recto[75]
295, May 1	?At Damascus	*Mos. et Rom. legum collatio* 6.4 = *CJ* 5.4.17[76]

ference of a mint from the former to the latter and back again, see C. H. V. Sutherland, *RIC* 6 (1967), 54 ff.; 486 ff.; 501 ff.; H. P. Laubscher, *Der Reliefschmuck des Galeriusbogens in Thessaloniki* (*Archäologische Forschungen* 1, 1975), 14 n. 95. On the archaeological remains of the palace buildings, M. Vickers, *JRS* 62 (1972), 25 ff.; 63 (1973), 111 ff.

72. Residence in Serdica before the Conference of Carnuntum in November 308 is implied by *Origo* 8. It is a permissible inference that Galerius moved his residence back to Thessalonica as soon as the new emperor Licinius began to reside in Sirmium.

73. The place is inferred from Diocletian's movements in early 293 (above, at n. 29). Seston, *Dioclétien* 88 ff., argued that Galerius assumed the purple on 21 May at Nicomedia, from which it would follow that he was created emperor in the absence of Diocletian (so I. König, *Chiron* 4 (1974), 567 ff.). Seston adduced two items of evidence. First, the Paschal Chronicle, which states that Galerius and Constantius were made emperors at Nicomedia on 21 May 293 (521 = *Chr. Min.* 1.229). Second, Lactantius, *Mort. Pers.* 19.2: "erat locus altus extra civitatem (sc. Nicomedia) ad milia fere tria, in cuius summo Maximianus ipse purpuram sumpserat." But the *dies imperii* of Galerius was 1 March 293 (*Pan. Lat.* 8(5).3.1), and, even if artificial *dies imperii* are attested (as, e.g., for Aurelian), there is no close parallel or obvious motive for the artifice postulated in 293 (see Jones, *LRE* 3.3 n.4). Nor is the hypothetical investiture in absence convincing. Moreover, both items of evidence adduced by Seston are vulnerable. Lactantius is speaking both of Diocletian and of the place where Diocletian was proclaimed emperor; therefore, the name "Maximianus" should be deleted as a later gloss. The Paschal Chronicle is never authoritative for events in this period outside Egypt: either it is simply mistaken about the place, or 21 May may be the day on which the laureled picture of the new emperors arrived in Alexandria (for the *laureata imago,* see P. Bruun, *Studia Romana in honorem P. Krarup* (Copenhagen, 1975), 122).

74. The papyrus, in Latin and from Oxyrhynchus, appears to be a receipt and mentions "[equit]ibus promotis dd. nn. Diocletiani et Ma[x]imian[i Augg.] et [Constantii et Maximiani] nobilissimorum Caesarum ag["—which indirectly implies the proximity of an emperor. (I am grateful to Dr. P. Brennan for drawing this evidence to my attention.)

75. On this papyrus, see A. K. Bowman, *BASP* 15 (1978), 27, 31 ff. In *Phoenix* 30 (1976), 180 ff., I improperly adduced *P. Oxy.* 43 as if it documented an emperor's presence in Egypt in 293/4.

76. The document describes itself as an edict (*Collatio* 6.4.1, 7, 8): according to conventional doctrine, therefore, it must be ascribed to Diocletian (Mommsen, *Ges. Schr.* 2.288). Admittedly, Diocletian's attested movements permit the hypothesis of an otherwise unknown visit to Syria in 295 (above, at n. 34), but geography and the division of the empire in 293 (Chapter XI) suggest

?295	Campaign on the Persian frontier	Tables 4, 5
296, late–297, spring	On campaign against the Persians; defeated between Carrhae and Callinicum	*P. Argent.* 480, 1 verso 1 ff.; Victor, *Caes.* 39.34; Eutropius, *Brev.* 25, Jerome, *Chronicle* 227^c
297	Collects a new army from the Danube	Victor, *Caes.* 39.34; Eutropius, *Brev.* 9.24; Festus, *Brev.* 25
298	Successful campaign against the Persians: attacks through Armenia, marches down the Tigris through Media and Adiabene, advances to Ctesiphon, and returns up the Euphrates	Arch of Galerius at Thessalonica; Lactantius, *Mort. Pers.* 9.6; Tables 4–7; Victor, *Caes.* 39.34; Eutropius, *Brev.* 9.25.1; Festus, *Brev.* 25 (Armenia); Constantine, *Oratio* 16; *HA, Carus* 9.3 (Ctesiphon); Ammianus 24.1.10 (return)[77]
?298/9, winter	Negotiates with a Persian envoy in Mesopotamia	Petrus Patricius, frag. 13
?299, spring	Meets Diocletian at Nisibis	Petrus Patricius, frag. 14
299, spring	With Diocletian at Antioch	Lactantius, *Div. Inst.* 4.27.4 f., cf. *Mort. Pers.* 10.1 ff.
299 or 300	Campaign against the Marcomanni	*Chr. Min.* 1.230, cf. Tables 4–7
?301, very late in the year	Campaign against the Carpi	Tables 4–7[78]

that Galerius was the emperor who issued the edict at Damascus — perhaps on the orders of Diocletian.

77. The chronology is established by two literary texts: Joshua the Stylite (translated by W. Wright (Cambridge, 1882), p. 6) dates the capture of Nisibis to year 609 of the Seleucid era, i.e. between 1 October 297 and 30 September 298; and Eumenius correlates Galerius' activities with those of his collelagues, when he remarks that men's minds contemplate "aut sub tua, Diocletiane Auguste, clementia Aegyptum furore posito quiescentem aut te, Maximiane invicte, perculsa Maurorum agmina fulminantem aut sub dextera tua, domine Constanti, Bataviam Britanniamque squalidum caput silvis et fluctibus exserentem aut te, Maximiane Caesar, Persicos arcus pharetrasque calcantem" (*Pan. Lat.* 9(4).21.2). The revolt is over, but Diocletian is still in Egypt: therefore, Eumenius was speaking during the summer or autumn of 298 (above, at nn. 36–38).

78. Four victories over the Carpi are attested between late 301 and 7 January 306 (Table 6). In *Phoenix* 30 (1976), 193, I assigned them to 302, 303, 304, and 305 — which might be correct. Moreover, any victory over the Carpi in 304 may have been won by Diocletian rather than Galerius (above, n. 43).

302	Campaigns against the Carpi and Sarmatians	Tables 4–7; Lactantius, *Mort. Pers.* 13.2; *RIC* 6.510, Thessalonica 10 (VICTORIAE SARMATICAE)
302/3, winter	At Nicomedia with Diocletian	Lactantius, *Mort. Pers.* 10.6 ff.; Eusebius, *HE* 8.5 (303, Feb. 24)
303, March 12	Still at Nicomedia	Eusebius, *HE* 8.6.2 ff., cf. *PO* 10.14
303, c. March 14	Leaves Nicomedia	Lactantius, *Mort. Pers.* 14.6 f.
303, autumn	Campaign against the Carpi	Tables 6, 7; Lactantius, *Mort. Pers.* 38.6
304/5, winter	Meets Maximian at an unknown location	Lactantius, *Mort. Pers.* 18.1
305, March–May	At Nicomedia	Lactantius, *Mort. Pers.* 18.1 ff.
306, late, or 307, early	Campaign against the Sarmatians	Tables 6, 7[79]
307, late summer/autumn	Invades Italy	Lactantius, *Mort. Pers.* 27.2 ff.; *Origo* 6–7
308 (or 309)	Campaign against the Carpi	Tables 6, 7[80]
308, Oct.	At Serdica	*Origo* 8[81]
308, Nov. 11	At Carnuntum	Lactantius, *Mort. Pers.* 29.1 f.; *Chr. Min.* 1.231
308, Nov.	Returns to Serdica	*Origo* 8
311, late April or early May	Dies in the province of Dardania, and is buried at Romulianum on the Danube	*Chr. Min.* 1.148; *Epitome* 40.16 (places); Lactantius, *Mort. Pers.* 35.4 (date)

79. *ZPE* 20 (1976), 149 f.; *Phoenix* 30 (1976), 192.
80. *ZPE* 20 (1976), 150; *Phoenix* 30 (1976), 192.
81. *Origo* 8: "Galerius in Illyrico Licinium Caesarem fecit. deinde illo in Pannonia relicto, ipse ad Serdicam regressus, morbo ingenti occupatus sic distabuit, ut...moreretur." Observe that this passage does not (as is assumed by Millar, *Emperor* 52) state that Galerius died in Serdica.

SEVERUS

Principal Residence

305–307   Milan

Attested Movements

305, May 1	Invested with the purple by Maximian at Milan	Lactantius, *Mort. Pers.* 18.12, 19.4, 26.10; Eutropius, *Brev.* 9.27.2
306/7, winter	Confers with Galerius, and prepares to march on Rome	Lactantius, *Mort. Pers.* 26.5
307, early	Begins his attack from Milan	Zosimus 2.10.1
307, spring	Advances close to Rome, but is forced to retreat and flees to Ravenna, where he abdicates	Lactantius, *Mort. Pers.* 26.8 ff.; Eutropius, *Brev.* 10.2.4; Zosimus 2.10.1

MAXIMINUS[82]

Principal Residences

305–306   Antioch[83]
306–308   ?Caesarea[84]
309–311   Antioch
311–312   Nicomedia
312–313   Antioch

Attested Movements

305, May 1	Proclaimed Caesar at Nicomedia	Lactantius, *Mort. Pers.* 19.1 ff.
305, ?May/ June	Goes to the East	Eusebius, *HE* 9.9a.2

---

82. The subject of Maximinus' movements is not adequately discussed in the recent studies of H. Castritius, *Studien zu Maximinus Daia* (*Frankfurter Althistorische Studien* 2, 1969), and T. Christensen, *C. Galerius Valerius Maximinus: Studier over Politik og Religion i Romerriget 305–313* (Copenhagen, 1974). The identification of his residences is largely conjectural.

83. G. Downey, *History of Antioch* 331 ff.

84. Note especially Eusebius, *Mart. Pal.* (S) 7.7.

?305, Nov. 5	?At Apollonopolis in the Thebaid	*CJ* 3.12.1[85]
306, Nov. 20	At Caesarea in Palestine	Eusebius, *Mart. Pal.* 6.1 ff.
307/8, winter	At Caesarea	Eusebius, *Mart. Pal.* (S) 7.7
308, spring or early summer	At Caesarea	Eusebius, *Mart. Pal.* (S) 8.3
310	Campaign against the Persians	Tables 6, 7; *RIC* 6.636, Antiochia 134 (IOVIO PROPAGAT ORBIS TERRARUM)
311, spring	In Syria when he learns of Galerius' death (which occurred c. 1 May)	Lactantius, *Mort. Pers.* 36.1
311, early summer	Crosses Asia Minor rapidly to Bithynia, and negotiates with Licinius at the Bosporus	Lactantius, *Mort. Pers.* 36.1 ff.
311, summer	Returns to Nicomedia and resides there	Eusebius, *HE* 9.9a.4; cf. Lactantius, *Mort. Pers.* 36.3 ff.
312, Jan. 7	At Nicomedia	Eusebius, *HE* 9.6.3; *Chr. Pasch.* 519–520 (place and year); *PO* 10.12; *Acta Sanctorum,* Nov. 2.2 (Brussels, 1931), 29, cf. John Chrysostom, *PG* 50.519 ff. (day)
?312	Visits Stratonicea in Caria	*Sylloge*³ 900
312, July/ Aug.	At Antioch	Malalas 311.12 ff. Bonn, cf. Eusebius, *HE* 9.3 (undated)
312, autumn	Campaign against the Armenians	Eusebius, *HE* 9.8.4; ?*RIC* 6.594, Cyzicus 107 (VICTORIAE MAXIMINI AUG)
313, Feb.	In Syria	Lactantius, *Mort. Pers.* 45.2

85. The heading reads "Impp. Constantius et Maximianus AA. et Severus et Maximinus nobilissimi CC. Verino," the subscription (as restored by P. Krüger) "d. non...Apollonio superioris Constantio V et Maximiano V CC. conss." On the place of issue, J. Morris, *Klio* 46 (1965), 363; *PLRE* 1.950, Verinus 1. Apollonopolis appears (in the locative case) as *Apollonos superioris* in the *Notitia Dignitatum* (Or. 31.34). As for the date, *Nov.* can easily be supplied after *d. non.*

313, late winter/spring	Crosses Asia Minor from Syria to Bithynia	Lactantius, *Mort. Pers.* 45.2
313, April	Captures Byzantium	Lactantius, *Mort. Pers.* 45.4 f.
313, c. April 20	Advances to Heraclea	Lactantius, *Mort. Pers.* 45.5
313, April 30	Defeated near Adrianople	Lactantius, *Mort. Pers.* 46.8 ff.[86]
313, May 1	Crosses the Bosporus	Lactantius, *Mort. Pers.* 47.5[87]
313, May 2	At Nicomedia	Lactantius, *Mort. Pers.* 47.5
313, May	Flees to Cappadocia	Lactantius, *Mort. Pers.* 47.6
313, c. July	Kills himself at Tarsus	Lactantius, *Mort. Pers.* 49.1 ff.; cf. *P. Oxy.* 3144; *P. Cairo Isid.* 103.20

APPENDIX: EUSEBIUS' CHRONOLOGY, 311–313

Eusebius states no precise dates in the ninth book of the *Ecclesiastical History,* which concerns itself almost exclusively with the policies and actions of Maximinus between the summer of 311 and his death c. July 313. But several of the documents which he quotes contain chronological cross-references, and it ought to be clear that a consistent and accurate chronology underlies Eusebius' account.[88] The problem was solved, in all essentials, by N. H. Baynes, who took the crucial step of identifying the "most perfect law on behalf of the Christians" issued by Constantine and Licinius (*HE* 9.9.12, cf. 9a.12) with the letter which Lactantius implies that Constantine wrote to Maximinus shortly after 28 October 312 (*Mort. Pers.* 44.11).[89] Nevertheless, some scholars continue to assert that Eusebius refers to a hypothetical "Edict of Milan," which Constantine and Licinius issued jointly when they conferred there, i.e. in February 313.[90] But this is chronologically impossible: in late spring or early summer 313, Maximinus described as written "last year" (*HE* 9.10.8) letters which

86. On the site of the battle, H. Grégoire, *Byzantion* 13 (1938), 585 f. He emends "campus...quem vocant serenum" to "Ergenum" (*Mort. Pers.* 46.9).

87. With the supplement of Tollius, accepted by J. Rougé: "at ille Kalendis Mais id est una nocte atque una die ⟨ad fretum⟩, Nicomediam alia nocte pervenit."

88. For an attempt at elucidation, based on some doubtful assumptions, see H. J. Lawlor, *Eusebiana* (Oxford, 1912), 211 ff. The arguments which R. M. Grant, *TU* 115 (1975), 417 f., adduces in order to accuse Eusebius of falsifying the order of events fall very far short of proof.

89. N. H. Baynes, *CQ* 18 (1924), 193 f. (disproving the chronology argued by H. J. Lawlor in 1912). When Lawlor reasserted his views in the following year (*CQ* 19 (1925), 94 f.), Baynes was allowed a rejoinder, to which G. W. Richardson added an exegesis of Eusebius' chronology in the *Martyrs of Palestine* (*CQ* 19 (1925), 95 ff.).

90. E.g., M. V. Anastos, *REB* 25 (1967), 23 ff., who argues that Licinius was in Milan in January 313, perhaps even before the end of 312. But Theomnestus, *Hippiatrica Berolinensia* 34.12, establishes a *terminus post quem* of the beginning of February (below, n. 144).

he ordered to be dispatched after he received the "most perfect law" (9.12–9a.12), and the order to write these letters itself refers to his arrival in Nicomedia in summer 311 as occurring "last year" (9a.4).[91] Moreover, the fact that Maximinus' death was known in Karanis by 13 September 313 (*P. Cairo Isid.* 103.20) precludes an escape from Baynes's conclusion by the hypothesis that Maximinus issued the latest document in the autumn of 313 and calculated by regnal years which began c. 1 September or c. 1 October.[92]

Since Baynes's brief note is sometimes still overlooked or ignored,[93] a restatement may be apposite. The following sections of Eusebius, *HE* 9 are either implicitly dated or datable from other evidence:

1.1–7	May/June 311	Maximinus' reaction to Galerius' proclamation of toleration
2	November 311	Resumption of persecution
6.2	26 November 311	Martyrdom of Peter of Alexandria[94]
6.3	7 January 312	Martyrdom of Lucian of Antioch[95]
7.3–14	summer 312	Rescript to Tyre
8	autumn 312	Famine, plague, and Armenian war
9	autumn 312	Constantine defeats Maxentius
9a.1–9	December 312	Letter to Sabinus (cf. 9a.12)
10.7–11	May 313	Edict restoring privileges and property to the Christians (cf. 10.12: less than a full year after 7.3–14)

CONSTANTINE[96]

Principal Residences

306–316   Trier,[97] and perhaps Arles[98]

91. H. Castritius, *Studien* 63 ff.; T. Christensen, *C. Galerius Valerius Maximinus* 222 ff.; Millar, *Emperor* 580 f.

92. As argued respectively by H. J. Lawlor and J. E. L. Oulton, *Eusebius: Ecclesiastical History* 2 (London, 1928), 289, 301, 303; E. Schwartz, *Gött. Gel. Nach.,* Phil.-hist. Klasse 1904.526 f.

93. It is nowhere acknowledged in the long discussion of Eusebius, *HE* 9.9.12, by R. Klein, *RQ* 67 (1972), 1 ff.

94. For the year, Eusebius, *HE* 7.32.31 (in the ninth year of persecution); for the day, the Egyptian evidence (which deserves priority) indicates 29 Athyr, which, in 311, corresponds to 26 November, see B. Kettler, *RE* 19 (1938), 1283.

95. Eusebius, *HE* 9.6.3; *Chr. Pasch.* 519–520; *PO* 10.12; *Acta Sanctorum,* Nov. 2.2 (Brussels, 1931), 29.

96. For earlier attempts to establish Constantine's movements, see especially Seeck, *Regesten* 159 ff. (311 onward); P. Bruun, *Studies in Constantinian Chronology* (*NNM* 146, 1961), 32 ff. (314–329); *RIC* 7 (1966), 76 ff.; T. D. Barnes, *JRS* 63 (1973), 36 ff. (314–317).

97. *Pan. Lat.* 6(7).22.5 ff., 5(8).1.1 ff., cf. E. M. Wightman, *Roman Trier* 58 ff., 98 ff.

98. *Pan Lat.* 6(7).14.6, 16.1 ff.; Lactantius, *Mort. Pers.* 29.5.

316/7	On campaign	
317–324	Sirmium, Serdica, and perhaps Thessalonica[99]	
324–330	?Nicomedia	
330–337	Constantinople[100]	

Attested Movements

306, July 25	Proclaimed emperor at York	*CIL* 1², pp. 268, 269; *Chr. Min.* 1.231; Socrates, *HE* 1.2.1 (day); Eutropius, *Brev.* 10.1.3; Jerome, *Chronicle* 228ᵍ (place)
306, autumn, or 307 early	Campaign against the Franci	*Pan. Lat.* 7(6).4.2; 6(7).10.2 ff.; 4(10).16.5 ff.; Tables 6–8[101]
?307, March 1	At Beauvais	*CTh* 7.20.2 = *CJ* 12.46.1 (emended)[102]
307	Visits Britain	*RIC* 6.129, Londinium 82 (AD-VENTUS AUGG, with obverse FL VAL CONSTANTINUS NOB C)
307, c. Sept.	Marriage to Fausta and investiture as Augustus by Maximian, presumably at Trier	*Pan. Lat.* 7(6); Lactantius, *Mort. Pers.* 27.1; *RIC* 6.205–206, 213, Treveri 639–641, 744–746[103]

99. Constantine used to call Serdica "my Rome," according to Petrus Patricius, *Excerpta Vaticana* 190 = Anon. post Dionem, frag. 15.1 Müller. Cedrenus 1.496 Bonn asserts that Constantine resided in Thessalonica for two years before he defeated Licinius. Constantine delivered his *Speech to the Assembly of the Saints* in one of these two cities on a Good Friday shortly before making war on Licinius in 324, but I am no longer convinced that the exact year and place can be conclusively established (cf. *JTS*, n.s. 27 (1976), 414 ff., arguing for delivery in Serdica on 12 April 317).

100. See G. Dagron, *Naissance d'une capitale: Constantinople et ses institutions de 330 à 451* (Paris, 1974), 19 ff.

101. On the date, *ZPE* 20 (1976), 149; *Phoenix* 30 (1976), 191 f.

102. As transmitted, the subscription reads "dat. kal. Mart. in civitate Velovocorum Constantino Aug. VI et Constantino [or *Constantio*] Caes. conss.," i.e. 1 March 320. If the date is correct, then the *civitas Velovocorum* must be an unidentified town near Serdica (Millar, *Emperor* 122 n. 90). But the place ought to be the well-attested *civitas Bellovacorum*, i.e. Beauvais in northern France (Mommsen, ad loc.; Seeck, *Regesten* 106). If so, the date must be wrong and I propose, with due hesitation, that the correct date is 307, with the consuls originally named as Galerius for the seventh time and Constantine as Caesar (cf. Chapter VI.1; Table 1).

This law is of great significance for the interpretation of Constantine's religious policies. Seeck, *Regesten* 176, emended the date to 326, and Jones, *LRE* 1.81, deduced that Constantine's army was still pagan in 324. The argument ought to proceed in the opposite direction. If his soldiers greeted the emperor with the words "Constantine Auguste, dei te nobis servent" (so *CTh*, but changed to "deus te nobis servet" in *CJ*), then the law should antedate his public profession of Christianity on 28 October 312.

103. The speech celebrates a double ceremony: the marriage of Constantine to Fausta, and his

308	Raids the territory of the Bructeri and builds bridge over the Rhine at Cologne	*Pan. Lat.* 6(7).12.1 ff.; 4(10).18.1 ff.; Tables 6–8[104]
310, summer	On campaign against the Franci	*Pan. Lat.* 6(7).18.1 ff.; Lactantius, *Mort. Pers.* 29.3
310, c. July	Marches south to Massilia on receiving news of Maximian's usurpation	*Pan. Lat.* 6(7).18.1 ff.; Lactantius, *Mort. Pers.* 29.7
310, August	At Trier	*Pan. Lat.* 6(7)[105]
?310, late	Visits Britain	*RIC* 6.134–135, Londinium 133–145 (ADVENTUS AUG(G) N(N))[106]
311, ?spring	Visits Autun	*Pan. Lat.* 5(8).7.2 ff.; 9.1 ff.
311, July 25	At Trier	*Pan. Lat.* 5(8)[107]
312	Invasion of Italy and campaign against Maxentius' forces in northern Italy	*Pan. Lat.* 12(9).5.1 ff.

---

investiture as Augustus by Maximian (1.1, cf. 2.1, 5.3, 8.1). The simultaneity of the two events disproves the dates of 31 March and 25 December 307 argued by W. Seston, *REA* 39 (1937), 197 ff.; J. Lafaurie, *CRAI* 1965.192 ff.; *Mélanges A. Piganiol* 2 (Paris, 1966), 795 ff. For Constantine appears still to have styled himself Caesar on 25 July 307 (*RIC* 6.213, Treveri 744–746, cf. R. Strauss, *Rev. Num.*[5] 16 (1954), 26 ff.), and he married Fausta when Galerius was about to invade Italy (Lactantius, *Mort. Pers.* 27.1 f.) — presumably, therefore, in the late summer or early autumn of 307.

104. On the date, *ZPE* 20 (1976), 150; *Phoenix* 30 (1976), 192.

105. The speech was delivered shortly after 25 July (2.3) on the *natalis dies* of Trier (22.4, cf. 1.1, 13.1) — perhaps 1 August, the birthday of the emperor Claudius, who made the city a *colonia* (E. Wightman, *Roman Trier* 40 f.). The year is deduced from the structure of the speech, which implies that Maximian has died very recently, see E. Schwartz, *Gött. Gel. Nach.,* Phil-hist. Klasse 1904.522 f.

106. Eusebius, *VC* 1.25 speaks of a victory over barbarians on the Rhine followed by a visit to Britain, both before 312; either visit implied by the coins of London would suit the context.

107. The date is established by the following passage: "Quinque annorum nobis reliqua remisisti! O lustrum omnibus lustris felicius! O lustrum quod merito hanc imperii tui aequavit aetatem! Nobis ergo praecipue te principem di immortales creaverunt, quibus singulis haec est nata felicitas, ex quo tu imperare coepisti. Quinquennalia tua nobis, et iam [my emendation of the transmitted *etiam*] perfecta, celebranda sunt. Illa enim quinto incipiente suscepta omnibus populis iure communia, nobis haec propria quae plena sunt" (13.1/2). Since Constantine's *dies imperii* was 25 July 306, his *quinquennalia* were celebrated from 25 July 310 (*quinto incipiente*) to 25 July 311

312, Oct. 28	Battle of the Milvian Bridge	*CIL* 1², p. 274
312, Oct. 29	Enters Rome	*CIL* 1², p. 274; *Pan. Lat.* 12(9).16.2, 19.1 ff.
312, Oct. 29– 313, Jan.	In Rome	*Pan. Lat.* 12(9).19–20; 4(10).33.6 (*bimestris fere cura*); *CTh* 10.10.2ˢ (Dec. 1), 15.14. 3ˢ (Jan. 6)
313, early Feb.	Marries his sister to Licinius at Milan	Lactantius, *Mort. Pers.* 45.1, 48.2; Eusebius, *HE* 10.5.4; *Origo* 13 (place); Theomnestus, *Hippiatrica Berolinensia* 34.12 (date);[108] *RIC* 6.296, Ticinum 111 (FELIX ADVENTUS AUGG NN)
313, Feb. 16	At Sirmio	*CTh* 7.22.1ˢ
313, March 10	At Milan	*CTh* 10.8.1
313, spring	Goes to Gaul	*Origo* 13
313, May 28– June 16	At Trier	*Frag. Vat.* 291ˢ; *CJ* 11.62.1ˢ
313, summer	Goes to the lower Rhine	*Pan. Lat.* 12(9).21.5
313, July 1	At Cologne	*CTh* 11.3.1ˢ
313, Aug. 3	At Trier	*CTh* 1.16.1ˢ
313, c. Aug.	At Trier	*Pan. Lat.* 12(9)
313	?Visit to Britain	*RIC* 7.97–98, London 1, 2, 21 (ADVENTUS AUG N)[109]
313, Nov. 3– 314, June 1	At Trier	*CTh* 9.40.1, 11.30.2, 11.36.1 (Nov. 3), 1.12.1, 1.12.3, 8.10.1, 10.15.1, 11.1.2, 11.7.1 (Nov. 8: some emended by Seeck), 11.29.1ˢ, 11.30.1ˢ (Dec. 27); *CJ* 7.32.10 (314, Jan. 22); *CTh* 3.30.1 (March 26), 11.30.4, 13.5.2, 13.5.3 (June 1: all partly emended by Seeck)

(*iam perfecta*). The orator's references to a harsh census five years earlier (5.4 ff., 10.5) also indicate 311 as the year (Chapter XIV).

108. Below, n. 144.
109. Also implied by *ILS* 8942; 696 (discussed below, n. 145).

314, August 1	Present at the Council of Arles	Eusebius, *VC* 1.44; Optatus, App. 4, p. 208.16 Ziwsa (presence);[110] *HE* 10.5.23 (date)
314, autumn	German campaign	Eusebius, *VC* 1.46; *RIC* 7.124, 163–164; 166–167; 362–364; Table 8
?314	Supervises the building of a fort on the east bank of the Rhine	*ILS* 8937[111]
314, Oct. 29–315, April 28	At Trier	*CTh* 6.35.1 (Oct. 29); 1.2.1 (Dec. 30); *RIC* 7.164, Trier 12 (FELIX PROCESSUS COS IIII AUG N); Optatus, App. 8 (April 28, year not stated)[112]
315, June 2	?At Sirmio	*CTh* 2.30.1 (emended)[113]
315, July 18	At Aqua Viva	*CTh* 8.18.1ˢ
315, July 21 (or 18)	Enters Rome	*CIL* 1², p. 268[114]
315, July 21–Sept. 27	In Rome	*Frag. Vat.* 33, 274 (Aug. 13); *CTh* 11.30.3, 1.2.2 (Aug. 25, 29), 10.1.1 (Sept. 13)
315, Sept. 27	Leaves Rome	*CIL* 1², p. 272

110. The context of *VC* 1.44 ("How he was present at councils of bishops") indicates that the primary reference must be to the Council of Arles in 314, not to the Council of Nicaea in 325 (*VC* 3.11 ff.), cf. S. Calderone, *Costantino e il Cattolicesimo* 1 (Rome, 1962), 293.

The purport of *VC* 1.44 was seen by Cardinal Baronius in the sixteenth century (*Annales Ecclesiastici, anno* 314, § 53). Baronius, however, dated the Battle of Cibalae to 317 (*anno* 317, §§ 1–10). When the date of October 314 for the battle became canonical with Gothofredus' classic *Chronologia Codicis Theodosiani*, published in 1665, then Constantine's presence at Arles seemed to be precluded. O. Seeck, *ZKG* 10 (1889), 507 ff., accepted it, but as a corollary redated the council to 316—a hypothesis easily refuted by L. Duchesne, *MEFR* 10 (1890), 640 ff. The modern redating of the War of Cibalae to 316/7 removes any rational grounds for declining the clear implication of Eusebius.

111. On the inscription (known only from Renaissance reports), see O. Hirschfeld, on *CIL* 13.8502; A. von Domaszewski, *Rh. Mus.*, n.f. 59 (1904), 379 f. A date c. 309 is preferred by D. Hoffmann, *Das spätrömische Bewegungsheer und die Notitia Dignitatum* (*Epigraphische Studien* 7.1, 1969; 7.2, 1970), 1.178; 2.64 n. 190. But Constantine is styled *maximus,* which implies a date later than November 312 (Chapter III, at n. 13).

112. The year is certain, since Domitius Celsus is named as *vicarius Africae* (Chapter IX). *RIC* 7.162, Trier 1, probably implies Constantine's presence there on 1 January 315, cf. M. R. Alföldi, *JNG* 9 (1958), 109 f.

113. The manuscripts have "dat. IIII non. Iun. Sirmio Constantino A. IIII et Licinio conss.," which Seeck retained (*Regesten* 163). But in 315 Sirmium was under the control of Licinius: therefore, either Licinius issued the law (C. Habicht, *Hermes* 86 (1958), 370) or *Sirmio* must be emended to *Sirmione* (as in *CTh* 7.22.1, of 16 February 313).

114. The Chronographer of 354 records *advent(us) divi* on both 18 and 21 July; it is not cer-

315, Oct. 19	At Milan	*Frag. Vat.* 273 (Oct. 19, in either 313 or 315); Augustine, *Epp.* 43.7.20 (place, but not exact date)[115]
316, Jan. 11	At Trier	*CTh* 1.22.1
316, March 21	At Cabillunum (Châlons-sur-Saône)	*CTh* 9.40.2[s]
316, May 6	At Vienne	*CTh* 2.6.1
316, Aug. 7	Presumably at Arles when his son Constantinus was born there	*Epitome* 41.4; Zosimus 2.20.2; *CIL* 1², p. 271
316, Aug. 13	At Arles	*CTh* 11.30.5, 11.30.6
?316, Sept. 29	At Verona	*Frag. Vat.* 290 (the year is missing in the ms.)
316, Oct. 8	At the battle of Cibalae	*Origo* 16; *Chr. Min.* 1.231 (year wrongly given as 314)
316, Dec. 4	At Serdica	*CTh* 9.1.1
316, Dec. 8	?At Serdica	*CJ* 1.13.1 (emended)[116]
c. 316, Dec.	At Philippi	*Origo* 17
c. 317, Jan.	Fights at the battle of the Campus Ardiensis, then advances toward Byzantium	*Origo* 17–18
317, Feb.	Returns to Serdica	*Origo* 19
317, March 1–April 17	At Serdica	*Chr. Min.* 1.232; *Origo* 19; *CTh* 8.12.2[s], 9.10.1
317, June 6–Aug. 7	At Sirmium	*CTh* 11.30.7; Julian, *Orat.* 1, 5d
?317, Dec. 27	At Thessalonica	*CJ* 6.1.4 (emended)[117]

tain which entry refers to 315 and which to 326. P. Bruun, *RIC* 7 (1966), 76, assumes that the coinage of Trier attests Constantine's presence there beyond 25 July.

115. Constantine's visit to Milan is probably the occasion of the issue of *RIC* 7.368, Ticinum 53 (LIBERALITAS XI IMP IIII COS PPP). Constantine became *imperator XI* on 25 July 315 (Table 3).

116. The heading reads "Imp. Constantinus A. ad Protogenem episcopum"; the subscription, as transmitted in the manuscripts, "d. VI id. Iun. Sabino et Rufino conss." If Protogenes is (as seems likely) the known bishop of Serdica (Millar, *Emperor* 591), *Iun.* should be emended to *Ian.*, and Constantine's presence in Serdica may be inferred.

117. As transmitted, the subscription reads "d. VI k. Iul. Thessalonicae Gallicano et Basso conss." and the law is addressed *ad Valerianum*. Seeck, *Regesten* 180, identified the recipient as

?318, Jan. 23	At Sirmium	*CTh* 6.22.1 (emended)[118]
318, Feb. 7–9	At Sirmium	*CJ* 3.11.3, 3.11.4
318, May 23– July 30	At Aquileia	*CTh* 9.16.3ˢ, 11.30.9ˢ (June 22), 12.1.6ˢ (July 1), 7.22.2ˢ, cf. *RIC* 7.396, Aquileia 27 (ADVENTUS AUGUSTI N)
318, Sept. 7	At Milan	*CTh* 8.18.2ˢ
318, Oct. 12	At Aquileia	*CTh* 3.17.1ˢ
318, Oct. 24– 319, April 13	At Sirmium	*CTh* 1.16.3ˢ, 2.6.2ˢ (Oct. 24), 5.2.1ˢ (Dec. 1), 14.25.1ˢ (Dec. 12); 2.6.3ˢ, ?11.35.1ˢ (Dec. 19), 2.4.1 (319, Feb. 4), 11.29.2 (Feb. 10), 10.8.2 (March 11), 2.19.1 (April 13)[119]
319, July 25	At Naissus	*CTh* 2.15.1; 2.16.2ˢ
?319, Aug. 18	At Serdica	*CTh* 5.10.1ˢ
?319, Sept. 29	At Serdica	*CTh* 12.1.16ˢ
319, Nov. 1– 320, May 19	At Serdica	*CTh* 2.10.1, 2.10.2 (Nov. 1), 9.37.1 (Nov. 26), 2.22.1ˢ; *CJ* 6.7.2ˢ (320, Jan. 30); *CTh* 3.2.1, 4.12.3ˢ, 8.16.1, 11.7.3; *CJ* 6.23.15ˢ, 6.37.21ˢ (Jan. 31); *CTh* 10.1.4 (May 19)
320, May 22– Aug. 10	At Sirmium	*CTh* 9.1.5ˢ (May 22), 15.1.4ˢ (July 22), 7.21.1ˢ (Aug. 10)
320, Dec. 17–31	At Serdica	*CTh* 16.10.1, 9.3.1ˢ
321, Feb. 6–27	At Serdica	*CTh* 2.19.2, 9.42.1
321, April 17	At Sirmium	*CTh* 11.19.1
321, May 21	At Viminacium	*CJ* 8.10.6

the *vicarius* Valerianus who received *CTh* 3.5.3 (29 April 330) and emended the date to *Gallicano et Symmacho conss.*, i.e. 330 (accepted in *PLRE* 1.938). But that necessitates the implausible hypothesis that Constantine left Constantinople shortly after its formal dedication on 11 May 330 and returned by 16 July. Accordingly, I retain the consular date, but emend the day, with hesitation, to *VI k. Ian.*

118. So *PLRE* 1.836, Severus 25. The ms. has 321: Seeck, *Regesten* 173, preferred 324.

119. P. Bruun, *RIC* 7 (1966), 76, deduces that Constantine was in Aquileia on 1 January 319 from *RIC* 7.396, Aquileia 28 (FELIX PROCESSUS COS IIII AUG N). The inference is not imperative: the mints of Ticinum, Aquileia, and Sirmium all greeted the following New Year with the legend "FELIX PROCESSUS COS VI AUG N" (*RIC* 7.375, Ticinum 104; 397, Aquileia 34; 467, Sirmium 1, 4)—but on 1 January 320 Constantine was in Serdica.

Seeck, *Regesten* 166, cf. 434, also lists *CTh* 11.35.1 under 19 May 318.

321, June 12–Sept. 14	At Sirmium	*CTh* 2.18.1ˢ, 11.30.11ˢ (June 12), 13.13.1 (Aug. 1), 1.4.1, 9.43.1 (Sept. 14)
?322, April 11	At Sirmium	*CTh* 15.1.2 (emended: 321 mss.)
322, May 23–July 20	At Sirmium	*CTh* 2.4.2, 2.18.2 (May 23), 4.8.4 (June 12), 4.8.3 (July 20)
322, Dec. 18	At Serdica	*CTh* 3.32.1
323, Feb. 15 or May 18	At Thessalonica	*CTh* 4.8.6 = *CJ* 8.46.10
323, spring	At Thessalonica when Roman territory is invaded	*Origo* 21, cf. *CTh* 7.1.1, 7.12.1 (April 28)
323, summer	Campaign against the Sarmatians: successively at Campona, Margus, and Bononia	Publilius Optatianus Porfyrius, *Carm.* 6.16 ff. (places); *RIC* 7.115, 135, 201/2, 262, 475 (SARMATIA DEVICTA); Zosimus 2.21; Petrus Patricius, *Excerpta Vaticana* 187[120]
323, Dec. 25	At Sirmium	*CTh* 16.2.5ˢ
324 (or 321), Jan. 19	At Sirmium	*CTh* 12.17.1 (emended)[121]
324, March 8–April 9	At Thessalonica	*CTh* 13.5.4; 2.17.1ˢ
324, spring–summer	Prepares and begins the campaign against Licinius from Thessalonica	Zosimus 2.22.1 ff.
324, July 3	Battle of Adrianople	*CTh* 7.20.1; *CIL* 1², p. 268; *Chr. Min.* 1.232
324, ?July–Sept.	Siege of Byzantium	*Origo* 27; Zosimus 2.23.1, 25.1.
324, Sept. 18	Battle of Chrysopolis	*CIL* 1², p. 272; *Origo* 27; *Chr. Min.* 1.232; Socrates, *HE* 1.4.2; Zosimus 2.26.3

120. On the date (and against the hypothesis of both a Sarmatian campaign in 322 and a Gothic campaign in 323), see H.-G. Opitz, *ZNW* 33 (1934), 139; T. D. Barnes, *ZPE* 20 (1976), 152.

121. The transmitted date is obviously corrupt: "dat. XIIII Kal. Feb. Sirmio Crispo III et Constantino II Conss." Mommsen, ad loc., and Seeck, *Regesten* 173, emend to "Crispo III et Constantino III conss." (324), but the emendation "Crispo II et Constantino II conss.," i.e. 321, may be preferable.

324, Sept. 19	Receives the surrender of Licinius at Nicomedia	Praxagoras, *FGrH* 219 = Photius, *Bibliotheca* 62; *Origo* 28; Zosimus 2.28.1
324, Nov. 8	Founds Constantinople and proclaims Constantius Caesar	Themistius, *Orat.* 4, p. 63a Dindorf; *CIL* 1², p. 276; *Chr. Min* 1.232[122]
c. 324, Dec.	Visits Antioch	*RIC* 7.685, Antioch 48 (ADVENTUS AUGUSTI N);[123] Constantine, Opitz, *Urkunde* 17.15 = Eusebius, *VC* 2.72;[124] Malalas 318 Bonn
325, Feb. 25	At Nicomedia	*CTh* 1.15.1
325, May 23– late June	At Nicaea	*CTh* 1.2.5 (May 23); Eusebius, *VC* 3.10–14, cf. Schwartz, *Ges. Schr.* 3.79–82 (on and before June 19);[125] Opitz, *Urkunden* 23.2, 25.2, 26.1, 27.13 (before and after June 19)
325, July 25– c. Sept. 15	At Nicomedia	Jerome, *Chronicle* 231ᵉ (July 25); *CTh* 12.5.1 (July 30), 9.1.4 (shortly before Sept. 17)[126]
325, Sept. 17	At Nassete (between Nicomedia and Chalcedon)	*CTh* 11.39.1ˢ
325, Oct. 13	At Constantinople	*CTh* 7.20.3
325, Oct. 19	At Aquae	*CTh* 7.4.1
326, Feb. 3	At Heraclea	*CTh* 9.3.2, 9.7.1

122. On *P. Oxy.* 889, which J. D. Thomas, *Ancient Society* 7 (1976) 306 f., conjecturally restores as attesting Constantine's presence in Nicomedia on 12 December 325, see Chapter XIV.3. Coins minted in Nicomedia c. 325 proclaiming "FELIX ADVENTUS AUG N" do not seem to aid in reconstructing Constantine's movements (P. Bruun, *RIC* 7 (1966), 609, on Nicomedia 52).

123. Observe, however, that the mint of Antioch exhibits, in late 324, some clearly inappropriate and tralatician legends (*RIC* 7.682–684, Antioch 37–41).

124. On the interpretation of this document, *AJAH* 3 (1978), 54 ff. Preparations for an impending imperial visit to Egypt are attested in January and May 325 (*P. Oxy.* 1261; 1626 = *FIRA*² 3.151).

125. Seeck, *Regesten* 175, dates the opening of the council of Nicaea to May 20, adducing Socrates, *HE* 1.13.13. But Socrates has merely misread πρὸ ιγ´ καλανδῶν Ἰουλίων as Ἰουνίων: his source was the creed subscribed on June 19 (Schwartz, *Ges. Schr.* 3.81).

126. Opitz, *Urkunde* 27.15, shows that Constantine was still in or near Nicomedia when he exiled Eusebius of Nicomedia, "three months" after the Council of Nicaea (Philostorgius, *HE* 1.10)—i.e., depending on the base date and method of counting, between late August and October 325.

326, March 5	At Heraclea	*CTh* 10.4.1[s]
326, March 8	At Constantinople	*CTh* 2.10.4
326, April 1–4	At Aquileia	*CTh* 9.24.1[s]; 9.8.1[127]
326, July 6	At Milan	*CTh* 9.21.3
326, July 18 (or 21)–Aug. 3	In Rome	*CIL* 1², p. 268; Jerome, *Chronicle* 231[e]; *Chr. Min.* 1.232 (July 25); *CTh* 10.8.3 (Aug. 3)
326, Sept. 25	At Spoletium	*CTh* 16.5.2
326, Oct. 23	At Milan	*CTh* 4.22.1
?326, Nov. 22	At Aquileia	*CJ* 2.19(20).11 (emended)[128]
326, Dec. 31	At Sirmium	*CJ* 10.1.7
327, Feb. 27	At Thessalonica	*CTh* 11.3.2
327, June 11	At Constantinople	*CTh* 2.24.2
327, July 30	At Nicomedia	*CTh* 12.5.1[s]
327, Dec./ 328, Jan.	Attends church council at Nicomedia	Opitz, *Urkunde* 31 (council); Eusebius, *VC* 3.23 (Constantine present); Philostorgius, *HE* 2.7, 7[a] (date and place); Opitz, *Urkunde* 29 + Athanasius, *Apol. Sec.* 59.5 (date)[129]
?328, Jan. 7	Refounds Drepanum in Bithynia as Helenopolis	*Chr. Pasch.* 527[130]
328, March 1	At Nicomedia	*CTh* 14.24.1
328, May 18	At Serdica	*CTh* 11.7.4[s]
328, July 5	At Oescus	*CTh* 6.35.5[s]
328, Sept. 27	At Trier	*CTh* 1.4.2[s]
328/9	Campaign on the Rhine	Table 8

127. *CTh* 9.7.2, posted at Nicomedia on 25 April, and *CJ* 5.26, posted at Caesarea on 14 June, are clearly fragments of the same law (Seeck, *Regesten* 63).

128. The subscription, as transmitted, reads "d. X k. Oct. Aquileiae Constantino A. VII et Constantio conss." Seeck originally emended the month from *Oct.* to *Dec.* (*ZSS*, Rom. Abt. 10 (1889), 236 f.), but later proposed to change the consular date to 340 (*Regesten* 189, reporting the ms. reading as "Constantio A. VII et Constantio conss."). The address *ad Evagrium pp.* precludes a date after 337 (Chapter VIII).

129. For the inference, *AJAH* 3 (1978), 60 f.

130. The Paschal Chronicle dates the refoundation of Drepanum to 327, which can hardly be correct, since Helena was still alive in January 327; the day must have been the anniversary of the martyrdom of Lucian in 312 (*PO* 10.12; *Acta Sanctorum,* Nov. 2.2 (Brussels, 1931), 29).

328, Dec. 29	At Trier	*CTh* 1.16.4, 7.20.5
329, March 9– April 18	At Sirmium	*CTh* 6.4.1ˢ (March 9), 2.16.1ˢ, 3.30.3ˢ; *CJ* 5.72.4ˢ (March 15), *CTh* 9.12.2ˢ (April 18)
329, May 13	At Naissus	*CTh* 11.27.1ˢ
329, May 29– June 19	At Serdica	*CTh* 9.9.1ˢ, 11.30.18ˢ
329, Aug. 3	At Heraclea	*CTh* 11.30.13ˢ
329, Oct. 18	At Bergule	*CTh* 16.8.1 (emended)[131]
329, Oct. 25	At Heraclea	*CTh* 12.1.17
330, Feb. 5	At Serdica	*CTh* 16.2.7; Optatus, App. 10
330, Feb. 22	At Bessapara	*CTh* 2.26.1ˢ
330, spring	Goes to Constanti- nople	*RIC* 7.576, Constantinople 41 (AD- VENTUS AUGUSTI N)
330, May 11	Formal dedication of Constantinople	*Chr. Min.* 1.233, 643; *Scriptores originum Constantinopolitanarum* pp. 18, 143 Preger
330, July 16– 331, June 30	At Constantinople	*Frag. Vat.* 248 (July 16); *CTh* 16.8.2 (Nov. 29), 16.8.4 (Dec. 1), 5.9.1 (331, April 17); *MAMA* 7.305, col. 3.1 ff. (June 30)
?331	Visits Nicomedia	*RIC* 7.626, Nicomedia 160 (AD- VENTUS AUG N)[132]
331 Nov. 1	At Constantinople	*CTh* 1.16.6, 1.16.7
331, c. Nov. 1– 332, Jan.	Tries Athanasius at Psamathia (a suburb of Nicomedia)	Athanasius, *Apol. Sec.* 60.4, 65.4 (place); *Festal Letter* 4.5 (date); Socrates, *HE* 1.27.10[133]

131. *CTh* 16.8.1 = *CJ* 1.9.3 has "dat. XV Kal. Nov. Murgillo Constantino A. IIII et Licinio IIII conss." (315). The place of issue has traditionally been identified as Mursella, in Pannonia Superior (M. Fluss, *RE* 16 (1935), 660 f., 677 f.), and Seeck emended the date to 13 August 339, taking *CTh* 16.8.6 and 16.9.2 (transmitted date 13 August 353) as coming from the same original document (*Regesten* 187). But Evagrius, to whom *CTh* 16.8.1, 8.6, 9.2 are addressed, was praetorian prefect before the death of Constantine (Chapter VIII). *PLRE* 1.284/5, Evagrius 2, emends the date to 329 ("Constantino A.VIII et Constantio C. IIII conss.") and *Murgillo* to *Bergulis,* i.e., the town of Bergule, between Adrianople and Constantinople (E. Oberhummer, *RE* 3 (1899), 293).

132. Constantine's presence in Nicomedia in 330 or 331 seems also to be implied by Epiphanius, *Pan.* 68.5/6.

133. The Index to *Festal Letter* 3 states that Constantine tried Athanasius in 330/1 – whence it has been erroneously deduced that Athanasius was tried in both 330/1 and 331/2 (e.g., Millar, *Emperor* 602).

332, April 12	At Marcianopolis	*CTh* 3.5.4, 3.5.5
332, April 20	Victory over the Goths	*Origo* 31;[134] Jerome, *Chronicle* 233ᶜ; *Chr. Min.* 1.234; Table 8; *RIC* 7.333, Rome 306 (VICTORIA GOTHICA)
332, Oct. 17–333, May 5	At Constantinople	*CJ* 6.1.6 (Oct. 17); *CTh* 4.8.8 (Oct. 26), 3.30.5 (333, April 18), 8.12.5 (May 4); *Const. Sirm.* 1 (May 5)[135]
333, late Oct.–Nov. 11	At Aquae	*CTh* 1.32.1, 1.2.6
334	At Nicomedia	*CJ* 6.21.15 (wrongly dated *III id. Aug.*)
334, June 17	At Constantinople	*CTh* 1.22.2
334, July 5	At Singidunum	*CTh* 10.15.2
334, Aug. 4	At Viminacium	*CTh* 12.1.21
334, Aug. 25	At Naissus	*CTh* 11.39.3
334	Campaign against the Sarmatians	*Chr. Min.* 1.234; Table 8
335, March 22–Oct. 21	At Constantinople	*CTh* 10.10.3 (March 22); 8.9.1 (April 17); 11.16.6ˢ (May 7); *Chr. Min.* 1.235 (July 25); *CTh* 16.8.5, 16.9.1 = *Const. Sirm.* 4 (Oct. 21)
335, Oct. 23	At Nicopolis	*CJ* 1.40.4[136]
335, Nov. 6	Returns to Constantinople	Gelasius, *HE* 3.18.4; Festal Index 8
335, Nov. 7	In Constantinople	Festal Index 8; cf. Athanasius, *Apol. Sec.* 87.1 f.[137]

134. The *Origo* has *per Constantinum Caesarem*, presumably using *Caesarem* in a non-technical sense (*ZPE* 20 (1976), 151 n.5).

135. *CTh* 3.5.6 may attest Constantine's presence in Constantinople on 15 July 332 (Chapter IX, n. 17).

136. P. Krüger, ad loc., emended *d. X k. Nov. Nicopoli* to *pp.* But Constantine's letter of 6 November 335 reveals that on that day he had just returned to Constantinople from elsewhere (Gelasius of Cyzicus, *HE* 3.18.4: (sc. Athanasius) εἰσιόντι μοι ἀπὸ προκέσσου ἐπὶ τὴν ἐπώνυμον ἡμῶν καὶ πανευδαίμονα Κωνσταντινούπολιν πρόσεισι ἐν μέσῳ τῆς λεωφόρου)· Athanasius, *Apol. Sec.* 86.2–12, deliberately omits parts of Constantine's letter, among them the precise and technical phrase ἀπὸ προκέσσου, cf. N. H. Baynes, *JEA* 11 (1925), 61 ff.

137. For a cogent defense of the transmitted date (often emended to 5 February 336), see P. Peeters, *Bull. Acad. Roy. de Belgique,* Classe des Lettres⁵ 30 (1944), 131 ff.

335, after Nov. 7	In Constantinople	Eusebius, *VC* 4.33, 46[138]
?336	Visits Thessalonica	*RIC* 7.527, Thessalonica 203 (ADVENTUS AUG N)
336	Campaigns north of the Danube, and recovers part of the lost province of Dacia	Festus, *Brev.* 26; Julian, *Caesares* 329b–d; Table 8; *RIC* 7.221, Trier 578 (VICTOR OMNIUM GENTIUM)
336, July 25– 337, April 3	At Constantinople	Eusebius, *Triac.* 1–10, cf. *VC* 4.46;[139] *CTh* 12.1.22 (Aug. 22); 3.1.2 (337, Feb. 4); Eusebius, *VC* 4.60.5 (April 3)
337, April or May	Visits Aquae and Helenopolis	Eusebius, *VC* 4.61.1
337, May 22	Dies at Ancyrona, a suburb of Nicomedia	Eusebius, *VC* 4.61.2, 64; *Chr. Min.* 1.235; Socrates, *HE* 1.39.2, 40.3; Festal Index 10; *Chr. Pasch.* 532

LICINIUS[140]

Principal Residences

308–316	Sirmium[141] and perhaps Naissus[142]
316/7	On campaign
317–324	Nicomedia[143]

Attested Movements

308, Nov. 11	Invested as Augustus at Carnuntum	Lactantius, *Mort. Pers.* 29.1 f.; *Chr. Min.* 1.231

---

138. On the speech to which Eusebius refers (not *Triac.* 11–18), *GRBS* 18 (1977), 343 ff.

139. For the date, H. A. Drake, *Historia* 24 (1975), 345 ff.

140. For earlier attempts to establish the movements of Licinius, see especially R. Andreotti, *Diz. ep.* 4 (1959), 981 ff.

141. *Origo* 8 (*in Pannonia relicto* in late 308); 16/17 (family and *thesauri* at Sirmium in October 316). The construction of *Thermae Licinianae* appears to be proved by *CIL* 3.10107, cf. M. Mirković, *Sirmium: Archaeological Investigations in Syrmian Pannonia* 1 (Belgrade, 1971), 37, 59.

142. [Julian], *Epp.* 185–187 (in 'Thrace' c. 315), cf. *GRBS* 19 (1978), 102 ff. What appears to be the palace of a pagan Roman emperor built c. 300 and soon abandoned has been found at Gamzigrad near Niš, *Illustrated London News,* October 1975, 97–99.

143. [Julian], *Epp.* 184, 416d–417b; Socrates, *HE* 1.6.33; Sozomen, *HE* 4.16.6.

310, June 27	Victory over the Sarmatians	*ILS* 664; Tables 6, 7
311, June 9	At Serdica	*FIRA*² 1.93
311, summer	Negotiates with Maximinus at the Bosporus	Lactantius, *Mort. Pers.* 36.1 f.
313, early Feb.	Leaves Carnuntum and travels posthaste to Italy	Theomnestus, *Hippiatrica Berolinensia* 34.12[144]
313, Feb.	Marries Constantine's sister at Milan	Lactantius, *Mort. Pers.* 45.1, 48.2; Eusebius, *HE* 10.5.4; *Origo* 13; Zosimus 2.17
313, April 30	Defeats Maximinus near Adrianople	Lactantius, *Mort. Pers.* 46.8 ff
313, early May	Advances to Nicomedia	Lactantius, *Mort. Pers.* 48.1
313, June 13	At Nicomedia	Lactantius, *Mort. Pers.* 48.1
313, summer	Crosses Asia Minor	Lactantius, *Mort. Pers.* 49.1
313, autumn	At Antioch	Lactantius, *Mort. Pers.* 50.6; Eusebius, *HE* 9.11
313 or 314	Campaigns on the Persian frontier	*ILS* 8942; 696[145]

144. Edited by E. Oder and K. Hoppe, *Corpus Hippiatricorum Graecorum* 1 (Leipzig, 1924), 183. The emperor is not named, but the allusion seems certain, see M. Haupt, *Opuscula* 3 (Leipzig, 1876), 491 ff.

145. These two inscriptions attribute to Constantine a combination of victory titles so unexpected that they have been dismissed either as aberrant and unreliable (O. Seeck, *Rh. Mus.*, n.f. 48 (1893), 200 n. 2) or as a version of the titles of Constantius illegitimately transferred to Constantine (C. Habicht, *Hermes* 86 (1958), 371). But the victory titles run closely parallel:

Ger. max.	Ger. maximo III	Med. max.	Med. max.
Sar. max.	Sarm. max.		Armen. max.
Brit. max.	Brit. max.	Gotico max.	Goth. max.
Per. max.	Capp. max	(*ILS* 8942: Semta,	(*ILS* 696: near
Aiab. max.	Arab. max.	315)	Sitifis, 318)

Since the correspondence of titles is very close (*Aiab.* and *Arab.* presumably being mistakes of transcription for *Adiab(enicus)*), each inscription tends to confirm the other, and, once the principle of collegiality in the taking of victory titles is recognized (Chapter III.2), it seems clear that the titles of Constantine reflect victories won either by himself or by his colleague Licinius, and hence that those relating to the East were earned by Licinius (*ZPE* 20 (1976), 154). The dates of the campaigns are fixed by *ILS* 8942 and by the fact that *Per(sicus)/Capp(adocicus) max(imus)* follows *Brit(tanicus) maximus,* thus implying that Licinius' campaigns are later than Constantine's expedition to Britain in autumn 313 (above, at n. 109).

314 or 315	Campaigns against the Goths	*ILS* 8942; 696
Between 314 and 316	At Tropaeum Traiani	*ILS* 8938[146]
316, Sept./ Oct.	At Sirmium	*Origo* 16; [Julian], *Epp.* 181, 449a[147]
316, Oct. 8	At Cibalae	*Origo* 16; *Chr. Min.* 1.231 (year wrongly given as 314)
316, Oct. 9	At Sirmium	*Origo* 16
316, after Oct. 9	Flees to Dacia and then to Adrianople	*Origo* 17; [Julian], *Epp.* 181, 449a
c. 317, Jan.	Defeated at the battle of the Campus Adriensis and withdraws to Beroea	*Origo* 18
c. 318	Campaign against the Sarmatians	*P. Oxy.* 889[148]
318, June 23	?At Byzantium	*CTh* 1.27.1[149]
323, April 13	?At Byzantium	*CTh* 11.30.12^s, 12.1.8^s
324, July 3	Defeated at Adrianople	*Origo* 24; Zosimus 2.22.4 ff., cf. *CIL* 1², p. 268; *Chr. Min.* 1.232
324, ?July–Sept.	Besieged in Byzantium	*Origo* 25; Zosimus 2.23.1 ff.
324, Sept.	Flees to Chalcedon	*Origo* 27; Zosimus 2.25.1
324, Sept. 18	Retreats to Nicomedia	Praxagoras, *FGrH* 219; Zosimus 2.26.3; Philostorgius, p. 180.13 ff. Bidez
324, Sept. 19	Abdicates and is then sent to Thessalonica	*Origo* 28–29; *Epitome* 41.7; Zosimus 2.28

146. *CTh* 2.30.1 might attest Licinius' presence at Sirmium on 30 June 315 (above, n. 113).
147. *GRBS* 19 (1978), 100 f.
148. Reprinted and discussed in Chapter XIV.3.
149. The subscription is transmitted as "data VIIII Kal. Iulias Constantinopoli A. et Crispo Caes. conss." Seeck emended *Constantinopoli* to *ipso* and attributed the law to Constantine (*Regesten* 166). For ascription of the law to Licinius, Millar, *Emperor* 591 n. 7.

CRISPUS

Principal Residences

317–318   ?With Constantine
318–323   Trier[150]
323–324   With Constantine and on campaign
324–326   ?Trier

Attested Movements

317, March 1	Proclaimed Caesar at Serdica	*Origo* 19; *Chr. Min.* 1.232
?319	Campaign against the Franci	*Pan. Lat.* 4(10).17.2, cf. 37.3; *RIC* 7.185, Trier 237–241; *P. Oxy.* 889[151]
321, Jan. 1	?At Serdica	*RIC* 7.470, Sirmium 19 (FELIX ADVENTUS CAESS NN), Sirmium 20A (FELIX PROCESSUS COS II)[152]
321, March 1	With Constantine, presumably at Serdica	*Pan. Lat.* 4(10).36.4 ff.
323	?Campaign on the Rhine	*RIC* 7.196, Trier 362–363, 365–366; 475, Sirmium 49–52 (ALAMANNIA DEVICTA)[153]
324, Jan. 1	?At Sirmium	*RIC* 7.476, Sirmium 57 (FELIX PROCESSUS COS III)
324, summer	In command of Constantine's fleet: destroys Licinius' fleet at the Hellespont and then sails to the Bosporus	Publilius Optatianus Porfyrius, *Carm.* 19.35 f., with the *versus intexti;* Eusebius, *HE* 10.9.4–6; *Origo* 23–27; Petrus Patricius, *Excerpta Vaticana* 188; Zonaras 13.2

150. Nazarius in 321 alludes to Crispus' normal separation from his father: "cui tanto intervallo videre filium licuit" (*Pan. Lat.* 4(10).37.1).

151. Reprinted and discussed in Chapter XIV.3. The date of the campaign is not certain: although Seeck once preferred 320 (*RE* 4 (1901), 1722), either 318 or, more probably, 319 appears to be established by the imperial coinage (P. Bruun, *RIC* 7 (1966), 76).

152. Referred to Serdica on the grounds that Serdica had no mint, and Constantine seems to have spent the winter of 320/1 there, not at Sirmium.

153. The inference is uncertain; but if it is correct, then Publilius Optatianus Porfyrius, *Carm.* 8.33, 10.24 ff., should refer to 323 rather than to Crispus' earlier campaign c. 319 (*AJP* 96 (1975), 180 f.).

| 325, March 6 | At Trier | *CTh* 12.9.1[154] |
| 326, c. May | Executed at Pola | Ammianus 14.11.20 (place); *Epitome* 41.11; Zosimus 2.29.2 (implied date)[155] |

LICINIUS CAESAR

If Licinius Caesar was twenty months old when he became Caesar on 1 March 317 (*Epitome* 41.4; Zosimus 2.20.2), he was only a boy of nine when he was deposed in September 324; presumably, therefore, he normally resided and traveled with his parents.

CONSTANTINUS

Principal Residences

317–328 With Constantine[156]
328–340 Trier[157]

Attested Movements (to 337)

323	?Takes part in Constantine's Sarmatian campaign	*RIC* 7.195–196, Trier 358–361, 364, 364A; 204, Trier 446 (PRINCIPIA IUVENTUTIS linked with SARMATIA)
326	?Remains in the East while Constantine visits Rome	*RIC* 7.207, Trier 467–468, cf. 328, Rome 279[158]
?330	Campaign against the Alamanni	*MAMA* 7.305, col. 3.7 (*Alaman(nicus)* by 30 June 331); *AE* 1934. 158[159]

154. Seeck, *Regesten* 174, emends *dat.* to *pp.* in order to attribute the law to Constantine.
155. A. Piganiol, *L'Empire chrétien* (Paris, 1947), 35.
156. *Pan. Lat.* 4(10).37.3.
157. Constantine's journey to Trier late in 328 was presumably to set Constantinus up with his own establishment.
158. A conjectural inference: the Trier coins allude to the imperial visit to the West with the legend "AETERNA GLORIA SENAT P Q R," but depict a quadriga with only two emperors (i.e. Constantine and Constantius), and it may be relevant that Evagrius remained in Nicomedia as praetorian prefect (Chapter VIII.3).
159. The campaign is dated to 328 by O. Seeck, *Geschichte* 4.381; *Regesten* 178; P. Bruun, *RIC* 7 (1966), 78, 213 f. But Constantine himself does not have the title *Alamannicus maximus* on

332, July 27	At Cologne	*CTh* 2.19.3; 4.10.1[160]
336, July 25	In Gaul	Eusebius, *Triac.* 3.4[161]
337, June 17	At Trier	Athanasius, *Apol. Sec.* 87.4
337, c. Sept.	Confers with Constantius and Constans in Pannonia	Julian, *Orat.* 1, 19a

CONSTANTIUS

Principal Residences

324–c. 330	With Constantine
c. 330–335	?With Constantine[162]
335–350	Antioch[163]

Attested Movements (to 337)

324, Nov. 8	Proclaimed Caesar at Byzantium	Themistius, *Orat.* 4, p. 63a Dindorf; *CIL* 1², p. 276; *Chr. Min.* 1.232
326	Accompanies Constantine to Rome	*RIC* 7.207, Trier 467–468, cf. 328, Rome 279
336, July 25	In Constantinople	Eusebius, *VC* 4.49, cf. *Triac.* 3.4[164]

AE 1934.158 = Chapter III, no. 8; therefore, the campaign should have been waged in his absence, not in 328 (despite *RIC* 7.213, Trier 516–517).

160. In order to attribute the law to Constantine himself, Seeck emended the date to 313 (*Regesten* 92, 156).

161. The translation and commentary of H. A. Drake, *In Praise of Constantine* (Berkeley, 1976), 87, 159, does not bring out the full force of Eusebius' conceit, that, just as the rays of the sun illumine both east and west, so Constantine illumines the whole world through his Caesars, of whom one resides in the east (i.e. Constantius), another illumines "the other race of men" (i.e. Constantinus in the far west), and a third is elsewhere (i.e. Constans).

162. Julian, *Orat.* 1, 11d–13d, alleges that Constantine gave Constantius charge of the Gallic provinces while still a boy, and later transferred him to stand guard on the eastern frontier. Hence Seeck, *Geschichte* 4.4, 382, argued that Constantius briefly replaced Constantinus in Gaul while the latter fought the Goths on the Lower Danube in spring 332. But *AE* 1934.158 does not give Constantinus the title *Sarmaticus:* hence the Gothic victory of 332 was won by Constantine himself (Table 8). Moreover, Libanius implies that Constantius remained with his father until 335 (*Orat.* 59.42 f.). Nevertheless, Julian might be correct in asserting that Constantius resided apart from his father before 335.

163. For 335–337, Eusebius, *Triac.* 3.4; Julian, *Orat.* 1, 13b; Sozomenus, *HE* 3.5.1, and the division of the empire in 335 (Chapter XI); for the years after 337, see Seeck, *Regesten* 184 ff., with the minor modifications proposed in *Phoenix* 34 (1980), 160 ff.

164. H. A. Drake, *Historia* 24 (1975), 354; *In Praise of Constantine* (1976), 159.

337, spring	In Antioch when he learns of Constantine's last illness	Zonaras 13.4
337, May	Travels to Nicomedia, but finds that Constantine is already dead	Julian, *Orat.* 1, 16d; Zonaras 13.4
337, shortly after May 22	Escorts Constantine's body to Constantinople and supervises the funeral	Eusebius, *VC* 4.70; Libanius, *Orat.* 59.74; *Chr. Min.* 1.236
337, c. Aug.	At Viminacium	Athanasius, *Apol. ad Const.* 5[165]
337, c. Sept.	Confers with Constantinus and Constans in Pannonia	Julian, *Orat.* 1.19a
337	Campaign against the Sarmatians	*ILS* 724 (Troesmis)[166]
337, c. Oct.	Returns to Constantinople and convenes a council of bishops	Socrates, *HE* 2.7
337, late	Travels to Antioch	Julian, *Orat.* 1, 20c; Socrates, *HE* 2.7[167]

CONSTANS

Principal Residences

333–335   With Constantine[168]
335–337   ?Milan[169]
337–340   Naissus[170]

Attested Movements (to 337)

337, Aug. 29   ?At Aquileia   *Frag. Vat.* 35[171]

165. Athanasius was in Trier on 17 June (Athanasius, *Apol. Sec.* 87.4) and entered Alexandria on 23 November 337 (Festal Index 10), cf. *AJAH* 3 (1978), 65 f.
166. *Phoenix* 34 (1980), 162.
167. For the date, *AJAH* 3 (1978), 66.
168. Libanius, *Orat.* 59.42 f.
169. Inferred from the division of the empire in 335 (Chapter XI).
170. Zonaras 13.5.9, cf. Seeck, *Regesten* 187 ff. The Sarmatian campaign of Constans implied by *ILS* 724 (Troesmis) should probably be dated to 338, see *Phoenix* 34 (1980), 164 f.
171. As transmitted, the subscription reads "Data IIII kal. Sept. a praefecto ⟨praetorio⟩ ad

337, c. Sept.	Confers with Constantinus and Constantius in Pannonia	Julian, *Orat.* 1, 19a

DALMATIUS

Principal Residence

335–337   ?Naissus

Attested Movements

337, summer   At Naissus   *CJ* 5.17.7[172]

---

correctorem Piceni Aquileia. Accepta XIIII kal. Oct. Albae Constantino Aug. III cons." (313). But sections 3–5 are virtually identical, word for word, with *CTh* 3.1.2, issued from Constantinople on 4 February 337 to Gregorius, praetorian prefect in Africa. The correct date, therefore, ought to be 337 (*PLRE* 1.1019, Anonymus 88). The presence of a praetorian prefect implies the presence of an emperor, who could only be Constantinus or Constans. Since Italy had been assigned to Constans in 335 (*Origo* 35; *Epitome* 41.20), he is here identified as the latter.

172. The law is addressed *ad Delmatium,* with the subscription *d(ata)...Naisso Feliciano et Titiano conss.* Seeck supposed that the Caesar Dalmatius was the recipient of the law (*Regesten* 127). That is impossible (cf. Chapter III, no. 8). The recipient ought to be identified as the Caesar's father, Fl. Dalmatius, cos. 333, who was presumably killed with his son, i.e. between 2 August and 9 September 337 (Chapter I, at n. 34). Hence the emperor who issued the law should be Dalmatius Caesar, between 22 May and 9 September 337.

PART TWO

HOLDERS
OF
OFFICES

CHAPTER VI

ORDINARY CONSULS

In the late Roman Empire the eponymous consulate retained and even increased its prestige, while the suffect consulate, though it continued to exist until at least 400, ceased to count as a real consulate and was no longer normally deemed worthy of record in the formal statement of a senator's career.[1] The names of the consuls of each year, therefore, have a clear historical importance: both imperial consulates and those of others often reflect political events, while the identity of private citizens who held an ordinary consulate is highly relevant to the political and social standing of individuals and families. Unfortunately, however, the ancient lists are all in some way incomplete or defective, while no modern list does full justice to the complexity of the available evidence.[2] The present chapter attempts to remedy this lack. It falls into two parts: a list of ordinary consuls from 284 to 337, and prosopographical notes on consuls other than emperors.

1. ORDINARY CONSULS, 284–337

The basis for any modern reconstruction of the consular fasti must be the various lists of consuls which survive from late antiquity. Theodor Mommsen provided a synopsis of these lists (*Chr. Min.* 3.515–520, for A.D. 284–337), and

---

1. On this development, see A. Chastagnol, *Rev. Hist.* 219 (1958), 221 ff.; *La Préfecture urbaine à Rome sous le Bas-Empire* (Paris, 1960), 398 f., 406. He postulates a sudden degrading of the suffect consulate, by deliberate imperial policy, between 301 and 310.

2. W. Liebenam, *Fasti Consulares Imperii Romani* (*Kleine Texte* 42–43, 1909), 31–36 (still useful for its references to epigraphic attestation of consular dates); A. Degrassi, *I fasti consolari dell'Impero romano* (Rome, 1952), 75–80, and *PLRE* 1.1042–44 all require revision for most years

the following calendars, chronicles, and fasti are utilized below without individual acknowledgment:

1. Chronographer of 354 (*Chr. Min.* 1.60–61: list of consuls; 62–63: Easter cycle; 66–68: consular dates in the list of *praefecti urbis;* 75–76: consular dates in the list of bishops of Rome)
2. *Consularia Constantinopolitana* and Paschal Chronicle (*Chr. Min.* 1.229–236)
3. *Fasti Vindobonenses* (*priores* and *posteriores*) (*Chr. Min.* 1.290–293)
4. Barbarus Scaligeri (A. Schoene, *Eusebi Chronicorum libri duo* 1 (Berlin, 1875), 230–240 = *Chr. Min.* 1.290–293)
5. Prosper Tiro (*Chr. Min.* 1.445–452) — the source of the consular lists in Victorius of Aquitania (*Chr. Min.* 1.708–712) and Cassiodorus (*Chr. Min.* 2.149–151)
6. Theo of Alexandria (*Chr. Min.* 3.379–380)
7. *Fasti Heracliani* (*Chr. Min.* 3.395–398)

Also used without acknowledgment are the index and the headings to the Easter Letters which Athanasius wrote to his Alexandrian congregation each year from 329 onward. Inscriptions and papyri which attest the consuls of individual years are adduced where (and only where) they supplement the more systematic evidence.[3]

Three features of the following list should be noted carefully: emperors are entered under their conventional modern names with iterations marked in Roman figures; in the years for which more than two ordinary consuls are attested (284, 285, 307–313, 321–325), the reconstruction offered sometimes goes beyond the explicit evidence; and the names of consuls other than emperors are entered in the fullest form which the evidence for the consular date attests, regardless of whether a more precise identification can be proved. It should also be observed that no attempt is here made to establish what consuls were recognized under the regimes of Carausius and Allectus in Britain (286–296) or of Domitius Alexander in Africa (308/9).[4] Nor are datings by the *post consulatum* formula in Egyptian documents registered, except in 322 and 323.[5]

---

in which more than two consuls are attested. Mommsen was fully aware of both the difficulties and the importance of the task (*Hermes* 32 (1897), 538 ff., on the years 307–313).

3. For consular dates in papyri, see R. S. Bagnall and K. A. Worp, *Chronological Systems of Byzantine Egypt* (*Studia Amstelodamensia* 8, 1978), 103 ff., with addenda and corrigenda in their *Regnal Formulas in Byzantine Egypt* (*BASP*, Supp. 2, 1979), 75 f., and a series of articles with the collective title "Chronological Notes on Byzantine Documents." Unfortunately, the list of consuls in Bagnall and Worp's "Synoptic Chronological Table" is based too closely on Degrassi (*Chronological Systems* 69 ff.).

4. Carausius himself was consul at least four times, in 287, 288, 289 and 290 (Chapter II).

5. For use of the formula μετὰ τὴν ὑπατείαν in other years, see F. Preisigke, *Wörterbuch der griechischen Papyrusurkunden* 3 (Berlin, 1931), 73 ff.; R. S. Bagnall and K. A. Worp, *Chronological Systems* 107 ff.; *BASP* 17 (1980), 27 ff.

284	(a) Carinus II, Numerianus
	(b) Diocletian, Bassus (from 20 November)[6]
285	(a) Carinus III, Aristobulus
	(b) Diocletian II, Aristobulus
286	M. Junius Maximus II, Vettius Aquilinus[7]
287	Diocletian III, Maximian
288	Maximian II, Januarianus
289	M. Magrius Bassus, L. Ragonius Quintianus[8]
290	Diocletian IV, Maximian III
291	C. Junius Tiberianus II, Cassius Dion[9]
292	Hannibalianus, Asclepiodotus
293	Diocletian V, Maximian IV
294	Constantius, Galerius
295	Nummius Tuscus, Annius Anullinus[10]
296	Diocletian VI, Constantius II
297	Maximian V, Galerius II
298	Anicius Faustus II, Virius Gallus[11]
299	Diocletian VII, Maximian VI
300	Constantius III, Galerius III
301	Flavius Postumius Titianus II, Virius Nepotianus[12]
302	Constantius IV, Galerius IV
303	Diocletian VIII, Maximian VII
304	Diocletian IX, Maximian VIII
305	Constantius V, Galerius V
306	Constantius VI, Galerius VI
307–313	Different consuls are attested for the following jurisdictions:
	(a) Galerius (until 311), Licinius (from 308), and Maximinus
	(b) Constantine
	(c) Maxentius (until 312)

6. The Paschal Chronicle (509 = *Chr. Min.* 1.229), followed by Syncellus (p. 725 Bonn), enters Διοκλητιανοῦ καὶ Βάσσου between the consuls of 283 and 284: they could perhaps be regarded as suffect rather than as ordinary consuls, but the date of 284 seems certain (cf. *PLRE* 1.151, 157, 254).

7. *ILS* 4936 (Rome).

8. *ILS* 4175 (Baiae); *CIL* 10.4631 (fasti of Cales).

9. *ICUR* 1.18 (of 291) has *Tiberiano et Dione* without the iteration (recorded in *ICUR* 1.17). A Roman epitaph from the period 311–320 has the names of the consuls of 291 in the fuller form *Gaio I[unio Tiberianio II et] Cassio Dione* (*ICUR* 1.32).

10. *P. Lips.* 29; *P. Oxy.* 23 verso; 43 recto 6.25.

11. The *nomina* of both consuls are well attested in papyri, see R. S. Bagnall and K. A. Worp, *Chronological Systems* 104. *ICUR* 1.24 has *Fausto et Virio Gal(lo)*.

12. The name Postumius is clearly attested by *PSI* 1037.36. Flavius and Virius can be documented in the consular dating formula only by *P. Flor.* 3.23 = *Chrestomathie* 1.391: [ὑπατείας] Φλ. Ποστουμίου Τιτι[ανοῦ τὸ β′ καὶ] Ο[ὐιρίου Νεπωτ]ιανοῦ (see J. R. Rea, on *P. Oxy.* 3304.3).

307   (a) Severus (until late September), Maximinus[13]

       (b) ?Galerius VII, Constantine (January–c. September)[14]

          Maximian IX, Constantine (c. September–December)

       (c) Galerius VII, Maximinus (January–April)

          post sextum consulatum (April–December)[15]

308   (a) Diocletian X, Galerius VII

       (b) Diocletian X, Galerius VII

       (c) *consules quos iusserint dd. nn. Augusti* (1 January–19 April)

          Maxentius, Valerius Romulus (from 20 April)

309   (a) Licinius, Constantine

       (b) *post consulatum X et VII*

       (c) Maxentius II, Valerius Romulus II

310   (a) Tatius Andronicus, Pompeius Probus[16]

       (b) *II post consulatum X et VII*

       (c) Maxentius III

311   (a) Galerius VIII (until May), Maximinus II[17]

       (b) Galerius VIII, Maximinus II

       (c) *consules quos iusserint domini nostri* (January–September)

          Rufinus, Volusianus (from September)[18]

13. Maximinus appears as sole consul in *P. Merton* 31; *P. Col.* 138 (both 24 December). That reflects the death of Severus, which probably occurred on 16 September (Chapter I, n. 13).

14. For Constantine's consuls in 307, before his open alliance with Maxentius, there are at least three possibilities:

    1. Severus and Maximinus, i.e. Galerius' consuls

    2. Galerius VII and Maximinus, i.e. the consuls proclaimed by Maxentius

    3. Constantine himself and a senior colleague from among the legitimate emperors

It is arguable, therefore, that *CTh* 7.20.2 originally bore the consular date of 307 in the form "Maximiano Aug. VII et Constantino Caes. conss." (Chapter V, n. 102).

15. The Chronographer of 354 is most informative on 307: "Maximiano VII et Maximino. ex mense Aprili factum est ⟨post⟩ sextum consulatum quod est novies et Constantino" (*Chr. Min.* 1.66 f.). Two Roman epitaphs of December 307 confirm the lack of consuls during the latter part of the year (*ICUR* 1.29: *post VI*[; 30: ἐπὶ Μαξεντίῳ).

16. R. S. Bagnall and K. A. Worp, *Chronological Systems* 106.

17. For the dropping of Galerius' name in papyri, R. S. Bagnall and K. A. Worp, *Chronological Systems* 106.

18. The order of names cannot be established with certainty. The Chronographer of 354 and the *Consularia Constantinopolitana,* which provide the only evidence for Maxentius' consuls in 311, present the date in three different forms:

    1. "consules quos iusserint dd. nn. Aug., ex mense Septembri factum est Rufino et Eusebio," where the second name appears to result from confusion with the consuls of 347 (*Chr. Min.* 1.67)

    2. "Maximiano VIII solo, quod fuit mense Sep. Volusiano et Rufino" (*Chr. Min.* 1.76)

    3. "Maximiano VIII, quod est Rufino et Volusiano" (*Chr. Min.* 1.231)

(The omission of Maximinus reflects the *damnatio memoriae* ordained by Constantine and Licinius in 313.)

312	(a) Constantine II, Licinius II
	(b) Constantine II, Licinius II
	(c) Maxentius IV (until 28 October)
313	(a) Maximinus III, Constantine III (January–April)
	Constantine III (April–c. August)
	Constantine III, Licinius III (c. August–December)
	(b) Constantine III, Maximinus III (January–May)
	Constantine III (May–c. August)
	Constantine III, Licinius III (c. August–December)[19]
314	Rufius Volusianus, Petronius Annianus[20]
315	Constantine IV, Licinius IV
316	Antonius Caecinius Sabinus, Vettius Rufinus[21]
317	*consules quos iusserint dd. nn. Augusti*
	Ovinius Gallicanus, Caesonius Bassus (from 17 February)[22]
318	Licinius V, Crispus
319	Constantine V, Licinius Caesar
320	Constantine VI, Constantinus
321–324	From 321 until the defeat of Licinius on 18 September 324, the consuls recognized by Constantine (a) were not acknowledged in the territory subject to Licinius (b)[23]

19. The evidence for the consuls of 313 appears complicated, but readily falls into the following pattern:

1. In the early months of the year, Maximinus and Constantine were recognized as consuls everywhere, but Maximinus was the senior consul in his own territory (*P. Oxy.* 3144; *P. Princeton Roll* 3.1; *PSI* 1038), and presumably in Licinius' too, while Constantine claimed seniority in the west (*AE* 1969/70.119: Caieta, 22 January; *CIL* 6.507: Rome, 14 April).

2. Constantine is attested as sole consul in his own territory by *Frag. Vat.* 34 (21 July): *IG* 14.956, A 1; B 24/5 (Rome: no diurnal date). Note, however, that Augustine, *Epp.* 88.4 (15 April) probably originally had Maximinus as Constantine's colleague (Chapter XV nos. 4, 5). As for Licinius' territory, a fragmentary dedication near Carnuntum may attest Constantine as sole consul on 11 June 313 (W. Jobst, *Sb. Wien,* Phil.-hist. Klasse 335 (1978), 27 no. 4).

3. Licinius replaced Maximinus as Constantine's colleague, and is attested as such on 13 September (*P. Cairo Isid.* 103.20). Hence the *Fasti Heracliani* appear to enter both Constantine and Maximinus and Constantine and Licinius as consuls in 313 (*Chr. Min.* 3.397 – where Mommsen wished to remove the doublet by emendation).

20. Attested by numerous papyri: R. S. Bagnall and K. A. Worp, *Chronological Systems* 107.

21. Mommsen emended the first consul's middle name to Caecina (*Chr. Min.* 3.397), but papyri consistently attest the form Caecinius, see J. R. Rea, *JEA* 60 (1974), 294; R. S. Bagnall and K. A. Worp, *Chronological Systems* 107.

22. *P. Theadelphia* 57 = *P. Sakaon* 50 has Gallicanus and Bassus as consuls on 8 January: it must have been written later and antedated. For the *nomina* of the consuls, *P. Princeton Roll* 8.20; *P. Vindob. Worp* 8.15; J. F. Gilliam, *Historia* 16 (1967), 252 ff. *ICUR* 1.33 (*idibus Aug. Gallicano cons.*) could imply that Bassus died before 15 August.

23. For the forms of dating attested by Egyptian papyri, see D. Hagedorn, *ZPE* 10 (1973), 121

321	(a) Crispus II, Constantinus II[24]
	(b) Licinius VI, Licinius Caesar II
322	(a) Petronius Probianus, Anicius Julianus[25]
	(b) *post consulatum Licinii VI et Licinii II*[26] *qui fuerint (nuntiati) consules II*
323	(a) Severus, Vettius Rufinus[27]
	(b) *II post consulatum Licinii VI et Licinii II*[28] *qui fuerint (nuntiati) consules III*
324	(a) Crispus III, Constantinus III
	(b) *qui fuerint (nuntiati) consules IV*
325	Proculus, Paulinus (January–May)[29]
	Anicius Paulinus, †ionius† Julianus (May–December)[30]
326	Constantine VII, Constantius[31]
327	Flavius Constantius, Valerius Maximus[32]
328	Flavius Januarinus, Vettius Justus[33]
329	Constantine VIII, Constantinus IV
330	Flavius Gallicanus, Aurelius Valerius Tullianus Symmachus [Phospho]rius[34]

ff.; R. S. Bagnall and K. A. Worp, *Chronological Systems* 108 f.

The Latin formula "qui fuerint (nuntiati) consules" is modeled on some later dates in the *Codex Theodosianus* (Seeck, *Regesten* 22). It corresponds more closely than Seeck's "consules quos iusserint domini nostri Augusti" (*Rh. Mus.*, n.f. 62 (1907), 517; *Regesten* 170 ff.) to the attested Greek versions, viz.

a. μέλλουσιν ὑπάτοις δευτέρᾳ ἀμοιβῇ
τρίτον / τέταρτον μέλλουσιν ὑπάτοις

b. τοῖς ἀποδειχθησομένοις ὑπάτοις τὸ β΄/γ΄

c. τρίτον ἐσομένοις ὑπάτοις
τοῖς ἐσομένοις ἐκ τρίτου ὑπάτοις
τοῖς ἐσομένοις ὑπάτοις τὸ δ΄.

24. *ILS* 6111 (Rome) shows Crispus and Constantinus as consuls on 13 March, but the fragmentary *ICUR* 1.34 has "]Kal. Mar. Licino VI["—which implies that Constantine recognized Licinius and his son as consuls at the beginning of the year.

25. *ILS* 6111ᶜ (Rome).

26. *P. Oxy.* 3122, 3123; *P. Panopolis* 26.

27. *CIL* 10.407 (Volcei).

28. *P. Oxy.* 42, cf. O. Seeck, *Hermes* 36 (1901), 32; T. Mommsen, *Hermes* 36 (1901), 604; O. Seeck and T. Mommsen, *Hermes* 37 (1902), 155 ff.

29. *P. Oxy.* 3125 (between 27 March and 25 April); *CTh* 2.25.1 = *CJ* 3.38.11 (29 April). Perhaps also *P. Oxy.* 889 (Chapter XIV. 3).

30. *P. Strasbourg* 137, 138 = *Sammelbuch* 8019, 8020.

31. Publilius Optatianus Porfyrius, *Carm.* 12.1, 18.2, seems to indicate that in 324 Constantine had been expected by some to assume his seventh consulate in 325, cf. *AJP* 96 (1975), 181, 182.

32. *P. Col.* 178; *PSI* 309; *P. Flor.* 53, cf. G. Vitelli, in his introduction to *PSI* 716.

33. *P. Flor.* 14; *P. Oxy.* 3126; *P. Theadelphia* 56; *Stud. Pal.* 2, pp. 33/4.

34. The papyri which attest Gallicanus' *nomen* present his colleague's name in a variety of forms: Aurelius Symmachus (*Sammelbuch* 7666); Valerius Symmachus (*PSI* 224, as also the

331	Junius Bassus, Flavius Ablabius
332	Papius Pacatianus, Mecilius Hilarianus
333	Flavius Dalmatius, Domitius Zenophilus
334	Flavius Optatus, Anicius Paulinus
335	Julius Constantius, Rufius Albinus
336	Virius Nepotianus, Tettius Facundus
337	Flavius Felicianus, Fabius Titianus[35]

2. THE CAREERS OF NONIMPERIAL CONSULS[36]

284 Bassus

If Bassus was Diocletian's colleague in his first consulate, then the pair must have assumed the *fasces* at Nicomedia on 20 November 284. Bassus, therefore, may be identified as the L. Caesonius Ovinius Manlius Rufinianus Bassus whose career is revealed by an inscription from Atella (*AE* 1964.223). Since the epigraphically attested Bassus was twice consul, *praefectus urbi* and *comes Augg.* (not necessarily in this temporal order or its reverse), it is an attractive conjecture that he accompanied the Persian expedition of Carus in 283, was still with the court when Numerianus died in 284, and was present when Diocletian was proclaimed emperor.[37] It follows that Diocletian installed him as *praefectus urbi* in the summer of 285 after defeating Carinus, and it can be rendered probable that he left office c. February 286.

285   T. Cl. Aurelius Aristobulus

One inscription attests Aristobulus' full name (*ILAlg.* 1.2048: Madauros). Praetorian prefect and consul under Carinus, he was retained in office by Diocletian (Victor, *Caes.* 39.15). His known subsequent career can be stated succinctly: proconsul of Africa, 290–294; *praefectus urbi,* 11 January 295–18 February 296.

---

heading to Athanasius' Easter letter of 330, cf. E. Schwartz, *Ges. Schr.* 3.16 n. 2); Valerius Tullianus (*CPR* 1.19 = *Stud. Pal.* 20.86; *BGU* 2252 – the *cognomen* is also attested by *ICUR* 1.37; Firmicus Maternus, *Math.* 8.15.4); and as Οὐαλερίου [Τυλλιανοῦ Συμμάχου Φωσφο]ρίου (*P. Theadelphia* 12.20–22, with P. Jouguet's conjectural restoration (on p. 87), cf. G. Polara, *PP* 29 (1974), 266).

35. The names of the consuls for 331–337 are relatively well attested in the papyri: R. S. Bagnall and K. A. Worp, *Chronological Systems* 109 f. (For 336, add *PSI* 804, cf. J. R. Rea, on *P. Oxy.* 3304.) The *nomen* of the second consul of 332 is Mecilius rather than Maecilius, see J. R. Rea, on *P. Oxy.* 3127.2.

36. Evidence is not normally adduced for posts which are documented and discussed in Chapters VII–IX – nor are detailed cross-references given to those chapters.

37. For discussion of his career, G. Barbieri, *Akte des IV. Internationalen Kongresses für griechische und lateinische Epigraphik* (Vienna, 1964), 41 ff.; *PLRE* 1.156-7, Bassus 18. One earlier post (not discussed here) is peculiarly problematical, see R. Syme, *Emperors and Biography: Studies in the Historia Augusta* (Oxford, 1971), 240 n.2.

286   M. Junius Maximus
Otherwise known only as *praefectus urbi* from 286 to 27 February 288.[38]

286   Vettius Aquilinus
Not otherwise attested.[39]

288   Januarianus
Clearly identical with Pomponius Januarianus, who became *praefectus urbi* on 27 February 288. Previously attested as prefect of Egypt in 283 and 284 (*P. Theadelphia* 18; *P. Oxy.* 1115; *Sammelbuch* 7206); in the interval he could have served briefly as a praetorian prefect.

289   M. Magrius Bassus
Not otherwise known.

289   L. Ragonius Quintianus
Not otherwise known.

291   C. Junius Tiberianus
Ordinary consul in 281, *praefectus urbi* from 18 February 291 to 3 August 292.

291   Cassius Dion
Proconsul of Africa for 294–295, *praefectus urbi* on 11 February 296.

292   Hannibalianus
Clearly identical with Afranius Hannibalianus, who is attested as praetorian prefect between 285 and 292 and as *praefectus urbi* in 297–298.[40]

292   Asclepiodotus
Julius Asclepiodotus, attested as praetorian prefect with Hannibalianus before 292; but not necessarily identical with the Asclepiodotus who was praetorian prefect of Constantius in 296.

295   Nummius Tuscus
Curator aquarum et Miniciae (*ILS* 643: Rome), *praefectus urbi* from 19 February 302 to 12 September 303.

295   Annius Anullinus
Probably identical with the Annius Anullinus who was *praefectus urbi* in 306/7.

---

38. For apparent ancestors, *PIR*[2] J 774/5.

39. The full name of the Christian poet Juvencus, who wrote under Constantine, was Vettius Aquilinus Juvencus *v. c.* (*CSEL* 24.v): presumably, therefore, a grandson of the consul of 286.

40. Perhaps the father of Maximian's first wife (Chapter IV, at n. 19).

298 Anicius Faustus II
The iteration implies that Anicius Faustus was previously consul suffect in an unknown year. Subsequently *praefectus urbi* in 299–300. Faustus' fuil name probably included the *nomen* Junius and the *cognomen* Paulinus.[41]

298 Virius Gallus
Known otherwise only as *corrector* of Campania.

301 Flavius Postumius Titianus II
Clearly identical with the T. Flavius Postumius Titianus, whose career, as far as his proconsulate of Africa, is known from a Roman dedication by a protégé (*ILS* 2941). It can be supplemented from an acephalous Roman inscription (*CIL* 6.1419b). Titianus held the following known posts:

> quaestor *candidatus*
> praetor *candidatus*
> *curator* of Cales, Can[usium], Lugdunum
> suffect consul
> *corrector Italiae* (attested before 1 March 293)
> *corrector Italiae reg(ionis) Tra[nspadanae]* (?293)[42]
> *corrector* of Campania
> *consularis aquarum et Miniciae*
> proconsul of Africa in 295–296
> *cos. II ord.* 301
> *praefectus urbi* from 12 February 305 to 19 March 306

301 Virius Nepotianus
Career otherwise unknown. Presumably father of the consul of 336.

308, 309 Valerius Romulus
Son of Maxentius: he bore the title *nobilissimus vir* and died in the course of 309 (*ILS* 672: Sardinia; *RIC* 6.377 ff., 400 ff.).

310 Tatius Andronicus
Certified as praetorian prefect in the papyri which record his consulate; otherwise unknown.

310 Pompeius Probus
Also praetorian prefect in 310: presumably identical with the Probus whom Galerius sent to negotiate with Maxentius in 307 (*Origo* 7).

---

41. His full name is stated as M. Junius Caesonius Nicomachus Anicius Faustus Paulinus by W. Liebenam, *Fasti Consulares* (1909), 32; E. Groag, *PIR*[2] A 601; G. Barbieri, *L'Albo senatorio da Settimio Severo a Carino (193–285)* (Rome, 1952), no. 1802 (retracted in the addenda, p. 640); Chastagnol, *Fastes* 31 ff.
42. The post is possibly identical with the preceding *correctura* (Chapter IX.1).

311 Rufinus
Conventionally identified as the Aradius Rufinus whom Maxentius appointed *praefectus urbi* on 9 February 312.[43] He might, however, be Statius Rufinus, *praefectus urbi* from 13 April 308 to 30 October 309 (otherwise unknown).

311 Volusianus
The career of C. Ceionius Rufius Volusianus is known principally from a Roman dedication to him in 314 or 315 (*ILS* 1213) and from literary sources (Firmicus Maternus, *Math.* 2.29.10–12 (without the name);[44] Victor, *Caes.* 40.18; Zosimus 2.14.2 ff.). It can be reconstructed as follows:

> born c. 240/250
> suffect consul c. 280
> *corrector Italiae* c. 282–c. 290 (He was *corrector* for eight years (*ILS* 1213, and was *iterum corrector* under Carinus and Numerianus (*CIL* 10.1655: Puteoli).)
> proconsul of Africa (?305/6)
> praetorian prefect of Maxentius in 309
> *praefectus urbi* from 28 October 310 to 28 October 311
> ordinary consul in 311
> *comes* of Constantine
> *praefectus urbi* from 8 December 313 to 20 August 315
> ordinary consul in 314
> exiled by senatorial decree (?315)

314 Rufius Volusianus
See 311.

314 Petronius Annianus
Attested as praetorian prefect from 315 to 317. Analogy suggests that he assumed this office before he became consul.

316 Antonius Caecinius Sabinus
No other office attested.

316 Vettius Rufinus
Clearly the C. Vettius Cossinius Rufinus whom the town of Atina thanked for protection during the reign of Maxentius (*ILS* 1217). The dedication names the following posts:

43. Chastagnol, *Fastes* 59 ff.; *PLRE* 1.775, 1043.
44. For the identification and its implications, *JRS* 65 (1975), 40 ff.

proconsul provinciae Achaiae sortito (The word *sortito* suggests that Rufinus was designated proconsul but never governed the province; if so, he
will presumably have been prevented by the rupture between Maxentius
and Galerius, and therefore proconsul designate for 307–308.)
curator of the Via Flaminia
curator alvei Tiberis et cloacarum sacrae urbis
corrector of Venetia and Histria
corrector of Tuscia and Umbria
corrector of Campania (between 306 and 312)
comes Augg. nn., i.e. of Constantine and Licinius
praefectus urbi (from 20 August 315 to 4 August 316)

317   Ovinius Gallicanus
The only offices attested for Ovinius Gallicanus are *curator* of Teanum Sidicinum between 293 and 300 (*CIL* 10.4785) and *praefectus urbi* from 4 August
316 to 15 May 317. The consul of 317 (rather than the consul of 330) may confidently be identified as the Gallicanus who donated Italian estates to the Church
of Saints Peter, Paul, and John the Baptist at Ostia (*Liber Pontificalis* 34.29,
p. 184 Duchesne).[45]

317   Caesonius Bassus
Otherwise unknown, unless he can be presumed identical with Septimius Bassus, *praefectus urbi* from 15 May 317 to 1 September 319. It is possible that the
consuls of 317 are brothers, and are the sons of L. Caesonius Ovinius Manlius
Rufinianus Bassus, presented above as consul in 284.

322   Petronius Probianus
Symmachus' father saluted Probianus as *Augustis notus et hospes* (*Epp.* 1.2.6),
but only two offices are attested for him besides the consulate: proconsul of
Africa from 315 to 317, and *praefectus urbi* from 8 October 329 to 12 April
331. In addition, Probianus received an imperial letter issued from Serdica on
27 February 321 (*CTh* 9.42.1), which discloses no real clue to his official position at the time.

322   Anicius Julianus
The fullest known form of Julianus' name is Amnius Anicius Julianus (Symmachus, *Epp.* 1.2.5); he was the father of the consul of 334 (*ILS* 1220) and

---

45. E. J. Champlin, "Saint Gallicanus (consul 317)" (forthcoming). Champlin rightly dis-
misses as historical romance the *Acta Gallicani* (*BHL* 3236), adduced in *PLRE* 1.383. Chastagnol,
Fastes 70, unfortunately accepts the identification of the Christian benefactor at Ostia as Flavius
Gallicanus, consul in 330, argued by H. Grégoire and P. Orgels, *Bull. Acad. Roy. de Belgique,*
Classe des Lettres[5] 42 (1956), 125 ff. Hence he holds the consul of 317 to be "probablement païen."
In fact, he may well be the first private citizen to be both a Christian and ordinary consul.

presumably a son of the Julianus proconsul of Africa in 301–302. Two posts are documented: proconsul of Africa in 320–321, and *praefectus urbi* from 13 November 326 to 7 September 329.

323 Severus

Presumably the Acilius Severus, *praefectus urbi* from 4 January 325 to 13 November 326.[46] There is no valid evidence that he was a praetorian prefect.

323 Vettius Rufinus

Otherwise unattested.

325 Proculus

Proculus was dismissed from his consulate and disgraced, apparently shortly after April 325; the date suggests that he may have been implicated in the alleged plot of Licinius and executed at the same time as the former emperor. Proculus appears to have possessed the *nomen* Valerius;[47] he is presumably identical with the Proculus who was proconsul of Africa in 319–320.

325 Anicius Paulinus

The *praenomen* Sextus is explicitly attested (*CIL* 6.1680), but he may also have borne the names Junius Caesonius Nicomachus, like other members of the same family.[48] Only two posts are otherwise known: proconsul of Africa for two years (probably 322–324), and *praefectus urbi* from 12 April 331 to 7 April 333.

325 †ionius† Julianus

The Julianus known as consul in 325 was identified by Otto Seeck as M. Ceionius Julianus, *praefectus urbi* in 333.[49] Subsequently two papyri revealed Julianus' *nomen*, but in a corrupt form: ὑπατείας Ἀνικίου Παυλίνου καὶ Ἰωνίου Ἰουλιανοῦ τῶν λαμπροτάτων (*P. Strasbourg* 137, 138 = *Sammelbuch* 8019, 8020). Paleographically, καὶ ⟨Κα⟩ιωνίου appears to be the easiest emendation. But M. Ceionius Julianus was proconsul of Africa after 325; therefore, he cannot be one of the consuls of that year. Hence it is more plausible to emend to καὶ Ἰουλίου and to identify the consul as Julius Julianus, the former praeto-

46. Chastagnol, *Fastes* 65; 77. However, neither of the items of evidence which he adduces to document the *nomen* Acilius has any probative force: the consul's *nomen* is lacking on *CIL* 10.407 (Volcei), and *P. Geneva* 10.20 attests the consuls of 316 (not 323).

D. M. Novak, *Ancient Society* 10 (1979), 306 ff., argues that the consul of 323 belongs to the noble family of the Acilii Glabriones.

47. *ZPE* 21 (1976), 280, adducing *P. Oxy.* 889 (re-edited in Chapter XIV.3).

48. Punctuate *CIL* 6.1680: "Sex. Anicio Paulino, procons. Africae bis, cos., praef. urb." Chastagnol, *Fastes* 84, punctuates "procons. Africae, bis cos." Polyonymity is implied by *P. Oxy.* 889, cf. Chapter XIV.3.

49. O. Seeck, *RE* 3 (1899), 1960, reaffirmed by J. R. Rea, on *P. Oxy.* 3125.9. A. Degrassi, *Fasti consolari* (1952), 79, misstates his *praenomen* as Publius.

rian prefect of Licinius, whom Constantine is known to have maintained in a position of honor and respect (Libanius, *Orat.* 18.9).[50] Julianus' known career, therefore, comprises the following posts:

prefect of Egypt (attested between 15 January and 29 August 314)
perhaps *vicarius* of Oriens
praetorian prefect (attested in office from 28 April 315 to September 324)
consul in 325

327 Flavius Constantius

Attested as praetorian prefect from 324 to 327; perhaps identical with the Constantius whom Constantine used on a diplomatic mission in 315 or 316 (*Origo* 14).

327 Valerius Maximus

Attested as praetorian prefect in 327/8, 332/3, and 337; previously *vicarius Orientis* (325). It may be inferred, from a general statement in Eusebius, that Maximus was a Christian (*VC* 2.44).

328 Flavius Januarinus

Possibly identical with the Januarinus who was *vicarius* of the diocese of Moesiae in 319, and also apparently *vicarius urbis Romae* in November-December 320 (*CTh* 9.21.2, 9.34.3).[51] The Christian sarcophagus of his wife, Marcia Romana Celsa, who died after 328, has been found at Arles.[52]

328 Vettius Justus

Otherwise unknown.[53]

330 Flavius Gallicanus

Nothing apart from the consulate is attested.

330 Aurelius Valerius Tullianus Symmachus [Phospho]rius

The consul of 330 is the grandfather of the orator Symmachus, and he has sometimes been claimed as a barbarian by birth whom Constantine advanced to the consulate and introduced into the Senate.[54] But there are good reasons

---

50. Chastagnol, *Fastes* 85; *PLRE* 1.478 f. The two papyri were read by G. Tschantz and J. Schwartz (*Bulletin de la Faculté des Lettres de Strasbourg* 15 (1937), 173 f., nos. 137, 138). Dr. J. R. Rea subsequently inspected them and confirms the reading (letter of January 1976).

51. *PLRE* 1.453, Ianuarinus 1, emending "dat. XII kal. Dec. Rom(ae) Crispo et Constantino CC. II conss." (*CTh* 9.21.2) to "dat. XII kal. Dec.... ⟨pp.⟩ Rom(ae) Crispo" etc.

52. J.-M. Rouquette, *CRAI* 1974.257 ff.

53. Perhaps grandfather of Justina, the wife of Valentinian (Chapter IV, at n. 71).

54. O. Seeck, *Hermes* 41 (1906), 533; *RE* 4A (1931), 1141; E. A. Thompson, *The Historical Work of Ammianus Marcellinus* (Cambridge, 1947), 80. Seeck's interpretation of Ammianus

for believing that the consul of 330 was a senator by birth.[55] He can easily be identified as the Symmachus who received two imperial letters dated 319: one does not specify Symmachus' title or status but was received by him at Corinth (*CTh* 2.4.1), whereas the other was apparently addressed either *ad Symmachum vic.* or *ad Symmachum v.c.* (*CTh* 2.15.1). Hence Symmachus was either *vicarius* of the diocese of Moesiae, or a *vir clarissimus,* i.e., proconsul of Achaea.[56] Now both the consul of 330 and his son, *praefectus urbi* in 364/5, possessed the *signum* Phosphorius (*ILS* 1257), while two inscriptions, which on epigraphical criteria seem to belong to the early fourth century, attest a Phosphorius as proconsul of Achaea (*IG* 7.96: Megara; *AE* 1901.125: Argos); hence Phosphorius may be presumed identical with Symmachus, proconsul of Achaea in 319.[57] As for the consul's origin and status in Roman society, he almost certainly comes from a well-established senatorial family. The Aristotelian commentator Elias records that the senator Chrysaorius to whom Porphyry dedicated his *Isagoge* had an ancestor named Symmachus (*In Porphyrii Isagogen,* pr. 15);[58] the Symmachi of the fourth century were probably descendants of these senators of the third century.

331   Junius Bassus
Praetorian prefect from 318 to 332.[59]

331   Flavius Ablabius
A Cretan of humble birth, Ablabius began his career on the staff of the governor of Crete (Libanius, *Orat.* 42.23; Eunapius, *Vit. Phil.* 6.3.1-7, pp. 463-464). The intervening stages are unknown, but Ablabius was *vicarius* of Asiana between 324 and 326, then praetorian prefect from at least 329 to 337. His daughter Olympias was betrothed to Constans (Athanasius, *Hist. Ar.* 69; Ammianus 20.11.3), perhaps before 333 (cf. *Cons. Sirm.* 1). A Christian (Athanasius, *Festal Letter* 4; *Const. Sirm.* 1).

21.10.8, 12.25, on which he based the hypothesis, is rightly criticized and rejected by A. Cameron, *JRS* 54 (1964), 21 f.

55. G. Polara, *PP* 29 (1974), 261 ff. The present paragraph is also indebted to an unpublished paper by Alan Cameron on the ancestry of Symmachus.

56. Both Seeck, *Regesten* 166, and *PLRE* 1.863, Symmachus 1, opt for the vicariate, emending the date of one or both of the laws to 318.

57. G. Polara, *PP* 29 (1974), 262 ff. On the inscriptions, see T. Reinach, *BCH* 24 (1900), 324 ff.; A. von Premerstein, *Zeitschrift für deutsches Altertum und deutsche Literatur* 60 (1923), 73 ff.

58. Edited by A. Busse, *Commentaria in Aristotelem Graeca* 18 (Berlin, 1900), 39. The passage is noted in *PLRE* 1.204, Chrysaorius; for its relevance to the later Symmachi, J. F. Matthews, *CR,* n.s. 24 (1974), 101.

59. Normally held to be a Christian (cf. Chastagnol, *Fastes* 151). But R. von Haehling, *Die Religionszugehörigkeit der hohen Amtsträger des Römischen Reiches seit Constantin I. Alleinherrschaft bis zum Ende der Theodosianischen Dynastie (Antiquitas* 3.23, 1978), 289, argues from the pagan deities on the mosaics of the basilica of which *CIL* 6.1737 = *ILCV* 59 is the dedication that he was a pagan.

332 Papius Pacatianus

The *praenomen* Lucius is attested (*ILT* 814).[60] Pacatianus' known career spans almost thirty years, even though only three posts can be documented apart from the consulate: *praeses* of Sardinia under Domitius Alexander (308/9); *vicarius Britanniarum* on 20 November 319; and praetorian prefect (attested from 332 to 337, but almost certainly appointed before 13 May 329).

332 Mecilius Hilarianus

Two posts are attested before the consulate: *corrector Lucaniae et Bruttiorum* on 20 January 316, and proconsul of Africa in 324–325. Hilarianus became *praefectus urbi* under Constans (13 January 338–14 July 339), and fifteen years later emerged from retirement as praetorian prefect (*CTh* 6.4.3^s, 4^s, 7^s).

333 Flavius Dalmatius

The consul of 333 was a son of Constantius and Theodora.[61] He lived for a period at Toulouse in an honorable retirement indistinguishable from exile (Ausonius, *Professores* 17(16).11–12).[62] When Constantine recalled him (perhaps during the summer of 326), he lived at court for some years (Ausonius, *Professores* 17(16).13 ff.). Between the spring of 333 and the spring of 334, Constantine revived the antique title of *censor* and bestowed it on Dalmatius (Athanasius, *Apol. Sec.* 65.1 ff., cf. *P. Oxy.* 1716).[63]

In 334, Dalmatius was residing at Antioch, apparently with wide executive powers: he investigated a charge of murder against Athanasius (*Apol. Sec.* 65.1 ff.; Socrates, *HE* 1.27.20 f.) and suppressed the revolt of Calocaerus in Cyprus, burning the insurgent alive at Tarsus (Theophanes, a. 5825, p. 29 de Boor).[64] He presumably left Antioch when Constantius set up court there in 335. In 337, Dalmatius received an imperial letter, either issued or published at Naissus, whose author ought to be his son, the Caesar Dalmatius (*CJ* 5.17.7), with whom he perished in the purge of that year (Julian, *Ep. ad Ath.* 270d).[65]

The Paschal Chronicle reports that Dalmatius (whom, like Theophanes, it confuses with his son) was στρατηγὸς Ῥωμαίων καὶ ὕπατος (531.19 ff.). On the strength of this it has been argued that Dalmatius was *praetor* at Rome in 324 (adducing *CTh* 12.17.1) or the first known *magister militum*.[66] It seems more prudent to disallow the evidence—even if it may derive from a much earlier and well-informed source.[67]

60. Reprinted in Chapter VIII.4.
61. On his identity and career, W. Ensslin, *Rh. Mus.*, n.f. 78 (1929), 199 ff.
62. On the text of this passage, D. Shackleton Bailey, *AJP* 97 (1976), 252.
63. *AJAH* 3 (1978), 61 f. Millar, *Emperor* 602 n. 71, impugns the title.
64. Chapter II.
65. On *CJ* 5.17.7, see Chapter V, n. 172.
66. Respectively, W. Ensslin, *Rh. Mus.*, n.f. 78 (1929), 207 ff.; Stein, *Bas-Empire* 1².476 n. 144. *PLRE* 1.241 also makes Dalmatius the recipient of *CTh* 12.17.1, for which it adopts the transmitted date of 321.
67. As argued by P. Batiffol, *RQ* 9 (1895), 57 ff.; J. Bidez, *Philostorgius Kirchengeschichte*

333   Domitius Zenophilus

Three posts are explicitly attested for Zenophilus: he was *corrector* of Sicilia (*CIL* 10.7234: Lilybaeum), *consularis* of Numidia in December 320 (Optatus, App. 1; *AE* 1915.30: Lambaesis), and proconsul of Africa between 326 and 333 (*ILS* 5359: Thignica). He was probably also the recipient of the following acephalous dedication:

> *eximiae* potesta-
> 2   tis et moderatio-
>   nis et bonitatis
> 4   ac praedicabili c.v. post cor-
>   recturas et consularem dig-
> 6   nitatem Acaiae Asiae iterum
>   et Africae IIII procos., sacro iudicio
> 8   Constantini maximi victo-
>   ris ac triumfatoris semper Au[g.
> 10   et beatissimorum Caes ////
>   ENE AS[
> 12   TUS A [

(*AE* 1917/18.99 = *ILAfr*. 456: Bulla Regia)[68]

On the normal interpretation of the Latin, the honorand was proconsul of Achaea, proconsul of Asia for two years, and then proconsul of Africa for four years. Now the date of the inscription is between 324 and 337 (lines 8/9), and a proconsul of Asia could have become proconsul of Africa only before 306 or after 324. Hence the number of possible identifications is very small. A. Chastagnol considered five, of which he preferred the first: (1) Ceionius Julianus, who would then be proconsul of Africa from 327 to 331; (2) Mecilius Hilarianus, from 322 to 326; (3) Tertullus, from 325 to 329; (4) Zenophilus, from 326 to 330; and (5) an unattested proconsul from 332 to 336, who might be Antonius Marcellinus (cos. 341).[69] Of these five, the *Prosopography* correctly eliminates Hilarianus who is attested as proconsul of Africa on 9 July 324 (*CTh* 12.1.9), and defines the choice as lying among the other four.[70] Another three can be eliminated. If the consul of 341 is identical with the Antonius Marcellinus, *praeses* of Lugdunensis Prima in 313 (*CTh* 11.3.1ˢ: the mss. have

---

(*GCS* 21, 1913), cl ff., 207.

68. Published by L. Carton, *CRAI* 1917.153. In favor of attribution to Domitius Zenophilus, see also M. T. W. Arnheim, *The Senatorial Aristocracy in the Later Roman Empire* (Oxford, 1972), 173 f.; D. M. Novak, *Ancient Society* 10 (1979), 308 ff.

69. Chastagnol, *Fastes* 89. Marcellinus' proconsulate (attested by *CIL* 8.25524: Bulla Regia) need not belong to the reign of Constantine.

70. *PLRE* 1.1012, Anonymus 37.

319), then he held a post (namely *praeses*) not recorded on the inscription. And even if he is not, the Marcellinus who was consul in 341 is only attested as holding one of the six different posts which are recorded.[71] Tertullus is attested as proconsul of Africa on 6 July 326 (*CTh* 9.21.3 = *CJ* 9.24.2): even if he was proconsul from 326 to 330, he cannot before 326 have been proconsul of Asia for two years. Ceionius Julianus was *consularis* of Campania late in 324 (*AE* 1939.151: near Abellinum) and became *praefectus urbi* on 10 May 333. Hence, if he were the subject of the inscription, the seven proconsulates would be of necessity run without any intermission (Achaea 325–326, Asia 326–328, Africa 328–332). Although that appears theoretically possible, in practice it is surely improbable. The career of the inscription can, however, be ascribed to Domitius Zenophilus without any apparent difficulty or implausibility:

corrector of Sicilia
corrector of another province
consularis of Numidia in 320
proconsul of Achaea no later than 323–324
proconsul of Asia from 325 to 327
proconsul of Africa from 328 to 332
consul in 333

334   Flavius Optatus

Although no precise official posts are attested, Optatus was an extremely important person. After serving as *grammaticus* to Licinius' son, be obtained high position and great wealth under Constantine (Libanius, *Orat.* 42.26/7), who created him *patricius* — the first bearer of the refurbished honor (Zosimus 2.40.2).

Since Optatus was killed in 337 (Zosimus 2.40.2), it is tempting to surmise kinship with the emperor, and allegations made about Optatus' wife may be significant. Libanius affirms that she was the daughter of a Paphlagonian innkeeper and that her influence gained Optatus his position after the fall of Licinius (*Orat.* 42.26/7). Either Optatus or his wife might be a relative of Helena, who came from Drepanum (in Paphlagonia on a generous or tendentious definition) and who was alleged to be a *stabularia* (Ambrose, *De Obitu Theodosii* 42).

334   Anicius Paulinus

Called *Amnius iunior* and *Anicius Paulinus iunior* to distinguish him from his relative, consul in 325 (*ILS* 1221, 698; *CIL* 6.1142). His full name was Amnius Manius Caesonius Nicomachus Anicius Paulinus, with the *signum* Honorius, and an inscription describes his career (*ILS* 1220: Rome):

71. Viz. proconsul of Africa in an unknown year (*CIL* 8.25524: Bulla Regia).

legatus Carthaginis while his father Anicius Julianus (i.e. the consul of 322)
  was proconsul of Africa
proconsul prov. Asiae et Hellesponti, probably c. 330
consul
praefectus urbi from 27 April 334 to 30 December 335

335 Julius Constantius
Son of Constantius and Theodora, father of Gallus and Julian; *patricius* by
335, created *nobilissimus* in 335 (Zosimus 2.39.2), and killed in 337 (Julian,
Ep. ad. Athen. 270c; Libanius, *Orat.* 18.31; Zosimus 2.40.2).

335 Rufius Albinus
An inscription reveals that the consul of 335 was Ceionius Rufius Albinus, a
philosopher and the son of Rufius Volusianus, consul in 311 and 314 (*ILS*
1222: from manuscript reports of an inscription seen by a pilgrim in Rome).
Moreover, he was *praefectus urbi* from 30 December 335 to 10 March 337.
These well-attested facts identify Albinus as the subject of a horoscope which
Firmicus Maternus discusses in detail (*Math.* 2.29.10–20).[72] Mainly from this
discussion, his life can be reconstructed as follows:

born on 14 or 15 March 303
tried by Constantine and exiled on charges of magic and adultery in 326
recalled from exile shortly thereafter
consularis of Campania
proconsul of Achaea
proconsul of Asia
consul in 335
praefectus urbi from 30 December 335 to 10 March 337

336 Virius Nepotianus
No career known except for a possible mention as a general in Phrygia in a hagiographical text which probably dates from the fifth century.[73] Nepotianus is
presumably the son (or possibly the grandson) of Virius Nepotianus, consul in
301, and can be presumed the father of Julius Nepotianus, who briefly wore
the purple at Rome in June 350.[74] If that inference is correct, the consul of 336
was a brother-in-law of Constantine, for the usurper of 350 was the son of
Eutropia (Eutropius, *Brev.* 10.11; *Epitome* 42.3; Socrates, *HE* 2.25.10; Sozomenus, *HE* 4.1.2; Zosimus 2.43.2).

72. *JRS* 65 (1975), 42 f., 47 f.
73. *Phoenix* 28 (1974), 226, adducing G. Anrich, *Hagios Nikolaos: Der heilige Nikolaos in der
griechischen Kirche* 1 (Leipzig and Berlin, 1913), 67, 77, 83, 162, 226, 252, 278, 404.
74. *PLRE* 1.625, Nepotianus 7.

336   Tettius Facundus
Unknown except as a consular date.

337   Flavius Felicianus
Constantine allegedly appointed Felicianus, who was a Christian, as the first
comes Orientis (Malalas 318–319 Bonn).

337   Fabius Titianus
An inscription from Rome gives Titianus' career as far as his first prefecture of
the city (*ILS* 1227), and the other evidence is relatively abundant.[75] The known
career is as follows:

corrector of Flaminia and Picenum
consularis of Sicilia
proconsul of Asia
comes primi ordinis
consul in 337
praefectus urbi from 25 October 339 to 25 February 341
praetorian prefect in Gaul from 341 to 349
praefectus urbi for the second time from 27 February 350 to 1 March 351
envoy of Magnentius to Constantius in summer 351 (Zosimus 2.49.1/2)

75. Chastagnol, *Fastes* 107 ff.; *PLRE* 1.918–919, Titianus 6.

CHAPTER VII

PREFECTS OF THE CITY OF ROME

The basis of any discussion of the *praefecti urbis* under Diocletian and Constantine must be the list of prefects from 254 to 354 which the Chronographer of 354 included in his almanac (*Chr. Min.* 1.66–68).[1] There are also the modern fasti of A. Chastagnol, who furnishes a detailed discussion of the family and career of each prefect.[2] The present chapter represents both an attempt to understand more fully the nature of the ancient list and a revision of Chastagnol's conclusions about some problematical careers and identifications.

1. THE TRANSMITTED LIST OF PREFECTS

284, 285	Ceionius Varus
286, 287, until 288, February 27	Junius Maximus
288, February 27, 289	Pomponius Januarianus
290, until 291, February 18	Turranius Gratianus
291, February 18–292, August 3	Junius Tiberianus
292, August 3–293, March 13	Cl. Marcellus
293, March 13–295, January 11	Septimius Acindynus

1. Both *praefectus urbis* and *praefectus urbi* are attested. Largely for the sake of euphony, I normally employ the dative with the singular, the genitive with the plural.

2. Chastagnol, *Fastes* 15–102 (particularly valuable for its full quotation of the evidence and discussion of modern opinions). No fewer than seven entries need to be expunged from the list in *PLRE* 1.1053–54, viz. 'Aelius Cesettianus' in 275, 'Fabianus' in 286/7, 'Laodicius,' 'Symphronius,' 'Plautianus' in 303, Anonymus 11 (? = Junius Flavianus), Anonymus 12 (= Ceionius Rufius Albinus).

295, January 11–296, February 11	Aristobulus
296, February 11–297, ?	Cassius Dion
297, ?–298, ?	Afranius Hannibalianus
298, ?–299, ?	Artorius Maximus
299, ?–300, March 1	Anicius Faustus
300, March 1–301, ?	Pompeius Faustinus
301, ?–302, February 19	Aelius Dionysius
302, February 19–303, September 12	Nummius Tuscus
303, September 12–304, January 4	Junius Tiberianus
304, January 4–305, February 12	Aradius Rufinus
305, February 12–306, March 19	Postumius Titianus
306, March 19–307, August 27	Annius Anullinus
307, August 27–308, April 13	Insteius Tertullus
308, April 13–309, October 30	Statius Rufinus
309, October 30–310, October 28	Aurelius Hermogenes
310, October 28–311, October 28	Rufius Volusianus
311, October 28–312, February 9	Junius Flavianus
312, February 9–312, October 27	Aradius Rufinus
312, October 27–312, November 29	Annius Anullinus
312, November 29–313, December 8	Aradius Rufinus
313, December 8–315, August 20	Rufius Volusianus
315, August 20–316, August 4	Vettius Rufinus
316, August 4–317, May 15	Ovinius Gallicanus
317, May 15–319, September 1	Septimius Bassus
319, September 1–323, September 13	Valerius Maximus Basilius
323, September 13–325, January 4	Lucer. Verinus
325, January 4–326, November 13	Acilius Severus
326, November 13–329, September 7	Anicius Julianus
329, September 7–329, October 8	Publilius Optatianus
329, October 8–331, April 12	Petronius Probianus
331, April 12–333, April 7	Anicius Paulinus
333, April 7–333, 10 May	Publilius Optatianus
333, May 10–334, April 27	Ceionius Julianus Kamenius
334, April 27–335, December 30	Anicius Paulinus
335, December 30–337, March 10	Rufius Albinus
337, March 10–338, January 13	Valerius Proculus

2. ADDITIONAL NAMES

The Chronographer's list is clearly complete from 302 at the latest: for every prefect after Aelius Dionysius he conscientiously provides the exact days on which he entered and left office. It also seems probable that the list is complete from 288, where the first diurnal date occurs.[3] The earlier part of the list is another matter. Before 288 there are no diurnal dates, and the list appears to name the prefect in office on a particular day each year (perhaps 21 April, the *natalis* of Rome).[4] Two names can be added from inscriptions. Pomponius Bassus, *consul ordinarius* in both 259 and 271, was also *praefectus urbi* (*CIL* 6.3836 = *IG* 14.1076 = *IGRR* 1.137); since a literary allusion indicates that he was in office near the end of the reign of Claudius (*Epitome* 34.3: "sententiae in senatu dicendae primus"), his tenure can be dated to 270.[5] Aurelian presumably replaced him very rapidly. L. Caesonius Ovinius Manlius Rufinianus Bassus has recently been revealed as both *cos. II* and *praefectus urbis* (*AE* 1964.223). If Bassus was consul for the second time with Diocletian for the last weeks of 284, then he presumably replaced Ceionius Varus as prefect of the city after Carinus was defeated and killed in the spring of 285.[6]

3. PATTERNS OF TENURE

Prefects of the city of Rome did not serve for a fixed term; within the period 284 to 337 the attested length of tenure ranges from one month to four years. Nevertheless, certain patterns of appointment can be detected (Table 9). Maxentius clearly aimed at strictly annual appointments running from one *dies imperii* (28 October) to the next. The deviations from this pattern can be explained in political terms: Insteius Tertullus took office in August 307 when Galerius was about to march on Rome, and he left office in the same month as Maximian attempted to depose Maxentius, while Junius Flavianus, who left office on 9 February 312, a mere three and a half months after his appointment, probably did so after his wife committed suicide.[7] Under Constantine, too, there is a tendency for appointments to last for approximately a whole number of years, despite some obvious irregularities. It may be legitimate, therefore, to project this tendency backward into the reign of Diocletian. Between 288 and 302, the Chronographer's list shows that the office of prefect changed hands in the following months:

288	February	296	February
289	unknown	297	unknown

3. G. Tomassetti, *Museo Italiano di Antichità Classica* 3 (1890), 58 n. 1.

4. Ibid., 547 f.; G. Barbieri, *Akte des IV. Internationalen Kongresses für griechische und lateinische Epigraphik* (Vienna, 1964), 48; 50; T. D. Barnes, *JRS* 65 (1975), 46 n. 64. Although all three supposed that before 288 the list recorded the prefects in office on the Kalends of January, the facts set out in the present discussion make a later date preferable.

5. Claudius died in August 270, see J. R. Rea, *Oxyrhynchus Papyri* 40 (London, 1972), 15 ff.; T. D. Barnes, *Phoenix* 26 (1972), 180 f.; *GRBS* 17 (1976), 66 ff.

6. For the date, Chapter V: Diocletian.

7. Below, at n. 18.

290	no new appointment	298	unknown
291	February	299	unknown
292	August	300	March
293	March	301	unknown
294	no new appointment	302	February
295	January		

Hence, if there was any regularity of tenure, the list of *praefecti urbis* from 284 to 304 can be conjecturally completed as follows (with unattested dates in italics):

Ceionius Varus	*autumn 283–summer 285*
L. Caesonius Ovinius Manlius Rufinianus Bassus	*summer 285–c. February 286*
Junius Maximus	*c. February* 286–27 February 288
Pomponius Januarianus	27 February 288–*c. February 290*
Turranius Gratianus	*c. February* 290–18 February 291
Junius Tiberianus	18 February 291–3 August 292
Cl. Marcellus	3 August 292–13 March 293
Septimius Acindynus	13 March 293–11 January 295
Aristobulus	11 January 295–11 February 296
Cassius Dion	11 February 296–*c. February 297*
Afranius Hannibalianus	*c. February 297–c. February 298*
Artorius Maximus	*c. February 298–c. February 299*
Anicius Faustus	*c. February* 299–1 March 300
Pompeius Faustinus	1 March 300–*c. February 301*
Aelius Dionysius	*c. February* 301–19 February 302

This reconstruction (it may be observed) is consistent with the hypothesis that the early part of the list names the prefects in office on 21 April in each year.[8]

4. PREFECTS WHO WERE *CONSULES ORDINARII* BETWEEN 284 AND 337

More than half the prefects who held office between 284 and 337 were ordinary consuls under Diocletian and Constantine.[9] They are listed below with the date of their prefecture or prefectures preceding the name, and the date of their ordinary consulate or consulates following it.

8. Above, at n. 4.
9. On their careers, and problems of identification, see Chapter VI.

285–286	L. Caesonius Ovinius Manlius Rufinianus Bassus	284
286–288	M. Junius Maximus	286
288–289	Pomponius Januarianus	288
291–292	C. Junius Tiberianus	281, 291
295–296	T. Cl. Aurelius Aristobulus	285
296–297	Cassius Dion	291
297–298	Afranius Hannibalianus	292
299–300	Anicius Faustus	298
302–303	Nummius Tuscus	295
305–306	T. Flavius Postumius Titianus	301
306–307	Annius Anullinus	295
310–311, 313–315,	C. Ceionius Rufius Volusianus	311, 314
312, 312–313	Aradius Rufinus	?311
315–316	C. Vettius Cossinius Rufinus	316
316–317	Ovinius Gallicanus	317
325–326	Acilius Severus	323
326–329	Amnius Anicius Julianus	322
329–331	Petronius Probianus	322
331–333	Sex. Anicius Paulinus	325
334–335	Amnius Manius Caesonius Nicomachus Anicius Paulinus	334
335–337	Ceionius Rufius Albinus	335

5. PROSOPOGRAPHICAL NOTES ON THE OTHER PREFECTS

283–285   Ceionius Varus
Nothing else known; presumably a relative of C. Ceionius Rufius Volusianus, cos. 311, 314, probably his uncle.

290–291   Turranius Gratianus
Gratianus' prefecture is also attested by an inscription of 290 (*CIL* 6.1128 + p. 845 = 31241). He is presumably to be identified with the L. Turranius Gratianus who, as *corrector provinciae Achaeae,* honored Diocletian at Athens (*CIL* 3.6103), probably very early in his reign.[10] Identity with the Turranius who appears on a fragmentary list from Rome (*NdS* 1917.22) is less than certain.[11]

292–293   Cl. Marcellus
Nothing else is known about Marcellus' career.

10. E. Groag, *Die Reichsbeamten von Achaia in spätrömischer Zeit* (*Dissertationes Pannonicae* 1.14, 1946), 14; Chastagnol, *Fastes* 16; *PLRE* 1.403, Gratianus 3.
11. Below, Section 6(c).

293-295 Septimius Acindynus
Career totally unknown apart from his prefecture.

298-299   L. Artorius Pius Maximus
The prefect Artorius Maximus is clearly identical with L. Artorius Pius Maximus of Ephesus, whom inscriptions certify as *legatus pro praetore* of Diocletian and Maximian at Heliopolis (*AE* 1939.58) and as proconsul of Asia (*CIL* 3.14195.27; *JÖAI* 44 (1959), Beibl. 349/50 = *I. Ephesos* 307, 621).

300-301   Pompeius Faustinus
Previously *corrector Campaniae* (*CIL* 10.4785: Teanum Sidicinum); probably not identical with, but father of, the Pompeius Appius Faustinus attested as *praetor urbanus* (*CIL* 6.314 d).[12]

301-302   L. Aelius Helvius Dionysius
Dionysius' career before his prefecture is known from a Roman inscription of which several seventeenth-century reports survive (*ILS* 1211), supplemented by other evidence relating to single posts. The attested career runs as follows:

> *curator operum publicorum* (also *ILS* 621, 622)
> *curator aquarum et Miniciae* (also *ILS* 626)
> *curator utriusque Italiae*
> *praeses* of Syria Coele
> *iudex sacrarum cognitionum totius Orientis*
> proconsul of Africa from 296 to 300

Dionysius' name is erased on the three African inscriptions which record his proconsulate (*CIL* 8.12459; *ILAfr.* 441, 531), and L. Poinssot acutely conjectured that he was disgraced and executed after his prefecture.[13] That conjecture would provide substance for Lactantius' charge that Maximian destroyed the *lumina senatus* through faked allegations of conspiracy (*Mort. Pers.* 8.4).[14]

303-304   Junius Tiberianus
Previously proconsul of Asia (*JÖAI* 44 (1959), Beibl. 267/8 = *I. Ephesos* 305).

304-305   Aradius Rufinus
Conventionally identified with the Aradius Rufinus who was *praefectus urbi* in 312 and 312-313.[15] He ought rather to be his father.

---

12. Below, Section 6(a).
13. L. Poinssot, *MSNAF* 76 (1919-23), 316 ff.
14. Moreau, *Lactance* 253, argues that the charge on which Lactantius alleges that senators were executed ("qui...affectasse imperium dicerentur") is "un véritable τόπος de l'historiographie."
15. Chastagnol, *Fastes* 41, 60 f.; *PLRE* 1.775, Rufinus 10. In favor of the identification, both

307-308 Attius Insteius Tertullus

Tertullus was appointed prefect when Galerius was about to attack Rome, and left office at the same time as Maximian fled to Gaul. His earlier career is known from a dedication by the corporation of *magnarii* for protecting them as prefect at a time of danger (*CIL* 6.1696). It runs as follows:

> quaestor (restored)
> praetor *candidatus*
> consul, i.e. suffect consul
> *corrector* of Venetia and Histria (the province is restored from *CIL* 5.2818: Padua)
> *praepositus fabri*[---

The last post lacks any parallel in a senatorial career.[16] Moreover, if the name of the factory (reading *fabri[cae]*) ought to be supplied, then there is no room on the stone for the proconsulate of Africa in 306-307, which some scholars have attributed to Tertullus (inferred from *CIL* 8.876: *Insteius Tertullus v. c.*).[17]

308-309 Statius Rufinus

Otherwise unknown. Nevertheless, there is a chance that the Rufinus consul in 311 is Statius Rufinus rather than Aradius Rufinus.

309-310 Aurelius Hermogenes

Previously proconsul of Asia (*CIL* 3.7069).

311-312 Junius Flavianus

Otherwise unknown. But the apparent dismissal of Flavianus before his year of office expired may be significant: he can be identified as the unnamed prefect whose wife (it is alleged) killed herself to escape the lust of Maxentius (Eusebius, *HE* 8.14.15-17; *VC* 1.34).[18]

312 Annius Anullinus

The Anullini of the late third and early fourth century present problems of identity which probably cannot be solved on the available evidence. For clarity, the attested bearers of the name in high office should be listed individually:

Chastagnol and *PLRE* adduce the fact that the Chronographer of 354 notes that Rufinus was *iterum praefectus urbis* (*Chr. Min.* 1.67). If relevant, *iterum* rather than *tertio* might tend to indicate the opposite. But the writer is surely doing no more than noting that Aradius Rufinus became prefect for the second time in 312 (after a mere month out of office).

16. Perhaps, therefore, an emergency appointment in 306/7 when Maxentius and Maximian were arming Italy to resist Galerius and Severus.

17. For discussion, Chastagnol, *Fastes* 49.

18. Chastagnol, *Fastes* 59. E. J. Champlin has suggested to me that Flavianus may be a brother of Anicius Faustus, cos. 298, whose full name is often presumed to be M. Junius Cae-

1. Annius Anullinus, consul, 295
2. C. Annius Anullinus, proconsul of Africa, 303–305
3. Annius Anullinus, *praefectus urbi,* 306–307
4. Anullinus, praetorian prefect of Severus, spring 307
5. Annius Anullinus, *praefectus urbi,* 312
6. Anullinus, proconsul of Africa, 312–313

The last is clearly a different person from any of the rest, but it has become conventional to identify the first three and the fifth.[19] On this hypothesis, however, Anullinus would be a unique and anomalous case of a proconsul of Africa after 295 who had already been ordinary consul.[20] By 303, the proconsulate normally preceded an ordinary consulate; therefore, either the identification is erroneous or Anullinus was appointed proconsul for a special reason (namely, to enforce imperial legislation against the Christians).[21] Moreover, the *praefectus urbi* of 312 could easily be the praetorian prefect of 307, whom Maxentius appointed on the day before he fought Constantine for partially superstitious reasons.[22] On present evidence, therefore, it is reasonable to distinguish four Anullini, of whom the first and second (or second and third) might be identical:

1. consul, 295; *praefectus urbi,* 306–307
2. proconsul of Africa, 303–305
3. praetorian prefect, 307; *praefectus urbi,* 312
4. proconsul of Africa, 312–313

317–319   Septimius Bassus
Bassus' prefecture is also attested by numerous laws.[23] The man is otherwise unknown, unless he can be identified with Caesonius Bassus, consul in 317 (*P. Columbia inv.* 173).[24]

319–323   Valerius Maximus Basilius
Maximus' prefecture is also attested by numerous laws,[25] but he is otherwise

---

sonius Nicomachus Anicius Faustus Paulinus (Chapter VI, n. 41).

19. Chastagnol, *Fastes* 45 ff., 63. *PLRE* 1.79, Anullinus 3, conflates this composite character with the fourth Anullinus, arguing that Zosimus errs in styling him praetorian prefect. In disproof, cf. *Phoenix* 27 (1973), 139.

20. The fasti are complete or virtually complete from 290 to 305 (Chapter IX).

21. Compare the apparent demotion of Sossianus Hierocles from *vicarius* of Oriens to *praeses* of Bithynia and his later appointment as prefect of Egypt (*HSCP* 80 (1976), 243 f.).

22. Seeck, *Geschichte* 1³.131.

23. See the lists (based on Seeck's *Regesten*) offered by Chastagnol, *Fastes* 71 n. 22; *PLRE* 1.157, Bassus 19.

24. Seeck, *Regesten* 115; Chastagnol, *Fastes* 72, proposed the identification before the consul's *nomen* was known.

25. Chastagnol, *Fastes* 73 n. 36; *PLRE* 1.590, Maximus 48 (largely based on Seeck's *Regesten*). But *CTh* 9.5.1 ought to be referred to a praetorian prefect of Licinius (Chapter VIII, at nn. 17–22).

unknown. The *praefectus urbi* is not identical with the Valerius Maximus who was consul in 327.[26] A pagan (*CTh* 16.10.1).

323-325   Lucer. Verinus

Verinus' *nomen* is uncertain: the Chronographer has *Lucer.* (nominative), laws *Lucrium* (accusative), *Locrio,* and *Lucrio* (dative). On this evidence, Chastagnol proposes *Lucer(ius)* for the name, while the *Prosopography* accepts *Locrius,* suggesting that Verinus may be the son of Sallustius Verianus and Locria Magna, who were Christians (*CIL* 11.2558, 2580: Clusium).[27] Even if that is a sheer guess, the *nomen* is definitely Etruscan.[28]

Apart from the prefecture (also *CTh* 2.17.1, 2.24.1, 14.4.2), only one post is securely attested for Verinus: he was *vicarius* of Africa from 318 to 321 (*CTh* 9.15.1, 9.21.1, 9.34,1, 3.19.1; Augustine, *Brev. Coll.* 3.22.40, 3.24.42; *Contra partem Donati post gesta* 31.54, 33.56; *Epp.* 141.9). Otherwise there are two problematical pieces of evidence. A law addressed to Verinus, with no office given, bears the publication date 30 January 314 (*CTh* 12.11.1): it might attest a governorship or an earlier vicariate.[29] The father of Symmachus wrote a poem about the prefect:

> Virtutem, Verine, tuam plus mirer in armis,
> Eoos dux Armenios cum caede domares,
> an magis eloquium morum vitaeque leporem,
> et — nisi in officiis, quotiens tibi publica curae —
> quod vitam innocuis tenuisti laetus in agris?
> nullum ultra est virtutis opus, quam si esset, haberes.

> (Symmachus, *Epp.* 1.2.7)

When did Verinus fight in Armenia? Seeck argued that it was during Maximinus' Mesopotamian campaign of 312, Chastagnol that it must have been later than the defeat of Licinius in 324.[30] Neither hypothesis is convincing.[31] A conjecture can be made which will explain Verinus' documented career: if his service in Armenia belongs to Galerius' Persian War,[32] then his association with

26. As Chastagnol supposes (*Fastes* 73).

27. Chastagnol, *Fastes* 74; *PLRE* 1.951–952, Verinus 2. This entry appears to be the work of J. Morris, see *Klio* 46 (1965), 363 f.

28. W. Schulze, *Zur Geschichte der lateinischen Eigennamen* (*Abh. Göttingen,* Phil.-hist. Klasse, n.f. 5.5, 1904), 182, 297, on names in Lucer- and Lucr-.

29. *PLRE* 1.952, rejecting Seeck's emendation of the date to 320 (*Regesten* 75, 169).

30. Seeck, *Geschichte* 1³.148, 503; Chastagnol, *Fastes* 76.

31. H. Castritius, *JAC* 11/12 (1968/69), 98 ff.; D. M. Novak, *Ancient Society* 10 (1979), 300.

32. As proposed by H. Castritius, *JAC* 11/12 (1968/69), 102. A law dated 294 is addressed *ad Verinum praesidem Syriae* (*CJ* 2.12.20), while one of 305 addresses *Verine carissime* (*CJ* 3.12.1). There is no compelling reason to identify either with the Verinus who was *praefectus urbi*.

Constantine goes back to 298. The vicariate of Africa and the prefecture of the city each came at a significant time: between 318 and 321 Constantine was attempting to repress Donatism, in 323 he was preparing for war against Licinius.

329, 333 Publilius Optatianus Porfyrius

The career of Optatianus is badly documented, but the fact that he sent a cycle of twenty poems to Constantine in 324 begging to be restored from exile permits a tentative reconstruction of his life:[33]

born, c. 260–270
proconsul of Achaea, before 306
sends poems (not extant) to Constantine with the extant *Epistula Porfyrii* and receives in reply the extant *Epistula Constantini,* November/December 312
exiled (?at the same time as Rufius Volusianus), ?in 315
sends Constantine *Carmina* I–XX from exile, autumn 324
recalled from exile, early 325
praefectus urbi, 329 and 333

333–334 M. Ceionius Julianus Kamenius

Two earlier posts are definitely attested: Julianus was *consularis* of Campania in late 324 (*AE* 1939.151), and proconsul of Africa between 326 and 331 (*CIL* 8.14436 = *ILS* 5518; *CIL* 8.14431, 15269, 25525; *ILAlg.* 1.4011 = *AE* 1922.16).

337–338 L. Aradius Valerius Proculus *signo* Populonius

Proculus' career down to his ordinary consulate in 340 is well documented by several Roman inscriptions (*CIL* 6.1690–94):

praetor *tutelaris*
legatus propraetore provinciae Numidiae, i.e. legate of a proconsul of Africa, almost certainly of his presumed relative Proculus, who was proconsul in 319–320
peraequator census provinciae Gallaeciae, during or soon after the census of 321
praeses of Byzacena
consularis Europae et Thraciae
consularis of Sicilia
comes ordinis secundi
comes ordinis primi

---

33. *AJP* 96 (1975), 174 ff. Observe that *Carm.* 2.31/2 ("Respice me falso de crimine, maxime rector,/exulis afflictum poena") implies that Porfyrius was not exiled by Constantine, but rather, like Volusianus, by the Roman Senate (cf. Firmicus Maternus, *Math.* 2.29.12).

proconsul of Africa in 332–333 and, for at least part of his proconsular
  year, concurrently praetorian prefect for all the African provinces
  comes iterum ordinis primi intra palatium
  praefectus urbi, from 10 March 337 to 13 January 338
  consul, 340

Proculus probably retired after his consulate, but he emerged from retirement
to be *praefectus urbi* for a second time under Magnentius (from 18 December
351 to 9 September 352).

6. SOME PROBLEMATICAL INSCRIPTIONS FROM ROME

The careers of men discussed in this chapter and the preceding one are very
relevant to the dating of certain inscriptions from Rome and to the identification of the persons whom they name.

(a) *CIL* 6.314

An altar to Hercules is reported by two Renaissance antiquaries as exhibiting
on its four sides dedications to Hercules by four urban praetors, viz. T. Flavius
Iulian{i}us Quadratianus, M. Nummius Ceionius Annius Albinus, Jul(ius) Festus, and Pompeius Appius Faustinus. Both Chastagnol and the *Prosopography
of the Later Roman Empire* date the altar to the late third century and identify
the fourth man as the Pompeius Faustinus who was *praefectus urbi* in 300–
301.[34] But a closely similar dedication appears to belong to 20 September 321:

(front)	*(side)*
Deo Herculi inv.	d. d.
M. Iun. Caesonius	XII Kal. Octob.
Nicomachus Anicius	Crispo et Constantino
Faustus Paulinus	Caes. II cons.
c. v., p. u., d. d.	

(*CIL* 6.315 = *ILS* 3409)

The inscription on the side survives, but the front of the altar now bears merely
the letters *D.O.M.* over an erasure. The inscription on the front is reported by
the same two Renaissance antiquaries, of whom one reports it alone, the other
with the inscription on the side.[35] The conjunction ought to be accepted; there
is no call to dismiss the date of 321 as irrelevant to the dedication on the front

---

34. Chastagnol, *Fastes* 33; *PLRE* 1.756–757, Quadratianus; 34, Albinus 7; 336, Festus 9;
327–328, Faustinus 7. Also G. Barbieri, *L'Albo senatorio da Settimio Severo a Carino (193–285)*
(Rome, 1952), 333 no. 1908/9; A. Illuminati, *Rendiconti Lincei*[8] 27 (1972), 470 ff.
   35. See W. Henzen, in annotation on *CIL* 6.315.

of the altar.[36] Moreover, M. Nummius Ceionius Annius Albinus possesses a set of names which appears to indicate that he is the brother of Ceionius Rufius Albinus, who was born in March 303.[37] Accordingly, it is preferable to date the four praetors in the vicinity of 320, so that Pompeius Appius Faustinus will not be the *praefectus urbi* of 300–301, but an apparently otherwise unattested son.

(b)   *CIL* 6.2153

> Rufius Volusianus v. c. xv [s. f.
> 2   Rufius Festus v. c. xv s. f.
> Sebasmius philos[opus
> 4   ///////////pon[t
> Brittius Praesens v. c. p. m[
> 6   Evagrius   philosopus
> Fl.   Atticus v.c.

The *Prosopography* dates the inscription c. 320.[38] But if Rufius Volusianus is (as all agree) the consul of 311 and 314, then the inscription must antedate his exile in or shortly after 315 (Firmicus Maternus, *Math.* 2.29.10, 12). The other names afford no aid toward a precise dating. But the erasure in line 4 excites curiosity; it could conceal Helvius Dionysius, whose name is erased on African inscriptions. He is known to have been a *pontifex dei Solis* (*ILS* 1211), which can be restored in line 4. If his name did originally stand on the inscription, its date would be prior to 305.[39.]

The precise nature of the list has not yet received a satisfactory elucidation.

(c)   *Notizie degli Scavi*[5] 16 (1917), 22 = *Bull. Comm.* 45 (1917), 225

> Turraniu[s]
> 2   Crepereius Ro[gatus
> Publilius Optatian[us
> 4   Ceionius Rufius Volusi[anus
>]n. Anicius P[aulinus
> 6   A]cilius
> PR

Chastagnol dates the list c. 320.[40] But if the third and fourth names belong to the poet Publilius Optatianus Porfyrius and the consul of 311 and 314, then the inscription must antedate their exiles, which can be dated (albeit tentatively) to 315 or shortly thereafter.[41] Nothing precludes dating the inscription some years

36. As Chastagnol, *Fastes* 32 (identifying the praetor as Anicius Faustus, cos. II 298).
37. *JRS* 65 (1975), 45.
38. *PLRE* 1.123, Atticus 2, etc.
39. Above, at nn. 13, 14.
40. Chastagnol, *Fastes* 16, 57, 81, 92.
41. *JRS* 65 (1975), 47; *AJP* 96 (1975), 176, 186.

earlier than 315, and E. Groag attractively identified the names as belonging to members of a priestly college whom Maxentius compelled to contribute to the building or restoration of a temple.[42] If that is so, the first name could be that of Turranius Gratianus, *praefectus urbi* in 290–291, the fourth that of the Anicius Faustus who was consul for the second time in 298 — though in both cases alternative identifications are possible, such as L. Turranius Venustus Gratianus, attested as *praetor urbanus,* [43] and Anicius Paulinus, consul in 325.[44] The second, sixth, and seventh names do not aid in dating.[45]

42. E. Groag, *Wiener Studien* 45 (1926–27), 102 ff.

43. *PLRE* 1.402, Gratianus 4, cf. 925.

44. F. Fornari, *NdS*[5] 16 (1917), 22, read the first element of his name as "[I]un.," but Chastagnol, *Fastes* 92, reads "[Am]n." and identifies the man as Amnius Manius Caesonius Nicomachus Anicius Paulinus *signo* Honorius, cos. 334.

45. *PLRE* 1.767, Rogatus 2; 10, Acilius 1; 1001 s.v. PR (perhaps part of the name Apronius or Sempronius).

CHAPTER VIII

PRAETORIAN PREFECTS

Augustus or Caesar, residing in his capital or touring the provinces, on campaign or in his cups, a Roman emperor of the late third and early fourth centuries was normally accompanied by a praetorian prefect.[1] The reign of Constantine also witnessed the first praetorian prefects who operated independently of the emperor and possessed a specific territorial jurisdiction.[2] There are, however, woeful gaps and uncertainties in documentation, and it is sometimes difficult to assign an attested prefect to the emperor whom he served or to the area which he administered. The present chapter adopts a rigorous prosopographical approach and attempts to establish the nature of the praetorian prefecture in the period of Diocletian and Constantine by tackling the problem in a strictly chronological order before attempting a synthesis.[3]

1. E.g., *Pan. Lat.* 12(9).11.4 (Constantine on campaign): *Origo* 11 (Galerius at dinner). The jurist Charisius declared that a prefect served his emperor just as the Republican *magister equitum* had served a dictator (*Dig.* 1.11.pr.).

2. Note *Cons. Sirm.* 4 (21 October 336): "ad Felicem praefectum praetorii...volumus ut excellens sublimitas tua litteris suis per dioecesim sibi creditam commeantibus iudices moneat."

3. For earlier attempts to establish such a list for the years 284–337, either in whole or in part, see B. Borghesi, *Œuvres complètes* 10, revised by A. Cuq and A. Héron de Villefosse (Paris, 1897), 145 ff., 189 ff., 435 ff., 489 ff., 673 ff.; O. Seeck, *Rh. Mus.*, n.f. 69 (1914), 1 ff.; *Regesten* 141 ff.; J.-R. Palanque, *Essai sur la préfecture du prétoire du Bas-Empire* (Paris, 1933), 1 ff. (on which, cf. E. Stein, *Byzantion* 9 (1934), 327 ff.; M. J. Higgins, *Byzantion* 10 (1935), 621 ff.); L. L. Howe, *The Pretorian Prefect from Commodus to Diocletian (A.D. 180–305)* (Chicago, 1942), 84 ff.; J.-R. Palanque, *Mélanges H. Grégoire* 2 (Brussels, 1950), 483 ff.; *Mélanges A. Piganiol* 2 (Paris, 1966), 837 ff.; C. Dupont, *Studi in onore di G. Grosso* 2 (Turin, 1968), 517 ff.; A. Chastagnol, *Recherches sur l'Histoire Auguste* (Bonn, 1970), 30 ff.; C. Dupont, *Études offertes à*

1. EMPERORS AND THEIR ATTESTED PREFECTS, 285–317

Diocletian
285   T. Cl. Aurelius Aristobulus, cos. 285
Praetorian prefect of Carinus, retained in office by Diocletian (Victor, *Caes.*
39.14).

Between 285 and 292   Afranius Hannibalianus, cos. 292
A dedication to Diocletian at Oescus attests Hannibalianus and a colleague:
Afranius Hannibalianus, Iul. Asclepiodotus v[v]. eemm. prae[ff. praet.] (*ILS*
8929). The inscription antedates 1 January 292, when the two prefects became
consuls and hence *viri clarissimi.*[4]

The inscription itself provides no explicit indication of which prefect belongs to which emperor; nevertheless, it may be argued that, since the order
of names presumably reflects the order of appointment to office, the senior
prefect is more likely to belong to the senior of the two emperors. In that case,
Hannibalianus was the prefect of Diocletian, Asclepiodotus of Maximian.[5]

302   Asclepiades
Prudentius presents the martyr Romanus as being tried and condemned at Antioch by the *praefectus* Asclepiades (*Peristephanon* 10.41 etc.), while Eusebius
reports that Diocletian was in Antioch at the time of Romanus' first trial,
which occurred long before his execution in November 303, and he alludes to a
magistrate without specifying either his name or his official post (*Mart. Pal.*
2.2–4: complementary details in each recension).[6] Asclepiades, therefore, was
the praetorian prefect of Diocletian in autumn 302.[7]

Maximian
Between 285 and 292   Julius Asclepiodotus, cos. 292
Colleague of Afranius Hannibalianus (*ILS* 8929). Not necessarily identical
with the Asclepiodotus known as praetorian prefect of Constantius in 296.[8]

J. Macqueron (Aix-en-Provence, 1970), 251 ff.; *PLRE* 1.1047 f.; C. Dupont, *Studi in onore di G.
Scherillo* 2 (Milan, 1972), 819 ff.
   4. The fact that Diocletian is *Germanicus maximus,* but not *Sarmaticus maximus,* does not
prove a date before 290, as urged in *PLRE* 1.407 (cf. Tables 4, 5).
   5. *Pan. Lat.* 10(2).11.4 does not, as is often supposed, allude to Hannibalianus (below, at nn.
9–13).
   6. *PLRE* 1.114, Asclepiades 2 adduces two other items of evidence: a private rescript of 294
(*CJ* 6.24.10) and the fictitious *Acta Agathonici* 4 (*BHG* 40, ed. G. van Hooff, *Anal. Boll.* 2 (1883),
103–4).
   7. Flaccinus, attested as prefect in 303, is assigned below to Galerius.
   8. As often assumed (e.g., *PIR*[2] J 179; *PLRE* 1.115–116, Asclepiodotus 3).

288-293   Constantius

Two Gallic panegyrics can be combined to render it highly probable that Constantius was praetorian prefect of Maximian for several years before his elevation as Caesar. The orator who addressed Constantius on 1 March 297 alludes to his first appearance before Maximian through the aid of Constantius: "praesertim cum favente numine tuo ipse ille iam pridem mihi, qui me in lucem primus eduxit, divinarum patris tui aurium aditus evenerit" (*Pan. Lat.* 8(5).1.5). He then speaks of his experiences in an office to which Constantius appointed him, when he apparently accompanied Constantius on a campaign before 293: "Quamquam multa mihi ex illis quoque hoc in tempore necessario transeunda sunt ac potissimum ea quibus officio delati mihi a divinitate vestra honoris interfui, captus scilicet rex ferocissimae nationis inter ipsas quas moliebatur insidias et a ponte Rheni usque ad Danubii transitum Guntiensem deusta atque exhausta penitus Alamannia; nam et maiora sunt quam ut enarrari inter alia possint et, ne meis quoque stipendiis videar gloriari, sufficit conscientiae meae illa vidisse" (*Pan. Lat.* 8(5).2.1).

If Constantius could introduce the orator to the emperor's presence, make or secure him an appointment and conduct military operations, he must have held high office under Maximian. An earlier speech, delivered before Maximian on 21 April 289, has an allusion which is both less and more specific: "tantum esse in concordia bonum statuis, ut etiam eos qui circa te potissimo funguntur officio necessitudine tibi et adfinitate devinxeris, id pulcherrimum arbitratus adhaerere lateri tuo non timoris obsequia sed vota pietatis" (*Pan. Lat.* 10(2).11.4). The most natural interpretation of the text is that Maximian has allied himself by marriage to his praetorian prefect.[9] Two explanations of the allusion have been advanced: either the prefect is Afranius Hannibalianus, and it is argued that Maximian's wife Eutropia was previously married to Hannibalianus,[10] or the prefect is Constantius, whose marriage to Theodora is implicitly dated to 293 by several narrative sources (Victor, *Caes.* 39.24; Eutropius, *Brev.* 9.22.1; Jerome, *Chronicle* 225[g]; *Epitome* 39.2).[11] The latter identification is correct. The date in these narrative sources deserves no respect, for they de-

---

9. Seeck, *Geschichte* 1[3].452. Seeck, however, harmed his case by taking the plural literally and deducing that Diocletian and Maximian each had two prefects. The panegyrical literature of the Late Empire is full of such hyperbolic plurals referring to a single person or episode (see, e.g., A. Cameron, *Claudian: Poetry and Propaganda at the Court of Honorius* (Oxford, 1970), 80).

10. *PLRE* 1.316, Eutropia 1; 407-408, Hannibalianus 3; 1128-29, Stemmata 1 and 2.

11. O. Seeck, *RE* 4 (1901), 1041; *Geschichte* 1[3].452. Seeck's conclusions were rejected by L. Cantarelli, *Memorie della Pontificia Accademia Romana di Archeologia*[3] 1.1 (1923), 31 ff., with the subsequent approval of most scholars (e.g., Seston, *Dioclétien* 89; J. Moreau, *JAC* 2 (1958), 158). But Cantarelli's arguments have two fatal weaknesses: he assumed that it was impossible to take "qui circa te potissimo funguntur officio" to refer to a single person, and he felt compelled to interpret the office as "il tirocinio di due Cesari" (p. 35)—which corresponds exactly to the function of a praetorian prefect.

rive from a single source written c. 337, which muddled the chronology of the 290s, and described Maximian's daughter Theodora as his stepdaughter.[12] The reliable evidence indicates that Constantius was the praetorian prefect and son-in-law of Maximian by 288; the orator of 21 April 289 refers to a recent campaign waged by him against the Franks (*Pan. Lat.* 10(2).11.4 f). Constantius presumably continued in office until he became Caesar in 293.

Constantius
296   Asclepiodotus
Named as praetorian prefect and as responsible for recovering Britain in 296 (Victor, *Caes.* 39.26; Eutropius, *Brev.* 9.22.2; Jerome, *Chronicle* 227[a]). He is normally identified with the Julius Asclepiodotus who was praetorian prefect before he became consul in 292. He might, however, be this man's son. In any event, this Asclepiodotus is the prefect of Constantius, not of Maximian.

Galerius
303   Flaccinus
Praefectus at Nicomedia in 303 (Lactantius, *Mort. Pers.* 16.4). Presumably the prefect in command of *praetoriani* who demolished a church in Nicomedia on 23 February 303 (*Mort. Pers.* 12.1 ff.), and hence praetorian prefect of either Diocletian or Galerius, who were both in the city.

310   ?Tatius Andronicus, cos. 310
Papyri of 310 attest Tatius Andronicus and Pompeius Probus as consuls and praetorian prefects.[13] They should, therefore, be the prefects of Galerius and Licinius. Since the order of their names in consular dates presumably attests Andronicus' prior appointment to the prefecture, and Licinius had only been emperor since 11 November 308, Andronicus was probably the prefect of Galerius.

Severus
307, early   Anullinus
Praetorian prefect with the army of Severus when he marched against Maxentius (Zosimus 2.10.1).

Maximinus
311, May–312, December   Sabinus
Eusebius, *HE* 9.1.3, 9.9a.1.

12. Chapter IV, at nn. 15–18. The proclamation of the Caesars in 293 is stated to be the result of the revolt of Achilleus in 297 by Victor, *Caes.* 39.22 ff.; Eutropius, *Brev.* 9.22.1; Jerome, *Chronicle* 225[g].

13. For papyri attesting the consuls of 310, 327, 331, and 332 as praetorian prefects in office in those years, see R. S. Bagnall and K. A. Worp, *Chronological Systems of Byzantine Egypt* (*Studia Amstelodamensia* 8, 1978), 108 ff.

Constantine

Before 314, 1 January–after 317, 1 March   Petronius Annianus, cos. 314

Attested in office on 28 April 315 (Optatus, App. 8), between 314 and September 316 (*ILS* 8938: Tropaeum Traiani) and after 1 March 317 (*AE* 1938.85 = *I. Ephesos* 312).). Analogy suggests that Annianus became praetorian prefect before his consulate, and there is no obvious obstacle to identifying him with the prefect who was with Constantine at the siege of Aquileia in 312 (*Pan. Lat.* 12(9).11.4).

Maxentius

Shortly after 306   Manilius Rusticianus[14]

Describes himself as *v. em., praef. praet.* on a dedication to Maxentius (*ILS* 8934: Rome).

309   C. Ceionius Rufius Volusianus, cos. 311, 314

Sent to Africa by Maxentius as praetorian prefect to suppress Domitius Alexander (Victor, *Caes.* 40.18; Zosimus 2.14.2 ff.)

312   Ruricius Pompeianus

Praefectus of Maxentius killed near Verona in 312 (*Pan. Lat.* 12(9).8.1, 10.3, 4(10).25.4 ff.).

Licinius

310   ?Pompeius Probus, cos. 310

Colleague of Tatius Andronicus as prefect and consul in 310. Since Galerius had used Licinius and Probus as envoys during his invasion of Italy in 307 (*Origo* 7), Probus must be the prefect of either Galerius himself or Licinius: the latter is here preferred because of Andronicus' seniority. A law with the unusual heading *Imp. Constantinus et Licinius AA. ad Probum* (*CJ* 6.1.3) may have been addressed to Pompeius Probus as praetorian prefect in 310 or 311,[15] but there is no reason to identify him as the Probus (office not stated) who received an imperial letter written on 1 April 314 (*CTh* 4.12.1).[16]

314, January 1   Maximus

The *Codex Theodosianus* and the *Codex Justinianus* contain a law addressed *ad Maximum p. u.* and published on 1 January 314 (*CTh* 9.5.1 = *CJ* 9.8.3). Either the date or the office must be wrong, and it has been normal to emend

14. *ILS* 8934 has Manli(us): identity is here assumed with Manilius Rus[ticianus], who commanded the praetorian cohorts, probably before October 306 (*CIL* 14.4455 (Ostia): *a. v. pra[eff. praetorio] eemm. vv.,* cf. Chapter XIII, n. 61).

15. Compare *FIRA*[2] 1.93 (issued in the name of Constantine and Licinius alone on 9 June 311). Although *CJ* 6.1.3 stands between laws of 294 and 317, P. Krüger, ad loc., proposed the date "a. 317–323."

16. As do Seeck, *Regesten* 162; *PLRE* 1.740, Probus 6.

the date to 320, and to identify the recipient of the law as Valerius Maximus Basilius, *praefectus urbi* from 319 to 323.[17] But the consular date is by nonimperial consuls (*Volusiano et Anniano*): therefore, of the contradictory elements, it is the designation of Maximus as *p(raefectus) u(rbi)* which must be regarded as the more liable to have been corrupted in transmission.[18] Emendation to ad *Maximum p(raefectum) p(raetori)o,* with the consequent attribution of the law to Licinius, is recommended by three powerful considerations.[19] First, the law survives not only in the law codes but also on stone: five copies are known, all from the territory of Licinius (viz. *I. Cret.* 1.226–228 no. 188: Lyttus; *CIL* 3.12133: Tlos in Lycia; *CIL* 5.2781: probably from Asia; *AE* 1957.180: Sinope; and an unpublished fragment from Pergamum).[20] Second, the law prescribes crucifixion as a punishment for slaves who denounce their masters—a form of punishment which Constantine abolished on religious grounds (Victor, *Caes.* 41.4; Sozomenus, *HE* 1.8.13).[21] Third, the content of the law, which refers to accusations for *maiestas,* fits appropriately into the circumstances following the defeat and death of Maximinus in 313.[22]

315–324   Julius Julianus

Prefect of Egypt in 314 (*P. Cairo Isid.* 73), but attested as praetorian prefect with Petronius Annianus on 28 April 315 (Optatus, App. 8), and by two inscriptions, one earlier than October 316 (*ILS* 8938: Tropaeum Traiani), the other later than 1 March 317 (*AE* 1938.85 = *I. Ephesos* 312). He appears to have remained in office until Licinius abdicated in September 324 (Libanius, *Orat.* 18.9).

2. 317–324

Between 1 March 317 and his abdication, Licinius seems to have retained Julius Julianus as his praetorian prefect (*I. Ephesos* 312; Libanius, *Orat.* 18.9). The Caesars Licinius and Constantinus were both infants who resided

---

17. Seeck, *Regesten* 75, 169; Chastagnol, *Fastes* 75 n. 36; *PLRE* 1.590, Maximus 49.

18. As demonstrated in other cases by Seeck, *Regesten* 111 ff.

19. *ZPE* 21 (1976), 275 ff.

20. In *ZPE* 21 (1976), 275, I inexcusably overlooked the fragment from Sinope, which was originally published by J. Moreau, *Historia* 5 (1956), 254 ff. Professor Habicht most kindly showed me a photograph of the fragment found at Pergamum. It confirms the reading *etiam ad praesides* which I proposed in line 47. Observe the contrast between the plural *ad praefectos nostros* and the singular *ad...rationalem et magistrum privatae* (lines 46 ff.): the former reflects the fact that the law was issued in the joint name of Constantine and Licinius, the latter the fact that Licinius had one official bearing each of the titles.

21. On these grounds, A. A. T. Ehrhardt, *TU* 64 (1957), 117 f., also retained the date of 314 and attributed the law to Licinius—though he assumed that Constantine too must have promulgated the law in the West.

22. For the purge of prominent pagans in 313, Eusebius, *HE* 9.11.3 ff.

with their parents and hence had no separate establishment.[23] The prefects of Constantine and the Caesar Crispus, however, present problems. The names attested and alleged will be considered in the alphabetical order of their last names.

1. Petronius Annianus, cos. 314

Still in office after 1 March 317, with Julius Julianus as his only colleague in the prefecture (*I. Ephesos* 312).

2. Junius Bassus, cos. 331

Attested as prefect by laws whose transmitted dates run from 18 March 320 (*CJ* 7.57.7) to 20 October 331 (*CTh* 1.5.3),[24] and styled praetorian prefect by papyri which name him as one of the consuls of 331. Since an inscription records that Bassus was *praefectus praetorio per annos XIIII* (*AE* 1964.203 = 1975.370: Aqua Viva, in Etruria), it may be inferred that Bassus was prefect from 318 to early 332.[25] The date of his appointment suggests that he was praetorian prefect of Crispus in Gaul — where he may have remained during the war of 324.[26]

3. Menander

Five laws are addressed *Menandro* with no office specified (*CTh* 15.1.2 (11 April 321), 4.13.2 (13 July 321), 4.13.3 (1 August 321), 11.27.2 (6 July 322), 8.5.4 (22 June 326)). Since Menander is clearly in Africa and superior to provincial governors including the proconsul of Africa, it has been argued that he must be a praetorian prefect.[27] But he could equally well be a *comes* with authority over the African diocese.[28] If so, then the transmitted date of the earliest of the five laws will need to be emended to 11 April 322.[29]

4. Petronius Probianus, cos. 322

A praetorian prefecture has been inferred, albeit with hesitation, from a law of 27 February 321 which neither names his office nor gives any real clue to its identification (*CTh* 9.42.1).[30] The inference appears to be contradicted by

23. Chapter V.

24. On the laws addressed to Bassus, see G. Evrard, *MEFR* 74 (1962), 641 ff.; *PLRE* 1.154-5, Bassus 14; A. Giardina, *Helikon* 11/12 (1971/2), 253 ff. Seeck, *Regesten* 52; 166 ff., had emended away all the evidence that Bassus was praetorian prefect before 329.

25. J.-R. Palanque, *Mélanges A. Piganiol* 2 (1966), 837 ff.

26. *PLRE* 1.1048.

27. So Seeck, *Regesten* 18. He accordingly emended the date of *CTh* 8.5.4 from 326 to 320.

28. So *PLRE* 1.595/6, Menander 2.

29. Locrius Verinus was still *vicarius* of Africa on 5 May 321 (Augustine, *Contra partem Donati post gesta* 31.54, 33.56).

30. Chastagnol, *Fastes* 84; *PLRE* 1.733-734, Probianus 3; 1048; D. M. Novak, *Ancient Society* 10 (1979), 298.

the silence of an inscription honoring his grandson as "nepoti Probiani, filio Probini vv. cc. praef[f]. urbis et conss." (*ILS* 1266: Verona).

5. Vettius Rufinus, cos. 323

Several modern treatments register Vettius Rufinus as praetorian prefect from 1 December 318 to 10 August 320.[31] The evidence comprises four laws addressed to a praetorian prefect named Rufinus, whose dates in the manuscripts of the Theodosian Code are, respectively, 1 December 319 (*CTh* 5.2.1), 27 April 319 (*CTh* 6.35.3), 21 May 326 (*CTh* 13.3.2), and 10 August 313 (*CTh* 7.21.1). A date in the vicinity of 350 seems probable for all four.[32] There is no valid evidence, therefore, that the consul of 323 was ever a praetorian prefect.

6. Severus

One law dated 18 December 322 (*CTh* 3.32.1) and another dated 13 April 323 (*CJ* 3.12.3) are addressed *ad Severum* but do not give the title of his office. It has been conventional to identify him as a praetorian prefect and also as the recipient of a law which the manuscripts transmit as issued on 23 January 321 and addressed *ad Severum p. u.* (*CTh* 6.22.1: Seeck emended the year to 324).[33] The Severus of the first two laws might equally well be a *vicarius,* and the Severus of the third the Julius Severus attested as *vicarius Italiae* at this period[34] — indeed the first Severus and the second may be identical. In any event, it is not prudent to infer from these three laws alone that Acilius Severus, cos. 323, was praetorian prefect in 322–324.

7. Volusianus

A law of 1 August 321 or 324 is addressed *ad Volusianum* (*CTh* 13.3.1). The correct date has been suggested as c. 314 or 354, in order to make the recipient of the law either C. Ceionius Rufius Volusianus, cos. 311, 314, as *praefectus urbi* or a later C. Ceionius Rufius Volusianus as praetorian prefect of Illyricum.[35] But emendation is not necessary: Volusianus could be either a praetorian prefect or a *vicarius* in 321 (the law deals with the immunity of doctors and teachers), and may be identified as a son of the consul of 311 and 314.[36]

31. Seeck, *Regesten* 166 ff., emending the dates of the laws of 319, 326 and 313 to 318, 320 and 320; J.-R. Palanque, *Essai* (1933), 4 f.; E. Groag, *Die römischen Reichsbeamten von Achaia in spätrömischer Zeit* (*Dissertationes Pannonicae* 1.14, 1946), 20; W. Ensslin, *RE* 22 (1954), 2496; Stein, *Bas-Empire* 1.473; Chastagnol, *Fastes* 66.

32. *PLRE* 1.774; 783.

33. Seeck, *Regesten* 172 f.; W. Ensslin, *RE* 22 (1954), 2496; Stein, *Bas-Empire* 1.473; Chastagnol, *Fastes* 77.

34. So *PLRE* 1.831, Severus 3; 836, Severus 25.

35. Respectively, T. Mommsen, *Codex Theodosianus* 1.1 (Berlin, 1904), ccxvi; *PLRE* 1.978–980, Volusianus 5.

36. *JRS* 65 (1975), 47. The identification of this Volusianus as the consul of 311 and 314 holding a second praetorian prefecture (Seeck, *Regesten* 465; Chastagnol, *Fastes* 57 f.) is disproved by the allusions to his career in Firmicus Maternus, *Math.* 2.29.10, 12, cf. *JRS* 65 (1975), 47.

The results of the preceding discussion can easily be summarized: only three prefects are attested with certainty between 317 and 324, viz. Petronius Annianus (prefect of Constantine: length of tenure unknown), Julius Julianus (prefect of Licinius for the whole period), and Junius Bassus (?prefect of Crispus), whose prefecture probably began in 318.

3. SEPTEMBER 324–22 MAY 337

Toward the end of Constantine's life, Eusebius remarks, each of his sons possessed a separate imperial establishment of armies, military commanders, and civilian counselors to administer the territory which he had been assigned (*VC*4.51/52). It may be assumed that each Caesar also had a praetorian prefect of his own. At the same time, however, some prefects received a specific geographical area to govern—and others perhaps transferred their services from one emperor to another. The prefects from September 324 to May 337, therefore, will be discussed in the order in which they are attested for the first time.

1. Junius Bassus, cos. 331
   Prefect from 318 to 332.[37]

2. Fl. Constantius, cos. 327
   First attested by a law annulling the laws and constitutions of Licinius which bears the transmitted date *XVII Kal. Iun.*, i.e. 16 May, of 324 (*CTh* 15.14.1), but which was presumably issued on 16 December 324 (*XVII Kal. Ian.*).[38] Also attested as praetorian prefect on 29 August or 28 September 325 (*CTh* 1.5.1: the ms. has *p. u.*), on 7 October 325 (*CTh* 12.1.11 + *CJ* 11.68.1), on 28 April 326 (*CTh* 8.4.1[5]: the ms. has 315), on 22 December 326 (*CTh* 4.4.1), and on 11 June 327 (*CTh* 2.24.2). One law specifically concerns the east (*CTh* 15.14.1), and another was probably published at Antioch (*CTh* 1.5.1).

3. Evagrius
   Evagrius is attested as praetorian prefect at four different dates:

a. In 326, in the east while Constantine visited Italy. Named as prefect on 27 May (*CTh* 12.1.13) and 22 November (*CJ* 2.19(20).11), Evagrius also received two imperial letters dated to 326 which omit the title (*CTh* 9.3.2:3 February; 9.7.2: 25 April) and possibly two others.[39]
b. On 18 October 329 (*CTh* 16.8.1: date emended from 315).[40]

---

37. Above, at n. 25.
38. Seeck, *Regesten* 99.
39. Viz. *CTh* 12.1.1 (mss.: 13 March 313, emended by Seeck to 326); 7.20.7 (mss.: 11 August 353, emended by Seeck to 339, but assigned to 326 in *PLRE* 1.284/5, Evagrius 2). On the date of *CJ* 2.19(20).11, Chapter V, n. 128.
40. Chapter V, n. 131. *PLRE* 1.284/5 also dates *CTh* 12.1.1 (mss. 313); 16.8.6 + 9.2 (mss.

c. On 4 (or 12) August 331 (*CTh* 7.22.3 + 12.1.19 (office not given) + 12.1.20).
d. On 22 August 336 (*CTh* 12.1.22).

It seems reasonable to infer a continuous prefecture from 326 to 336 and perhaps beyond.[41]

4. Valerius Maximus, cos. 327
   Maximus is attested as praetorian prefect at three separate dates:

a. Between 21 January 327 and 29 December 328 (*CTh* 1.5.2, 1.4.2ˢ (27 September 328), 1.16.4 + 7.20.5).
b. Between May 332 and 5 May 333 (*CJ* 7.36.7; *CTh* 8.1.3).
c. On 2 August 337 (*CTh* 13.4.2).

5. Aemilianus
   Addressed as praetorian prefect in the heading to a document read at Rome on 9 May 328 (*CTh* 11.16.4).

6. Fl. Ablabius, cos. 331
   Attested as praetorian prefect from 329 to 337 by abundant and varied evidence:

329   *CTh* 11.27.1ˢ (13 May: office not stated, the law concerns Italy), 16.2.6ˢ (1 June), 13.5.5ˢ (18 September

330   *CTh* 16.8.2 (29 November)

331   *CTh* 5.9.1 (17 April), 3.16.1

332   Athanasius, *Festal Letter* 4.5 (at Constantine's court c. January)

333   *Const. Sirm.* 1 (5 May); *CTh* 7.22.5 (13 November)

337   *AE* 1925.72 = *ILT* 814 (summer); Eunapius, *Vit. Phil.* 6.3.9–13, p. 464 (dismissal by Constantius)

Not precisely dated   Eunapius, *Vit. Phil.* 6.2.10 ff., p. 463 (at the court in Constantinople); Ammianus 20.11.3; Palladius, *Hist. Laus.* 56; *Vita Olympiadis* 2 (ed. A.-M. Malingrey, *SC* 13ᵇⁱˢ (1968), 408); Zosimus 2.40.3

7. L. Papius Pactianus, cos. 332
   Attested as praetorian prefect from 332 to 337:

332   *CTh* 3.5.4 + 5 (12 April)

334   *CTh* 14.4.1 (8 March), 10.15.2 (5 July)

335   *CTh* 8.9.1 (17 April)

337   *AE* 1925.72 = *ILT* 814 (summer 337)

---

339); 14.8.1 (mss. 315) to 329.
    41. W. Ensslin, *RE* 22 (1954), 2499 f.; A. Chastagnol, *REA* 70 (1968), 352.

It should be noted that two of the laws specifically concern the city of Rome (*CTh* 14.4.1, 8.9.1).

8. L. Aradius Valerius Proculus, cos. 340

Two Roman inscriptions which record Proculus' career disclose a very important fact about the praetorian prefecture:

> proconsuli provinciae Africae vice sacra iudicanti eidemq(ue) iudicio sacro per provincias proconsularem et Numidiam Byzacium et Tripolim itemque Mauretaniam Sitifensem et Caesariensem perfuncto officio praefecturae praetorio (*ILS* 1240)

> praefectus et idem
> hic Libyae, idem Libyae proconsul et ante (*ILS* 1241)

Taken together, the two inscriptions indicate that Proculus became praetorian prefect of Africa while he was proconsul in 332–333.[42]

9. Felix

Attested as praetorian prefect of the African diocese from 333 to 336:

333   *CTh* 3.30.5, 1.32.1 (18 April and October: neither gives the office)

334   *CTh* 12.1.21[5] (4 August: concerns African *curiales*); 13.4.1(27 August: *pp. Karthagine* and contains the injunction "sublimitas tua in provinciis Africanis ad hoc studium impellat"); 13.5.6 (7 September: *pp. Karthagine*)

335/6   *Const. Sirm.* 4 = *CTh* 16.8.5 + 9.1 (issued 21 October 335, published at Carthage on 9 March 336; contains the clause "volumus ut excellens sublimitas tua litteris suis per dioecesim sibi creditam commeantibus iudices moneat" etc.); *CJ* 4.62.4 (9 March 336)

10. Gregorius

Attested as praetorian prefect on 9 October 336 (*CTh* 11.1.3), and denounced by Donatus as *dedecus praefectorum* (Optatus 3.3, p. 73.22–23 Ziwsa). The other evidence does not record his office (*CTh* 4.6.3 (21 July 336), 3.1.2 (4 February 337); Optatus 3.10, p. 96.21: *sub Gregorio*). Presumably the successor of Felix.

---

42. No earlier year is open if Domitius Zenophilus was proconsul from 328 to 332 (Chapter IX).

11. C. Annius Tiberianus

Under the thirtieth year of Constantine, i.e. 335/6, Jerome notes, "Tiberianus vir disertus praefectus praetorio Gallias regit" (*Chronicle* 233ᵐ). The date is approximately correct, since Tiberianus is attested as praetorian prefect in summer 337 (*AE* 1925.72 = *ILT* 814), but the description of his functions could be anachronistic.

12. C. Caelius Saturninus

Saturninus' existence is known only from two Roman dedications in his honor by his son, of which one gives his career before he became praetorian prefect (*ILS* 1214), while the other describes him simply as *v. c., praefecto praetorio* (*ILS* 1215).⁴³ The date of the first inscription is between 324 and 337; unless the hypothesis of an honorary prefecture is invoked, Saturninus can plausibly be identified as Tiberianus' predecessor.⁴⁴

4. THE COLLEGE OF PREFECTS IN 337

An inscription from Tubernuc in proconsular Africa preserves a list of prefects which requires close attention (*AE* 1925.72 = *ILT* 814). Since the date is important and the number of prefects has too often been miscounted, the text must be quoted:

> Virtute clementia m[emor]ando pie-
> 2 tate omnes a[ntecellenti] d. n. Fl. Clau-
> dio Consta[n]t[ino iu]niori
> 4 ‖Aug.‖
> L. Pap. Pacatianus Fl. Ablabius ////
> 6 //// C. Annius Tiberianus Nes-
> [to]ri[u]s Timonianus viri cla-
> 8 [rissimi p]raefecti pretorio.

The erasure after the name of Fl. Ablabius was originally believed to conceal a phrase describing his status, such as *adfinis Caes(aris)*.⁴⁵ It is more plausible to

43. The fullest discussion of Saturninus' long career remains that by T. Mommsen, *Memorie dell'Istituto di Corrispondenza Archeologica* 2 (Leipzig, 1865), 298 ff.

44. So *PLRE* 1.806, 1048. The first validly attested honorary prefect is Libanius in 383/4 (*Orat.* 1.219, 30.1, 45.1). The *Suda* alleges that Constantine made a certain Theon, who was a sophist at Sidon, καὶ ἀπὸ ὑπάτων καὶ ὕπαρχος (Θ 208, 2.702 Adler), but *PLRE* 1.906, Theon 1, rightly dismisses the titles as "probably fictitious." In Eusebius *VC* 4.1.2, although F. Winkelmann prints ὑπαρχικῶν ἀξιωμάτων, the paradosis is probably ὑπατικῶν: the former stands in one manuscript only, and that a manuscript which offers many conjectures (see Winkelmann's preface (*GCS*, 1975), p. xii).

45. L. Poinssot and R. Lantier, *CRAI* 1924.232 (publishing the inscription but not venturing a precise supplement); A. Piganiol, *REA* 31 (1929), 142 ff. (proposing that Ablabius was officially styled *adfinis* or *necessarius Caesaris*).

suppose that the name of a praetorian prefect has been erased.[46] The inscription was first engraved after Constantine died (22 May 337) but before the younger Constantinus became Augustus (9 September) — or at least between the news of these two events reaching Africa. The text was subsequently revised, with *Aug.* engraved over the deleted *nob. Caes.* (line 4). It is easy to suppose that the name of the third prefect (lines 5/6) was erased at the same time. Hence the inscription originally listed a college of five praetorian prefects — not four, as some discussions of the prefects of Constantine have mistakenly assumed.[47]

The erased name can be supplied. The prefects are clearly listed in the order of their entry into the college. That is the order in two similar inscriptions of 341 and c. 343,[48] and Pacatianus (cos. 332) precedes Ablabius (cos. 331). (Hence, incidentally, it follows that Pacatianus became prefect before 13 May 329, when Ablabius is first attested as prefect.) Annius Tiberianus cannot have been appointed before 17 October 332, when he is attested as *comes* of Hispaniae (*CJ* 6.1.6);[49] therefore, the third name is that of a prefect who had entered office between c. 325 (when Ablabius was still *vicarius* of Asiana) and c. 336 (when Tiberianus was appointed). Among the attested prefects the only candidates appear to be Evagrius, attested as prefect in 326, 331, and 336, and Valerius Maximus, attested in 327–328, 332–333, and 337, and of these Maximus deserves the preference because he is attested as prefect on 2 August 337 — during the very months when the inscription of Tubernuc was engraved. The erasure in lines 5/6, therefore, conceals the name of Val. Maximus.

The functions of the prefects in 337 must be inferred from their number. Since the college of prefects numbers five, it is plausible to suppose that one prefect was attached to each emperor, while one administered the diocese of Africa. Furthermore, the evidence seems to permit the identification of the precise function of each prefect:

1. Papius Pacatianus: prefect of Constans, since he received two laws concerning Rome, which belonged to the territory formally assigned to Constans.
2. Fl. Ablabius: prefect of Constantius (Eunapius, *Vit. Phil.* 6.3.9–13, p. 464).
3. Valerius Maximus: prefect of Dalmatius. The erasure of his name implies that he suffered *damnatio memoriae* at the same time as Dalmatius was killed.
4. Annius Tiberianus: prefect of Constantinus in Gaul.
5. Nestorius Timonianus: praetorian prefect of Africa (by elimination).

46. A. Chastagnol, *REA* 70 (1968), 330 ff.

47. E.g., N. H. Baynes, *JRS* 15 (1925), 204 ff.; Jones, *LRE* 1.102; *PLRE* 1.1048, etc.

48. In 341 the college of prefects comprised Domitius Leontius (cos. 344), Antonius Marcellinus (cos. 341) and Fabius Titianus (cos. 337) (*ILS* 8944: Traiana in Thrace), about two years later Domitius Leontius, Fabius Titianus, and M. Maecius Memmius Furius Baburius Caecilianus Placidus (cos. 343) (unpublished inscription from Delphi reported in *PLRE* 1.502, 705, 918).

49. On the date of *CTh* 3.5.6, usually assumed to attest Tiberianus as *vicarius* of Hispaniae in

If these identifications are correct, it follows that no regional prefectures other than the African existed in summer 337, and it should accordingly be doubted whether Constantine created any others.[50]

5. OTHER POSSIBLE PREFECTS

1. Ulpius Silvinus, attested as praetorian prefect (*TAM* 3.126: Termessus in Pisidia). Date uncertain, but possibly between 284 and 311.[52]

2. Pomponius Januarianus was prefect of Egypt in 283/4, ordinary consul in 288, and *praefectus urbi* on 27 February 288. Either his initial status or the rapid promotion demands explanation — and the possibility that he was praetorian prefect may be entertained.[53]

3. Allectus may have been the praetorian prefect of Carausius.[54]

4. Galerius' career before 293 is totally unknown; the parallel of Constantius suggests that he was Diocletian's praetorian prefect.[55]

5. In 299 Veturius ordered the soldiers under his command to sacrifice or be dismissed from the army (Eusebius, *HE* 8.4.3, cf. *Chronicle* 227 Karst; Jerome, *Chronicle* 227[d]).[56] Although Jerome calls him *magister militiae* and Eusebius applies to him a word which he elsewhere uses of a mere *dux* (viz. ὁ στρατοπεδάρχης, cf. *HE* 9.5.2; *Mart. Pal.* (S) 13.1-3), Veturius might be the praetorian prefect of Galerius.[57]

6. At least one version of the *Passio Sabini*, which has not yet been edited critically (*BHL* 7451-54), presents Hermogenianus as a praetorian prefect with Maximian in Rome in late April 304.[58] It is not impossible that the jurist Her-

---

335, see Chapter IX, n. 17.

50. T. Mommsen, *Ges. Schr.* 6 (Berlin, 1906), 288; Jones, *LRE* 1.102.

51. The following list omits the anonymous pair of prefects attested at Rome under Maximian (*CIL* 6.36947), and the anonymous prefects attested at Rome (*CIL* 6.31387a) and Perinthus (*ILS* 665 = E. W. Bodnar and C. Mitchell, *Cyriacus of Ancona's Journeys in the Propontis and the Northern Aegean 1444-1445* (*Mem. Amer. Phil. Soc.* 112, 1976), no. 5). Rufinus, alleged as praetorian prefect when Constantine visited Antioch in 324/5 by Malalas 318/9 Bonn, appears to result from confusion with the prefect Rufinus who visited Antioch in 393, see G. Downey, *A History of Antioch in Syria* (Princeton, 1961), 650 ff.

52. H. Dessau, *PIR*[1] V 510.

53. *PLRE* 1.452/3, Ianuarianus 2.

54. Chapter II, n. 4.

55. He may have married Diocletian's daughter before 293 (Chapter IV, at nn. 45-47).

56. The date emerges from Lactantius, *Mort. Pers.* 10.1-5, with *Div. Inst.* 4.27.4-5, cf. Moreau, *Lactance* 266. The episode which provoked the purge occurred when Diocletian was in the East (*Mort. Pers.* 10.1) in the presence of both Diocletian and Galerius (*Div. Inst.* 4.27.4-5) — who departed to the Danube in 299.

57. *HSCP* 80 (1976), 246.

58. Viz. that quoted by Baronius, *Annales Ecclesiastici, anno* 301, §§ 18, 19. However, other versions style Hermogenianus *praefectus urbi:* see D. Liebs, *Hermogenians Iuris Epitomae* (*Abh. Göttingen,* Phil.-hist. Klasse[3] 57.3, 1964), 32 f.

I am grateful to Mr. W. Turpin for showing me the draft of an article on the *Passio Sabini,* in

mogenianus, who must have been at the court of Diocletian while he compiled his legal code between 293 and 295,[59] subsequently became prefect of the western Augustus.[60] However, the *Passio Sabini* can hardly be regarded as adequate attestation of his prefecture.[61]

7. The Caesar Severus commanded troops before 1 May 305 (Lactantius, *Mort. Pers.* 18.12) — conceivably as praetorian prefect of Galerius (or alternatively of Maximian).

8. Licinius may have been the praetorian prefect of Galerius. When Galerius invaded Italy in 307, he sent Licinius and Probus as envoys to Maxentius (*Origo* 7): the latter is next attested as praetorian prefect in 310.[62]

9. On 9 June 311 at Serdica, Licinius wrote a letter bestowing tax privileges on soldiers and veterans of the armies of Illyricum (*FIRA*[2] 1.93). Its recipient was a man whose full name and office are not stated, but who is twice addressed as *Dalmati carissime nobis;* he was presumably either praetorian prefect or *vicarius* of the diocese of Pannonia.

6. ATTESTED PREFECTS AND THEIR DATES

Ancient evidence and modern reconstructions must always be distinguished. To avoid confusion of the two, the following chronological list is provided; it comprises those praetorian prefects between 285 and 337 whose names are known and whose prefectures are explicitly attested by reliable evidence.

T. Cl. Aurelius Aristobulus, cos. 285	285
Afranius Hannibalianus, cos. 292	between 285 and 292
Julius Asclepiodotus, cos. 292	between 285 and 292
Flavius Valerius Constantius	288–293
Asclepiodotus	296
Asclepiades	302
Flaccinus	303
Anullinus	307
Manilius Rusticianus	shortly after 306
C. Ceionius Rufius Volusianus, cos. 311, 314	309
Tatius Andronicus, cos. 310	310
Pompeius Probus, cos. 310	310
Sabinus	311–312

---

which he defends Baronius' version and argues that the *passio* incorporates authentic documents of the early fourth century.

59. A. M. Honoré, *JRS* 69 (1979), 58 ff.

60. D. Liebs, *Hermogenians Iuris Epitomae* (1964), 34 ff.

61. It was written no earlier than the late fifth century, see F. Lanzoni, *RQ* 17 (1903), 1 ff.; A. Dufourcq, *Étude sur les Gesta Martyrum romains* 3 (Paris, 1907), 87 ff.

62. E. Groag, *RE* 14 (1930), 2432, 2439, held that Licinius and Probus were colleagues in the praetorian prefecture in 307.

Ruricius Pompeianus	312
Maximus	314
Petronius Annianus, cos. 314	313–317
Julius Julianus, cos. 325	315–324
Junius Bassus, cos. 331	318–332
Fl. Constantius, cos. 327	324–327
Evagrius	326, 329, 331, 336
Valerius Maximus, cos. 327	327/8, 332/3, 337
Aemilianus	328
L. Papius Pacatianus, cos. 332	329–337
Fl. Ablabius, cos. 331	329–337
L. Aradius Valerius Proculus, cos. 340 (Africa)	332/3
Felix (Africa)	333–336
Gregorius (Africa)	336/7
C. Annius Tiberianus	337
C. Caelius Saturninus	before 22 May 337
Nestorius Timonianus (Africa)	337

7. A HYPOTHETICAL RECONSTRUCTION

From 285 to 324 all the known praetorian prefects functioned as deputies of the emperor to whom they were attached. But when only eighteen prefects are indubitably attested over a period of forty years, for most of which at least four emperors ruled at a time, it is clear that many prefects must have vanished from the historical record. Accordingly, it becomes legitimate to speculate about the gaps, and this chapter has suggested that three emperors besides Constantius had served as praetorian prefect immediately before their elevation to the purple—Galerius with Diocletian before spring 293, Severus before 1 May 305, and Licinius with Galerius before 11 November 308. If these conjectures are well-founded, they will emphasize the importance of military affairs in understanding the achievement of Diocletian and his colleagues.

At the very end of Constantine's reign, likewise, all the praetorian prefects, except the prefect who administered the African diocese, were attached to emperors. Hence by extrapolation from an inscription which records the prefects in office in the summer of 337 (*AE* 1925.72 = *ILT* 814), the college of prefects can be reconstructed as it existed from the proclamation of Dalmatius (18 September 335) to the death of Constantine (22 May 337):

prefect of Constantine	Evagrius (whose prefecture automatically lapsed when the emperor died)
prefect of Constantinus	Annius Tiberianus
prefect of Constantius	Fl. Ablabius
prefect of Constans	L. Papius Pacatianus

| prefect of Dalmatius | Valerius Maximus |
| prefect in Africa | Felix, then Gregorius |

The functions of the praetorian prefects of the intervening period are less clear.[63] Too many are attested for all to be assigned to emperors,[64] and at least one besides the prefect in Africa operated independently of an emperor: Fl. Constantius, who probably resided at Antioch between 324 and 326.[65] But Constantine did not divide the empire permanently into regional prefectures, as Zosimus alleged (2.23.1 ff.);[66] except in Africa from 332/3 onward, he gave prefects primarily territorial jurisdictions only as a temporary measure. The regional prefectures of the late fourth century came into permanent existence only after Constantine's sons frustrated his plans for the division and administration of the empire by a harmonious college of emperors.[67]

63. The hypothesis of collegiate prefectures (invoked by W. Ensslin, *RE* 22 (1954), 2499 f.) no longer needs to be considered seriously, see A. H. M. Jones, *JRS* 54 (1964), 78 ff. = *Roman Economy* (Oxford, 1974), 375 ff.

64. The attempt to do so in *PLRE* 1.1048, etc., involves too many transfers from one emperor to another to be convincing.

65. Constantius' functions passed to Dalmatius, the half-brother of Constantine, who resided at Antioch with the title of *censor* (Chapter VI, at nn. 63, 64).

66. For modern formulations of the idea (which Zosimus has merely repeated from Eunapius), see O. Seeck, *Rh. Mus.,* n.f. 69 (1914), 1 ff.; J.-R. Palanque, *Essai* (1933) 14 ff.; Stein, *Bas-Empire* 1².117 f.

67. Jones, *LRE* 1.370.

CHAPTER IX

ADMINISTRATORS OF DIOCESES
AND GOVERNORS OF PROVINCES

The lists of provincial governors in the first volume of the *Prosopography of the Later Roman Empire* have been commended by a reputable historian as "a model of what can be achieved by the patient collation of all the primary evidence, combined with secure technical principles of interpretation."[1] That favorable verdict is not at all justified, at least for the reigns of Diocletian and Constantine, where the lists are not merely inaccurate in detail, but often misleading in principle: the editors have usually forgotten that proconsulates normally lasted for approximately a twelvemonth;[2] they enter many governors on the strength of dubious *acta martyrum* alone, even when they possess fictitious or anachronistic titles;[3] and they fail to present some combined provinces (such as Phrygia et Caria) and some divided provinces (such as the two Numidias) as the separate entities which they really were.[4] Revised fasti of *vicarii, comites,* and praetorian prefects in charge of dioceses and of governors of provinces are here offered for the period between Diocletian's accession (20 November 284) and the day on which Constantine's sons were proclaimed Augusti (9 September 337). Provinces are grouped by diocese, the dioceses are considered in the order in which they occur in the Verona List, and the provinces within each in a rough geographical order.

1. J. F. Matthews, *CR*, n.s. 24 (1974), 100.
2. See the fasti of the proconsular provinces, *PLRE* 1.1072–1077.
3. Chapter X.
4. Chapter XIII. Observe, however, the separate list of governors of Lycia et Pamphylia (*PLRE* 1.1100).

It should be noted that these lists are exclusive rather than inclusive. Although some names have been included on the basis of conjectural arguments or attributions, the underlying principles of compilation are moderately rigorous: bogus names are all excluded, while many officials whose date or precise post is uncertain have been either omitted or relegated to footnotes under the appropriate diocese or province. The lists are not intended to be definitive; their function is rather to provide a framework for interpreting doubtful cases and for studying imperial administration during a period of rapid change.[5]

1. *VICARII* AND *COMITES* OF DIOCESES

ORIENS

Vicarii

298	Aemilius Rusticianus	*P. Oxy.* 1469[6]
shortly before 303	Sossianus Hierocles	Lactantius, *Mort. Pers.* 16.4 (*vicarius*); Eusebius, *Contra Hieroclem* 4, p. 373.10/11; 20, p. 386, 30/1 (date and diocese implied)[7]
?	Julianus	*P. Oxy.* 2952

If Julianus is identical with Julius Julianus, the date must be between 15 January 314 and 28 April 315.[8]

?	?Festianus	Malalas 314 Bonn (confused and unreliable)
325, June 17– Dec. 25	Valerius Maximus	*CTh* 7.20.4 (17 June), 12.1.10 (11 July), 15.12.1 (1 Oct.), 12.1.12 (25 Dec.); *CJ* 11.50.1 (undated)
326, April 17– Sept. 1	Dracilianus	*CTh* 2.33.1[s] (17 April), 16.5.1 (1 Sept.); Eusebius, *VC* 2.31.2

---

5. For *duces* of provinces and other military commanders, see *PLRE* 1.1117 ff. (not wholly reliable).

In the following lists a date in the form, e.g., "293/305" means "at some time between 1 March 293 and 1 May 305" (for the relevant imperial colleges, see Chapter I), whereas a date in the form, e.g., "290–294" means "continuously from 290 to 294." Detailed cross-references within this chapter or to Chapters VI–VIII, X, and XV are not given.

6. On Rusticianus' office, Vandersleyen, *Chronologie* 62 f.

7. *HSCP* 80 (1976), 244 f.

8. Identity is assumed by A. K. Bowman, *JRS* 66 (1976), 162 n. 96.

Comites[9]

?before 332	Flavius Felicianus	Malalas 318/9 Bonn

Malalas states that Constantine appointed Felicianus as the first *comes Orientis* in 335; either the date is wrong or Felicianus is probably not the first *comes*.

325, Oct. 7/ 337	Januarius	*CJ* 11.68.2 (undated, but later than *CJ* 11.68.1, cf. *CTh* 12.1.11)
c. 330/336	Q. Flavius Maesius Egnatius Lollianus	Firmicus Maternus, *Math.* 1 praef. 7; *ILS* 1225 (Rome)

Lollianus was subsequently proconsul of Africa, in 336–337.

PONTICA

Vicarius

?	Lucilius Crispus	*AE* 1924.89 (Ancyra)

Crispus' dedication to a single Augustus seems strictly to imply a date of 324/337 or 350/361.[10] Nevertheless, the correct date might be 311/313.

ASIANA

Vicarii

324/326	Flavius Ablabius	*ILS* 6091 = *MAMA* 7.305 (Orcistus)
334, May 19– 335, May 7	Veronicianus	*CTh* 8.1.4 + 8.15.2, 11.6.6^s

Comes

330, Feb. 22	Tertullianus	*CTh* 2.26.1

THRACIA

None attested

---

9. G. Downey, *A Study of the Comites Orientis and the Consulares Syriae* (Diss. Princeton, 1939), 8 ff. A law of 331 contains the clause "nec prius praefecti praetorio aut comitis Orientis vel alterius spectabilis iudicis imploret auxilium" (*CJ* 3.13.4). With appeal to T. Mommsen, *Memorie dell'Istituto di Corrispondenza Archeologica* 2 (1865), 306, Downey holds that the mention of the *comes Orientis* is there interpolated — so that he may sustain Malalas' date of 335 for the creation of the office. Archelaus, whom Downey dates to 335, was probably *comes Orientis* after 337, see *PLRE* 1.100, Archelaus 1.

10. *PLRE* 1.233, Crispus 5.

MOESIAE[11]

Vicarii

319	Januarinus	*CTh* 9.1.2 (13 Jan.: office not stated, but *acc(epta) V Kal. Aug. Corintho*); *CJ* 6.1.5 (15 Feb.: *ad Ianuarium,* office not stated); *CTh* 9.37.1 (26 Nov.: *ad Ianuarinum p. u.*)[12]
c. 321	C. Caelius Saturninus	*ILS* 1214 (Rome)

PANNONIAE

None explicitly attested[13]

BRITANNIAE

319, Nov. 20   L. Papius Pacatianus   *CTh* 11.7.2

GALLIAE

None validly attested

VIENNENSIS

None validly attested

ITALIA

Correctores Italiae

(a) active in the south

c. 282–c. 290   C. Ceionius Rufius Volusianus   *ILS* 1213 (Rome); *CIL* 10.1655 (Puteoli)

(b) active in the north

284   M. Aurelius Julianus Sabinus   Victor, *Caes.* 39.10

Proclaimed Augustus *cum Venetos correctura ageret:* Zosimus 1.73.1 alleges that he was praetorian prefect.[14]

---

11. Acacius is attested as *comes Macedoniae* on 27 February 327 (*CTh* 11.3.2). Not necessarily a *comes* in charge of a diocese (as *PLRE* 1.1081): rather, a *comes* in charge of confiscating temple treasures in the province of Macedonia (cf. Eusebius, *Triac.* 8.2) — a function he performed in Palestine (Eusebius, *VC* 3.53.2, 62.1).

12. On Januarinus' post, *PLRE* 1.453, Ianuarinus 1; G. Polara, *PP* 29 (1974), 262.

13. The Dalmatius who received a letter of Licinius dated 9 June 311 could be a *vicarius Pannoniarum* (*FIRA*[2] 1.93).

14. *PLRE* 1.474, Julianus 24; 480, Julianus 38, postulates two homonymous and contemporaneous usurpers. In favor of identity, *PIR*[2] A 1538.

286	Acilius Clarus	*CIL* 5.8205 (near Aquileia)
287	T. Aelius Marcianus	*CIL* 11.1594 (Florence)
289, Aug. 19– 290, Feb. 14	Paetus Honoratus	*CJ* 7.56.3 + 9.2.9, 2.10.1 (no office stated); *ILS* 614 (Patavium: 284/ 290)
290, Sept. 10	Numidius	*CJ* 7.35.3 (area of activity neither stated nor implied)
before 293, March 1	T. Flavius Postumius Titianus	*AE* 1919.52 (Comum)

(c) *corrector utriusque Italiae*

| ?290/293 | L. Aelius Helvius
Dionysius | *ILS* 1211 (Rome) |

(d) regional *correctores*

| ?293 | T. Flavius Postumius
Titianus | *ILS* 2941; *CIL* 6.1419b (Rome) |

corrector Italiae Transpadanae (*ILS* 2941) / *reg. Tra*[(*CIL* 6.1419b)[15]

Vicarii[16]

| c. 300/c. 325 | Caecilianus | *ILS* 1218 (Mutina) |
| ?318, Jan. 23–
Sept. 7 | Julius Severus | *CTh* 6.22.1 (emended), 6.35.4 (emended), 11.30.9^s, 7.22.2^s, 8.18.2^s |

The ms. attestation of Severus' date, name, and office is as follows:

CTh	6.22.1	23 Jan. 321	*ad Severum p. u.*
	6.35.4	15 Mar. 321	*ad Iulium Verum vic(ari)um Italiae*
	11.30.9	22 June 319	*ad Severum vic(ari)um*
	7.22.2	30 July 326	*ad Severum*
	8.18.2	7 Sept. 319	*Iulio Severo*

| 325, Feb. 25 | ?Silvius Paulus | *CTh* 1.15.1 (stating the office as the otherwise unknown *mag*[i] *Italiae*) |

15. A. Chastagnol, *La Préfecture urbaine à Rome sous le Bas-Empire* (Paris, 1960), 21 ff.; *Fastes* 43; *Historia* 12 (1963), 351, takes *ILS* 2941 and *CIL* 6.1419b to refer to the same post as *AE* 1919.52 (*corr. Ital.*), which he dates to 291. It is here proposed that Titianus may have been *corrector* in 293 when Diocletian divided Italy into provinces (cf. Chapter XIII).

16. *CTh* 9.8.1 (4 April 326) is addressed *ad Bassum vic. Italiae*. This is accepted by A. Chastagnol, *Historia* 12 (1963), 354, who also adduces *CTh* 2.10.4 (8 March 326: *ad Bassum p. u.*); 16.5.2 (25 September 326: *ad Bassum*). The recipient of all three laws is identified as the praetorian prefect Junius Bassus by *PLRE* 1.154.

For *vicarii* of the city of Rome, see A. Chastagnol, *Préfecture* 463 ff.

HISPANIAE

Vicarii

298, Oct. 30	Aurelius Agricolanus	*Passio Marcelli* (G. Lanata, *Byzantion* 42 (1972), 513 ff.)
306/337	Q. Aeclanius Hermias	*CIL* 2.2203 (Corduba)
?324/326	Septimius Acindynus	*CIL* 2.4107 = *I. Tarraco* 97

Acindynus dedicated a statue to a Caesar whose name has been erased, probably Crispus, while the governor Badius Macrinus dedicated two statues, of Constantine as *victor* and Constantius Caesar, with virtually identical wording (*CIL* 2. 4106, 4108 = *I. Tarraco* 95, 96)

?332, July 15	C. Annius Tiberianus	*CTh* 3.5.6[17]

Comites

316, Dec. 4– 317, Jan. 19	Octavianus	*CTh* 9.1.1, 12.1.4
332, Oct. 17	C. Annius Tiberianus	*CJ* 6.1.6
333, May 4– 336, May 19	-us Severus	*CTh* 8.12.5 + 11.39.2, 8.18.3 (30 March 334); *AE* 1915.33 = 1935.4 (Emerita: 333/335); *CTh* 13.5.8

AFRICA

Vicarii

303–308	Valerius Alexander	*AE* 1942/3.81 (Aqua Viva: 303); *IRT* 464 (Lepcis: under Maxentius); Victor, *Caes.* 40.17; Zosimus 2.12.2 (the usurper L. Domitius Alexander as *vicarius* of Africa)
312–313	Patricius	Eusebius, *HE* 10.6.4 (winter 312/3, implying appointment in Nov. 312)
314, spring	?Aelafius[18]	Optatus, App. 3

17. *CTh* 3.5.6 is addressed "ad Tiberianum vicarium Hispaniarum" and the subscription reads "dat. id. Iul. Constant(ino)p(oli). accepta XIIII k. Mai. Hispali Nepotiano et Facundo conss." Since the date of publication is given as 18 April 336, the year of issue would normally be assumed to be 335 (so Seeck, *Regesten* 183). But Severus is attested as *comes Hispaniarum* from 333 to 336 (though *PLRE* 1.831, Severus 4, emends the date of *CTh* 13.5.8 from 336 to 335), and the official in charge of the diocese was a *comes* in 337/340 (*AE* 1927.165, re-edited by A. Chastagnol, *MEFR (A)* 88 (1976), 260 ff.). It seems simpler, therefore, to postulate that, though published at Hispalis in April 336, the constitution was issued in July 332.

18. The name (attested by a single careless ms.) is "unmöglich," according to O. Seeck, *ZKG*

314, summer and autumn	Aelius Paulinus	Optatus, App. 2, p. 197.17/8, 26; p. 200.20/1 Ziwsa
315, Feb.	Verus	Augustine, *Epp.* 88.4; *Contra Cresconium* 3.70.81
315, April 28– 316, Jan. 11	Domitius Celsus	Optatus, App. 8 (28 April, year not stated); *CTh* 9.18.1 = *CJ* 9.20.16 (1 Aug. 315); Optatus, App. 7 (c. Nov. 315); *CTh* 1.22.1 (11 Jan. 316)
316, Mar. 21– Nov. 10	Eumelius	*CTh* 9.40.2ˢ (21 March 315 mss.); Augustine, *Contra Cresconium* 3.71.82; *Brev. Coll.* 3.19.37; *Contra partem Donati post gesta* 33.56 (10 Nov. 316)
318, Nov. 16– 321, May 5	Locrius Verinus	*CTh* 9.15.1 (16 Nov. 318), 9.21.1 (18 March 319), 9.34.1 (29 March 319), 2.19.1 (13 April 319); Augustine, *Epp.* 141.9; *Brev. Coll.* 3.22.40, 3.24.42; *Contra partem Donati post gesta* 31.54, 33.56 (5 May 321)

Comites

321, July 13– 326, June 22	Menander	*CTh* 4.13.2 (13 July 321), 4.13.3 (1 Aug. 321), 15.1.2 (11 Apr. 322: the mss. have 321), 11.27.2 (6 July 322), 8.5.4 (22 June 326)
326, July 30– 327, Apr. 21	C. Annius Tiberianus	*CTh* 12.5.1, 12.1.15; cf. *Karthago* 1 (1950), 200, frag. 11 (c. 369)

Praefecti praetorio (from Chapter VIII.3,4)

332/3	L. Aradius Valerius Proculus
333, April 18–336, Mar. 9	Felix
336, July 21–337, Feb. 4	Gregorius
337, June/Sept.	Nestorius Timonianus

Dated *Vicarii* Whose Diocese Is Unknown

314, March 6– 315, Feb. 5	Ursus	*CTh* 2.7.1; *CJ* 3.26.5

---

30 (1909), 200. L. Duchesne, *MEFR* 10 (1890), 645 f., had plausibly suggested that *Aelafio* is merely a corruption of *Aelio Paulino* (not noted in *PLRE* 1.16).

Vicarius of a western diocese, cf. Eusebius, HE 10.6.1 (rationalis of Africa in winter 312/3)

314, April 29– 315, May 15	Dionysius	CJ 7.22.3, 3.1.8 (office not stated)

Probably vicarius of an eastern diocese[19]

322, Dec. 18– 323, April 13	?Severus	CTh 3.32.1; CJ 3.12.3 (office not stated)
330, April 29	Valerianus	CTh 3.5.3[20]

2. PROVINCIAL GOVERNORS

DIOCESE OF ORIENS

Libya Superior

None attested

Libya Inferior

None attested

Thebais (praeses)[21]

295, Feb.	Herodianus	P. Oxy. 43 recto, col. 6.3/4, 10/1, as revised by T. C. Skeat, Papyri from Panopolis (Dublin, 1964), xviii
298–300	Julius Athenodorus	P. Beatty Panopolis 1 (Sept. 298), 2 (Jan. 300)
301, Dec.	Aurelius Reginus	P. Lacau, Annales du Service des Antiquités de l'Égypte 34 (1934), 30, figs. 8–10, cf. J. Lallemand, L'administration 250, with Planche I

---

19. Seeck, *Regesten* 53, 162.

20. Seeck, *Regesten* 180; *PLRE* 1.938, identify Valerianus as the recipient of *CJ* 6.1.4 (mss.: 27 June 317), whose date they emend to 330. But *CJ* 6.1.4 does not state its recipient's office, and its original date may be 28 December 317 (Chapter V, n. 117).

21. For the governors of all the Egyptian provinces, Lallemand, *L'administration* 236 ff.; A. K. Bowman, *JRS* 66 (1976). 162.

The statement by Epiphanius that Culcianus was "prefect of the Thebaid" while Hierocles was prefect of Egypt, i.e. in 310/11, should be disregarded (*Panarion* 68.1.4). Anysius, whom *PLRE* 1.79 enters as "governor of the Thebaid ?c.a. 323," is more probably a retired member of the governor's staff (*P. Giessen* 117).

305/306–307, Feb./March	Satrius Arrianus	*P. Oxy.* 2665 (305/306); *P. Grenfell* 78 (Oasis Magna); *P. Flor.* 33 (Hermopolis Magna: 305/311)[22]
313, Nov. 20–314	Antonius Gregorius	*CPR* 1.233 (Hermopolis Magna: 20 Nov. 313); *P. Panopolis* 23.12 (314 or later), 24.8 (undated)[23]
?	Aurelius Aeneas	*P. Panopolis* 25 (undated, but apparently early fourth century)
322, Mar. 29–326, Nov. 19	Valerius Victorinianus	*P. Oxy.* 3123 (29 March 322); *P. Panopolis* 27 (April or May 323); *P. Strasbourg* 296 (Hermopolis: 19 Nov. 326); *P. Panopolis* 24 (undated); *P. Cairo inv.* 10466; *Stud. Pal.* 20.100 (both from Hermopolis and undated)[24]
329, July 9	Flavius Gregorius	*P. Panopolis* 28
332, July–Aug. 5	Flavius Quintilianus	*P. Panopolis* 29.4 (between Jan. and 24 July), 30 (5 Aug.)

Aegyptus (praefectus)[25]

285 or 286, early	M. Aurelius Diogenes	*P. Oxy.* 1456 (Diocletian as sole emperor); *P. Cairo inv.* 10531, quoted by A. Stein, *Die Präfekten von Ägypten der römischen Kaiserzeit* (Bern, 1950), 156 (undated)
before 287	Peregrinus	*P. Oxy.* 2343

22. On *P. Flor.* 33, see J. R. Rea, *CE* 46 (1971), 142 ff. Arrianus is also prominent as a persecutor in Coptic hagiography (Vandersleyen, *Chronologie* 86 ff.).

23. *P. Panopolis* 20–31 were published by L. C. Youtie, D. Hagedorn, and H. C. Youtie, *ZPE* 10 (1973), 101 ff.

24. An abnormally long tenure, see D. Hagedorn, *Proceedings of the Twelfth International Congress of Papyrology* (*American Studies in Papyrology* 7, 1970), 210.

25. For prefects down to 299, G. Bastianini, *ZPE* 17 (1975), 318 ff. The following prefects should be removed from the list in *PLRE* 1.1083/4: Aurelius Mercurius, see J. D. Thomas, *JHS* 84 (1964), 207; A. K. Bowman, *BASP* 6 (1969), 35 ff.; Apollonius, who appears to result from conflating the martyr Apollonius with the unnamed prefect who tried him (*Historia Monachorum in Aeypto* (Greek) 19.9); 'Eustratius'; 'Armenius'; Titinnius Clodianus, cf. G. Bastianini, *ZPE* 17 (1975), 313 f. The present list excludes the prefects attested without a precise date by *P. Rein.* 51 (Aurelius Proculinus): *P. Amherst* 82 (-banus); *P. Oxy.* 1504 (anonymous); [Julian], *Epp.* 201 (Himerius, cf. *PLRE* 1.437).

287–290	C. Valerius Pompeianus	*P. Oxy.* 888 (before 25 Oct. 287); 2343 (287/8); 1503 (288/9); *P. Amherst* 137 (288/9); *P. Oxy.* 1642 (March/April 289); *P. Oxy.* 1252 (15 Sept. 289); *PSI* 461 (Feb./March 290); *P. Oxy.* 2612 (undated)
291, June 10–292, Feb.	Titius Honoratus	*P. Oxy.* 3296; *BGU* 2069 (Jan. 292); *P.Oxy.* 2704 (Feb. 292); *Sammelbuch* 7205 (Great Oasis: undated)
292/3	Rupilius Felix	*P. Oxy.* 2712 (292/3); *PSI* 298 (undated)[26]
297, Mar. 16	Aristius Optatus	*P. Cairo Isid.* 1; *P. Oxy.* 2713 (undated)

During the revolt of 297/8, a *corrector* is attested:

297, Sept. 5–9	Aurelius Achilleus	*P. Cairo Isid.* 62 (Karanis); *P. Mich.* 220 = *Sammelbuch* 7252 (Philadelphia)

After the revolt, *praefecti* of undivided Egypt are attested until 314:

298–299	Aelius Publius	*P. Cairo Isid.* 66, 67 (Karanis: 298/9); *P. Oxy.* 1204 (autumn 299); *OGIS* 718 = *Sammelbuch* 8278 (Alexandria: after 298); *P. Oxy.* 1416, 2133; *P. Amherst* 82 (undated)
300	Claudius Cleopatrus	*P. Oxy.* 3301 (300), 3302 (29 Aug. 300/6 June 301), 3303 (undated)
301, 6 June–307, Feb. 4	Clodius Culcianus	*P. Oxy.* 3304 (6 June 301); 71 (28 Feb. 303); 2187 (Jan. 304); 895 (spring 305); 1104 (29 May 306); *PSI* 716 (?306); *Acta Phileae* (*P. Bodmer* XX: 4 Feb. 307); *P. Oxy.* 2558; *?P. Amherst* 83; Eusebius, *HE* 9.11.4
308	Valerius Victorinus	*P. Oxy.* 2674 (308); *P. Lond. inv.* 2226 (Oxyrhynchus: before Sept. 308)

26. G. Bastianini, *ZPE* 17 (1975), 320, n. 1. The papyrus was previously read as attesting a prefect whose name ended in "-elius" (so *PLRE* 1.998).

308, Sept.– 309, June 22	Aelius Hyginus	*P. Lond. inv.* 2226; *P. Oxy.* 2667, 2666 (undated)
310, April– 311	Sossianus Hierocles	*P. Oxy.* 3120 (April 310): *P. Cairo* *Isid.* 69 (310); *P. Berol. inv.* 21654 = *P. Coll. Youtie* 75 (Jan./July 311);[27] Eusebius, *Mart. Pal.* (L) 5.3; Epiphanius, *Pan.* 68.1.4
312, Aug. 17	Aurelius Ammonius	*P. Flor.* 36 + Addenda, p. xi = *Chrestomathie* 2.64 (Theadelphia); *PSI* 886 (Oxyrhynchus: after 310– 311), 449 (undated)
314, Jan. 15/ Aug. 28	Julius Julianus	*P. Cairo Isid.* 73 (Karanis: 314); *Sammelbuch* 9192 (undated); Ju- lian, *Epp.* 60 Bidez[28]

Aegyptus Iovia (315–324)

None attested

Aegyptus Herculia (315–324) (praeses)

315, Dec. 27– 316, April 1	Aurelius Antonius	*P. Cairo Isid.* 74 (Karanis: 27 Dec. 315); *P. Merton* 91 (Karanis: 30 Jan. 316); *P. Oxy.* 2113 (Jan. 316); 896, col. 2.29 (1 April 316); *P. Oxy.* 29 4B. 48/G(6–7)a (undated)
318, April 13– 321, Dec. 12	Valerius Ziper[29]	*Sammelbuch* 9187 (Karanis: 13 April 318); 9188 = *P. Cairo Isid.* 76 (Karanis: 15 July 318); *P. Ryl-* *ands* 653 (?Theadelphia: 3 June 318, 319, or 320); *P. Cairo Isid.* 77 (Karanis: 320); *P. Theadelphia* 13 (12 Dec. 321); *P. New York* 1a (Karanis); *P. Theadelphia* 19; *CPR* 5.7 (all three undated)

27. On the date, H. Maehler, *Collectanea Papyrologica: Texts Published in Honor of H. C.*
Youtie 2 (Bonn, 1976), 531: the consular date presents Galerius as still alive, while the earliest
known Egyptian document which reflects his decease is dated 12 July 311 (*P. Cornell* 13.24–26, cf.
J. D. Thomas, *ZPE* 6 (1970), 181 f.).

28. On the text of this letter, see J. Bidez, *Mélanges P. Thomas* (Bruges, 1930), 57 ff.

29. For the name of the prefect, J. R. Rea, on *CPR* 5.7.2. *PLRE* 1.464; 993, registers Q. Iper
and Valerius Ziper as separate governors (in 321–322 and 318–320 respectively).

323, Aug. 17– 324	Sabinianus	*P. Oxy.* 60 = *Chrestomathie* 2.43 (17 Aug. 323); *P. Oxy.* 3260 (324); *PSI* 452; *P. Rylands* 659 (undated)

Arabia Nova (?315–324)

None attested

Aegyptus (reunited in or soon after 324) (praefectus)

?c. 325	Caecilius -ultius	*P. Strasbourg* 560
before 328 (possibly be- fore 315)	Aurelius Apion	*PSI* 685 (Oxyrhynchus)

Apion is διασημότατος (as is the preceding prefect); all prefects after 339 were λαμπρότατοι and all prefects between 328 and 339 are probably known.

328, Aug. 19– 329, April 6	Septimius Zenius	*P. Oxy.* 3126; Athanasius, *Festal Letter* 1, heading
330, April 19	Flavius Magnilianus	Athanasius, *Festal Letter* 2, heading; *P. Oxy.* 2562 (undated)
331, April 11	Florentius	Athanasius, *Festal Letter* 3, heading
332, April 2	Flavius Hyginus	*PSI* 767 (Nov. 331 or 332); Athanasius, *Festal Letter* 4, heading (2 April 332); *P. Theadelphia* 17 (undated); Sozomenus, *HE* 2.25.3 (before 335)
333, April 15	Paterius	Athanasius, *Festal Letter* 5, heading; Opitz, *Urkunde* 34.43 (undated)
334, April 7– 336, Feb./ March	Flavius Philagrius	Athanasius, *Festal Letter* 6, heading (7 April 334); 7, heading (30 March 335); *Sammelbuch* 8246 (Arsinoite nome: probably c. 334); Athanasius, *Apol. Sec.* 76.1 ff. (Sept. 335); *P. Oxy.* 3129 (Sept. 335), 1470 (Feb./March 336)

Athanasius, *Hist. Ar.* 51.1 ff., implies that Philagrius was out of office before 22 May 337.

| ?337, April 3– 338, March 26 | Flavius Antonius Theodorus | Athanasius, *Festal Letter* 10, heading; *P. Oxy.* 67 = *FIRA*[2] 3.173 (338)[30] |

Arabia (praeses)[31]

284/305	Domitius Antoninus	*CIL* 3.14156.2 = *I. Gerasa* 160
293/305	M. Aurelius Aelianus	*AE* 1957.272 (Bostra)
293/305	Aurelius Asclepiades	*CIL* 3.14149 (Kasr Bcher)
293/305	Aurelius Felicianus	*I. Gerasa* 105, 106
293/305	Aurelius Gorgonius	*AE* 1930.105 = *I. Gerasa* 161

Palaestina (praeses)[32]

303, April–Nov.	Flavianus	Eusebius, *Mart. Pal.* (S) praef.; (L) 1.1, 1.5
304, spring–307/8, winter	Urbanus	Eusebius, *Mart. Pal.* 3–7
308, early–310, c. March	Firmilianus	Eusebius, *Mart. Pal.* 8–11, cf. (S) 13.1
310/311, c. June	Valentinianus	*AE* 1964.198 (Scythopolis)

---

30. The Festal Index enters the prefects from Zenius to Theodorus under the following consular dates:

328, 329 (praef., 1)	Zenius
330 (2)	Magnilianus
331, 332 (3, 4)	Hyginus
333, 334, 335 (5–7)	Paterius
336, 337 (8, 9)	Philagrius
338 (10)	Theodorus

The Index appears to be based on (and to distort) the information in the headings, see E. Schwartz, *Ges. Schr.* 3 (1959), 15 ff. In addition, under Letter 3, of 331, the Index describes events connected with Letter 4, of 332 (cf. Athanasius, *Apol. Sec.* 60.1 ff.; *Festal Letter* 4.5: the names of Athanasius' accusers), and under Letters 8 and 10 it describes events of 335 and 337, not 336 and 338 (for the dates, *AJAH* 3 (1978), 62 ff.). The heading to Letter 10 appears to imply that Theodorus had been prefect at the preceding Easter too.

31. For governors down to 305, H.-G. Pflaum, *Syria* 34 (1967), 143 f.; G. W. Bowersock, *JRS* 61 (1971), 236. The present list omits three governors of very uncertain date: Aurelius Antiochus (*CIL* 3.14157 = *I. Gerasa* 162; *AE* 1913.144); Bassaeus Astur (*AE* 1920.73); Ael. Flavianus (G. W. Bowersock, *JRS* 61 (1971), 236).

32. The present list omits four names from that in *PLRE* 1.1108, viz. 'Severus', Anonymus 130 (? = Firmilianus), Delphinius (whose status is uncertain), and the anonymous governor attested in 326 (Eusebius, *VC* 3.31).

Phoenice[33]

286/c. 295	L. Artorius Pius Maximus	*AE* 1939.58 (Heliopolis)
	leg(atus) eorum (sc. *Augustorum*) *pro pr(aetore)*	
292, Mar. 31	Crispinus	*CJ* 1.23.3

CJ 1.23.3 names Crispinus as *praeses provinciae Phoenices;* he may also be the recipient of *CJ* 7.35.4 (26 Feb. 292), 9.2.11 (25 March 292), 9.9.25 (28 Aug. 293), 10.62.3 (undated)

shortly before 324	Achillius	*AfP* 3 (1906), 168 = *P. Rylands* 4, p. 104 (Hermopolis)[34]
	ἡγεμ(ών)	
328, Oct. 21– 329, March 14	Flavius Dionysius	*CTh* 9.34.4 (Tyre), 8.18.4ˢ; *CJ* 6.9.8ˢ (Heliopolis)
	Title not attested	
334	Archelaus	Socrates, *HE* 1.29.2[35]
	ὑπατικός	

Augusta Libanensis (praeses)

293/c. 300	Sossianus Hierocles	*CIL* 3.133 = 6661; *AE* 1932.79 (Palmyra)

Syria (praeses, *after c. 325* consularis)[36]

290, May 10	Charisius	*CJ* 9.41.9, cf. 11.55.1 (286/293)
293, April 21/ Dec. 31	Primosus[37]	*CJ* 7.33.6 (undated: date inferred from 7.33.5, 7)

33. The present list omits the governor apparently attested by a very worn milestone, from the road between Tyre and Sidon, published by R. G. Goodchild, *Berytus* 9 (1948–49), 222/3, with Plate XXII, 2; the words "CI MAXIMO," from which *PLRE* 1.581 deduces that his name was Maximus, may be part of the emperor's name and titles. J. and L. Robert, *BE* 1956.335, argued that Aelius Statutus was a governor of Syria Phoenice; *PLRE* 1.852 identifies him as a *censitor.*

34. On the date, C. H. Roberts, *JEA* 31 (1945), 113; B. R. Rees, *BJRL* 51 (1968/9), 164 ff.

35. Socrates makes Archelaus governor when the allegedly murdered Arsenius was found alive: the date of that must be 334 (*AJAH* 3 (1978), 62).

36. J. F. Gilliam, *AJP* 79 (1958), 237 f. (to 305). The present list discards the following names from the list in *PLRE* 1.1105: L. Artorius Pius Maximus (see Phoenice); 'Publius'; Anonymus 127 (who is the praetorian prefect Asclepiades); Anonymus 128 (Philostorgius, *HE* 3.15); and Dyscolius (*P. Rylands* 623; 4, p. 104: status uncertain); Plutarchus (Malalas 318 Bonn, on which passage see G. Downey, *A History of Antioch in Syria* (Princeton, 1961), 348, 622).

37. *PLRE* 1.725 assumes identity with the senator Latinius Primosus (*CIL* 6.37118).

294, Sept. 22	Verinus	*CJ* 2.12.20
290/296	L. Aelius Helvius Dionysius	*ILS* 1211
329/335	Flavius Dionysius	Eusebius, *VC* 4.42.3; Libanius, *Orat.* 1.36; Socrates, *HE* 1.28.31

Augusta Euphratensis

None securely attested[38]

Cyprus (praeses)

293/305	Antistius Sabinus	*I. Salamis* 39, 40, 129–131[39]

Isauria (praeses)

305/311	Flavius Severianus	*AE* 1972.652 (Seleucia ad Calycadnum)

Cilicia (praeses)

303/305	Aemilius Marcianus	*CIL* 3.223 (near Tarsus: 293/305), cf. W. Lackner, *Vig. Chr.* 27 (1973), 53 ff.
303/313	?Lysias	*BHG* 2069, 2070, 2108 (W. Lackner, *Anal. Boll.* 87 (1969), 128 ff.; 90 (1972), 251 ff.)

Mesopotamia

None attested

Osrhoene

?309	?Mysianus	*BHO* 363
?310	?Ausonius	*BHO* 367

DIOCESE OF PONTICA

Cappadocia (praeses)

?316	Titianus	*CJ* 7.16.41 (undated, but issued by Constantine and Licinius)[40]

38. *PLRE* 1.499 argues that Leontius (*CTh* 8.1.1) was governor in 319, with appeal to A. H. M. Jones, *JRS* 39 (1949), 47. Seeck, *Regesten* 192, redated the law to 343.

39. On Sabinus as a persecutor in Cypriot hagiography, I. Michaelidou-Nicolaou, *Acta of the Fifth International Congress of Greek and Latin Epigraphy* (Oxford, 1971), 381 ff.

40. On the date, Seeck, *Regesten* 53 f.; Millar, *Emperor* 336, arguing from *CTh* 8.5.2 (14 May 316: *ad Titianum*). It could also be between 310 and 312.

Armenia

None attested

Pontus Polemoniacus

None attested

Galatia

None attested

Paphlagonia

None attested

Pontus, later Diospontus, from 328 Helenopontus (praeses)

293/305	Aurelius Priscianus	*CIL* 3.307, 13643, 14184.20, 21, 39; *BCH* 33 (1909), 27; *AE* 1961.26 (all milestones)
317/324	Valerius CIIPUS /// UR	*CIL* 3.14184.31 = *AE* 1900.152
333/335	Flavius Julius Leontius	*CIL* 3.14184.17, 37; *AE* 1908.1
before 337	Claudius Longinus	*CIL* 3.14184.24 = *AE* 1900.149 (a fragmentary milestone)[41]

Pontus et Bithynia (consularis)

324/c. 338	L. Crepereius Madalianus	*ILS* 1228 (Calama)

Bithynia (praeses, *after c. 325* consularis)[42]

303, spring	Sossianus Hierocles	Lactantius, *Mort. Pers.* 16.4, cf. *Div. Inst.* 5.2.12
303 or shortly after	Priscillianus	Lactantius, *Mort. Pers.* 16.4
329/c. 336	Julius Aurelianus	*AE* 1969/70.116 (Formiae)

41. Published by J. H. R. Munro, *JRS* 20 (1900), 159 f.: "]io[/]io[/ [nobilissi]mis C[ae]ss. / Cl. Longinus v. p. / p. [p.]."

42. Anonymous *praesides* are mentioned by Lactantius in 311/2 and on 13 June 313 (*Mort. Pers.* 40.1, 48.1).

DIOCESE OF ASIANA

Lycia et Pamphylia (praeses)

c. 275/c. 325	Terentius Marcianus	*TAM* 3.89 (Termessus); *AE* 1915.53 (Trebenna); *BCH* 7 (1883), 268 no. 12 (Sagalassus)[43]
311, June 1	Eusebius	*CTh* 13.10.2[s]
333/335	Aurelius Fabius Faustinus	*JRS* 57 (1967), 44 no. 11 (Choma in Lycia)

Since the province is not named, it is possible that Lycia et Pamphylia had been divided before 335, and that Faustinus governed Lycia only.[44]

Pisidia (praeses)

308, Nov./ 311, May– ?311 Nov./ 313 May	Valerius Diogenes	*ILS* 8932 (Apamea: honors Valeria as Augusta); *MAMA* 1.170 (Laodicea Combusta: persecuted Christians, apparently under Maximinus);[45] *CIL* 3.6807 (Pisidian Antioch); Ramsay, *JRS* 14 (1924), 197 no. 25 (near Antioch: both undated)

Phrygia (praeses)[46]

286/305	Ju-	*IGRR* 4.523 (Dorylaeum)

Perhaps governor of Phrygia et Caria

Phrygia et Caria[47]

286/293	Priscus	*CIL* 14191.2 (Docimium)
	v. c., pr[---	

43. On the date, see G. Bersanetti, *Aevum* 19 (1945), 384 ff.

44. Fl. Areianus Alypius (*I. Side* 54) is now attested as *praeses* of Augustamnica in 351 (*CPR* 5.12); he presumably governed either Pamphylia or Lycia et Pamphylia after 337.

45. W. M. Calder, *Gnomon* 10 (1934), 503 f. —contesting the claim of A. Wilhelm, *Sb. Berlin,* Phil.-hist. Klasse 1932.834 ff., that the tortures mentioned were merely mental or psychological ills. Millar, *Emperor* 576 n. 58, dates *MAMA* 1.170 to 305/6, adducing Eusebius, *Mart. Pal.* 4.8. The inference is illegitimate, since in 305/6 Asia Minor was under the control of Galerius, not of Maximinus (Chapter XI). However, ἐπὶ Μαξιμίνου could be a mistake for ἐπὶ Μαξιμιανοῦ (a common confusion—see *JTS,* n.s. 27 (1976), 420). If so, *MAMA* 1.170 attests Diogenes as *praeses* of Pisidia under Galerius, i.e. before May 311.

46. Hagiography attests one Eustathius as a governor at Myra late in the reign of Constantine (G. Anrich, *Hagios Nikolaos: Der heilige Nikolaos in der griechischen Kirche* 1 (Leipzig and Berlin, 1913), 70, 78 f., 84 f., 219, 253 f., 279, 301, 310, 404). In defense of his historicity, *Phoenix* 28 (1974), 227.

47. C. Roueché, *JRS* 71 (1981), 103 ff., publishes and discusses recently discovered inscrip-

?293/305	L. Castrius Constans	*MAMA* 6.94 = J. and L. Robert, *La Carie* 2 (Paris, 1954), 199 no. 123 (near Heraclea ad Salbacem); *ILS* 8881 (Eumeneia)[48]

λαμπρότατος ἡγεμών, of consular rank

shortly after 20 Nov. 301	Fulvius Asticus	*JRS* 65 (1975), 160 = *AE* 1975.805 (Aezani in Phrygia); *CIL* 3.480 (near Alabanda in Caria: 293/305)

praeses/ἡγεμών

Caria (praeses)

293/305	Aurelius Marcellus	*ILS* 635 (Halicarnassus)

v. p. praes. prov. Caria[e]

Lydia

None attested

Insulae (praeses)

294, Aug. 2	Diogenes	*CJ* 3.22.5
293/305	Aurelius Agathus Gennadius	*CIL* 3.450 (Mytilene); *AE* 1947.57 (Cos)
293/324	Attius ?Epinicius	*ILS* 3107; *CIL* 3.14199.1 (Samos: dedications to Juno and Jupiter by the governor)

Asia (proconsul)[49]

286/293	T. Flavius Festus	*I. Didyma* 89, 90 (286/293), 159 (proconsul before Asia was divided)
286/305	Aurelius Hermogenes	*CIL* 3.7069 = *I. Ilion* 98
287/298	L. Artorius Pius Maximus	*CIL* 3.14195.27; *JÖAI* 44 (1959), Beibl. 349–350 = *I. Ephesos* 307, 621

---

tions from Aphrodisias which appear to demonstrate that the province of Phrygia and Caria was not created by Diocletian, but in the 250s. Moreover, the anonymous senatorial *legatus pro praetore* of the province attested by *IGRR* 4.814 (Hierapolis) and *AE* 1932.56 (Laodicea) should, on purely epigraphical grounds, be dated close to the middle of the third century, rather than under Diocletian, as argued by J. G. C. Anderson, *JRS* 22 (1932), 24 ff.

48. On the date, see W. H. Buckler and W. M. Calder, *MAMA* 6 (1939), pp. 35 f.; L. Robert, *Noms indigènes dans l'Asie Mineure gréco-romaine* 1 (Paris, 1963), 361 ff.

49. B. Malcus, *Opuscula Atheniensia* 7 (1969), 91 ff.

293/303	Junius Tiberianus	*JÖAI* 44 (1959), Beibl. 267 = *I. Ephesos* 305
293/305	An- ? [Epi]phanius	*I. Ilion* 97[50]
311–313, May	?Peucetius	Eusebius, *HE* 9.11.4

Eusebius reports that Maximinus appointed Peucetius δὶς ὕπατος καὶ τρὶς ὕπατος καὶ τῶν καθόλου λόγων ἔπαρχος. Since the Egyptian papyri (from Maximinus' domains) show no trace of Peucetius' alleged three consulates, Eusebius has clearly misheard or misunderstood. Accordingly, a conjecture may be advanced: since the proconsulate of Asia was the only other office with a fixed (and therefore renewable) term which Maximinus could bestow, Peucetius may have been proconsul of Asia. If the conjecture is correct, the triennium 311–314 best fits the historical circumstances. Peucetius' function as *praefectus summarum rationum* was presumably to raise money for the war against Licinius in 313; he was executed after Maximinus' defeat (*HE* 9.11.4).

?325–327	Domitius Zenophilus	*ILAfr.* 456 (Bulla Regia)
c. 330/334	Ceionius Rufius Albinus	Firmicus Maternus, *Math.* 2.29.10
c. 330/336	Fabius Titianus	*ILS* 1227 (Rome); *I. Ephesos* 666d

Asia et Hellespontus (proconsul)

c. 330	Amnius Manius Caesonius Nicomachus Anicius Paulinus	*ILS* 1220, 1221 (Rome)[51]

Hellespontus (praeses)

293/305	Julius Cassius	*I. Ilion* 97

DIOCESE OF THRACIA

293/305	Domitius Domninus	*IGRR* 1.789–792 (Heraclea)

vir perfectissimus and governor: presumably, therefore, *praeses Europae*

---

50. The inscription is known only from the report of J. B. Lechevalier, who gives the proconsular date as επιαν.... / φανετοι του λανπροτανο / ασιας (*Voyage dans la Troade*² (Paris, 1799), 256, no. I).

51. The inscriptions imply that Hellespontus had been made a separate province again between Paulinus' proconsulate and 334/5, see Chastagnol, *Fastes* 91 n. 107; A. H. M. Jones, *Roman Economy* (Oxford, 1974), 268.

shortly after   L. Aradius Valerius   *CIL* 6.1690, 1691[52]
324   Proculus

    consularis Europae et Thraciae

DIOCESE OF MOESIAE

Moesia Superior
None attested

Praevalitana
None attested

Dardania
None attested

Dacia (praeses)
321, Feb. 6   Claudius   *CTh* 2.19.2

Dacia Ripensis
None attested

Macedonia (praeses)
304, Mar.-   Dulcitius   Μαρτύριον τῶν ἁγίων Ἀγάπης,
Apr.   Εἰρήνης καὶ Χιόνης (*BHG* 34)

Epirus Nova (praeses)
324/332   Flavius Hyginus   *CIL* 3.7320 (Lychnidus: fragmen-
                                     tary)

Epirus Vetus
None attested

Thessalia
None attested

---

52. Jones, *LRE* 3.11 n. 13, argues that *Thraciae* here means, not the province of Thracia, but "the rest of the diocese of Thrace" or "other provinces of the Thracian diocese." But the fragmentary *CIL* 8.24521 (Carthage) has "consular. [prov. Europae consula]r. prov. Thrac.," which might indicate that *ILS* 1240 runs together two separate posts.

Achaea (normally proconsul)[53]

?c. 285	L. Turranius Gratianus	*CIL* 3.6103 (Athens)
	v. c., corrector	
293/305	L. Sul. Paulus	*Corinth* 8.2.23–25
	v. p., praeses	
?before 306	Publilius Optatianus Porfyrius	*AE* 1931.6 = *SEG* 11.810 (Sparta)
?appointed for 307–308	C. Vettius Cossinius Rufinus	*ILS* 1217 (Atina)
318–320	Aurelius Valerius Tullianus Symmachus Phosphorius	*CTh* 2.4.1 (4 Feb. 319); 2.15.1 (25 July 319); *IG* 7.96 = *SEG* 13.297 (Megara); *IG* 4.1608 = *AE* 1901.125 (Argos)
?323–324	Domitius Zenophilus	*ILAfr.* 456 (Bulla Regia)
c. 330	Ceionius Rufius Albinus	Firmicus Maternus, *Math.* 2.29.10

Crete

286/293	Aglaus	*I. Cret.* 4.281 (Gortyn)

Proconsul, presumably of the as yet undivided province of Crete and Cyrene

293/305	M. Aurelius Buzes	*I. Cret.* 4.282, 283 (Gortyn)
	ἡγεμὼν τῆς Κρήτης	

Diocese of Pannoniae

?316/324	Valerius Catullinus	*ILS* 704 (near Poetovio: under Constantine, who is not yet *victor*)

v. p. p(raeses) p(rovinciae) {p} P(annonniae) S(uperioris)

?316/324	Fabius Claudius	*CIL* 3.5326 (Solva: dedication to Constantine, who is not yet *victor*)

v. p. p(raeses) p(rovinciae) N(orici) M(edi)t(erranei)[54]

53. E. Groag, *Die Reichsbeamten von Achaia in spätrömischer Zeit* (*Dissertationes Pannonicae* 1.14, 1946), 13 ff. The status and titles of two anonymous governors are important: a *praeses et corrector* probably belongs to the reign of Diocletian (*SEG* 11.887: Sparta), but Eunapius alludes to a proconsul who probably held office before 306 (Eunapius, *Vitae Phil.* 9.2.3–30, pp. 483–485).

54. On governors of Noricum in the fourth century, see G. Winkler, *Die Reichsbeamten von*

DIOCESE OF BRITANNIAE

296/305   Aurelius Arpagius   *RIB* 1.1912 (Birdoswald)

pr(aeses), presumably of Britannia Secunda

DIOCESE OF GALLIAE

294   Aurelius Proculus   *ILS* 640 (Vitudurum)

v. p. pr[--- : presumably *praeses* of Sequania

298, late   Anonymous   *Pan. Lat.* 9(4)
summer or
autumn

vir perfectissimus at Autun: presumably *praeses* of Lugdunensis Prima

313, July 1   Antonius Marcellinus   *CTh* 11.3.1[s] (319 mss.)

praeses Lugdunensis primae

DIOCESE OF VIENNENSIS

312/324   M. Alfius Apronianus   *CIL* 12.1852 (Vienne)

v. p. p(raeses) p(rovinciae) Fl(aviae) Vienn(ensis)

DIOCESE OF ITALIA[55]

Venetia(e) et Histria (corrector)

286/305   Attius Insteius Tertul-   *CIL* 5.2818 (Patavium); 6.1696
lus

c. 309   C. Vettius Cossinius   *ILS* 1217 (Atina)
Rufinus

318/c. 327   L. Nonius Verus   *ILS* 1218 (Mutina)

Noricum und ihr Personal bis zum Ende der römischen Herrschaft (*Sb. Wien*, Phil.-hist. Klasse
261.2, 1969), 103 ff. Two governors who are here rejected require discussion. (1) Aurelius Her-
modorus, *v. p. p. N(orici) M(edi)t(erranei)*, who is dated 311 by R. P. Harper, *Anatolian Studies*
14 (1964), 168; *PLRE* 1.422, belongs to the reign of Julian: he restored a temple of Mithras built in
311 which had been deserted for more than fifty years (*ILS* 4197). (2) 'Aquilinus' (not in *PLRE* 1),
alleged as *praeses* of Noricum Ripense c. 304 by the *Passio Floriani* (*BHL* 3054), is accepted by G.
Winkler, *Reichsbeamten* 110, with appeal to R. Noll, *Frühes Christentum in Österreich* (Vienna,
1954), 26 ff. But the *Passio Floriani* is worthless as evidence: an editor rightly denounced it as "ab
impostore confecta" and a "Carolingian forgery" (B. Krusch, *MGH*, Scriptores rerum Mero-
vingicarum 3 (1896), 65: *Neues Archiv* 28 (1903), 339 ff.), for it is a plagiarism of the *Passio
Irenaei*, itself of doubtful authenticity (*BHL* 4466).

55. A. Chastagnol, *Historia* 12 (1963), 348 ff.

| before 340 | M. Maecius Memmius Furius Baburius Caecilianus Placidus | *ILS* 1231 (Puteoli) |

Aemilia et Liguria (consularis)

321, July 1	Junius Rufus (or Rufinus)	*CTh* 4.13.1
323, May 21	Ulpius Flavianus	*CTh* 11.16.2
c. 327/c. 340	C. Julius Rufinianus Ablabius Tatianus	*ILS* 2942 (Abellinum)

Raetia (praeses)[56]

290	Septimius Valentio	*ILS* 618 (Augusta Vindelicum)
c. 275/c. 325	Aurelius Mucianus	*CIL* 3.5785 (Augusta Vindelicum)
c. 275/c. 325	Valerius Venustus	*CIL* 3.5862 (Zweifalten)

Alpes Cottiae (praeses)

| 286/305 | Aurelius Saturninus | *CIL* 5.7248, 7249 (Segusio) |

Tuscia et Umbria (corrector)

| c. 310 | C. Vettius Cossinius Rufinus | *ILS* 1217 (Atina) |
| c. 326/c. 340 | C. Julius Rufinianus Ablabius Titianus | *ILS* 2942 (Abellinum) |

Flaminia et Picenum (corrector)

325, Nov. 8 or 13	Claudius Uranius	*AE* 1937.119 (Amiternum); *CIL* 9.4517 (Amiternum: undated)
before 330, Feb. 5	M. Aurelius Valerius Valentinus	*CIL* 11.5381 (Assisi), cf. *CTh* 16.2.7
before 334	Fabius Titianus	*ILS* 1227 (Rome)
before c. 337	L. Crepereius Madalianus	*CIL* 14.4449 (Ostia); *ILS* 1228 (Calama)[57]

56. The present list omits the anonymous *v. p. p(raeses) p(rovinciae) R(aetiae)* attested by *CIL* 3.14370.12 (Regina). *PLRE* 1.1020, Anonymus 92, dates him "before c. 314 when Raetia was divided into two provinces." The date of the division (attested for 354 by Ammianus 15.4.1) is unknown, see R. Heuberger, *Klio* 24 (1931), 348; A. Chastagnol, *Historia* 12 (1963), 358 n. 27.

57. M. Aurelius Consius Quartus was successively *corrector* of Flaminia et Picenum and of

Campania (corrector, *from late 324* consularis)[58]

c. 294	T. Flavius Postumius Titianus	*ILS* 2941 (Rome)
293/298	Virius Gallus	*ILS* 6310 (Capua)[59]
293/300	Pompeius Appius Faustinus	*CIL* 10.4785 (Teanum Sidicinum)
c. 311	C. Vettius Cossinius Rufinus	*ILS* 1217 (Atina)
before 324	P. Helvius Aelius Dionysius	*ILS* 1212 (Formiae)[60]
324, Oct. or Nov.	L. Aelius Proculus	*AE* 1969/70.107 (Puteoli: Constantine is *victor*)[61]

corrector

324, Nov. or Dec.	M. Ceionius Julianus	*AE* 1939.151 (near Abellinum)

consularis, attested before news arrived of Constantius' proclamation as Caesar on 8 Nov. 324

325/337	C. Caelius Censorinus	*ILS* 1216 (Atella)
325/337	?Junius Valentinus	*CIL* 10.1482 (Naples: all letters in the name are dotted or supplemented)
?337	Julius Aurelianus	*AE* 1969/70.108 (Puteoli); 116 (Formiae)[62]

Venetia et Historia, *consularis* of Belgica Prima, *vicarius* of the diocese of Hispaniae, and proconsul of Africa (*AE* 1955.150: Hippo). On his career, A. Chastagnol, *Libyca* 7 (1959), 191 ff. It is difficult to date precisely, but it seems probable that even the earliest attested post falls after the death of Constantine.

58. One anonymous *consularis* is attested before 337 (*CIL* 9.2206: Telesia).

59. A. Chastagnol, *Historia* 12 (1963), 363; *PLRE* 1.384, Gallus 2, date the *correctura* after Gallus' ordinary consulate in 298.

60. A. Chastagnol, *Historia* 12 (1963), 363, adduces *CTh* 8.18.4; *CJ* 3.1.8, 7.22.3 to establish a date of 314. But the first of these laws, dated 339 in the manuscripts, probably belongs to 329 (Seeck, *Regesten* 179; *PLRE* 1.259), while the second and third, both dated 314, are addressed "ad Dionysium vice praefectorum agentem" (*CJ* 7.22.3). Seeck held, very plausibly, that they are fragments of a law of Licinius (*Regesten* 53, 162).

61. E. Guadagno, *Rendiconti Lincei*[8] 25 (1970), 112 ff.

62. *AE* 1969/70.108 honors a Caesar whose name has been erased: "Fl. Iulio [---nob]ilissimo ac [amant]issimo [omnium] Caesari." The missing name is supplied as *Constanti* by E. Guadagno, *Rendiconti Lincei*[8] 25 (1970), 119; as *Crispo* by G. Camodeca, *Atti dell'Accademia di Scienze morali e politiche, Napoli* 82 (1971), 24 ff. The latter is rendered virtually impossible by the fact that Aurelianus was *consularis* of Bithynia before he became *consularis* of Campania (*AE*

?before 338	?T. Antonius Marcellinus	*ILS* 6506 (Beneventum)[63]

Apulia et Calabria (corrector)

305, May/306, Oct.	Ulpius Alenus	*CIL* 9.687 = *AE* 1967.91 (Herdonia
c. 300/c. 325	Caecilianus	*ILS* 1218 (Mutina)
317/324	L. Nonius Verus	*CIL* 9.1115 (Aeclanum: 312/324), 1116 (317/326); *ILS* 1218 (Mutina)
before 333	Clodius Celsinus Adelfius	*ILS* 1239 (Beneventum: *corr. regionum duarum*)[64]
326/333	Volusius Venustus	*ILS* 5557a (Canusium: *ddd. nnn. Constantino Aug. et filiis eius Caes.*)

Lucania et Bruttii (corrector)[65]

?before 306	-vius Bassus	*AE* 1975.261a (Paestum)

v. p. corr(ector) [*re*]*gionum Lucaniae* [*et*] *Brittiorum:* the fact that Bassus is a *vir perfectissimus* rather than a *vir clarissimus* probably points to a date before Maxentius or Constantine ruled Italy.

c. 300/c. 320	Brittius Praesens	*CIL* 10.468 (between Velia and Paestum: undated)
313, Feb. 16–Oct. 21	Rufinus Octavianus	*CTh* 7.22.1ˢ (319 mss.), 1.16.1ˢ (3 Aug. 315 mss.), 16.2.2ˢ (319 mss.)
313, Dec. 27–314, Feb. 6	Claudius Plotianus	*CTh* 11.29.1ˢ + 11.30.1ˢ

1969/70.116). On the other hand, Guadagno's arguments for a date in the summer of 335 are not compelling (p. 120 f.). The extravagant formula perhaps suggests rather the summer of 337 (cf. *ILT* 814, reproduced in Chapter VIII.4).

63. Known only from Renaissance copies (T. Mommsen, on *CIL* 9.1589): the date is obtained by emending the reported *Tanonio* to *T. Antonio* and assuming identity with Antonius Marcellinus, cos. 341. *PLRE* 1.548/9, Marcellinus 16, 22, enters the *consularis Campaniae* as a different person from the consul.

64. For the identification of the *regiones duae* as the province of Apulia et Calabria, see Chastagnol, *Fastes* 133; *PLRE* 1.192–193, Celsinus 6; A. Chastagnol, *Latomus* 36 (1977), 801 ff. Beneventum was in the province of Campania by 333 (*Itinerarium Burdigalense* p. 610.8 ff. Wesseling).

65. L. Turcius Apronianus has been deleted from the list in *PLRE* 1.1095: the Turciu[s] of *CIL* 10.407 (Volcei: 323) is a landowner, not a provincial governor, see E. J. Champlin, "The Volcei land-register (*CIL* X.407)" (forthcoming).

| 316, Jan. 16 | Mecilius Hilarianus | *CTh* 9.19.1 + 12.1.3 |
| 324/326 | Alpinius Magnus | *ILS* 708 (Salernum) |

Sicilia (corrector , *after c. 324* consularis)

| 293/304 | C. Valerius Apollinaris | *EE* 8.696 (Lilybaeum) |

v. p.: all the other attested *correctores* are *viri clarissimi*

304, April 29–Aug. 12	Calvisianus	*Acta Eupli* (*BHG* 629)
314, spring	Domitius Latronianus	Eusebius, *HE* 10.5.21; *ILS* 677 (Panormus: 312/324); *AE* 1966.166 (Lilybaeum: 312/337); *IG* 14.296 (Panormus: undated)
before 320, Dec. 13	Domitius Zenophilus	*CIL* 10.7234 (Lilybaeum: undated)
312/324	Betitius Perpetuus	*CIL* 10.7204 (Mazara); *ILS* 8843 (Rome: undated)
293/c. 324	?Zoilus	*CIL* 10.7112 = *AE* 1959.23 (Catana)[66]
after c. 324	Alpinius Magnus ὑπατ(ικός)	*AE* 1966.167 (Lilybaeum)
before 332	L. Aradius Valerius Proculus	*CIL* 6.1690, 1691
c. 324/335	Fabius Titianus	*ILS* 1227 (Rome)
c. 324/c. 335	C. Caelius Censorinus	*ILS* 1216 (Atella)

Sardinia (praeses)[67]

| 286/305 | Valerius Fl[. . .]nus | *EE* 8.759 (Rotili Pioni) |

Not necessarily a governor

---

66. L. Cantarelli, *Studi e Documenti di Storia e Diritto* 24 (1903), 278, argued that *Zoilo corr.* was an error for or contraction of *Zenophilo corr.* Identity is vigorously denied by S. Grasso, *Epigraphica* 15 (1953), 151 n. 4; G. Manganaro, *Archivio Storico per la Sicilia Orientale* 4 (1958), 13 ff.

67. P. Meloni, *L'amministrazione della Sardegna da Augusto all'invasione vandalica* (Rome, 1968), 229 ff. The present list omits one known anonymous *v. e. pres. provinc. Sard.* (*EE* 8.764: Rotili Pioni), and Helennus, who was *v. p., proc.* between 335 and 337 (*AE* 1889.49: Telti).

293/305	Aurelius Marcus	*EE* 8.777, 778 = *AE* 1889.24, 30 (Sbrangatu); Sotgiu 1.388 (Olbia: name partly restored)
305	Valerius Domitianus	*AE* 1948.178 = Sotgiu 1.241 (Turris Libisonis: before May 305); *CIL* 10.8030 (between Caralis and Olbia: May 305/Sept. 306, apparently styling Domitianus *proc(urator)*)
305/6	Maximinus	*EE* 8.780 = *AE* 1889.25 (Sbrangatu)
306, Nov./ 308	Cornelius Fortunatianus	*ILS* 672 (near Terranova)
308/9	L. Papius Pacatianus	*AE* 1966.169 = Sotgiu 1.372 (between Caralis and Sulci)
312/324	T. Septimius Januarius	*EE* 8.783 = *AE* 1889.35 (Sbrangatu); *CIL* 10.7950 (Turris Libisonis); 7974, 7975 (Olbia)
319, July 29	Festus	*CTh* 9.40.3
323	Florianus	*AE* 1889.34 (Sbrangatu: *Fl. Iul. Cos[tan]tino [no]b. Ces. Aug. tr. p. VII cos.*)
335/337	Flavius Octavianus	*CIL* 10.8015 (= *ILS* 720), 8021 (milestones)

Corsica (praeses)

?c. 300	-s Magnus	*AE* 1962.144 d (Aleria)[68]
318, Oct. 24	Felix	*CTh* 1.16.3ˢ = 2.6.2ˢ (319 mss.)

Perhaps still governor on 28 July 320 if he is identical with the Furius Felix of *CTh* 2.11.1 (no office stated)

DIOCESE OF HISPANIAE[69]

Hispania Citerior (praeses)

286/293	Julius Valens	*AE* 1929.233 = *I. Tarraco* 91

68. On the date, J. Jehasse, *CRAI* 1961.376. *PLRE* 1.534/5, Magnus 8, assumes identity with Alpinius Magnus and a date of 317/324.

69. A. Balil, *Emerita* 27 (1959), 289 ff. (to 300). Two Spanish governors cannot be assigned to a specific province: Fortunatus in 298 (*Passio Marcelli*), and Exsuperius, between 335 and 337 (Ausonius, *Professores* 18(17).12–13).

288 or 289	Postumius Lupercus	*CIL* 2.4104 = *I. Tarraco* 92

Hispania Tarraconensis (praeses)

312	Valerius Julianus	*CIL* 2.4105 = *I. Tarraco* 94
316, May 6	Julius Verus	*CTh* 2.6.1
324/?326	Badius Macrinus	*CIL* 2.4106, 4108 = *I. Tarraco* 95, 96 (324/337); cf. *CIL* 2.4107 = *I. Tarraco* 97 (?317/326)

Carthaginiensis

None attested

Gallaecia (praeses)

before 338	Aco Catullinus	*CIL* 2.2635 (Asturica: undated)[70]

Lusitania (praeses)[71]

293/305	Aurelius Ursinus	*CIL* 2.5140 (Ossonoba)
c. 300/c. 320	Caecilianus	*ILS* 1218 (Mutina)
315/319	C. Sulpicius -s	*CIL* 2.481 (Emerita)
336	Numerius Albanus	*ILS* 5699 (Olisipo)

Baetica (praeses)

306/312	Octavius Rufus	*CIL* 2.2204 (Corduba)

Mauretania Tingitana

None attested

DIOCESE OF AFRICA[72]

Tripolitana (praeses)[73]

shortly after 300	C. Valerius Vibianus	*IRT* 577 (Lepcis); *ILS* 9352 (Tibubuci)

70. Catullinus had become *vicarius* of Africa by 27 July 338 (*PLRE* 1.187/8, Catullinus 3).

71. An anonymous *praeses provinciae Lusitan[iae]* is attested between 333 and 335 (*AE* 1935.4).

72. A. C. Pallu de Lessert, *Fastes des provinces africaines sous la domination romaine* 2: *Bas-Empire* (Paris, 1901).

73. The present list excludes at least two anonymous *praesides* who belong to the period 293–337: one before 305 (*AE* 1954.184: Arae Philaenorum), the other between 324 and 337 (*CIL* 8.22767: Talalati).

shortly after   Aurelius Quintianus   *ILS* 9352
300

Successor of Vibianus, and attested as governor of Numidia
Cirtensis on 20 Nov. 303.

306, Nov./ 308, summer	Volusius Donatianus	*IRT* 465 (Lepcis: under Maxentius —a twin of *IRT* 464 which attests Valerius Alexander as *vicarius*)
324, Nov./ 326, summer	Laenatius Romulus	*IRT* 468 (Lepcis); 467 (312/337); 101 (Sabratha: undated); 574 (Lepcis: undated)[74]

(Valeria) Byzacena (praeses, *after c. 324* consularis)

293/305	-cius Flavianus	*CIL* 8.23179 = *ILAlg.* 1.3832 (between Theveste and Thelepte)
293/c. 324	Vibius Flavianus	*AE* 1953.45 (Mactar)
313, Nov. 3– 314, April 17	Aco Catullinus	*CTh* 9.40.1 + 11.30.2 + 11.36.1 (published at Hadrumetum: Catullinus' title is not stated)
312/c. 324	Agricola	*AE* 1946.45 (Chusira: *v. c. praeses*)
312/c. 324	-tianus	*CIL* 8.701 (Chusira: *v. c. p(raeses)*)
321, Mar. 13– Aug. 29	Q. Aradius Rufinus Valerius Proculus	*CIL* 6.1684–1689 (partly reprinted as *ILS* 6111–6111 c)
321/c. 324	L. Aradius Valerius Proculus	*CIL* 6.1690 (= *ILS* 1240), 1691; 8.24521 (Carthage)
after 328	Cezeus Largus Maternianus	*ILAlg.* 1.4012 (Madauros), cf. *ILS* 5518 (near Vaga)

Africa (proconsul)[75]

285/290, for two years	Aurelius Antiochus	*ILAfr.* 513 (Thugga)

74. A. Chastagnol, *Latomus* 25 (1966), 541 ff.

75. L. Poinssot, *MSNAF* 76 (1919–23), 264 ff. (295–307); T.D. Barnes, *HSCP* 80 (1976), 248 ff. (290–305). In these articles Poinssot assumed that the proconsular year began on approximately 1 July, while I entertained 1 June as a possibility. But Symmachus, *Epp.* 2.24 (a proconsul of Asia about to set out from Rome on 28 February 383) and the evidence relating to the African proconsuls of 315–320 imply that the proconsular year probably began at a variable date in the second half of April. Accordingly, the present fasti of Asia, Achaea, and Africa assume that the proconsular year began in April throughout the period 284–337.

The proconsul Claudius A— (*IRT* 522: Lepcis), who held office before 293, might belong to the reign of Diocletian rather than earlier—indeed, he might even be Aristobulus, proconsul

290–294	T. Claudius Aurelius Aristobulus	*ILAlg.* 1.179 = *ILS* 5477 (Calama: attests four-year tenure); *ILAlg.* 1. 1032 = *ILS* 5714 (Thagora); *CIL* 8.23413 + *AE* 1946.119 = *Kartha-go* 8 (1957), 100–103 (Mactar); *ILAlg.* 1.2048 (Madauros); *CIL* 8.11774 (Mididi) (all four before 293); *ILS* 637 (Mididi: 294);*CIL* 624 + 11782 (Mactar); *ILAfr.*90 (Ksar-el-Hammam); *CIL* 8.23658 (Ksar Mdudja) (all three undated)
294–295	Cassius Dion	*Acta Maximiliani* (*BHL* 5813: 12 March 295)
295–296	T. Flavius Postumius Titianus	*CIL* 8.26566 (Thugga: 295), 26573 + 26567 + *ILAfr.* 532 (Thugga: 294/6); *CIL* 6.1419b
296–300	L. Aelius Helvius Dionysius	*CIL* 8.12459 (Maxula: *procos. p. A. IIII*); *Frag. Vat.* 41 (10 March 298); *CIL* 8.14401 = *ILAfr.* 441 (Vaga: 298); *CIL* 8.26562 = *ILAfr.* 531 (Thugga: undated)
300–301 or 302–303	M. Tullius T[...]nus	*CIL* 8.1550 + 15552 (Agbia: 293/ 305)
301–302	Julianus	*Mos. et Rom. leg. collatio* 15.3 (31 March 302, cf. Chapter V, n. 41)
303–305	C. Annius Anullinus	*Acta Felicis* (H. Delehaye, *Anal. Boll.* 39 (1921), 268–270: 5 June– 15 July 303); *Acta Crispinae* (*BHL* 1989 a/b: 5 Dec. 304); *ILT* 1308 = *AE* 1942/3.82 (Thignica: 293/305); Optatus 3.8, p. 90.15/16 Ziwsa
305–306 or 306–307	C. Ceionius Rufius Volusianus	*ILS* 1213 (Rome)
312, Nov.– 313, April 15	Anullinus	Eusebius, *HE* 10.5.15–17, 6.4, 7.1–2 (winter 312/3: 6.4 implies appointment by Constantine in Rome); Augustine, *Epp.* 88.2; Euse-

---

290-294. And an inscription of Calama records a proconsul whose name is lost, apparently in 325 or 334 (*CIL* 8.5357 = *ILAlg.* 1.270: *v. c. procons.* [...P]aulino conss.).

bius, *HE* 10.5.18–20 (summer 313, but not implying that Anullinus was still in office)

313–315	Aelianus	Optatus, *App.* 2

Aelianus is indubitably attested as proconsul only on 25 February 315, but the Theodosian Code contains eight fragments addressed to Aelianus and dated as follows:

1.12.1	dat. III k. Nov. Trev(iris) Constantino IIII et Licino IIII conss.
1.12.3	dat. k. Oct. Constantino A. et Constantio consul.
8.10.1	dat. VI id. Nov. Treviris, acc. XV kal. Mart. Carthagine Constantino A. IIII et Licinio IIII consulibus
9.34.2	pp. V. kal. Mar. Carthag(ine) Constantino A. VI et Constantino C. conss.
10.15.1	dat. VI id. Nov. Trev(iris(Constantino A. IIII et Licinio IIII conss.
11.1.2 + 7.1	dat. kal. Nov. Trev(iris) Constantino A. IIII et Licinio IIII conss.
11.36.3	pp. VI kal. Mai. Karthag(ine) Constantino A. VII et Constantio Caes. conss.

CTh 9.34.2 and 11.36.3 were probably published in 315, while all the other six fragments may come from a single imperial letter or rescript written in October or November 313.[76]

315–317	Petronius Probianus	Augustine, *Epp.* 88.4; *Contra Cresconium* 3.70.81; *Brev. Coll.* 3.23.41 (May 315); *CTh* 11.30.3 (25 Aug. 315), 11.30.5, 6 (13 Aug. 316); *ILS* 6809 (Vallis: undated)
317–319	Aco Catullinus	*CTh* 9.10.1 (17 April 317), 8.12.2[s] (20 April 317: the mss. have 316); *CJ* 3.11.4 (9 Feb. 318), 6.56.3[s] (27 July 318: the mss. have 315); *CTh* 11.16.1[s] (27 Aug. 318: the mss. have 319), 14.25.1[s] (12 Dec. 318: the mss. have 319(; *CIL* 8.14453 (near Vaga), 24582 (Carthage); *ILAfr.* 269 (Thuburbo Maius: all undated)

76. Seeck, *Regesten* 161, 163. Augustine's undated references to Aelianus are listed in *PLRE* 1.17, Aelianus 2.

319–320	Proculus	*CJ* 8.52.2 (24 April 319); *CTh* 15.3.1 (7 May 319), 6.35.2⁵ (27 July 319: the mss. have 315), 1.12.2 + 4.16.1 (26 Dec. 319)
320–321	Amnius Anicius Julianus	*ILS* 1220 (Rome)
?321–322	Domitius Latronianus	*CIL* 8.1016 (Carthage: before c. Nov. 324)
?322–324	Sex. Anicius Paulinus	*CIL* 6.1680, 1681 (Rome)
324–325	Mecilius Hilarianus	*CTh* 12.1.9 (9 July 324); *CIL* 8.1179 (Utica: after Sept. 324), 12524 (Carthage: undated)
326–327	Tertullus	*CTh* 9.21.3 = *CJ* 9.24.2 (6 July 326)
327–328	M. Ceionius Julianus	*ILS* 5518 (near Vaga: 326/333); *CIL* 8.14431 (near Vaga), 15269 (Thubursicu Bure), 25525 (Bulla Regia); *ILAlg.* 1.4011 (Madauros: all four undated)
328–332	Domitius Zenophilus	*ILAfr.* 456
332–333	L. Aradius Valerius Proculus	*ILS* 1240, 1241
336–337	Q. Flavius Maesius Egnatius Lollianus	Firmicus Maternus, *Math.* 1, praef. 8

Numidia (divided in 303) (praeses)[77]

?286	Flavius Flavianus	*CIL* 8.2480, 2481 (Ad Maiores), 4325 (Casae); *AE* 1916.18 (Cuicul), 21 (Lambaesis); Kolbe, *Statthalter* 30 no. 6 (Henchir Tamarik)

All the inscriptions are dated 286/293: in *CIL* 8.4325, Diocletian is given the implausible titles *t. pot. I, imp., cos., pro(consuli)*, which H. G. Kolbe has convincingly emended to *t. pot. III, p(atri) p(atriae), cos., pro(consuli)*

286/293	M. Aurelius Diogenes	*CIL* 8.2573–75 (Lambaesis); *AE* 1903.243 (Ain Karma)

---

77 Kolbe, *Statthalter* 28 ff. An anonymous *v. p. praeses* is attested between 286 and 293 (*CIL* 8.2718: Lambaesis).

?289/293	Aurelius Maximianus	*ILS* 5786, 5787 (Lambaesis); *CIL* 8.4224 (Verecunda), 7003 = *ILAlg.* 2.579 (Cirta);[78] Kolbe, *Statthalter* 40 no. 3 (Thamugadi)
293/305	Aurelius Pi[...]nus	*AE* 1917/18.30 (Lambaesis)
295, June 1	Valerius Concordius	*CJ* 9.9.27(28); *AE* 1920.15 (Cuicul: 293/305)
303	Valerius Florus	*AE* 1942/3.81 (Aqua Viva: 303); *CIL* 8.6700 (executed Christians at Milevis); Optatus 3.8, p. 90 Ziwsa; Augustine, *Contra Cresconium* 3.27.30 (as persecutor); *CIL* 8.4324 (Casae: 293/305)

v. p. p(raeses) p(rovinciae) N(umidiae) (*AE* 1942/3.81)

Numidia Militiana (303–314) (praeses)

303/305	Valerius Florus	*ILS* 631–633; *BCTH* 1907.272 (Thamugadi); *AE* 1955.81 (Lambaesis)

v. p., p(raeses) p(rovinciae) N(umidiae) M(ilitianae)

Numidia Cirtensis (303–314) (praeses)

303, Nov. 20	Aurelius Quintianus	*ILS* 644 (near Macomades Minores)[79]
305, spring–306	C. Valerius Antoninus	*CIL* 8.1870 (near Macomades: before May 305); *ILS* 651; *AE* 1895.80 (Thibilis: both after 1 Jan. 306); *ILAlg.* 2.31 (Rusicade: undated)

Numidia (reunited in 314) (praeses, *from 320 or earlier* consularis)[80]

314	Valerius Paulus	*CIL* 8.18905 (Thibilis: 10 Dec. 313/c. Sept. 314, cf. Table 3); *ILS* 688 = *ILAlg.* 2.582 (Cirta: 312/

---

78. The *terminus post quem* for Maximianus is deduced from the fragmentary victory titles of Diocletian and Maximian, viz.]*thicis Persicis Sarmati*[*cis*]. Whether the first title is to be restored as [*Par*]*thicis* (so G. Wilmanns in *CIL;* H.-G. Pflaum in *ILAlg.*) or as [*Go*]*thicis* (W. Ensslin, *RE* 7A (1948), 2430; Kolbe, *Statthalter* 41 n. 1), *Persicis* should refer to the diplomatic triumph of 287, *Sarmati*[*cis*] following *Persicis* to Diocletian's Sarmatian campaign in 289 (Chapter V: Diocletian).

79. On Florus and Quintianus, see especially the full discussion of Kolbe, *Statthalter* 48 ff.

80. The *consulares* (of whom the earliest known belongs to 320) are listed and discussed by A. Chastagnol, *Mélanges J. Carcopino* (Paris, 1966), 224 ff.

324), cf. Optatus, App. 3, p. 205.
33/4 Ziwsa (Numidia still divided
in spring 314)

v. p., p(raeses) p(rovinciae) N(umidiae)

314/316	Iallius Antiochus	*CIL* 8.2241 (Mascula: before c. Oct. 316), 7005 = *ILAlg.* 2.584 (Cirta)
?317/320	Aurelius Almacius	*CIL* 8.4469 (Nicivibus: fragmentary and with an erasure after [*Fla*]*vi Valeri Constant*[)

v. p. p(raeses) p(rovinciae) N(umidiae)

320, Dec. 13	Domitius Zenophilus	Optatus, App. 1; *AE* 1915.30 (Lambaesis: undated)

consularis

330, Feb. 5	M. Aurelius Valerius Valentinus	*CTh* 16.2.7, cf. Optatus, App. 10, p. 215 (5 Feb., but without year or name); *CIL* 11.5381 (Assisi)
333/337	Clodius Celsinus Adelfius	*ILS* 715 = *ILAlg.* 2.587 (Cirta)

Mauretania Sitifensis (praeses)

after 293	Titus Atilius	*CIL* 8.8484 (Sitifis)
315	Septimius Flavianus	*CIL* 8.8476, 8477 = *ILS* 695 (Sitifis: both style Constantine *trib. pot. X* and the latter alludes to his *decennalia*); *CIL* 8.8712 (Centenarium Solis: 312/324)
318	Flavius Terentianus	*CIL* 8.8412 = *ILS* 696 (between Sitifis and Saldae: Constantine is *trib. pot.XIIII imp. XIII cos. IIII*, cf. Table 3)

Mauretania Caesariensis et Sitifensis (praeses)

324/337	Flavius Terentianus	*CIL* 8.8932 (Saldae)

Mauretania Caesariensis (praeses)[81]

288	Flavius Pecuarius	*CIL* 8.8474 (Sitifis)

81. The present list omits an anonymous possibly Diocletianic *v. p. p. M. Caes.* (*CIL* 8.20964: Caesarea).

290–293	T. Aurelius Litua	*ILS* 627 (Auzia: year 251 of the provincial era), 628 (Caesarea: 286/305); *CIL* 8.8924 (Saldae: 286/305); *ILS* 6886 (Centenarium Aqua Frigida: 293/305); *AE* 1912.24 (undated)
293/305	Ulpius Apollonius	*ILS* 638 (Rapidum)
?297	-ianus	*CIL* 8.21447–49 (Gunugu: three fragments which appear to show Diocletian as *trib. pot. XIIII cos. VI*)
305, May/ 306, July	M. Valerius Victor	*AE* 1966.600 (Tipasa)
311, May/ 312, autumn	Valerius Faustus	*ILS* 671 (Caesarea)
?after 312	L. Junius Junillus	*AE* 1975.882 (Urev, in Africa Proconsularis)[82]

DATED GOVERNORS WHOSE PROVINCE IS UNKNOWN[83]

286/290	Sallustianus	*CJ* 9.41.18 (undated, but between rescripts of 286 and 290)
311/313	Theotecnus	Eusebius, *HE* 9.11.5
315 or 320, July 8–Oct. 1	Crispinus	*CTh* 11.30.10 (mss. 315), 12.1.2 (mss. 320)[84]
326, April 10	Florianus	*CTh* 7.20.1^s (318 mss.)[85]
334, Aug. 25	Julianus	*CTh* 11.39.3[86]
335, Oct. 23	Pericles	*CJ* 1.40.4[87]

82. On the date, J. Peyras, *BSNAF* 1973.27.

83. The list of "provincial governors (province unknown)," *PLRE* 1.1110, contains men who are probably private citizens—and some who may be *vicarii* (such as Lucretius Paternus (*CTh* 12.1.17: 25 October 329)).

84. Seeck, *Regesten* 199 f., emended both dates to 353 (accepted hesitantly by *PLRE* 1.232, Crispinus 4). In favor of a Constantinian date, J. Gaudemet, *Iura* 2 (1951), 66 f.

85. *PLRE* 1.366, Florianus 2, adopts Mommsen's emendation to 324.

86. Seeck, *Regesten* 182, identifies Julianus as a governor of Phrygia, adducing Libanius, *Epp.* 674.

87. P. Krüger, ad loc., emended *d. X. kal. Nov. Nicopoli* to *pp.,* on the grounds that Constantine was in Constantinople two days earlier (*CTh* 16.8.5, 9.1)—which would imply that Pericles was *praeses* of Moesia Inferior. Against the emendation, see Chapter V, n. 136.

CHAPTER X

NAMES IN *ACTA MARTYRUM*

More than a century ago, a scholar declared his intention of compiling a list of Roman officials named in hagiographical sources, but he was deterred by the magnitude of the task.[1] Something similar to part of this projected "Catalogus magistratuum utriusque imperii ex Actis Sanctorum" is incorporated in the first volume of the *Prosopography of the Later Roman Empire,* but the execution manifests serious shortcomings. First, many entries rely on inferior texts, so that the best evidence is sometimes overlooked for such vital matters as a person's name, status, or geographical location. Second, individual documents are sometimes treated capriciously: for example, the *Acta Sebastiani* name two bogus prefects of the city of Rome (*PL* 17.1114 ff.), but 'Agrestius Chromatius' is omitted while 'Fabianus' acquires an entry (322). Third, the editors fail to apply consistently the criterion for distinguishing between truth and falsehood which they announce at the outset.[2] Fourth, and most serious, the criterion of authenticity employed is inadequate. According to the list of "symbols and conventions" which prefaces the volume (xxii), a pair of asterisks and exclamation marks brands "persons known only from sources of doubtful reliability (principally the *Historia Augusta* and the *Acta Sanctorum*)." Yet genuine names can (and do) occur in "sources of doubtful reliability"; the distinction should be not between good and bad sources, but between genuine and invented persons.[3]

1. A. Tougard, *De l'histoire profane dans les actes grecs des Bollandistes* (Paris, 1874), 271.

2. Thus Atharidus (121) and Rhothesteus (765), both known only from the *Passio Sabae* (*BHG* 1607) lack the stigmata, but a *commentariensis* has them even though an inscription is adduced (86, *!Apronianus!*). One entry also makes an explicit distinction between the genuine *Acta Marcelli* and the "spurious *Acta Cassiani*" (31).

3. *Phoenix* 26 (1972), 141 ff. Significantly, A. Chastagnol misreports the stated rubric as "en-

Deficiencies of this nature indicate a failure of organization rather than mere lapses in the execution of detail. The editors of the *Prosopography* have not consistently observed the principles of hagiographical method, which the Société des Bollandistes has developed over the course of three centuries, and to which Hippolyte Delehaye gave succinct, lucid, and classic expression.[4] The purpose of the present chapter is to apply these principles to the problem of deciding which Roman officials and persons of high rank between 284 and 337 attested only by *acta martyrum* are genuine historical persons.

1. HAGIOGRAPHICAL METHOD AND PROSOPOGRAPHY

The relevant *acta martyrum* must first be classified according to their reliability and historical value. Delehaye made a sixfold division, which scarcely seems to admit of correction or refinement:

1. official reports of trials
2. accounts of eyewitnesses and of contemporaries reporting the accounts of eyewitnesses
3. *acta* of which the principal source is a written document belonging to categories 1 or 2
4. historical romances, including accounts plagiarized from the accounts of other martyrs
5. imaginative romances, in which even the hero has been invented
6. forgeries, i.e. legends composed with the conscious aim of deceiving readers[5]

An obvious corollary can immediately be drawn. If a document belongs to either of the first two categories, then the names which it contains need no external corroboration in order to be presumed authentic. But which *acta martyrum* really belong to these first two categories? The number admitted has been continually diminishing, despite the publication of new passions and of more primitive versions of passions already known.[6] For the years 284 to 337, T.

---

cadrement par astérisque et point d'exclamation pour les personnages apocryphes ou suspects d'inauthenticité" (*REL* 50 (1972), 383).

4. H. Delehaye, *Les légendes hagiographiques* (first published in 1905); *Les légendes grecques des saints militaires* (Paris, 1909); *Les passions des martyrs et les genres littéraires* (1921, reissued in a revised and corrected edition as *Subsidia Hagiographica* 13 B, 1966); *Cinq leçons sur la méthode hagiographique* (*Subsidia Hagiographica* 21, 1934). In this chapter, these four works will be cited with abbreviated titles, as *Légendes* (from the third edition, *Subsidia Hagiographica* 18, 1927, reprinted in a fourth edition, 1955), *Saints militaires, Passions,* and *Méthode.*

5. *Légendes* 101 ff.

6. For *acta* of the period before 250, *JTS*, n.s. 19 (1968), 509 ff. From the decade 250–260, the *Acta Acacii* (Knopf-Krüger 11 = *BHL* 25), the *Acta Maximi* (Knopf-Krüger 12 = *BHL* 5829) and the *Martyrium Cononis* (Knopf-Krüger 14 = *BHG* 361) must definitely be relegated from the highest two classes; see Delehaye, *Passions* 246 ff.; H. Leitzmann, *Kleine Schriften* 1 (*TU* 67, 1958), 241 ff.; A. Harnack, *Chronologie der altchristlichen Litteratur bis Eusebius* 2 (Leipzig,

Ruinart's *Acta primorum martyrum sincera et selecta* (first published in 1689, and reprinted as late as 1859) offered more than fifty texts in all. The two most recent collections of *acta martyrum* contain, respectively, fourteen and twelve documents from the same period,[7] and even some of the chosen dozen may need to be discarded before there remain only the completely reliable. The *acta* of Julius the veteran (*BHL* 4555),[8] of Dasius (*BHG* 491),[9] and of Irenaeus of Sirmium (*BHL* 4466)[10] are all seriously vulnerable. Further, the *acta* of Crispina (*BHL* 1989a/b) contain some interpolations,[11] while the most primitive version of the *Acta Eupli* (*BHG* 629) descends abruptly from reality to fiction (at p. 101.6 Knopf-Krüger = p. 312.16 Musurillo).[12] On the other hand, the Donatist *Sermo de passione Donati* (*BHL* 2303b = *Clavis*[2] 719) appears, on several criteria, to rank with authentic *acta* in the standard collections.[13]

A definitive judgment is not always possible. Yet the two most recent collections of *acta martyrum* contain seven documents which the historian may legitimately trust as wholly authentic, provided that he takes into account the quality of the text and the available editions. They are the following:

1. *Acta Maximiliani* (295): *BHL* 5813 = Knopf-Krüger 19 = Musurillo 17. Despite Delehaye's explicit insistence that "le texte laisse à désirer et devrait être revu sur les manuscrits,"[14] editors inexcusably continue to reprint Ruinart's text.

1904), 469 f. Between 260 and 284, recent collections contain only the *Acta Marini* = Eusebius, *HE* 7.15.

7. Viz. R. Knopf and G. Krüger, *Ausgewählte Märtyrerakten* (third edition 1929, with a fourth edition revised by G. Ruhbach: Tübingen, 1965), and H. Musurillo, *The Acts of the Christian Martyrs* (Oxford, 1972). Of the earlier collection, Musurillo rightly discards the *acta* of Cassianus (Knopf-Krüger 21 = *BHL* 1636) and of Claudius, Asterius, and their companions (Knopf-Krüger 28 = *BHL* 1829).

8. A subjective judgment. For a more favorable assessment, *Anal. Boll.* 10 (1891), 50; H. Delehaye, *Anal. Boll.* 31 (1912), 268 f.; *Comm. Mart. Rom.* 212.

9. Delehaye, *Passions* 230 ff. On the description of the Saturnalia in this passion, see S. Weinstock, *Mullus: Festschrift für Th. Klauser* (Münster, 1964), 391 ff.

10. These *acta* belong to the troublesome third category, see Delehaye, *Légendes* 115. Musurillo prints a text (his 23) which he describes as "ultimately based" on Ruinart, *Acta primorum martyrum* (Ratisbon, 1859), 432–434: here, as elsewhere, he conspicuously fails to provide the "new critical edition" which his preface promises.

11. P. Monceaux, *Mélanges Boissier* (Paris, 1903), 383 ff.; Delehaye, *Passions* 81 ff.; G. E. M. de Ste Croix, *HTR* 47 (1954), 91 f.; G. Lanata, *Gli atti dei martiri come documenti processuali* (Milan, 1973), 93 ff. The *acta* strongly imply that Crispina lacked the senatorial status which Augustine attributed to her (*Enarr. in Ps.* 120.13 (*CCL* 40.1799)).

12. On the relationship between the various recensions of the *Acta Eupli* (and for modern discussion), see F. Corsaro, *Orpheus* 4 (1957), 33 ff.

13. Delehaye, *Passions* 86. The piece was held to be a sermon delivered on 12 March 320 by P. Monceaux, *Histoire littéraire de l'Afrique chrétienne* 5 (Paris, 1920), 60 ff., but later interpolations and reworking of the text are detected by E. L. Grasmück, *Coercitio: Staat und Kirche im Donatistenstreit* (*Bonner Historische Forschungen* 22, 1964), 85.

14. Delehaye, *Passions* 77 n.1.

2. *Passio Marcelli* (298): G. Lanata, *Byzantion* 42 (1972), 513–516, reproduced with a slightly simplified *apparatus criticus* in her book *Gli atti dei martiri come documenti processuali* (Milan, 1973), 202–204. Knopf-Krüger 20 and Musurillo 18 reproduce the provisional edition by H. Delehaye, *Anal. Boll.* 41 (1923), 260–267, which has been rendered obsolete by subsequent work on the manuscript tradition.[15] Unfortunately, however, Lanata prints as part of her text a letter of a governor to the *vicarius* which cannot be genuine (3a).[16]

3. *Acta Felicis* (303): H. Delehaye, *Anal. Boll.* 39 (1921), 268–270 = Knopf-Krüger 22 = Musurillo 20. Musurillo prints an appendix (from Ruinart) which belongs to the later legend of Felix and has no historical value.[17]

4. Μαρτύριον τῶν ἁγίων Ἀγάπης Εἰρήνης καὶ Χιόνης (304): *BHG* 34 = P. Franchi de' Cavalieri, *Nuove note agiografiche* (*Studi e Testi* 9, 1902), 15–19 = Knopf-Krüger 24 = Musurillo 22. Apparently a documentary record of the trial, which a later redactor has equipped with an introduction and conclusion (1/2, 7).[18]

5. Letter of Phileas: Eusebius, *HE* 8.10 = Knopf-Krüger 30 = Musurillo 26.

6. *Acta Phileae* (307): (a) Greek: V. Martin, *Papyrus Bodmer* XX: *Apologie de Philéas évêque de Thmouis* (Geneva, 1963) = Musurillo 27A; (b) Latin: F. Halkin, *Anal. Boll.* 81 (1963), 19–27 = Musurillo 27B.[19]

7. *Testamentum XL martyrum: BHG* 1203 = Knopf-Krüger 32 = Musurillo 28.[20]

---

15. For a conspectus of manuscripts, editions, and studies, F. Masai, *Scriptorium* 20 (1966), 11 ff.; G. Lanata, *Byzantion* 42 (1972), 509 ff. It is not altogether certain that the extant recensions, which diverge substantially, permit the reconstruction of the original text undertaken by Lanata, see F. Dolbeau, *REL* 52 (1974), 572.

16. On this *elogium,* see especially B. de Gaiffier, *Études critiques d'hagiographie et d'iconologie* (*Subsidia Hagiographica* 43, 1967), 81 ff. It contains the phrase "natalis genuini dominorum nostrorum eorundem Augustorumque Caesarum," which was emended to "natalis gemini" and argued to be authentic by W. Seston, *Aux sources de la tradition chrétienne: Mélanges Goguel* (Paris, 1950), 239 ff.; *Historia* 1 (1950), 257 ff. But the reference to all four emperors together in the authentic part of the *Passio Marcelli* has the historically correct *diem festum imperatoris vestri* (2), i.e. the anniversary of Maximian's proclamation as Caesar (Chapter I, n. 5).

17. *Comm. Mart. Rom.* 473.

18. P. Franchi de' Cavalieri, *Nuove note agiografiche* (*Studi e Testi* 9, 1902), 4; Delehaye, *Passions* 103 f.

19. For subsequent discussion of the document, G. Lanata, *Gli atti dei martiri* (Milan, 1973), 227 ff.; *Museum Philologum Londiniense* 2 (1977), 207 ff. The intervention of Philoromus in the Latin *acta* (7) appears to be a later addition, see E. Schwartz, *Ges. Schr.* 3.102 n. 2; M. Simonetti, *Studi agiografici* (Rome, 1955), 109 ff.

20. On the problems posed by this document, P. Franchi de' Cavalieri, *Note agiografiche* 3 (*Studi e Testi* 22, 1909), 64 ff.; *Note agiografiche* 7 (*Studi e Testi* 49, 1928), 155 ff.

Roman officials named in these seven documents (and also those named in the *Acta Eupli* and *Acta Crispinae*) deserve to be regarded as historical even if no confirmatory evidence exists.

An equally clear decision can be given on magistrates named in documents of the last three categories. Whether he intends to deceive or not, the hagiographer who composes a historical romance around a real martyr, or a romance with an invented martyr for hero, is unlikely to transmit genuine names. Admittedly, he might sometimes use a genuine name from a reliable source, and known historical characters do appear in hagiographical fiction; but they have often undergone changes of status, date, and place.[21] The transformation of martyrs like Procopius and Theodorus suggests that genuine names and facts can be disengaged from thoroughly fictitious *acta* only with the aid of external evidence.[22] Hence, if a document contains the name of an authentic magistrate whose title and historical setting have been changed, purely internal criteria will not suffice to detect and rectify the deformation.

There remains the large and difficult category of *acta martyrum* whose principal source is an official report or contemporary account, however often the text has been remodeled, expanded, or even interpolated. Literary analysis quickly reveals that the best texts in the category are but little inferior to contemporary accounts or documentary records, while the worst are almost indistinguishable from entirely fictitious compositions.[23] Thus, at one extreme, the account of the trial of Agape, Irene, and Chione reproduces an official report without detectable alteration, but with additions at the beginning and end which can hardly be contemporary. Toward the other extreme, the version of the *Acta Felicis* printed by Ruinart illustrates the evanescence of genuine fact (*BHL* 2895). Anullinus, the proconsul of Africa, and the local *curator* Magnilianus survive unchanged from the more primitive *Acta Felicis,* which are clearly the main or only written source.[24] But the *legatus proconsulis* is in the process of disappearing and being replaced by the proconsul himself, and a praetorian prefect has been invented, to whom Felix is dispatched from Africa and by whom he is executed at Venusia.[25]

The literary classification of *acta martyrum* both reflects and indicates their historical reliability. But evidence external to the text must also be taken into ac-

21. Thus Annius Anullinus appears, not only correctly as proconsul of Africa (*BHL* 5809 = *Anal. Boll.* 9 (1890), 110-116; *BHL* 4279 = *Acta Sanctorum* Mai. 2³ (Paris, 1866), 138/9), but also in northern Italy, where his alleged date fluctuates widely, see B. de Gaiffier, *Anal. Boll.* 72 (1954), 379.

22. For these two striking cases, see Delehaye, *Légendes* 119 ff.; *Saints militaires* 11 ff.

23. Delehaye, *Légendes* 114 ff.; *Passions* 260 ff.

24. Magnilianus should be the *curator* attested by *CIL* 8.23964/5, cf. R. Duncan-Jones, *JTS,* n.s. 25 (1974), 106 ff., who shows that the town cannot be Thibiuca, as is commonly supposed.

25. Ruinart, *Acta primorum martyrum* (Ratisbon, 1859), 290 f. I cite this notoriously inaccurate reprint rather than the editions of 1689 or 1713, on the grounds that it is more widely available.

count. The "hagiographical coordinates" of a martyr sometimes provide decisive proof that officials whom his *acta* name are unhistorical.[26] For, if the cult of a martyr is attested at an early date in one place, while the extant passions or *acta* situate his trial and martyrdom elsewhere, then any Roman magistrates or officials whom they locate at a place where the martyr was neither tried nor executed are likely to be inventions.[27]

Two other types of criterion lend additional aid in exposing fiction. Hagiographical inventions are often betrayed by obvious ignorance of specific historical details, as when the magistrate who tries a martyr bears an impossible or anachronistic title: for example, a *praeses* governing Corsica and Sardinia as a single province, a governor of Lycaonia decades before the province existed, or an otherwise unattested *praefectus urbi* at a date when the names of all the prefects are known.[28]

More serious, at least in its effects on modern comprehension, was the hagiographers' overall conception of the period. Lactantius and Eusebius provide a clear outline of imperial policy toward the Christians.[29] After the capture of Valerian (260), although Christianity probably remained in theory a capital crime, Christians were in practice left largely unmolested. Diocletian only attacked the church toward the end of his reign, and then under the influence of Galerius. Even though Christians in the eastern armies were ordered to sacrifice in 299, Diocletian did not promulgate the first general persecuting edict until February 303, and universal persecution was a brief episode. In the west, the edict ordaining universal sacrifice (spring 304) was never promulgated and persecution ceased altogether in 306. In the Danubian provinces, the persecuting edicts remained in force until 311, and in the Asiatic provinces persecution was finally halted by Licinius' defeat of Maximinus (313). Finally, there were some executions of Christians under Licinius, between c. 320 and 324. These facts were too prosaic for generations of hagiographers, who replaced them with a "heroic age" of early Christianity in which Diocletian indulged in a vicious persecution throughout the twenty years of his rule. Many passions and *acta martyrum* depict Diocletian as ordaining persecution by imperial edict long before 303 — a fact which alone convicts them of invention and usually suffices to damn the magistrates whom they name.[30]

---

26. For the crucial importance of identifying saints by the day of their anniversary and the place of its celebration, see Delehaye, *Méthode* 5 ff.

27. E.g., 'Pyrrhus' (below, List C).

28. E.g., 'Barbarus,' 'Domitianus,' and 'Plautianus' (below, List C).

29. Lactantius, *Mort. Pers.* 5.1–48.13; Eusebius, *HE* 7.15–9.11.

30. Delehaye, *Légendes* 85 ff.; *Passions* 173 ff.

2. GENUINE AND FICTITIOUS NAMES

The three lists below attempt to apply sound principles of hagiographical method to the problem of segregating Roman officials attested by *acta martyrum* for the period 284–337 into the real and the bogus.

List A includes all persons appearing in the seven authentic *acta martyrum* listed above, and in the *acta* of Euplus and Crispina, who hold official posts in the Roman army or imperial administration or who possess senatorial status. They are listed whether their existence is confirmed by other evidence or not, and the list is intended to comprise all persons in this category.

List B contains holders of official posts in the Roman army or imperial administration attested solely by other *acta martyrum* who may be historical characters. This list is deliberately brief and select; some names in list C perhaps deserve promotion to list B.

List C contains names which the first volume of the *Prosopography of the Later Roman Empire* registers on the strength of *acta martyrum* alone but which should be rejected as fictitious.

The lists are thus diverse in both nature and comprehensiveness. Only the first aims at completeness; the second is by its very nature provisional; and the third is confined to existing entries in the *Prosopography*. Although a fuller collection of fictitious names could easily be compiled,[31] its usefulness for study of the period of Diocletian and Constantine seems questionable. Furthermore, two deliberate omissions must be avowed: first, genuine officials or senators on independent attestation who appear in unreliable *acta martyrum,* unless they qualify for lists A or B; and second, genuine persons named only in other types of hagiographical documents, such as Eusebius' *Martyrs of Palestine,* the poems of Prudentius, calendars, and martyrologies.[32]

A. GENUINE PERSONS OF HIGH RANK

Aurelius Agricolanus (31)[33]

Agens vices/vicem/vice praefectorum praetorio, at Tingi on 30 October 298 (*Passio Marcelli*).

Anullinus (79)

Proconsul of Africa, from at least June 303 (*Acta Felicis*) to December 304 (*Acta Crispinae*).

---

31. E.g., by recourse to the excellent index in the reprint of B. Mombritius, *Sanctuarium seu Vitae Sanctorum* 2 (Paris, 1910), 761 ff.

32. For some important names in calendars, see B. de Gaiffier, *Anal. Boll.* 75 (1957), 17 ff.

33. The numbers in brackets supply the page reference in *PLRE* 1. Cross-references are not normally given to the discussions of posts, careers, and identities in Chapters VI–IX.

Calvisianus (177)

ὁ λαμπρότατος κορρήκτωρ, at Catana in 304 (*Acta Eupli*), i.e. *corrector* of Sicilia. Calvisianus' title confirms the excellence of the source: after c. 324 the governor of Sicily bore the title *consularis,* not *corrector.*

Clodius Culcianus (233/4)

ἡγεμών, at Alexandria (*Acta Phileae*). The date of Phileas' martyrdom is probably 4 February 307.[34]

Cassius Dion (253)

Proconsul, of Africa, at Theveste in March 295 (*Acta Maximiliani*).

Dulcitius (273)

ἡγεμών, at Thessalonica in March 304 (Μαρτύριον τῶν ἁγίων Ἀγάπης, Εἰρήνης καὶ Χιόνης).

Fortunatus (370)

Praeses on 28 July 298 (*Passio Marcelli*). The version of the passion which presents Fortunatus as *praeses* at León, and therefore governor of Gallaecia (Recension N, ed. H. Delehaye, *Anal. Boll.* 41 (1923), 264–267), is secondary;[35] hence Fortunatus' province is unknown. As for his name, the *Prosopography* enters him as Astasius Fortunatus (as in Recension M, ed. H. Delehaye, *Anal. Boll.* 41 (1923), 260–263). But *Astasius* is an unjustified emendation.[36] Nor is the name *Manilius* (Recension N) adequately attested: in the edition by G. Lanata (*Byzantion* 42 (1972), 513–516), it occurs only in the interpolated letter of Fortunatus to Agricolanus (3a).

Maximus (not in *PLRE* 1)

ὁ λαμπρότατος, at Catana in 304 (*Acta Eupli* 1.2). Probably a member of the *consilium* of the governor Calvisianus.[37]

---

34. The day is attested by the *Martyrologium Hieronymianum* (*Acta Sanctorum,* Nov. 2.2 (Brussels, 1931), 77), while the year is inferred from the fact that Phileas wrote a letter from prison to Meletius which survives in a Latin translation (*EOMIA* 1.636/7, cf. K. Müller, *Abh. Berlin,* Phil.-hist. Klasse 1922, Abh. 3.12 ff.).

35. B. de Gaiffier, *Anal. Boll.* 61 (1943), 116 ff.

36. F. Masai, *Scriptorium* 20 (1966), 16 ff.

37. Or else a prominent local figure with access to the governor, see P. Franchi de' Cavalieri, *Note agiografiche* 7 (*Studi e Testi* 49, 1928), 6 f.; G. Lanata, *Gli atti dei martiri* 226. The Latin version of the *Acta Eupli* printed by Ruinart styles Maximus *unus ex amicis Calvisiani* (Ruinart, *Acta primorum martyrum* (1859), 437 = p. 101.26 Knopf-Krüger = p. 314.7 Musurillo). The phrase appears to be an interpolation by Baronius, see Franchi de' Cavalieri, *Note agiografiche* 7 (1928), 37 ff.

Philoromus (698)

Executed at Alexandria with Phileas, the bishop of Thmuis (*Acta Phileae* (Latin) 7), probably on 4 February 307. About Philoromus' status, the evidence diverges. Eusebius states that he held "an office of no small importance in the imperial administration of Alexandria" (*HE* 8.9.7). In his translation, Rufinus seems to have misunderstood Eusebius' further remark that, in virtue of his rank, Philoromus was escorted by soldiers at his trial: hence he makes him *vir turmam agens militum Romanorum,* and the Latin *Acta Phileae* may be dependent on Rufinus when they style him *tribunus Romanorum,* in a passage which is lacking in the Greek version and appears to be interpolated.[38]

Pompeianus (712)

Advocatus at Theveste on 12 March 295 (*Acta Maximiliani*). Presumably an *advocatus fisci.*[39]

?Valerius Quintianus (759)[40]

Praepositus Caesariensis, at Theveste in March 295 (*Acta Maximiliani* 1.1). In the absence of a critical edition of these *acta,* neither the name nor the office can be regarded as certain.[41]

Anonymous (not in *PLRE* 1)

Legatus, at Carthage in July 303 (*Acta Felicis* 23 ff.). Clearly legate of the proconsul Anullinus.[42]

B. Some Doubtful Cases

Ausonius (138)

Governor at Edessa, i.e. of Osrhoene, perhaps in 310 (*Acts of Habib, BHO* 367: English translation by F. C. Burkitt, *Euphemia and the Goth* (London, 1913), 112 ff.). The extant *acta* may be based on authentic information; hence the name of the governor may be genuine, even though its form is not unambiguously attested.[43]

38. Above n. 19.
39. Delehaye, *Passions* 78.
40. Valerius is an emendation: *PLRE* gives the first name as *Valesianus* following Ruinart, *Acta primorum martyrum* (Paris, 1689), 309 = (1859), 340, while Knopf-Krüger silently alter to *Valerianus* (p. 86.9).
41. For discussion, M. Durry, *Mélanges Ernout* (Paris, 1940), 129 ff.
42. Musurillo strangely alleges that he was "the *legatus* of the *legio III Augusta,* stationed at Carthage" (p. 269 n. 6).
43. On the date and the name, see Burkitt, *Euphemia* 29 f., 175 f. Opinions vary widely on the value of the *Acts of Habib* and the *Acts of Guriā and Shamōnā.* For a favorable estimate, Burkitt, *Euphemia* 9 ff.; J. B. Segal, *Edessa 'the Blessed City'* (London, 1970), 93; for a more skeptical view, P. Devos, *Anal. Boll.* 90 (1972), 432 f.

Bassus (151)

The *Prosopography* registers two separate Bassi from *acta martyrum:* one as *legatus* in Moesia Inferior in 303 (from the *Acta Dasii, BHG* 491 = Knopf-Krüger 23 = Musurillo 21). The other as "governor in Thrace" c. 304 (from the *Passio Philippi, BHL* 6834). The date of 303 for the former depends on the assumption that he is genuine.[44] As for the latter, the absence of Greek *acta* of Philippus is disturbing, and the Latin passion has some clearly invented characters (e.g., 'Mucapor,' cf.Victor, *Caes.* 36.2; *HA, Aurel.* 35.5 (the assassin of Aurelian)). Nevertheless, it is possible that there was a genuine governor named Bassus who persecuted Christians in the area in or soon after 303.

Dacianus or Datianus (244)

Prominent as a persecutor in several cycles of passions of Spanish martyrs, none of which merits any confidence.[45] But *acta* circulated as early as c. 400 which named Datianus as the governor who had executed Vincentius (Prudentius, *Peristephanon* 5.40, 130, 422; Augustine, *Sermo* 276.4 (*PL* 38.1257)).

Heraclianus (not in *PLRE* 1)

Dux at Nisibis (*Acts of Guriā and Shamōnā, BHO* 363: English translation by F.C. Burkitt, *Euphemia and the Goth* (1913), 90 ff.). Not named in the main narrative, only with a list of martyrs outside Edessa. The source and value of this list remains problematical.[46]

Lysias (523)

Lysias appears in a cycle of passions from Cilicia, which seem to have been composed no earlier than the division of Cilicia into two provinces some time after 381 (W. Lackner, *Anal. Boll.* 87 (1969), 115 ff.; 90 (1972), 241 ff.). Although the *acta* cannot be authentic (a date of 285 is alleged),[47] local tradition may have preserved the name of a real governor who executed Christians in the region in the early fourth century.

Marcellinus (545)

The *Sermo de passione Donati* records events leading to the deaths of Donatist bishops, apparently on 12 March 317 (*PL* 8.752–758).[48] The names of the persecutors are given thus: "Res apud Carthaginem gesta est Caeciliano pseudepiscopo[49] tunc instante, assentiente Leontio comite, duce Ursatio, Marcellino

44. The entry invokes F. Cumont, *Anal. Boll.* 16 (1897), 8.
45. B. de Gaiffier, *Anal. Boll.* 72 (1954), 378 ff.
46. P. Devos, *Anal. Boll.* 90 (1972), 15 ff.
47. As in the *Acta Claudii,* p. 109.15 Knopf-Krüger — which were damned by P. Franchi de' Cavalieri, *Nuovo Bullettino di Archeologia Cristiana* 10 (1904), 17 ff. = *Scritti agiografichi (Studi e Testi* 222, 1962), 86 ff.
48. P. Monceaux, *Histoire littéraire* 5 (1920), 61.
49. Migne prints the nonsensical *Eudinepiso,* from L. E. Dupin, *Sanctus Optatus de Schismate Donatistarum*[3] (Antwerp, 1702), 191.

tunc tribuno" (2, *PL* 8.753). Two opposing views of the three officials are possible. Either the names and posts are all genuine (as the *Prosopography* assumes),[50] or they are inventions based on three notorious enemies of the Donatists, who were active at different dates. Leontius and Ursacius are known from other evidence as persecutors of the Donatists (especially Optatus 3.1, 4, 10); while Ursacius cooperated with Domitius Zenophilus c. 320 (Augustine, *Contra Cresconium* 3.30.34), Optatus writes as if he and Leontius presided over different episodes (3.4, p. 85.3/4 Ziwsa: "sub Leontio, sub Ursacio..., sub Paulo et Macario."). As for Marcellinus, the *tribunus et notarius* who presided over the Conference of 411 also bore the name Marcellinus[51] — a coincidence which some have found not only suspicious but damning.[52]

Mysianus (615)

Governor at Edessa, i.e. of Osrhoene, perhaps in 309 (*Acts of Guriā and Shamōnā, BHO* 363). As likely to be genuine as Ausonius.[53]

C. Rejected Names

The following names of persons attested as magistrates or possessors of high status between 284 and 337 only by dubious *acta martyrum* should be expunged both from the main section of the *Prosopography* and, if they occur there, from the fasti (1.1041–1127).[54] The list normally enters (1) the name rejected; (2) a page reference to the first volume of the *Prosopography;* (3) a reference to the primary hagiographical document or documents which attest the name; and (4) the rank, title, or official position these allege (which is not necessarily that reported in the *Prosopography*). Where appropriate, brief annotation has been added.

50. *PLRE* 1.499–500, Leontius 4; 545, Marcellinus 3; 984, Ursacius 1.
51. Viz. Flavius Marcellinus, cf. W. Ensslin, *RE* 14 (1930), 1445 f.
52. Seeck, *Geschichte* 3².517 f.
53. On the date and the form of the name, see Burkitt, *Euphemia* 29 f., 165.
54. Persons entered under the rubric "L III" are here included (e.g. 'Acacius'). The following names from *acta martyrum* assigned to a date earlier than 284 should also be expunged: the consul 'Agesius' (*PLRE* 1.28); the former proconsul 'Clarus' (206); the conflated 'Claudius Cleobulus,' entered as a possible governor of Syria under Probus (216), cf. *Phoenix* 26 (1972), 172 n. 118; 'Crispinus,' *praeses* in Gaul under Aurelian (231.1); 'Lampadius,' consul three times (493.1); 'Silvanus,' *comes* in Bithynia under Aurelian (840).

On the other hand, the following persons whom the *Prosopography* stigmatizes (contrast 966, Vincentius 1) may be admitted as real persons whose status has been falsified: Mocius (604) is a genuine martyr whose cult is well attested, see H. Delehaye, *Les origines du culte des martyrs*² (*Subsidia Hagiographica* 20, 1933), 233 ff.; Mustiola (614) is attested as a saint at Clusium (*CIL* 11.2549 = *ILCV* 4553), but the evidence that she was related to the emperor Claudius is worthless (*BHL* 4455/6); Theodorus (896) is a genuine martyr, who was in reality a humble recruit, not a Roman general (Gregory of Nyssa, *PG* 46.735 ff. = *Acta Sanctorum,* Nov. 4 (Brussels, 1925), 25 ff.). The doctor Aristo (105) named by Prudentius *Peristephanon* 10.896 ff., may also be historical (cf. Chapter VIII.1, on Asclepiades).

'Acacius' (6)	*BHG* 279/80; *BHL* 1413	Father of 'Aglais'
'Aglais' (30)	*BHG* 279/80; *BHL* 1413	Descendant of 'Clarus,' who is alleged to have been a proconsul, apparently in the middle of the third century
'Agrianus' (30)	*BHG* 467	Governor of Crete in 304

Argued to be authentic by P. Franchi de' Cavalieri, *Note agiografiche* 9 (*Studi Testi* 175, 1953), 210 f. The Latin passions of the same martyr place his death "sub Decio imp., agente Lucio duce" (*BHL* 2070).

'Alexander' (40)	*BHG* 313y–318e	*Praeses* of Cilicia c. 304
'Amantius' (50)	*BHL* 7035	*Praeses* of Pannonia Prima c. 304

Jerome, *Chronicle* 229[e], dates the martyr's death to 307/8.

'Antiochus' (71)	*BHG* 1624	*Dux* of Augusta Euphratensis c. 304

The *Prosopography* enters 'Antiochus' as a genuine person, with appeal to A. H. M. Jones, *JRS* 44 (1954), 23 n. 32. But the passion of Sergius and Bacchus is clearly fictitious (*Comm. Mart. Rom.* 439), and the name 'Antiochus' is an obvious allusion to the Seleucid king of the second century B.C. against whom the Maccabees rebelled.

'Apellianus' (80)	*BHG* 2399	Proconsul, in Thrace
'Armenius' (108)	*BHO* 107, 578, etc.	*Dux* or *comes* of Alexandria c. 304

Vandersleyen, *Chronologie* 92, argues that 'Armenius,' who occurs often in the Coptic hagiography of Egypt, was *dux* of Egypt from 303 until 307 or even later, while the *Prosopography* states that "if he is genuine, he was presumably a *comes* sent by Diocletian or Galerius as an agent to prosecute the persecution." In fact, 'Armenius' appears to be a double of the historical Satrius Arrianus, who also appears frequently in fictitious Egyptian *acta martyrum* (H. Delehaye, *Anal. Boll.* 40 (1922), 139, cf. 27 ff.).

'Asterius' (118)	*BHL* 8569	*Praeses* and *praefectus,* at Massilia c. 304
'Barbarus' (146)	*BHL* 2156; 7490/1	*Praeses* of Corsica and Sardinia in 304
'Baudus' (159)	*BHG* 2280/1	*Praeses,* in Thrace shortly before 324
'Celsina' (190)	*BHG* 2280/1	*Clarissima femina,* at Beroea shortly before 324
'Claudius' (207)	*BHL* 8354	*Dux* or *comes* of Mauretania Caesariensis in 303 or 304

'Crispinus' (232.3)   *BHL* 2911/2   *Praeses,* at Vienne, no date stated

'Delphius' (247)   *BHL* 5092   *Praeses,* in Sardinia c. 304

'Diogenianus' (257)   *BHL* 4566–4569   *Praeses,* in Baetica, no clear indication of date

'Domitianus' (262)   *BHG* 314   *Comes,* made *praeses* of Lycaonia c. 304

    Lycaonia did not become a separate province until c. 370 (Basil, *Epp.* 138).

'Doncius' (269)   *BHL* 8354   *Praepositus,* at Tigavum in 303 or 304

'Dulcitius' (273.1)   *BHL* 1543–49   Governor at Aquileia under Diocletian

    Presumably inspired by a Latin translation (*BHL* 118-120) of the *acta* which record the genuine Dulcitius at Thessalonica in 304.

'Euphrates' (299)   *BHG* 1298   Quaestor and praetor at Rome before 287/8

'Eustathia' (310)   *BHG* 1298   Wife of 'Euphrates'

'Eustratius' (314)   *BHG* 1742   Governor at Alexandria c. 304

    Delehaye assigned the *acta* to the category of imaginative romance (*Légendes* 113 ff.).

'Euticius' (316)   *BHL* 8569   *Praeses* and *praefectus,* at Massilia c. 304

'Eutolmius' (316)   *BHG* 39/40   *Comes,* in Bithynia and Thrace under Galerius

'Eutychianus' (319)   *BHO* 578   Governor or *comes* of Pchati, i.e. Nikiu, when Arrianus was governor of the Thebaid

    Vandersleyen, *Chronologie* 89 f., argued that 'Eutychianus' was possibly prefect of Egypt in 308/9. That thesis being proven impossible (*P. Oxy.* 2666/7), the *Prosopography* suggests that he may have been governor of the Thebaid c. 306

'Eutychius' (321)   *BHL* 8627–40   Son of the consul 'Agesius'

'Fabianus' (322)   *BHL* 7543   *Praefectus,* at Rome in or shortly after 286

    The name was inspired by that of Fabianus, bishop of Rome, whose death was celebrated on the same day as St. Sebastian (Delehaye, *Méthode* 36).

'Firmilianus' (338)   *BHG* 1250   *Tribunus,* in Phrygia c. 304

'Flavianus' (343)   *BHL* 2567   Deputy of 'Julicus'

'Gaius' (381)   *BHL* 108/9   *Iudex,* at Augusta Vindelicum c. 304

'Julicus' (481)   *BHL* 2567   *Iudex,* in Sardinia c. 304

'Julicus' is the 'Oulcion' of Greek legends of Procopius, and his deputy 'Flavianus' the genuine Flavianus, governor of Palestine in 303 (Delehaye, *Légendes* 135 f.).

'Justinus' (489) *BHL* 6834 *Praeses* in Thrace c. 304

According to the *Passio Philippi,* successor of Bassus (List B).

'Lampadius' (493.2)	*Acta Sanctorum,* Nov. 3 (Brussels, 1910), 765–784	*Tribunus,* in Pannonia in November 302
'Laodicius' (495.1)	*BHG* 1298	Proconsul of Europa in 287/8
'Laodicius' (495.2)	*BHL* 5234/5	*Praefectus urbis* c. 304
'Leuco' (505)	*BHL* 6070–74	*Consiliarius* of 'Maximus' (*PLRE* 1.580.3)
'Marianus' (559)	*BHG* 2280/1	*Palatinus,* with Licinius in Thrace shortly before 324
'Maximinus' (576)	*BHG* 1298	Proconsul of Europa in succession to 'Laodicius'
'Maximus' (580.3)	*BHL* 6070–74	*Praeses,* in Campania, no clear indication of date

The martyrs in question belong in fact to Moesia (*Comm. Mart. Rom.* 224f.).

'Maximus' (580.4) *BHL* 4555 *Praeses,* at Durostorum *tempore persetionis*

The *Acta Julii* are pronounced "bonae notae iudicio peritorum" in *Comm. Mart. Rom.* 212.

'Maximus' (580.5) *BHL* 7035 *Praeses,* at Siscia c. 304

Jerome, *Chronicle* 229[e], dates the martyr's death to 307/8.

'Fl. Gaius Numerianus Maximus' (588)	*BHG* 1574, *BHL* 7981–7985[55]	*Praeses,* at Tarsus under Diocletian
'Megetius' (592)	*BHL,* Supp. 3001–6	*Augustalis,* in Umbria under Diocletian

The *Acta Firminae* appear to be no earlier than the seventh century and the martyr herself is fictitious (*Comm. Mart. Rom.* 542 f., 558).

---

55. Also F. Halkin, *Inédits byzantins d'Ochrida, Candie et Moscou* (*Subsidia Hagiographica* 38, 1963), 211 ff.

'Olympiades' (642)   *BHL,* Supp.   *Consularis* and *augustalis,* predecessor
                      3001–6   of 'Megetius'

'Pancratius' (664)   *BHL* 1637   Proconsul of Tuscia under Diocletian

The *Acta Cassiani* seem to be a deliberate forgery, probably of the six-teenth century (*Acta Sanctorum,* Aug. 3³ (Paris, 1867), 20 f.).

'Philippesius' (695)   *BHG* 1298   *Praefectus,* at Heraclea in Thrace in 287/8

'Philophron' (698)   *BHG* 619   Senator under Diocletian

'Plautianus' (706)   *BHL* 3315   *Praefectus* in Rome with Diocletian

'Plautianus' surely owes his name to Fulvius Plautianus, the praetorian prefect of Septimius Severus; the martyr Genesius seems to be bogus and his passion is a "roman d'imagination" (*Comm. Mart. Rom.* 359; Delehaye, *Légendes* 113f.).[56]

'Possidonius' (717)   *BHG* 2416   *Praepositus* of the legion II Traiana, in Hellespontus under Licinius

Modeled on the *ducenarius* 'Possidonius' in *acta* of Theodorus (Delehaye, *Saints militaires* 24f., 128, 139 f.).

'Priscus' (729)   *BHG* 619   Proconsul of Europa c. 304

'Probus' (736)   *BHL* 4466;   *Praeses Pannoniae* c. 304
                  6869

The *Passio Pollionis* (*BHL* 6869) is pronounced "bonae notae" in *Comm. Mart. Rom.* 106. I suspect that 'Probus' owes his existence to the fact that the emperor Probus was killed at Sirmium.

'Proculus' (745)   *BHL* 8072   Proconsul at Alexandria c. 304

'Proculus' corresponds to 'Eustratius' in the Greek *acta* of the same saints (*BHG* 1742).

'Publio' (754)   *BHG* 1574;   *Tribunus* or *princeps,* under Diocletian
                BHL 7981–85

'Publius' (754.1)   *BHG* 1761–   *Praeses,* at Antioch c. 304
                  1762d

The manuscripts of the earliest Greek version of the *Passio Theodori* give his name as both 'Publius' and 'Publius Strato' (*Acta Sanctorum,* Nov. 4 (Brussels, 1925), 32).

'Publius' (754.2)   *BHL* 6834   *Assessor praesidis,* i.e. of Bassus (List B)

---

56. The historicity of Genesius (but not of the *passio*) is defended by A. Amore, *I martiri di Roma* (Rome, 1975), 102 f.

'Pyrrhus' (756)   *BHG* 1250   Governor, at Cotyaeum c. 304

Menas, whose fictitious *acta* attest both 'Firmilianus' and 'Pyrrhus,' was an Egyptian saint whose cult was introduced to Cotyaeum toward the middle of the fifth century, see P. Peeters, *Orient et Byzance: Le tréfonds oriental de l'hagiographie byzantine* (*Subsidia Hagiographica* 26, 1950), 32 ff.).

'Rictiovarus' (766)   *Praeses* and *praefectus,* in northern Gaul, c. 304

'Rictiovarus' appears in many passions of Gallic martyrs (C. Jullian, *REA* 25 (1923), 367 ff.), but Lactantius expressly denies that any Christians were executed in Gaul under Constantius (*Mort. Pers.* 15.6).

'Severus' (831)   *BHL* 6702   *Praeses,* in Palestine under Galerius

'Simplicius' (843)   *BHL* 1413   *Iudex,* in Cilicia in 290

Not named in the Greek *acta* (*BHG* 279/80).

'Symphronius' (871)   *BHL* 156 =   *Praefectus* (*urbi*), some years before
                           *Clavis*² 2159   Constantine

'Theotecnus' (908)   *BHG* 1782   Governor, in Galatia c. 304

Clearly modeled on the genuine Theotecnus (Eusebius, *HE* 9.2.2, 3.4, 11.5 f.).[57]

'Thrason' (910)   *BHL* 2062   *Magister militum* at Rome in 298/9

The *Passio Cyriaci* which makes 'Thrason' a *magister militum* appears to be based on bogus *acta* of Marcellus, bishop of Rome, but these attest no official post (*BHL* 2056–59, cf. *BHL* 5234/5; *Comm. Mart. Rom.* 24).

'Zelicinthius' (990)   *BHG* 2416   *Tribunus* of the legion II Traiana, under Licinius

The *Prosopography* enters the name as 'Zelicentius' from the Latin translation of the *Passio Theagenis* (*BHL* 8106).[58]

'Anonymus' 3   *BHL* 2895   *Praefectus praetorio* in Italy in 303
(1005)

In a spurious addition to the genuine *Acta Felicis.*

'Anonymus' 4   *BHL* 2275   *Iudex, praefectus,* and *praeses Gallia-*
(1005)   *rum* c. 304

---

57. H. Grégoire and P. Orgels, *BZ* 44 (1951), 165 ff., argued that 'Theotecnus' in the *Passio Theodoti* "constitue un souvenir historique indépendant du texte d'Eusèbe." On the unhistorical nature of the text, H. Delehaye, *Anal. Boll.* 22 (1903), 320 ff.

58. For proof that the Latin *passio* is a mere translation from the Greek, P. Franchi de' Cavalieri, *Note agiografiche* 4 (*Studi e Testi* 24, 1912), 161 ff.

| 'Anonymus' 112 (1023) | *BHL* 7595 | *Rector provinciae* and *praeses,* at Sirmium c. 306 |
| 'Anonymus' 195 (1033) | *BHL* 7595 | *Domesticus Maximiani imperatoris* at Sirmium |

In epilogue, a note of caution must be sounded. The evaluation of *acta martyrum,* and of the historical information which they contain, must necessarily proceed from known and verifiable facts. Sometimes complete certainty can be attained, but the majority of cases fall far short of conclusive proof. The preceding lists attempt to apply general principles of hagiographical method to a large number of individual and varied problems. It cannot be assumed that the application will have been equally successful in every instance. The discovery of an inscription has sometimes confirmed the existence of a governor previously known only from late and unreliable documents whose debt to local tradition or a lost written source had passed undetected.[59] Other *acta martyrum* whose testimony has here been rejected may await the same vindication.[60]

59. E.g., the Marcianus in passions of Julianus of Anazarbus (*BHG* 965-967e) is Aemilius Marcianus, *praeses Ciliciae* (*CIL* 3.223, cf. W. Lackner, *Vig. Chr.* 27 (1973), 53 ff.), and a Sabinus of Cypriot hagiography is now certified as the *praeses* Antistius Sabinus (*I. Salamis* 39, 40, 129-131, cf. I. Michaelidou-Nicolaou, *Acta of the Fifth International Congress of Greek and Latin Epigraphy* (Oxford, 1971), 381 ff.).

60. Observe, e.g., C. Foss, *DOP* 31 (1977), 33 ff. (the hagiography of Ancyra); 86 (governors of Galatia and *vicarii* of Pontus from the *Vita Clementis* (*BHG* 353)). Elsewhere in the present volume, I have adduced the *Passio Quattuor Coronatorum* as putative evidence for the movements of Diocletian (Chapter V, n. 42), the *Passio Sabini* for the movements of Maximian (Chapter V, n. 61), and for a praetorian prefect (Chapter VIII, at nn. 58-61), and the hagiography of Myra for a governor of Phrygia (Chapter IX, n. 46).

THE
ADMINISTRATION
OF THE EMPIRE

CHAPTER XI

POLITICAL DIVISIONS

OF THE EMPIRE

Imperial pronouncements of all types were conventionally issued in the joint name of all the emperors who belonged to the imperial college; hence, for example, a letter of Constantius which speaks of "meus Constanti Caesaris ex Italia revertentis comitatus" can be described as "hae imperatorum et Caesarum litterae" (*Pan. Lat.* 9(4).14.1, 15.2). But a legal enactment of one emperor might not be enforced or even promulgated by his colleagues. The clearest case concerns the edicts which Diocletian issued against the Christians in 303 and 304: the first edict was promulgated throughout the empire, but Constantius declined to enforce it strictly in the territories which he ruled (Lactantius, *Mort. Pers.* 15.6-7), while the fourth and most severe edict was neither enforced nor (it seems) promulgated anywhere in the western half of the Roman Empire.[1] Since the identity of the emperor who exercised effective control over a particular area influenced the policies which impinged on its inhabitants, this chapter sets out to present as clearly as possible the evidence for the political divisions of the Roman Empire between 285 and 337.[2]

1. CHRONOLOGICAL SURVEY

285-293

Diocletian was proclaimed Augustus on 20 November 284 at Nicomedia and was at once recognized as ruler throughout Asia Minor, the east, and

1. G. E. M. de Ste Croix, *HTR* 47 (1954), 84 ff. Similarly, all the very numerous fragments the edict of 301 on maximum prices come from the eastern half of the empire, and there is no reason to believe that the edict was published in the west (J. and L. Robert, *BE* 1964.69).
2. Detailed cross-references are not given for statements based on Chapters I, II, and V.

Egypt.[3] He must also quickly have acquired the Danubian provinces closest to Asia. In 285, probably in the spring, Diocletian defeated Carinus and thus became recognized as ruler throughout the Roman Empire. On 21 July 285 he appointed Maximian Caesar and dispatched him to Gaul.

Maximian became Augustus on 1 April 286, but soon lost control both of Britain (which had its own emperor until 296) and of a large part of northwestern Gaul (until 293). A formal division of the empire between the two Augusti is nowhere explicitly attested, but the panegyrist of 289 may allude to such a division when he expresses the wish that "tuque potissimum (credo enim hoc idem Diocletianum Oriens rogat) has provincias tuas frequenter inlustres" (*Pan. Lat.* 10(2).14.4). If the empire was formally divided, then Maximian's portion comprised Italy, Africa, Gaul, and Spain.

293–305

Lactantius expressly states that the appointment of the Caesars entailed a fourfold division of the empire: "tres enim participes regni sui fecit [sc. Diocletianus] in quattuor partes orbe diviso" (*Mort. Pers.* 7.2).[4] Aurelius Victor (*Caes.* 39.30) and Praxagoras (*FGrH* 219) provide details, which can be supplemented from elsewhere (Lactantius, *Mort. Pers.* 8.3; *Pan. Lat.* 8(5).6.1). In the west, Maximian held Italy, Africa, and Spain, while the Caesar Constantius received most of Gaul in March 293, won the rest of Gaul in summer 293, and added the still rebellious Britain in 296. In the east, according to Victor and Praxagoras, the Caesar Galerius was assigned the Danubian provinces, while Diocletian retained Asia Minor and the diocese of Oriens (which included Egypt). But Diocletian spent the years 293 and 294 on the Danube frontier, while Galerius appears to have gone to Egypt. Moreover, the Persian War of 296–299 and a revolt in Egypt in 297–298 necessitated the presence of both Diocletian and Galerius in the oriental provinces. Victor and Praxagoras, therefore, describe a situation which obtained only from 299 to 305. The contemporary evidence indicates that in 293 Galerius had received the diocese of Oriens, with Diocletian retaining the Danube area and probably the whole of Asia Minor.[5]

Between 293 and 305, even if formally divided into four, the Roman Empire was in practice divided into two, but even this division was disregarded on

---

3. The earliest known papyrus attesting his control of Egypt belongs to 7 March 285 (*P. Oxy.* 3055). It refutes the hypothesis advanced by Vandersleyen, *Chronologie* 33 ff., that Diocletian was not recognized as emperor in Egypt until after the death of Carinus.

4. Lactantius' clear statement fortunately renders it irrelevant whether Victor wrote *quadripartito imperio* or *quasi partito imperio* (*Caes.* 39.30). The existence of a fourfold division of authority before 305 is denied by Seston, *Dioclétien* 231 ff.; G. E. M. de Ste Croix, *HTR* 47 (1954), 105 ff.

5. *Phoenix* 30 (1976), 187. Lactantius implies that in 305 Galerius had guarded the Danube for fifteen years (*Mort. Pers.* 18.6): either he is mistaken or the numeral is corrupt.

some occasions and for some purposes. Each Augustus and his Caesar cooperated in military and political crises, so that Maximian defended the Rhine
when Constantius invaded Britain (*Pan. Lat.* 8(5).13.3), while Diocletian and
Galerius not only acted together during the Persian War of 296–299, but also
conferred in Nicomedia in 303 and 305, while Diocletian probably campaigned
on the Danube in 304. But only two occasions are recorded on which an
eastern and western emperor entered the other half of the empire: Diocletian
visited Italy in 303/4 and Galerius had a meeting with Maximian late in 304 or
early in 305 at an unknown location. On the other hand, Diocletian is known
to have replied to a petition from Africa in September 293 (*Epitome Codicis
Hermogeniani* 2 (*FIRA*[2] 2.665)) and to a letter from the proconsul of Africa on
31 March 302 (*Mos. et Rom. legum collatio* 15.3).

305–306

After the abdication of Diocletian and Maximian on 1 May 305, the existing
fourfold division was altered. In the east, Galerius took Asia Minor in addition
to the Danubian provinces, while the new Caesar Maximinus received the diocese of Oriens (Eusebius, *HE* 9.1.1). In the west, Constantius added Spain to
Gaul and Britain, while the new Caesar Severus received Italy and Africa.

The evidence for the division of the west requires explicit discussion. Both
the emperor Julian and Orosius expressly state that Constantius ruled Spain
(*Orat.* 2, 51d; *Hist. Adv. Pag.* 7.25.15), and there is no reason to dispute their
testimony,[6] since the panegyric of 313 fails to praise Constantine for liberating
Spain (*Pan. Lat.* 12(9).25) and thus implies that it was never subject to Maxentius.[7] As for Severus, one source attributes to him the diocese of Pannoniae as
well as Italy and Africa (*Origo* 9). But the same source elsewhere limits Severus
to "Italiam et quicquid Herculius obtinebat" (*Origo* 5), and no other writer
hints at his possession of Pannonia; therefore, Eutropius' statement that Galerius retained the whole of Illyricum (*Brev.* 10.1.1) should be correct.

306–313

When Constantius died, his domains passed to Constantine; from 306 to
312, therefore, the latter ruled Britain, Gaul, and Spain.[8] On 28 October 306 a
revolt occurred at Rome; when Severus attempted to suppress it in spring 307,
he was deposed and Maxentius became the ruler of Italy and Africa. Maxen-

---

6. The standard edition of Orosius deletes *Hispaniaque* (K. Zangemeister, *CSEL* 5 (1882),
492). However, although Orosius has added the word to Eutropius, *Brev.* 10.1, which he is here
copying, he may, as a Spaniard himself, have derived his knowledge from valid local memories or
tradition.

7. The Maxentian coinage of Tarraco alleged by older scholarship belongs to Ticinum, see C.
H. V. Sutherland, *RIC* 6 (1967), 6 f., 43, 266 ff.; P. Bastien, *Latomus* 38 (1979), 90 ff.

8. Stein, *Bas-Empire* 1[2].83, 426, postulates a priori that in 306 Spain passed briefly under the
sway of Severus.

tius lost control of Africa to Domitius Alexander for a period (probably 308–309), and was defeated by Constantine in 312, who thus became master also of Italy, Africa, and the islands of the western Mediterranean.

Although Licinius became Augustus on 11 November 308, no formal assignment of territory is alleged in any source; he may have shared with Galerius the defense of the whole Danubian frontier, and hence the administration of all the Danubian provinces.[9] On the death of Galerius in 311, Maximinus seized Asia Minor; in 313 he invaded Europe, but was defeated, with the result that Licinius became emperor in Asia Minor and Oriens.

313–324

The division of the Roman Empire between Constantine and Licinius from 313 to 316 was almost the same as the twofold division under Diocletian. After the war of 316/7 Licinius lost all his European territories except the diocese of Thracia (*Origo* 18). Constantine thus acquired virtually the whole of the Danubian area, mainland Greece, and most of the Aegean islands. On 1 March 317, three Caesars were formally proclaimed. Two were infants and presumably had no separate establishments. Although the third, Crispus, conducted military operations in Gaul independently of Constantine, it is unlikely that there was any formal assignment of territory.

324–337

In 324 Licinius was defeated and the Roman Empire united again. Toward the end of his reign, Constantine divided the empire among several Caesars, each of whom had a separate apparatus of government (Eusebius, *VC* 4.51/52). Three sources indicate the areas which each received (Eusebius, *VC* 4.51.1, deliberately confusing the divisions of 335 and 337; *Origo* 35; *Epitome* 41.20): Constantinus had Gaul, Britain, and Spain; Constantius, Asia Minor and Oriens; Constans, Illyricum, Italy, and Africa; Dalmatius, the lower Danube and Greece.[10] Constantine himself, however, clearly retained overall control everywhere.[11] In the summer of 337, after Constantine died, Dalmatius was killed and his territories were reapportioned: Constantius gained Constantinople and the neighboring provinces (Philostorgius, *HE* 3.1ᵃ), while Constans appears to have acquired Macedonia and Achaea (Zonaras 13.5).

---

9. It is sometimes supposed that Licinius was formally appointed Augustus of the West (so, recently, A. Arnaldi, *Memorie dell'Istituto Lombardo,* Classe di Lettere, Scienzi Morali e Storiche 35 (1975), 217 ff.). That is a plausible, but not a necessary, corollary of the fact that he replaced Severus in the imperial college and was expected to suppress Maxentius (Lactantius, *Mort. Pers.* 29.2; *Origo* 13; Zosimus 2.11).

10. Zosimus 2.39.2 states that Constantinus and Constans jointly ruled Britain, Gaul, Spain, Italy, Africa, Illyricum, and the Danubian region, and he implies that Dalmatius controlled no territory. That probably reflects Eunapius' genuine ignorance of the difference between the divisions of 335 and 337.

11. Libanius, *Orat.* 59.46.

2. DIOCESES AND THEIR EMPERORS

Oriens:	284–293	Diocletian
	293–296	Galerius
	296–299	Diocletian and Galerius
	299–305	Diocletian
	305–313	Maximinus
	313–324	Licinius
	324–337	Constantine
	337–361	Constantius
Asiana and Pontica:	284–305	Diocletian
	305–311	Galerius
	311–313	Maximinus
	313–324	Licinius
	324–337	Constantine
	337–361	Constantius
Thracia:	284–299	Diocletian
	299–311	Galerius (from 308 with Licinius)
	311–324	Licinius
	324–337	Constantine
	337	Dalmatius
	337–361	Constantius
Moesiae:	285–299	Diocletian
	299–311	Galerius (from 308 with Licinius)
	311–316/7	Licinius
	316/7–337	Constantine
	337	Dalmatius
	337–350	Constans
Pannoniae:	285–299	Diocletian
	299–311	Galerius (from 308 with Licinius)
	311–316	Licinius
	316–337	Constantine
	337–350	Constans
Britanniae:	285–286	Maximian
	286–293	Carausius
	293–296	Allectus
	296–306	Constantius
	306–337	Constantine
	337–340	Constantinus
Galliae and Viennensis:	285–293	Maximian (with northwestern Gaul under rebel control from 286 to 293)
	293–306	Constantius
	306–337	Constantine
	337–340	Constantinus

Italia:	285–305	Maximian
	305–306/7	Severus
	306/7–312	Maxentius[12]
	312–337	Constantine
	337–350	Constans
Hispaniae:	285–305	Maximian
	305–306	Constantius
	306–337	Constantine
	337–340	Constantinus
Africa:	285–305	Maximian
	305–306/7	Severus
	306/7–308	Maxentius
	308–309	Domitius Alexander[13]
	309–312	Maxentius
	312–337	Constantine
	337–350	Constans[14]

12. Maxentius held some of the outlying provinces either more briefly or not at all: he probably never controlled Raetia, which was presumably administered with the diocese of Pannoniae from 307 until 312, and it seems that he lost the peninsula of Istria to Licinius in 309 or 310 (A. Jeločnik, *The Čentur Hoard: Folles of Maxentius and of the Tetrarchy* (Situla 12, 1973), 163 ff.; V. Picozzi, *Numismatica e antichità classiche* 5 (1976), 267 ff.). Whether or not Maxentius ever recovered Istria, it appears to have been under the control of Licinius, not of Constantine, between 312 and 316 (*Origo* 15).

13. Alexander also controlled, at least for a period, Sardinia, which belongs to the Italian diocese (Sotgiu 1.372 = *AE* 1966.169: undated).

14. But Constantinus issued a rescript from Trier to the proconsul of Africa on 8 January 339 (*CTh* 12.1.27). He appears to have been accorded, at least for some time, preeminence in the imperial college, see O. Seeck, *ZfN* 21 (1898), 44 ff.

THE VERONA LIST

A seventh-century manuscript in the library of the cathedral at Verona preserves a list of the provinces of the Roman Empire which has obvious relevance to Diocletian's administrative reforms. It was first published by Scipione Maffei in 1742, but subsequently escaped scholarly notice until 1862, when Theodor Mommsen republished it under the title "A List of the Roman Provinces Drawn Up c. 297."[1] Since then the document, conventionally styled the "Verona List" or the "laterculus Veronensis," has been the subject of much discussion, both as a whole and in detail.[2] This chapter offers a diplomatic text, a brief discussion of the date and nature of the list, and a reconstituted list of the provinces of the Roman Empire as they probably were when the Verona List was originally compiled.

1. DIPLOMATIC TEXT OF THE VERONA LIST

Manuscript
  Verona, Bibliotheca Capitolare II(2), fols. 255-256. (For a description of the manuscript, see E. A. Lowe, *Codices Latini Antiquiores* 4 (Oxford, 1947), 21, no. 477.)
Editions
  F. S. Maffei, *Istoria teologica delle dottrine e delle opinioni corse ne' cinque primi secoli in proposito della divina Grazia, del libero arbitrio e della*

---

1. T. Mommsen, *Abh. Berlin* 1862.489 ff. = *Ges. Schr.* 5 (1908), 561 ff.
2. For bibliography, E. Honigmann, *RE* 4A (1932), 1695 f.; Stein, *Bas-Empire* 1[2].437 f.; T. D. Barnes, *ZPE* 16 (1975), 275 f.

Predestinazione 2 (Trent, 1742), 84, reprinted in his *Opere* 11 (Venice, 1790), 159.

T. Mommsen, *Abh. Berlin* 1862. 491–492, reprinted in his *Gesammelte Schriften* 5 (Berlin, 1908), 563–564.

O. Seeck, *Notitia Dignitatum* (Berlin, 1876), 247–251.

A. Riese, *Geographi Latini Minores* (Heilbronn, 1878), 127–128.

Concerning these editions, it will suffice to say that the first is inaccessible, while the other three not only concur in several small errors (e.g. in reporting *syriae cohele* where the manuscript clearly divides the words *syria ecohele*), but also prejudge important historical questions, either by numbering the provinces, sometimes wrongly (Mommsen, Seeck), or by deleting parts of the text as interpolated (Riese).

Printed below is a transcript of the Verona List made from photographs kindly supplied by the Biblioteca Capitolare of Verona. The reports and emendations of earlier editors are deliberately ignored: I note only variants in the manuscript. (The stops printed here on the line (.) are raised in the manuscript (·).)

fol. 255, recto

14 Incipit eiusdem nomina prouinciarum omnium.
15 Diocensis orientis habet prouincias numero
16 XVIII. libia superior. libia inferior. thebais.
17 aegyptus. iouia. aegyptus. herculea. arabia.
18 item arabia. augusta libanensis: palestina.
19 fenicen. syria ecohele, augusta eupatenses.[3]
20 cilicia. isauria. tupus. mesopotamia. osroaena

fol. 255, verso

1   Diocensis pontica. habet prouincias. numero VII
2   bitinia. cappadocia. galatia. paᵐplagonia. nunc
3   in duas diuisas. diospontus. pontus polemiacus
4   armenia minor; nunc et maior addita.
5   Diocensis asiana. habet prouincias supra scribtas
6   VIIII. phanfilia. frigia prima. frigia secunda.
7   assa lidia. caria. insuluae. pisidiae. ellespontus.
8   Diocensis. tracoae. habet prouincias numero. VI
9   europa. rodo. petracia. emossanus. scitia.
10 misia inferiori[4] Diocensis misiarum habet.
11 prouincias numero. XI; dacias. misia superior

3. Altered from *eupatensis*.
4. There is a deletion sign above the last letter of *inferiori*.

12 margensis. dardania. macedonia. tessalia.
13 priantina. priualentina. epiros noua. epiros uetus.
14 creta Diocensis pannoniarum habet prouincias
15 numero VII. pannonia inferior. fauensis;
16 dalmatia. ualeria. pannonia. pannonia superior
17 noricus pariensis; noricus mediterranea
18 Diocensis brittaniarum habet prouincias
19 numero VI. primam secundam maxime caesariensis
20 aelauiae caesariensis Diocensis galliarum

fol. 256, recto

1 habet prouincias numero VIII. betica prima.[5]
2 betica secunda. germania prima. germania secunda.
3 sequania. lubdunensis prima. lubdunensis secunda.
4 alpes graiae et poeninae; Diocensis biennensis
5 habet prouincias numero. VII. biennensis
6 narbonensis prima. narbonensis secunda
7 nouem populi. aquitanica prima: aquitanica
8 secunda alpes maritimas; Diocensis italiciana
9 habet prouincias numero XVI. beteiam
10 histriam flaminiam. picenum tusciam
11 umbrenam. apuliam calabriam licaoniam
12 corsicam. alpes cotias. rectia; Diocensis
13 hispaniarum habet prouincias numero VI.
14 beticam. lusitaniam. kartaginiensis. gallecia
15 tharraconensis. mauritania tingitania.
16 Diocensis africae habet prouincias numero. VII.
17 proconsularis; bizacina. zeugitana. numidia cirtensis
18 numidia miliciana; mauritania caesariensis.
19 mauritania tabia; insidiana. felix saeculum;

2. THE DATE AND NATURE OF THE LIST

As the title of his article implies, Mommsen held that the Verona List is a homogeneous document datable c. 297.[6] Epigraphical discoveries have long rendered that view untenable, for it was during 303 that Numidia was divided into Numidia Cirtensis and Numidia Militiana (which both appear in the list).[7] Most scholars who have discussed the list during the present century adopt one

---

5. A probably contemporary half-uncial hand has added *belgica prima* above *betica prima*.
6. He argued that, apart from the two obviously later additions in fol. 255, verso, lines 2–4, the list had no features which were demonstrably later than 296 (*Ges. Schr.* 5.587 f.).
7. Kolbe, *Staathalter* 48 ff.

of two views. Some follow Mommsen in holding that the document is wholly homogeneous; on this basis its date has been argued to be c. 305 (G. Costa, E. Stein, H. Nesselhauf), between 304 and 314 (C. W. Keyes), between 308 and 315 (J. B. Bury), between 312 and 320 (A. H. M. Jones), between 312 and 314 (H. G. Kolbe), or 314 precisely (A. H. M. Jones).[8] Others deny total homogeneity, but argue that both the eastern and the western halves are homogeneous; on this basis, the eastern half has been dated to 312–324, the western to 303–306.[9]

The postulate of total homogeneity has always been very fragile, for it requires the Verona List to be dated within an ever-narrowing slot of time. On the one side, while two separate Numidias still existed in the spring of 314 when Constantine summoned the Council of Arles for 1 August (Optatus, App. 3, p. 205.33/34 Ziwsa), they were united before the end of the year and probably before the end of summer 314 (CIL 8.18905, cf. Table 3). On the other side, no governor of Aegyptus Herculia is yet attested before 27 December 315 (P. Cairo Isid. 74), while Egypt was certainly still undivided after 15 January 314, when the praefectus Aegypti was still the governor at Karanis, in the territory of the later Aegyptus Herculia (P. Cairo Isid. 73).[10] Hence, although the Verona List can theoretically be regarded as a wholly homogeneous document from the latter months of 314, more precise evidence for either the reunification of Numidia or the division of Egypt may at any moment disprove that view irretrievably.

The view that the eastern and western halves of the Verona List are each homogeneous, though different in date, requires, no less than the postulate of total homogeneity, that each separate diocesan list be internally consistent. The external evidence for the provinces of the diocese of Oriens appeared until recently to contradict this requirement. In the diocese of Oriens, there appear provinces called Arabia (arabia item arabia), Aegyptus Iovia, and Aegyptus Herculia. But while contemporary papyri indicate that Egypt was divided and that the Aegyptus Herculia and Aegyptus Iovia of the Verona List were created

8. G. Costa, Diz. ep. 2 (1912), 1834; C. W. Keyes, CP 11 (1916), 196 ff.; J. B. Bury, JRS 13 (1923), 127 ff.; Stein, Bas-Empire 1².437; H. Nesselhauf, Abh. Berlin, Phil.-hist. Klasse 1938, Nr.2.8 f.; A. H. M. Jones, JRS 44 (1954), 21 ff. = Roman Economy (1974), 263 ff. (unfortunately overlooking the earliest evidence for the reunification of Numidia (viz. CIL 8.18905); Kolbe, Statthalter 65 ff. (correcting Jones's oversight); Jones, LRE 1.43; 3.4, 381 (after the publication of P. Cairo Isid. 73).

9. A. Chastagnol, La Préfecture urbaine à Rome sous le Bas-Empire (Rome, 1960), 3 f. The much later dates advocated by J. Mispoulet, CRAI 1908.254 ff. ("la fin du règne de Constantin" for the whole list), and E. Schwartz, Abh. München, Phil.-hist. Abt., n.f. 13 (1937), 79 ff. (the eastern half between 328 and 337, the western after 364), are flatly impossible.

10. A. E. R. Boak and H. C. Youtie, The Archive of Aurelius Isidorus (Ann Arbor, 1960), 285 f.; L. de Salvo, Aegyptus 44 (1964), 34 ff.; Lallemand, L'administration 49 ff. However, Lactantius, Mort. Pers. 52.3 (adduced by de Salvo) concerns the titles of emperors, not the names of provinces.

no earlier than 314 (*P. Cairo Isid.* 73), the southern part of the Trajanic province of Arabia had been incorporated in Palaestina before 314.[11] Writing in 311 and again in 313, Eusebius reported that in 307 the governor of Palaestina sentenced Christians to work in "the copper mines of Palaestina" or "the copper mines at Phaeno in Palaestina" (*Mart. Pal.* 7.2 (both recensions)). If Phaeno belonged to Palaestina in 307 (or even in 311), then one of the two provinces of Arabia in the Verona List (so it seemed) must have passed out of existence before Aegyptus Herculia was created, whence it would follow that neither the list as whole nor either half of it can be regarded as homogeneous.[12]

An unpublished papyrus removes the basis of that attempt to disprove the homogeneity of the list of provinces in Oriens. For it reveals that there existed between 314/5 and 318 a province of Arabia Nova — which appears to be part of Egypt, where a nome called Arabia is well attested.[13] Hence the words *arabia item arabia* in the Verona List do not reflect a Diocletianic division of Arabia into an Arabia east of the Jordan and an Arabia Petraea.[14] They show rather that when the province of Egypt was divided in 314/5, it was not divided into two provinces (as has always been assumed), but into the three provinces of Aegyptus Iovia, Aegyptus Herculia, and Arabia Nova.[15] The available external evidence, therefore, indicates that the Verona List depicts the eastern provinces of the Roman Empire as they were between 314/5 and 324, the western provinces as they were between 303 and 314.

3. THE PROVINCES OF THE LIST

In the first column of the list below are the entries in the Verona List as they stand in the manuscript; in the second column, the correct names of the corresponding provinces during the decade 310–320.

Oriens

libia superior	Libya Superior
libia inferior	Libya Inferior
thebais	Thebais
aegyptus iovia	Aegyptus Iovia (created 314/5)
aegyptus herculea	Aegyptus Herculia (created 314/5)

11. R. E. Brünnow and A. von Domaszewski, *Die Provincia Arabia* 3 (Strassburg, 1909), 273 ff.

12. *ZPE* 16 (1975), 277 f.

13. *P. Oxy.* 29 4B. 48/G (6–7)a, to be published by Dr. J. R. Rea, who kindly brought it to my attention. For the nome Arabia, see A. H. M. Jones, *Cities of the Eastern Roman Provinces*[2] (Oxford, 1971), 298 f., 337 ff.

14. As argued in *ZPE* 16 (1975), 277, with appeal to A. Alt, *ZDPV* 71 (1955), 173 ff.; G. W. Bowersock, *JRS* 61 (1971), 242.

15. I owe the interpretation of the new papyrus adopted here entirely to G. W. Bowersock.

arabia	Arabia Nova (created 314/5)
item arabia	Arabia
augusta libanensis	Augusta Libanensis
palestina	Palaestina
fenicen	Phoenice
syria ecohele	Syria Coele
augusta eupatenses	Augusta Euphratensis
cilicia	Cilicia
isauria	Isauria
tupus	Cyprus
mesopotamia	Mesopotamia
osroaena	Osrhoene

Pontica

bitinia	Bithynia
cappadocia	Cappadocia
galatia	Galatia
pamplagonia	Paphlagonia
nunc in duas divisa{s}	after 384
diospontus	Diospontus
pontus polemiacus	Pontus Polemoniacus
armenia minor	Armenia
nunc et maior addita	after 381

Asiana

phanfilia	Lycia et Pamphylia
frigia prima	Phrygia Prima
frigia secunda	Phrygia Secunda
assa	Asia
lidia	Lydia
caria	Caria
fisidiae	Pisidia
ellespontus	Hellespontus

Thracia

europa	Europa
rodope	Rhodope
tracia	Thracia
emossanus	Haemimontus
scitia	Scythia
misia inferior[[i]]	Moesia Inferior

Moesiae

dacias	Dacia
	Dacia Ripensis
misia superior margensis	Moesia Superior *or* Margensis
dardania	Dardania
macedonia	Macedonia
tessalia	Thessalia
priantina	Achaea
privalentina	Praevalitana
epiros nova	Epirus Nova
epiros vetus	Epirus Vetus
creta	Creta

Pannoniae

pannonia inferior	Pannonia Inferior
favensis	Savensis (later Savia)[16]
dalmatia	Dalmatia
valeria	Valeria
pannonia pannonia superior	Pannonia Superior
noricus pariensis	Noricum Ripense
noricus mediterranea	Noricum Mediterraneum

Britanniae

primam	Britannia Prima
secundam	Britannia Secunda
maxime caesariensis	Maxima Caesariensis
aelaviae caesariensis	Flavia Caesariensis

Galliae

betica prima	Belgica Prima
betica secunda	Belgica Secunda
germania prima	Germania Prima
germania secunda	Germania Secunda
sequania	Sequania
lubdunensis prima	Lugdunensis Prima
lubdunensis secunda	Lugdunensis Secunda
alpes graiae et poeninae	Alpes Graiae et Poeninae

16. Athanasius calls it Siscia, presumably confusing province and metropolis (*Apol. Sec.* 1.2; *Hist. Ar.* 28.2).

Viennensis

biennensis	Viennensis
narbonensis prima	Narbonensis Prima
narbonensis secunda	Narbonensis Secunda
novem populi	Novem Populi
aquitanica prima	Aquitanica Prima
aquitanica secunda	Aquitanica Secunda
alpes maritimas	Alpes Maritimae

Italia

beteiam histriam	Venetia et Histria
	Aemilia et Liguria
flaminiam picenum	Flaminia et Picenum
tusciam umbrenam	Tuscia et Umbria
	Campania
apuliam calabriam	Apulia et Calabria
licaoniam	Lucania et Bruttii
	Sicilia
	Sardinia
corsicam	Corsica
alpes cotias	Alpes Cottiae
rectia	Raetia

Hispaniae

beticam	Baetica
lusitaniam	Lusitania
kartaginiensis	Carthaginiensis
gallecia	Gallaecia
tharraconensis	Tarraconensis
mauritania tingitania	Mauretania Tingitana

Africa

proconsularis	Africa Proconsularis
bizacina	(Valeria) Byzacena
zeugitana	Tripolitana
numidia cirtensis	Numidia Cirtensis ⎫ reunited in 314
numidia miliciana	Numidia Militiana ⎭
mauritania caesariensis	Mauretania Caesariensis
mauritania tabia insidiana	Mauretania Sitifensis (perhaps originally called Mauretania Tubusuctitana)

CHAPTER XIII

DIOCLETIAN AND THE PROVINCES

Provinces cut up into tiny pieces; many governors and their still more numerous staffs watching over every region, almost over every city; troops of *rationales, magistri,* and *vicarii praefectorum* busy with perpetual condemnations and confiscations — so Lactantius bitterly described Diocletian's administrative reforms as they affected the provinces of the Roman Empire (*Mort. Pers.* 7.4). The caricature is savage, but not altogether misleading: it is precisely during the reign of Diocletian that *magistri privatae* of provinces and dioceses and vicars of dioceses appear for the first time.[1] For the provinces, the Verona List and other evidence bring a welcome precision to Lactantius' rhetoric, and enable the details of Diocletian's administrative reorganization to be described province by province.

1. THE DIVISION OF SEVERAN PROVINCES

The individual discussions below present evidence for the division of the Severan provinces. They rely upon a rigorous sifting of good evidence from bad — a task all the more necessary since the standard treatment of the subject assumes that the *Historia Augusta,* in a fictitious passage (*Tyr. Trig.* 24.2), "probably refers to the position in the late third or early fourth century,"[2] and the fasti in the *Prosopography of the Later Roman Empire* are inflated by the inclusion of fictitious governors of provinces which either did not exist or may

1. *PLRE* 1.1063; Millar, *Emperor* 628 ff.
2. Jones, *LRE* 3.385.

not have existed at the relevant date.[3] The following items of evidence are employed without specific reference on every occasion:

1. the Verona List (Chapter XII)
2. the list of bishops who subscribed the Creed and Canons of Nicaea in June 325 (Tables 10 and 11)
3. the *Itinerarium Burdigalense* of 333, printed in *CCL* 175 (1961), 1–26, from the editions of P. Geyer, *CSEL* 39 (1898), 3–33 and O. Cuntz, *Itineraria Romana* 1 (Leipzig, 1929), 86–102 (the page and line numbers are those of P. Wesseling, *Vetera Romanorum Itineraria* (Amsterdam, 1735), 535–617, which are marked in all three modern editions)
4. the list of anti-Arian bishops who subscribed the Canons of the Council of Serdica in 343/4 (Table 12), and the list of provinces from which the Arian bishops came (Table 13)
5. the list of provinces in Festus' *Breviarium,* which describes the provinces of the Roman Empire as they were in 364 or slightly earlier[4]
6. the list of bishops who subscribed the decisions of the Council of Constantinople in July 381, which survives in Greek, Latin, and Syriac: C. H. Turner, *JTS* 15 (1914), 168–170 (Greek); *EOMIA* 2.433–464 (Latin); F. Schulthess, *Abh. Göttingen,* Phil.-hist. Klasse, n.f. 10.2 (1908), 113–119 (Syriac)
7. the *Notitia Dignitatum,* edited by O. Seeck (Berlin, 1876)
8. Polemius Silvius, edited by A. Riese, *Geographi Latini Minores* Heilbronn, 1878), 130–132; T. Mommsen, *Chr. Min.* 1 (1892), 535–542
9. the lists of governors of provinces printed above in Chapter IX

The conciliar lists of 325 and 381 (nos. 2 and 6) are normally assumed to be "of particular value since they show which cities belonged to each province."[5] Regrettably, that is not quite true even of the list of 381, which still shows a single Cappadocia, even though the secular province had been divided into Cappadocia Prima and Secunda in 371 (Gregory of Nazianzus, *Orat.* 43.58).[6] Nevertheless, the conciliar list of 381 appears in general to reflect the secular administrative divisions of the eastern Roman provinces in 381, since it depicts a state of affairs slightly earlier than that presented in the *Notitia Dignitatum,* whose eastern sections describe the eastern provinces and armies c. 393.[7] The Nicene

3. Chapter X.
4. R. Tomlin, *Britannia* 5 (1974), 309. The discussion of provincial lists in J. W. Eadie, *The Breviarium of Festus: A Critical Edition with Commentary* (London, 1967), 154–171, ignores several important items of evidence.
5. Jones, *LRE* 3.381.
6. It has been deduced that the Catholics deliberately retained the old ecclesiastical organization for some years after 371 because the Arian Valens had divided Cappadocia for partisan reasons (*EOMIA* 2.446).
7. On the *Notitia Dignitatum,* see especially Jones, *LRE* 3.347 ff.; E. Demougeot, *Latomus* 34 (1975), 1079 ff.
The following Oriental provinces in the list of 381 are divided in the *Notitia Dignitatum:*

subscriptions, however, do not provide authoritative evidence for Roman provinces in 325: it was demonstrated long ago that the bishops' names were not grouped in geographical order, province by province, until several decades after 325.[8]

It should be noted that minor alterations in provincial boundaries are normally ignored, unless they are obviously and directly relevant to the larger changes which form the subject of this chapter.

Achaea

Governors of Achaea are attested throughout the third and fourth centuries; hence the province's omission in the Verona List is presumably due to displacement by the meaningless *priantina*.[9]

Aegyptus

The abundance of evidence for Egypt — not only papyri, inscriptions and Ammianus (22.16.1 ff.), but also documents from the Arian controversy and the writings of Athanasius — permits a degree of precision attainable for hardly any other province. The following Egyptian provinces are attested:

1. Aegyptus: continues, though with loss of territory to the new province of Thebais, until 314/5, when it is divided into Iovia, Herculia, and Arabia Nova, which are recombined in 324 (cf. Opitz, *Urkunde* 15)
2. Aegyptus Iovia: no evidence except the Verona List, but the province is clearly the twin of Herculia
3. Aegyptus Herculia: created after January 314 (*P. Cairo Isid.* 73) but before 27 December 315 (*P. Cairo Isid.* 74)
4. Arabia Nova: attested between 314/5 and 318 (*P. Oxy.*: unpublished)[10]
5. Libya Inferior: first attested in early 309[11]
6. Thebais: a *praeses* of Thebais is certainly attested in September 298, and one is probably attested in January 295

Armenia, divided before 386 (*CTh* 13.11.2); Cilicia; Galatia, perhaps divided in 399 (Claudian, *In Eutr.* 1.585 ff., cf. *Phoenix* 32 (1978), 81 f.); Palaestina; Paphlagonia, divided between 384 and 387 (Libanius, *Orat.* 19.62); Phoenice; Syria Coele. On Theodosius' policy of dividing provinces, A. Lippold, *RE,* Supp. 13 (1973), 914.

8. L. Duchesne, *Bulletin critique* 1 (1880), 330 ff.; *Mélanges Graux* (Paris, 1884), 135; H. Gelzer, *Beiträge zur alten Geographie und Geschichte: Festschrift für H. Kiepert* (Berlin, 1898), 47 ff. Subsequent research has not justified the less discriminating rejection of all conciliar lists by C. Czwalina, *Über das Verzeichnis der römischen Provinzen vom Jahre 297* (Prog. Wesel, 1881), 6 ff.

9. T. Mommsen, *Ges. Schr.* 5 (Berlin, 1908), 579 n.1.

10. *P. Oxy.* 29 4B.48/G (6–7)a, of which Dr. J. R. Rea most kindly supplied me with a text in advance of publication.

11. By a group of four dedications to Galerius and Licinius as Augusti and to Maximinus and Constantine as Caesars by Aurel. Maximinus who describes himself as "v. p. dux Aeg(ypti) et Theb(aidos) utrarumq(ue) Lib(yarum)": P. Lacau, *Annales du Service des Antiquités de l'Égypte* 34 (1934), 22–23, nos. I–L. (Only two of the four are reprinted in *AE,* I as *AE* 1934.7, K as *AE* 1934.8.)

7. Augustamnica: created in 341 from the territory of Aegyptus (Festal Index 13), it corresponds to the earlier short-lived province of Arabia Nova

Africa

Although a proconsular province of Africa still existed into the fifth century, it was far smaller than the Severan province. The permanent changes under Diocletian were two. The boundary with Numidia was modified (before March 295, when the *Acta Maximiliani* show that Theveste was part of proconsular Africa), and the new provinces of Byzacena and Tripolitana (for both of which governors are attested before 305) were carved out of the old proconsular province, splitting it into three.[12]

The Verona List enters *proconsularis bizacina zeugitana* and omits Tripolitana. The omission clearly results from textual corruption: *tripolitana* has either dropped out through haplography or been displaced by *zeugitana*.[13] The word *zeugitana* is in itself problematical, for it is hard to imagine how it could be a corruption for the required *tripolitana*. The transmitted text is normally construed as designating two provinces, viz. Proconsularis and Byzacena, with Zeugitana being either an additional title of the former or an alternative name which it briefly bore.[14] It has also been suggested that *zeugitana* denotes a separate province — a hypothesis which would imply that the Verona List attests a short-lived division of the old proconsular Africa into four provinces.[15]

Alpes Maritimae, Alpes Cottiae, Alpes Graiae et Poeninae

No change.

Aquitania

There appears to be no early evidence against which to measure the Verona List, which registers Novem Populi, Aquitanica Prima, and Aquitanica Secunda as three provinces. Novem Populi presents no problems.[16] But Aquitanica was later a single province: a *praeses provinciae Aquitanicae* is attested in the

---

12. On these changes, see still R. Cagnat, *Klio* 2 (1902), 73 ff.; *Philologie et Linguistique: Mélanges Havet* (Paris, 1909), 65 ff. For the boundaries of the new provinces, Seston, *Dioclétien* 331 ff. (Africa); J. Desanges, *Cahiers de Tunisie* 44 (1963), 7 ff. (Byzacena).

13. Kolbe, *Statthalter* 65 ff. (with reference to earlier discussions).

14. E.g., respectively, Jones, *LRE* 3.383; R. Cagnat, *Mélanges Havet* (Paris, 1909), 67 f. After initially adopting the former view (*Ges. Schr.* 5.585 f.), Mommsen proposed to delete *zeugitana* (*CIL* 8, p. xvii n. 5).

15. T. D. Barnes, *Tertullian: A Historical and Literary Study* (Oxford, 1971), 86. But Zeugis was of old the name of the region around Carthage (Pliny, *NH* 5.23 f.; Orosius, *Hist. Adv. Pag.* 1.2.91), and Carthage must always have been in Africa Proconsularis.

16. E. Linckenheld, *RE* 17 (1937), 1181–85, s.v. Novempopulana. But *CIL* 13.412 (Tarbelli, in Aquitania) does not show that the province was created before Diocletian (as argued by J. B. Bury, *JRS* 13 (1923), 139).

340s (*ILS* 1255);[17] Ammianus enters it as a single province in a complete enumeration of the Gallic provinces in 355 (15.11.1 ff.); and Hilary of Poitiers appears to know of only one Aquitanica in 358 (*PL* 10.479). Moreover, the entry *(ex) provincia Aquitanica* in the subscriptions to the Council of Arles (*CCL* 148 (1963), 15.47, 16.39, 18.34, 20.36, 21.34) may imply that Aquitanica was already reunited as a single province in 314.[18]

Arabia

The evidence for the provincial divisions of Arabia in the late third and early fourth centuries appears to exhibit confusion over the provincial status of the territory which eventually became Palaestina Tertia, i.e. the southern part of the old Nabataean kingdom, which was made a Roman province in 106.[19] But the apparent confusion vanishes when the words *arabia item arabia augusta libanensis* in the Verona List are correctly interpreted. Some scholars have punctuated these five words as if they referred to two provinces only, viz. Arabia and Arabia Augusta Libanensis,[20] while others have diagnosed interpolation, deleting either the two words *item Arabia* or the four words *item Arabia Augusta Libanensis,* in order to remove the historical difficulties which they perceive in the transmitted text.[21] However, emendation is an arbitrary procedure when dealing with evidence like the Verona List, and a province of Arabia Augusta Libanensis is a geographical impossibility.[22] The manuscript text should be accepted, and the five words interpreted as listing three provinces, viz. two called Arabia, and one with the name of Augusta Libanensis. Accordingly, so it has widely been assumed, the Verona List attests the division of the Trajanic province of Arabia into two parts, one the northern part, with Bostra as its capital, the other Arabia Petraea.[23] A papyrus from Oxyrhynchus disproves this assumption: it attests the existence of a province named Arabia Nova between 314/5 and 318 and implies that a town called Eleutheropolis in

17. For the date, *PLRE* 1.814–817, Secundus 2.
18. For discussion of the division of Aquitania, see A. Chastagnol, *BSNAF* 1970. 272 ff. Two Aquitanicae are again attested from the late fourth century onward.
19. On Arabia in the fourth century and later, see still R. E. Brünnow and A. von Domaszewski, *Die Provincia Arabia* 3 (Strassburg, 1909), 251 ff. (with copious quotation of ancient evidence and modern opinions).
20. So Mommsen and Seeck, in their editions; W. Ohnesorge, *Die römische Provinzliste von 297. 1. Ein Beitrag zur Geschichte der römischen Provinzteilungen* (Duisburg, 1889), 33 ff.; Seston, *Dioclétien* 373 ff.
21. These deletions were first proposed by E. Bormann, *De Syriae provinciae Romanae partibus capita nonnulla* (Diss. Berlin, 1865), 30 (*item Arabia*); E. Kuhn, *Neue Jahrbücher* 115 (1877), 697 ff. (all four words). Riese's edition adopts Kuhn's deletion.
22. A. Alt, *ZDPV* 71 (1955), 173 ff.
23. J. Marquardt, *Römische Staatsverwaltung* 1 (Berlin, 1873), 268; 276 f. (retracted in the second edition); T. Nöldeke, *Hermes* 10 (1876), 166 ff. Their conclusion has recently been reiterated by A. Alt, *ZDPV* 71 (1955), 186; G. W. Bowersock, *JRS* 61 (1971), 242; T. D. Barnes, *ZPE* 15 (1976), 276.

Arabia Nova is close to Aegyptus Herculia.[24] On the natural interpretation of all the evidence, therefore, the first *arabia* of the Verona List should be identical with Arabia Nova, and a subdivision of the earlier Aegyptus, not of the province Arabia.

The other evidence for the southern part of the Trajanic province of Arabia now falls neatly into place:

1. Eusebius' *On the Place-Names in Holy Scripture* contains four entries which give a provincial designation for Petra, the former capital of the Nabataean kingdom. Three entries describe Petra as being in Arabia (viz. those for Petra (Judges 1.36), Rekem (Numbers 31.8), and Kadesh-Barnea (Numbers 32.8)),[25] while one describes Petra as belonging to Palaestina (that for Arkem (II Kings 17.30)). Since Eusebius compiled his biblical gazetteer by working through the text of the Bible, book by book (p. 2.17–20 Klostermann), the fourth of these entries (p. 36.13/14), though occurring before the other three in the completed work (respectively, pp. 112.8–12, 142.7/8, 144.7–9), must have been composed last. Consequently, it is possible that when Eusebius wrote "Petra, a city in Arabia" and "Petra, a famous city of Palaestina," both descriptions were accurate at the time of writing—that is, Arabia Petraea was incorporated in Palaestina while Eusebius was engaged on compiling the gazetteer in the 290s.[26]

2. Both recensions of Eusebius' *Martyrs of Palestine* (composed in 311 and 313, respectively) state that the area around Petra belonged to Palaestina in 307 (7.2).

3. Eusebius' *Commentary on Isaiah*, written between 324 and 337, describes Petra as "a city of Palaestina" (p. 273 Ziegler). Similarly, the Nicene subscriptions list the bishop of Aila under Palaestina.

4. Palaestina was divided while Clematius, the correspondent of Libanius, was governor: in 357 his province included Elusa, in 358 it did not (Libanius, *Epp.* 315, 334). In 357/8, therefore, Arabia Petraea became a separate province as the Palaestina Salutaris of the *Notitia Dignitatum*.[27]

---

24. *P. Oxy.* 29 4B.48/G (6–7)a. I owe the interpretation of the papyrus adopted here entirely to G. W. Bowersock.

25. The entry for Kadesh-Barnea (p. 112.8–12 Klostermann) is slightly problematical. The one Greek manuscript has ἔρημος ἡ παρατείνουσα Πέτρᾳ πόλει τῆς πόλεως Παλαιστίνης (*sic*), but Klostermann prints πόλει τῆς Ἀραβίας from Procopius of Gaza and Jerome's translation (*Petrae in Arabia*). That Eusebius here assigned Petra to Arabia is confirmed by a Syriac fragment published by I. E. Rahmani, E. Tisserant, E. Power, and R. Devreesse, *Revue de l'Orient syrien* 23 (1922–23), 248, frag. 46.

26. T. D. Barnes, *JTS,* n.s. 26 (1975), 412 ff.—though assuming a mistaken identification for the two Arabias in the Verona List.

27. Note Jerome, *Quaestiones in Genesim* 21.30 (*CCL* 72.26): "quae provincia ante non grande tempus ex divisione praesidum Palaestinae Salutaris est dicta."

Diocletian detached Arabia Petraea from the rest of the pre-Diocletianic province of Arabia and incorporated it in Palaestina in or not long after 293. He did not make Arabia Petraea a separate province, even for a brief period.[28]

Asia

Between 293 and 305, governors of the following provinces carved out of the old proconsular province of Asia are attested:

1. Asia, much reduced in territory but still governed by a proconsul
2. Phrygia et Caria, attested in the winter of 301/2
3. Caria
4. Insulae, attested on 2 August 294
5. Hellespontus

The Verona List has seven provinces corresponding to pre-Diocletianic Asia, viz. Phrygia Prima, Phrygia Secunda, Asia, Lydia, Caria, Insulae, and Hellespontus. Since recent discoveries appear to establish that the province of Phrygia et Caria was not created by Diocletian, but in the 250s,[29] it may be deduced that in 293 Diocletian divided the rest of the old proconsular province, adjusting boundaries (the proconsul of Asia, Festus, was active at Miletus, in the later Caria, between 286 and 293). Subsequently, after the winter of 301/2 and possibly before May 305, Phrygia et Caria was divided into the Phrygia Prima, Phrygia Secunda, and Caria of the Verona List.

Although the earliest indubitable evidence outside the Verona List for two Phrygias belongs to 358 (Hilary of Poitiers, *De Synodis* 33 (*PL* 10.506 f.)), the Nicene subscriptions, which have a single Phrygia, are probably in error.[30] A joint province of Asia et Hellespontus is attested c. 330.

Baetica

No change.

Belgica

As provinces in the diocese of Galliae, the Verona List enters *betica prima betica secunda,* i.e. Belgica Prima and Belgica Secunda. No governor of either is attested before c. 340.[31]

---

28. As argued by P. von Rohden, *RE* 2 (1896), 359 f., and accepted by T. D. Barnes, *ZPE* 16 (1975), 275 ff.; *JTS,* n.s. 26 (1975), 415.

29. C. Roueché, *JRS* 71 (1981), 103 ff.

30. W. M. Ramsay, *Cities and Bishoprics of Phrygia* 1 (Oxford, 1895), 80 ff., argued from Gelasius of Cyzicus, *HE* 2.38.9, that there were two Phrygias in 325. Unfortunately, the evidence of Gelasius is worthless, since he also has two Macedonias in 325 (*HE* 2.38.8).

31. The first is M. Aurelius Consius Quartus (*AE* 1955.150: Hippo), *consularis* of Belgica Prima; on the date, see A. Chastagnol, *Libyca* 7 (1959), 191 ff.

Britannia

Britain was divided into two provinces, Inferior (in the north) and Superior, early in the third century (Herodian 3.8.1 f. — slightly misdated). The Verona List has four provinces: Prima, Secunda, Maxima Caesariensis, and Flavia Caesariensis. The divisions were presumably made in 296, when Constantius reconquered Britain.

Cappadocia

The large Severan province of Cappadocia was divided into four main units: Pisidia, Cappadocia, Armenia Minor, and Pontus Polemoniacus. A part was also incorporated in a province which seems to have been called Pontus at its creation, then Diospontus (as in the Nicene subscriptions), and finally Helenopontus.

In this area, some division before Diocletian has long been attested: milestones found not far from Sinope bearing the date 279 (Probus is *trib. pot. IIII*) attest one Ael. Casinus Atianus as *v. p., pr(aeses) pr(ovinciae) P(onti)* (D. M. Robinson, *AJA* 9 (1905), 329 no. 78, with the corrections at *AJA* 10 (1906), 433; *AJP* 27 (1906), 449 no. 3, which was noted but not published as *AJA* 9 (1905), 329 no. 79).

Cilicia

Divided into Cilicia and Isauria (so the Verona List and the Nicene subscriptions).

Corsica

No change.

Creta et Cyrene

Divided into the provinces of Crete (in the diocese of Moesiae), Libya Superior, also called Pentapolis, and Libya Inferior (in the diocese of Oriens). The date of the division is indicated by the differing status of two governors attested in Crete: Aglaus was proconsul between 286 and 293, while M. Aur. Buzes was *praeses* of Crete between 293 and 305.

Cyprus

No change.

Dacia

Trajan's conquests north of the Danube were definitively abandoned by Aurelian, who appears to have established two new provinces south of the river: such at least is the implication of a bronze plaque which reads "Caro et Carino Augg. Gaianus preses finem posuit inter du[as Da]cias dila[" (*AE* 1912.200:

near Serdica).[32] Subsequently, the Verona List has *dacias* (plural), while an orator in 297 alludes to the singular (*Pan. Lat.* 8(5).3.3: *Dacia restituta*), and a *praeses Daciae* is attested in 321. But this need not imply a single Dacia, since the two provinces are called Dacia and Dacia Ripensis in 343/4. On the available evidence, it seems most reasonable to conclude that two Dacias existed continuously from Aurelian onward.[33] The name Dacia Mediterranea is first attested in the reign of Valentinian.[34]

Dalmatia

Part of the Severan province was detached and combined with territory from the adjacent provinces of Pannonia Superior and Moesia Superior to form the new province of Praevalitana.[35]

Epirus

Name changed to Epirus Vetus.

Galatia

The Severan province was divided into three parts: the new and diminished Galatia lost territory in the south to the new province of Pisidia, while the north of the old province was combined with some territory from Pontus et Bithynia to form Paphlagonia. A *v. p. praes(es) Pisid(iae)* is attested c. 310.

Gallia Lugdunensis

The Verona List divides Lugdunensis into two provinces, and a *praeses Lugdunensis primae* is probably attested in 313. A speech delivered before a governor at Autun in summer 298 is extant (*Pan. Lat.* 9(4)): unfortunately, the orator only addresses him as *vir perfectissime,* and the description of him in one manuscript as *v. p. Galliarum praeses* (*Pan. Lat.,* p. 230 Mynors) is clearly a fifteenth-century conjecture, so that the speech provides no evidence for his precise title. It seems that the division of Lugdunensis, once effected, was permanent.

Gallia Narbonensis

The Verona List has three provinces: Viennensis, Narbonensis Prima, and Narbonensis Secunda. The first of these was a permanent creation, and a *prae-*

32. Published and discussed by B. Filow, *Klio 12* (1912), 234 ff., cf. N. Vulić, *Le Musée Belge* 27 (1923), 253 ff. Sir R. Syme has cautioned me that the inscription could be a forgery.

33. H. Vetters, *Dacia Ripensis* (*Öst. Akad. d. Wiss., Schriften der Balkankommission,* Antiquarische Abt. 11.1, 1950), 6 ff.

34. *PLRE* 1.48, Alypius 11, adducing an inscription published in *Razkopki i Prouchvanija,* n.s. 1 (1948), 84–85. It is sometimes assumed that c. 300 Dardania and Dacia Mediterranea were alternative names for the same province (e.g., H. Vetters, *Dacia Ripensis* (Vienna, 1950), 205; Stein, *Bas-Empire*[2] 1, Carte II).

35. J. J. Wilkes, *Dalmatia* (London, 1969), 417.

ses of the province Flavia Viennensis is attested between 312 and 324. The two Narbonenses, however, were subsequently reunited, since Ammianus (15.11.14, 18.1.4, 22.1.2), Hilary of Poitiers (*De Synodis,* praef. (*PL* 10.479)), and Festus record a single province of Narbonensis between 355 and 364. The *Notitia Dignitatum* shows two provinces of Narbonensis again, as does the heading to a letter from the Council of Aquileia in 381 (*PL* 16.979).

Geographical considerations suggest that the later division was not the original one. Since the Narbonensis Secunda of the late fourth century was carved out of Viennensis (not out of Narbonensis), the choice of names seems explicable only if Narbonensis was originally divided into two parts, one of which was then incorporated in Viennensis before resuming a separate existence.[36]

Germania Inferior

Name changed to Germania Secunda.

Germania Superior

Divided into Germania Prima (in the north) and Sequania.

Hispania Tarraconensis

The Severan province was divided by Caracalla, but soon reunited, after which its normal designation became Hispania Citerior.[37] Diocletian made a division, which underwent no changes until long after 337, into the three provinces of Gallaecia (in the northwest), Tarraconensis (the northeast), and Carthaginiensis.[38] A senatorial *leg. Augg. pr. pr.* is attested as governor of Hispania Citerior in 283 (*ILS* 599: Tarraco), and governors styled *v. p. praeses Hispaniae Citerioris* after 286 and in 288 or 289, while the earliest *praesides* of the separate provinces are attested c. 300.

Italia

Before Diocletian, Italy was not a province of the Roman Empire and all its territory was exempt from provincial taxation. Its division into provinces can be dated quite closely from known senatorial careers. Until c. 290 there were two *correctores Italiae,* one in the north and one in peninsular Italy, while the first known *corrector* of an Italian province entered office no later than 294 (viz. T. Flavius Postumius Titianus in Campania). Between 290 and 293, L. Aelius Helvius Dionysius was *corrector utriusque Italiae,* while in or before 293 Postumius Titianus is attested as both *corr(ector) Ital(iae)* and *corrector Italiae regionis Transpadanae* (the two titles either refer to two separate, and presumably consecutive, posts or are variant descriptions of the same post).

36. H. Nesselhauf, *Abh. Berlin,* Phil.-hist. Klasse 1938, Nr. 2. 8 ff.

37. G. Alföldy, *Fasti Hispanienses* (Wiesbaden, 1969), 49 ff., 106 ff.

38. A. Albertini, *Les divisions administratives de l'Espagne romaine* (Paris, 1923), 117 ff.; A. Balil, *Hispania* 27 (1967), 287 ff.

The list of Italian provinces in the Verona List is very defective. Although the heading promises sixteen provinces in the *diocesis Italiciana,* only eight appear in the manuscript:

1. Venetia et Histria, of which a *corrector* is attested before 305
2. Flaminia et Picenum, of which no governor is known before 325
3. Tuscia et Umbria, of which the earliest known *corrector* can be dated c. 310
4. Apulia et Calabria, of which a *corrector* is attested in 305/6
5. Lucania (et Bruttii), of which the earliest known *corrector* probably held office before 306
6. Corsica: the Severan province
7. Alpes Cottiae: the Severan province
8. Raetia: the Severan province

In addition, the following Italian provinces are attested before 337:

9. Aemilia et Liguria in 321
10. Campania, which came into existence no later than 294
11. Sardinia: the Severan province
12. Sicilia: the Severan province.[39]

Lusitania
    No change.

Lycia et Pamphylia
    A *praeses Lyciae et Pamphyliae* is attested on 1 June 311, and it appears to have been the provincial council of a combined Lycia and Pamphylia which submitted a petition to Maximinus against the Christians, probably later in the same year (*CIL* 3.12132 = *TAM* 2.3.785: Arycanda). Although the Nicene subscriptions register two separate provinces, the phraseology of a letter probably written c. 320 suggests that they are anachronistic and that the division of the province into two separate provinces of Lycia and Pamphylia had not yet occurred (Opitz, *Urkunde* 14.59: καὶ Συρίας καὶ ἔτι Λυκίας καὶ Παμφιλίας). The Verona List has only the single entry *phanfilia,* which indicates either that an entry for a separate Lycia has been accidentally omitted or that the extant entry designates the still undivided province.[40] The earliest evidence for the separation of Lycia and Pamphylia comes from the 350s (Libanius, *Epp.* 366).[41]

---

39. For discussion of the provinces of Italy, see especially R. Thomsen, *The Italic Regions from Augustus to the Lombard Invasion* (Copenhagen, 1947), 196 ff.; A. Chastagnol, *Historia* 12 (1963), 348 ff.
    40. T. Mommsen, *Ges. Schr.* 5.577, opted strongly for the former alternative.
    41. *PLRE* 1.760–761, Quirinus.

Macedonia

Divided into Macedonia, Thessalia, and Epirus Nova (all three in the Verona List).

Mauretania Caesariensis

Caesariensis was divided into two new provinces, of which the western one continued to bear the old name, while Mauretania Sitifensis is attested as the name of the eastern one as early as 315. The Verona List has *mauritania caesariensis mauritania tabia insidiana*. Although Tabia or Zabia has been claimed as the original name of Sitifensis,[42] *insidiana* seems inexplicable except as a manuscript corruption, and it is possible that the original list called Sitifensis Mauritania Tubusuctitana.[43]

The date of the division requires discussion, for it has often been claimed that Diocletian divided Mauretania Caesariensis before 293.[44] Positive testimony appears to be provided by the following inscription:

> invictissimorum Aug[g(ustorum)
> 2 tam ex Mauret(ania) Caes(ariensi) quam
> etiam de Sitifensi adgres-
> 4 sus Quinquegentaneos
> rebelles caesos multos
> 6 etiam et vivos adpre-
> hensos sed et praedas
> 8 actas repressa despe-
> ratione eorum victo-
> 10 riam reportaverit
> Aurel(ius) Litua v. p. p(raeses) p(rovinciae)
> M(auretaniae) Caes(ariensis)
>
> (*CIL* 8.8924: Saldae)

The beginning can be supplied from a similar inscription from Caesarea (*CIL* 8.9324), which refers to "omnib(us) militibus dd. nn. Diocletiani et Maximiani Augg." The absence of the names of Constantius and Galerius indicates a date earlier than 1 March 293 and thus (so the argument runs) attests the division of the old Mauretania Caesariensis into the new Caesariensis and Sitifensis before that date. The inference is not peremptory. The fact that Litua bears the title *praeses* of Caesariensis, while Saldae is in Sitifensis, implies rather that he governed a still undivided Caesariensis. Moreover, whereas the inscription quoted

42. C. Jullian, *MEFR* 2 (1882), 86 ff.; Stein, *Bas-Empire* 1, Carte II.
43. G. Costa, *Diz. ep.* 2 (1912), 1836.
44. J. G. C. Anderson, *JRS* 22 (1932), 30; J. Carcopino, *Le Maroc antique* (Paris, 1943), 245; Seston, *Dioclétien* 326; B. H. Warmington, *The North African Provinces from Diocletian to the Vandal Conquest* (Cambridge, 1954), 1; P. Romanelli, *Storia delle province romane dell'Africa* (Rome, 1959), 515.

uses the third person (*reportaverit*), the one from Caesarea records a dedication in the first person ("Aurel. Litua v. p. p. p. M. C. votum libens posui"). Taken together, the two inscriptions suggest that Litua's expedition began before 1 March 293 when Caesariensis was as yet undivided, but that the inscription from Saldae represents a later re-engraving of the original dedication after the division of the province.[45] Indeed, it was argued long ago that the two dedications prove that Diocletian divided Caesariensis precisely in 293.[46]

Mauretania Tingitana

No change, at least in theory, but the real extent of effective Roman control is not easy to gauge.[47]

Mesopotamia

The eastern expeditions and policy of Septimius Severus and his son added the provinces of Mesopotamia and Osrhoene to the Roman Empire.[48] Although their fortunes can only be traced with difficulty during the third century,[49] two items of evidence indicate that both provinces probably existed in 293. First, the *Res Gestae Divi Saporis,* which list Assyria (i.e. Babylonia), Adiabene, Arabia, Armenia, and Albania as belonging to Persia, imply by their silence that the provinces of Mesopotamia and Osrhoene were in Roman hands when Shapur died (272). Second, an orator in 297 described Diocletian as having driven the Persians back beyond the Tigris in 287 (*Pan. Lat.* 8(5).3.3).

The Verona List agrees with Ammianus (14.3.2, 14.8.7, 18.7.3, 23.2.7, 24.1.2) and the conciliar list of 381 in recording Mesopotamia and Osrhoene as separate provinces. The Nicene subscriptions, however, enter only Mesopotamia, and that with Edessa, the capital of Osrhoene, as its metropolis. If the provincial designations for 325 were authoritative, that would imply that Osrhoene and Mesopotamia had been combined.[50] But such a combination produces an excessively large province, when Galerius' conquests of 298 are taken into account.[51] It is preferable to suppose that the rubric "Mesopotamia" in the Nicene subscriptions (which includes one bishop from Persian territory) does not correspond strictly with Roman provincial boundaries. Hence there is no reason to deny the existence of a separate Osrhoene in 325.

45. A. Poulle, *Annuaire de Constantine* 6 (1862), 169 ff.; *Recueil de Constantine* 18 (1876/7), 495; 20 (1879/80), 263.

46. R. Cagnat, *Mélanges Havet* (Paris, 1909), 72 ff.; *L'armée romaine d'Afrique* (Paris, 1913), 70 (misreported by Seston, *Dioclétien* 326).

47. For discussion, C. Courtois, *Les Vandales et l'Afrique* (Paris, 1955), 79 ff.

48. On the administration of these territories, see R. P. Duncan-Jones, *CP* 64 (1969), 229 ff.; 65 (1970), 107 ff.

49. A. Christensen, *L'Iran sous les Sassanides*[2] (Copenhagen, 1944), 221 ff., cf. H. Petersen, *TAPA* 107 (1977), 277 ff.

50. So Jones, *LRE* 3.390.

51. On Roman acquisitions in the war of 296–299, see M. L. Chaumont, *Recherches sur l'histoire d'Arménie de l'avènement des Sassanides à la conversion du royaume* (Paris, 1969), 113 ff.

Moesia Inferior

The Severan province lost territory in the west to Aurelian's new Dacia, and was divided into two provinces, which the Verona List calls Scythia and Moesia Inferior (later Moesia Secunda).[52] A *dux limit(is) prov(inciae) Scyt(hiae)* is attested between 293 and 305 (*ILS* 4103: Tomi).

Moesia Superior

Most of the territory of the new Dacia had formerly belonged to Moesia Superior; the remainder was then divided into two provinces eventually called Moesia Prima and Dardania.[53] The Verona List has *misia superior margensis:* presumably Moesia Superior and Margensis are alternative names for the later Moesia Prima.

Noricum

Divided into Noricum Ripense and Noricum Mediterraneum; a governor of the latter is attested c. 320.[54]

Numidia

By singular good fortune, the division and the reunification of Numidia can be dated precisely.[55] In 303 Valerius Florus was still governing the whole of Numidia, in which capacity he enforced anti-Christian legislation promulgated in Nicomedia on 24 February 303. But Florus is also attested as *v. p. p. p. N. M.,* i.e. as *vir perfectissimus, praeses provinciae Numidiae Militianae* before 1 May 305, whereas one Aurelius Quintianus is attested as *praeses* on 20 November 303 at Macomades Minores, i.e. as governor of Numidia Cirtensis. The division, therefore, occurred in 303, between c. June and November; Florus stayed on as the first governor of the new province of Numidia Militiana, and Quintianus came to govern Numidia Cirtensis. The reunification can be dated to 314: on the one hand an imperial letter of early 314 uses the words *de Byzacenae, Trispolitanae, Numidiarum et Mauritaniarum . . . provinciis* (Optatus, App. 3, p. 205.33/34 Ziwsa), and, on the other, Valerius Paulus appears as *v. p. p. p. N.,* i.e. as *praeses provinciae Numidiae,* on an inscription which probably antedates c. September 314 (*CIL* 8.18905, cf. Table 3).

Osrhoene

See Mesopotamia.

---

52. On the boundary changes in both Moesiae, see M. Fluss, *RE* 15 (1932), 2359; H. Vetters, *Dacia Ripensis* (Vienna, 1950), 5 ff.

53. A. Mócsy, *Pannonia and Upper Moesia* (London, 1974), 273 ff.

54. G. Alföldy, *Noricum* (London, 1974), 199, alleges that a governor of Noricum Ripense is attested in 304/5: he is the fictitious *praeses* 'Aquilinus' (Chapter IX, n. 54).

55. Kolbe, *Statthalter* 46 ff.; 65 ff.

Palaestina

Enlarged by the addition of territory formerly belonging to Arabia (see Arabia).

Pannonia Inferior

Divided into Valeria (north) and Pannonia Inferior (later Secunda);[56] the name Valeria was given in honor of Valeria, the daughter of Diocletian and wife of Galerius (Victor, *Caes.* 40.10; Ammianus 19.11.4). Aurelius Victor attributes the creation of Valeria to Galerius: if that were correct, it would entail a date no earlier than 299.

Pannonia Superior

Divided into Pannonia Superior (north) and Savensis. These are the names used in the Verona List; they were later changed to Pannonia Prima and Savia, of which the latter is attested in 343/4.

Phoenice

A single province of Phoenice is registered not only in the Nicene subscriptions and in 381, but also in Ammianus' account of the Oriental provinces in 354 (14.8.9), and in Polemius Silvius. The *Notitia Dignitatum* records both Phoenice and Phoenice Libanensis, which should be identical with, or at least correspond substantially to, Phoenice and Augusta Libanensis in the Verona List.

Pontus et Bithynia

The Verona List enters *bitinia* and *paplagonia nunc in duas divisa{s}*. The note of the division of Paphlagonia (by the creation of Honorias between 384 and 387 (Libanius, *Orat.* 19.62)) is clearly a later gloss. The single Severan province of Bithynia and Pontus was probably divided into two before 284 (see Cappadocia), while Diocletian further divided Bithynia into the separate provinces of Bithynia and Paphlagonia; the four *praesides* to whom Lactantius refers between 303 and 313 are presumably *praesides* of the reduced Bithynia (*Mort. Pers.*16.4, 40.1 — where *praesidi †eratineo* may conceal *praesidi Bithyniae;*[57] 48.1).

Raetia

A *praeses p(rovinciciae) R(aetiae)* is attested in 290 and the Verona List enters only one Raetia. Division into two provinces is first attested for 354 (Ammianus 15.4.1).

---

56. On the boundaries of the new provinces, A. Mócsy, *RE,* Supp. 9 (1962), 585 ff.; *Pannonia* (London, 1974), 273. The old names Inferior and Superior were still normal in 333, but Secunda is attested before 352 (*ILS* 1253, cf. *PLRE* 1.637). *PLRE* 1.454, Ianuarius 7; 1117, registers a *dux Pannoniae secundae Saviae* in 305: the relevant letters in *CIL* 3.10981 (*PSS*) should probably be construed as *pro salute sua,* see E. Ritterling, *RE* 12 (1925), 1355.

57. Moreau, *Lactance* 123.

Sardinia
No change.

Sicilia
No change.

Syria Coele
From the middle of the fourth century onward, the evidence consistently shows that the former Syria Coele was divided into the two provinces of Syria Coele and Euphratensis (note especially Ammianus 14.8.7, describing events of 353: "Commagena, nunc Euphratensis"; 8: "dein Syria"; 9: "post hanc... Phoenice"). But the conciliar list of 325 enters only Syria Coele, while the Verona List enters both Syria Coele and Augusta Euphratensis. Two resolutions of this divergence are possible: either the province was divided, later reunited, and then again divided, or the Nicene subscriptions are again misleading.[58]

Thracia
The Severan province had surrendered territory in the northwest to the new province or provinces of Dacia, and by the fourth century was divided into four smaller provinces, viz. Thracia, Haemimontus, Rhodope, and Europa (as in the Verona List). Two of the new provinces (Europa and Rhodope) are attested in 333.

2. IMPERIAL POLICY

Diocletian not only divided most of the provinces of the Roman Empire into smaller administrative units, but also grouped his new provinces into twelve dioceses. The dioceses were a new creation, and Diocletian created a new type of official to govern them: his title was *vicarius* or *vices/vicem/vice agens praefectorum praetorio* (i.e. a deputy of the praetorian prefects),[59] and his functions were primarily judicial (Lactantius, *Mort. Pers.* 7.4, cf. 48.10).[60] It follows that the creation of the dioceses, for which Lactantius implies a date later than 1 March 293 (*Mort. Pers.* 7.2 ff.), must precede the earliest attested *vicarii*. Two *vicarii* stand on incontestable documentation in 298: Aurelius Agricolanus as *agens vicem* (or *vices* or *vice*) *praefectorum praetorio* at Tingi on 30 October (*Passio Marcelli*), and Aemilius Rusticianus, apparently as *vicarius* of the dio-

---

58. *PLRE* 1.71, Antiochus 2; 499, Leontius 3, registers a *dux* and a governor of (Augusta) Euphratensis c. 304 and in 319 respectively. The *dux* is fictitious (Chapter X.2), and Seeck dated the governor to 343 (*Regesten* 192, on *CTh* 8.1.1). For what it is worth, Malalas attributes the creation of Euphratensis to Constantine (318 Bonn).

59. The equation of the two titles was established by E. Michon, *MSNAF* 74 (1914), 244 ff.

60. Also Eusebius, *Contra Hieroclem* 4, p. 373.10–11 Kayser; 20, p. 386.30–31. Jones was misled by the *Passio Marcelli* into thinking that *vicarii* were military officials (*LRE* 1.63).

cese of Oriens (*P. Oxy.* 1469).[61] W. Seston, therefore, argued that Diocletian created the dioceses all at once in 297/8,[62] and other scholars too have written of "the great administrative reform of 297/8."[63] But Seston's argument assumes a false chronology for the Persian War and related events.[64] In 297/8, so far from having won that war and thus being free to initiate any general administrative reform, Diocletian was occupied with suppressing a revolt in Egypt, after which he traveled to Upper Egypt (summer 298) before going to Syria to negotiate with the Persians (?spring 299).[65]

If *vicarii* and dioceses existed in 298, they should be presumed to have existed already in 296 when the Persian War began. But if the dioceses existed in 296, then it becomes reasonable to regard their creation as part of a comprehensive plan which also included the proclamation of the two Caesars and the division of the provinces. Several decades ago J. G. C. Anderson argued that "the administrative re-arrangements [sc. of Diocletian] were made gradually, as circumstances suggested, and were not completed till the close of the reign."[66] It is more probable that Diocletian ordained the division of provinces and the creation of dioceses in 293 at a single stroke, that his reforms were put into effect immediately, or at least with all deliberate speed, and that only minor changes were made thereafter.[67]

---

61. Septimius Valentio, attested as *v. p. a. v. praeff. praet. cc. vv.* at Rome between 1 January 293 and 31 December 295 (*ILS* 619), is not necessarily the *vicarius* of a diocese (Jones, *LRE* 3.4 n. 17) or a deputy praetorian prefect (Seston, *Dioclétien* 337 n. 4); he should be rather the commander of praetorian cohorts stationed in Rome, with the prefects permanently absent (A. Chastagnol, *Ancient Society* 3 (1972), 223 ff.).

62. Seston, *Dioclétien* 334 ff.

63. A. Chastagnol, *La Préfecture urbaine à Rome sous le Bas-Empire* (Paris, 1960), 26.

64. Seston believed that the Persian War was finished by the spring of 298, the revolt of Egypt a year earlier (*Dioclétien* 137 ff.).

65. Chapter V: Diocletian.

66. J. G. C. Anderson, *JRS* 22 (1932), 31.

67. For numismatic arguments in favor of the same conclusion, see M. Hendy, *JRS* 62 (1972), 75 ff.

CHAPTER XIV

THE IMPERIAL CENSUS

Roman taxation is an intricate and perplexing subject on which there has long been deep scholarly disagreement.[1] Yet, by paradox, almost universal agreement exists on one central issue. Theodor Mommsen decreed that, before Diocletian at least, there was no imperial census in the formal sense of the word, and his verdict has normally been regarded as authoritative.[2] This chapter will attempt to revive the earlier view (probably expounded best by J. Marquardt)[3] that even before Diocletian the imperial administration conducted a regular census of all the provinces of the Roman Empire. Its principal aim, however, is to document the existence of a five-year cycle of empire-wide censuses between 284 and 337, and to apply this fact to the interpretation of several important items of evidence concerning taxation during the period.

---

1. The most helpful collections and discussions of material for the Late Empire are A. Déléage, *La Capitation du Bas-Empire* (Macon, 1945), and Jones, *LRE* 1.61 ff., 411 ff.; *Roman Economy* (Oxford, 1974), 228 ff., 280 ff. The novel conclusions of W. Goffart, *Caput and Colonate: Towards a History of Late Roman Taxation* (Toronto, 1974) are unconvincing, and ignore (or misrepresent) much of the relevant evidence, see A. Chastagnol, *REA* 77 (1975), 390 ff.; R. Duncan Jones, *JRS* 67 (1977), 202; A. Chastagnol, *Armées et fiscalité dans le monde antique* (Paris, 1979), 279 ff.

2. T. Mommsen, *Römisches Staatsrecht* 2³ (Berlin, 1887), 417: "es hat...einen Reichscensus im formellen Sinne des Wortes überhaupt nicht und am wenigsten in der Kaiserzeit gegeben."

3. J. Marquardt, *Römische Staatsverwaltung* 2² (Berlin, 1884), 204 ff. Unlike previous writers on the subject, Marquardt quite properly declined to claim support from late and dubious evidence (e.g., Cassiodorus, *Variae* 3.52; Isidore, *Origines* 5.36.4).

1. THE FIVE-YEAR CYCLE IN THE EARLY FOURTH CENTURY

The *Codex Theodosianus* contains many laws relating to taxation and the census, from which Otto Seeck long ago demonstrated that the imperial government of the later fourth and early fifth centuries conducted an empire-wide census every five years.[4] In two respects, however, Seeck's conclusions require modification. First, he dated the censuses to the first, sixth, and eleventh years of each fifteen-year indiction period (i.e. 372–373, 377–378, 382–383, etc.). But much of the evidence he used concerns problems arising from a census which must have preceded the relevant law, and it will also support the more plausible conclusion that a census was taken every five years to come into effect at the start of the first, sixth, and eleventh years of each indiction, i.e. on 1 September 372, 1 September 377, 1 September 382, etc.[5] Second, Seeck believed that he could detect the cycle as early as 312/3 and 307/8, and he deduced that it originated with Diocletian.[6] But the earliest certain evidence for the five-year cycle which he identified belongs to 362.[7] There was indeed a five-year cycle in the early fourth century, but it fell one year earlier than the later cycle.

An empire-wide census was conducted in both 306 and 311. For 306 Lactantius provides an explicit description, or rather denunciation:

> census in provincias et civitates semel missus. censitoribus ubique diffusis et omnia exagitantibus hostilis tumultus et captivitatis horrendae species erant. agri glebatim metiebantur, vites et arbores numerabantur, animalia omnis generis scribebantur, hominum capita notabantur, in civitates urbanae ac rusticae plebes adunatae, fora omnia gregibus familiarum referta, unusquisque cum liberis, cum servis aderant, tormenta ac verbera personabant, filii adversus parentes suspendebantur, fidelissimi quique servi contra dominos vexabantur, uxores adversus maritos. (*Mort. Pers.* 23.1–2)

Whatever the nature of Galerius' innovation, Lactantius expressly depicts the census as embracing the whole of the Roman Empire (26.2: "cum statuisset censibus institutis orbem terrae devorare"): *censitores* were even sent to register the *plebs* of Rome (26.2). Other evidence corroborates Lactantius'

---

4. O. Seeck, *Deutsche Zeitschrift für Geschichtswissenschaft* 12 (1894), 279 ff.

5. Note especially *CTh* 13.10.5 (7 June 367), 11.4.1 (4 April 372), 7.6.3 (9 August 377), 13.11.13 (6 June 412), 13.11.15–17 (14 March 417), 11.28.13 (20 February 422).

6. O. Seeck, *Deutsche Zeitschrift* 12 (1894), 284 f.

7. Sozomenus, *HE* 5.4.5, cf. *CTh* 11.28.1 (remission of arrears on 26 October 362). The earlier evidence which Seeck adduced is not probative. Lactantius, *Mort. Pers.* 26.1 ff. relates to 306, not to 307/8; *CTh* 13.10.1 (18 January 313) provides no precise date for the preceding census; *CIL* 10.407, dated 323, need not be "das Fragment einer Schätzungsliste der Stadt Volcei" (O. Seeck, *Deutsche Zeitschrift* 12 (1894), 283).

highly rhetorical description: early in 306 a register of the citizens was compiled at Caesarea in Palestine (Eusebius, *Mart. Pal.* 4.8), and in the same year a census was held at Autun (*Pan. Lat.* 5(8).5.4 ff., 13.1). Five years later, in 311, varied evidence either states or implies that a census was conducted in Gaul (*Pan. Lat.* 5(8).10.5 ff.), in Illyricum (*FIRA* 1.93), in Bithynia (Lactantius, *Mort. Pers.* 36.1), in Lycia and Pamphylia, and in the diocese of Oriens (*CTh* 13.10.2⁵). In both 306 and 311, therefore, a census was conducted throughout all the provinces of the Roman Empire, with the probable exception of Egypt.

Positive evidence can be produced for at least one other empire-wide census between 284 and 337. Eusebius phrases a charge of rapacity against Licinius in slightly different ways in two parallel passages:

> What need is there to reckon up . . . the countless assessments that he devised against subject provinces, the manifold exactions of gold and silver, the revaluations of land, and the profit gained by fining men in the country who were no longer alive but long since dead? (*HE* 10.8.12)

> Then he devised reassessments of land, so that he might reckon the smallest plot larger in the assessment, through an insatiable desire for excessive exactions. Then he registered men in the country who were no longer alive but had long lain among the dead, by this means providing himself with ignoble profit. (*VC* 1.55)

Eusebius clearly alludes, however tendentiously, to the taking of a census: on the easiest hypothesis it will be a census which Licinius conducted in his domains in 321. In the west, L. Aradius Valerius Proculus was *peraequator census provinciae Gallaeciae* shortly after 320 (*ILS* 1240–1242).[8] It is legitimate to infer an empire-wide census in 321, and the evidence so far adduced indicates that there was an empire-wide census every five years at least from 306 onward.

2. THE ORIGIN OF THE FIVE-YEAR CYCLE

Was the five-year cycle introduced by Diocletian in order to raise imperial revenues more efficiently? That view was argued by Seeck and can, strictly speaking, not be refuted.[9] Yet evidence exists, albeit scanty, that censuses were held at regular intervals at a far earlier date.[10] And there is one well-known item

8. Chapter VII.5.

9. O. Seeck, *Deutsche Zeitschrift* 12 (1894), 285 ff., accepted by Stein, *Bas-Empire* 1².74. A series of provincial censuses stretching from the 290s to 311 is envisaged by Seston, *Dioclétien* 284; Jones, *LRE* 1.62. That hypothesis cannot accommodate the evidence for the censuses of 306 and 311.

10. Regularity is assumed in *CIL* 3, p. 945 (a contract of sale dated 6 May 159); *Dig.* 50.15.2 (Ulpian); Eusebius, discussing Luke 9.7 (*PG* 24.548: written between c. 304 and c. 308).

of evidence which alleges an empire-wide census, on the same cycle, almost three hundred years before Diocletian: "In those days a decree was issued by the Emperor Augustus for a registration to be made throughout the Roman world. This was the first registration of its kind; it took place when Quirinius was governor of Syria" (Luke 2.1–2, as translated in the New English Bible). Luke here states clearly that in A.D. 6 a census was conducted throughout the Roman Empire. Mommsen disbelieved Luke, and derided his testimony as the misapprehension of an ignorant provincial.[11] But why should Luke, who was probably writing no more than sixty years later, be mistaken about an institution which so directly affected provincials like himself? Even were he mistaken about the census of A.D. 6, the passage surely proves that Luke was familiar with an empire-wide census in his own day. Moreover, the census of A.D. 6 did not embrace the new province of Judaea alone: the fact that it was simultaneous with, and part of, a census of Syria (Josephus, *AJ* 17.355, cf. *ILS* 2683) tends to confirm, rather than to contradict, Luke's explicit statement that a census was held throughout the Roman Empire.

In the nineteenth century, many scholars accepted the existence of an empire-wide census in the early empire. Savigny, for example, assumed that Lactantius could be used as evidence for earlier conditions and deduced from Ulpian that c. 200 the interval between censuses was ten years (*Dig.* 50.15.4: the census-return should include fields sown within the last ten years and meadows cut within the last ten years).[12] P. E. Huschke collected most of the literary evidence adduced above and deduced that there was an empire-wide census every ten years, at least from the time of Domitian (he held that the interval may have been five years from Augustus to Domitian).[13] It was the authority of Mommsen which caused a change of opinion. He asserted flatly that no respectable evidence existed for an empire-wide census before Diocletian, and that such a practice was "incompatible with the essence of the principate."[14] J. Unger then produced a hypothesis which can accommodate almost all the evidence, viz. that a fixed interval of fifteen years between censuses first became standard c. 100, but that there was no empire-wide census, because different regions or provinces employed different starting points for their cycles of fifteen years.[15] But it is rash to reject Luke's testimony out of hand. In the early

11. T. Mommsen, *Staatsrecht* 2³ (1887), 1092 n. 1. For modern discussion of the passage, see H. Braunert, *Historia* 6 (1957), 192 ff.; E. Schürer, *History of the Jewish People in the Age of Jesus Christ* 1, revised by G. Vermes and F. Millar (Edinburgh, 1973), 399 ff.

12. F. K. von Savigny, *Vermischte Schriften* 2 (Berlin, 1850), 124 ff. (reprinted from a paper first published in *Abh. Berlin* 1822–23.27 ff.).

13. P. E. Huschke, *Über den Census und die Steuerverfassung der früheren römischen Kaiserzeit: Ein Beitrag zur Römischen Staatswissenschaft* (Berlin, 1847), 41 ff., 57 ff.

14. T. Mommsen, *Staatsrecht* 2³ (1887), 417: "kein einziges einigermassen achtbares Zeugniss in der massenhaften, wenn auch zertrümmerten Überlieferung spricht von demselben"; "nicht bloss unbezeugt, sondern mit dem Wesen des Principates unvereinbar."

15. J. Unger, *Leipziger Studien zur Classischen Philologie* 10 (1887), 64 ff.

empire, the evidence for taxation is abundant only for Egypt, which was administered in a fashion unlike all other provinces, and where a census cycle of fourteen years is attested from 33/34 to 257/8.[16] Although it is regrettably and undeniably true that "except for the fourteen-year cycle in Egypt [censuses] cannot be shown to have happened at regular intervals,"[17] lack of conclusive proof ought not, in this matter, to be regarded as decisive. Moreover, the hypothesis of an empire-wide census every five years might illuminate much sporadic evidence for census-taking before Diocletian.[18]

3. NOTES ON INDIVIDUAL DOCUMENTS

Whether or not the five-year cycle of censuses which included those of 306 and 311 can be traced back to Augustus, its existence provides the background against which some important documents relating to taxation under Diocletian and his successors should be interpreted.

(a) The Edict of Aristius Optatus

Eutropius reports that Diocletian reorganized the administration of Egypt after the revolt of Achilleus (*Brev.* 9.23),[19] and the activity of *censitores* can be documented in Egypt in 298–300 (and again in 309/10).[20] Hence it seemed natural to interpret the edict of the prefect Aristius Optatus, which was issued on 16 March 297 and orders the taking of a census (*P. Cairo Isid.* 1), as introducing a permanent reform of taxation in Egypt after the revolt — until it became clear that the revolt began in the summer of 297, and hence that the edict preceded it.[21] The edict may be construed rather as attesting an attempt to apply to the Egyptian census of 297 procedures and rules used in the census of the rest of the Roman Empire taken in the preceding year.

The substantive points of Optatus' pronouncement can be summarized succinctly. The edict orders the publication in every city and village of itself and

16. M. Hombert and C. Préaux, *Recherches sur le recensement dans l'Égypte romaine (P. Bruxelles Inv. E. 7616)* (*Papyrologica Lugduno-Batava* 5, 1952), 47 ff.; 172 ff.

17. F. Millar, *The Roman Empire and its Neighbours* (London, 1967), 93.

18. See, e.g., A. B. Bosworth, *Athenaeum*, n.s. 51 (1973), 49 ff. (71); J. Devreker, *Latomus* 30 (1971), 352 ff. (a survey of the territory of Pessinus in 216); Herodian 7.3.1 ff. (236).

19. Eutropius' translator Paeanius dates the introduction of an empire-wide census to this occasion: ἐκ ταύτης δὲ τῆς αἰτίας καὶ πάσης τῆς βασιλευομένης τὰς εἰσφορὰς ἐπέθηκε διαμετρησάμενος τὴν γῆν καὶ εἰς ἀπογραφὴν ἀναγαγὼν ἃ πάντα εἰς τόδε ἐκράτησαν (p. 165 Droysen). Paeanius may be the source of Lydus, *Mag.* 1.4: Διοκλητιανοῦ ὃς πρῶτος... ἀνεμετρήσατό τε τὴν ἤπειρον καὶ τοῖς φόροις ἐβάρυνεν.

20. For the principal evidence, *PLRE* 1.794, Sabinus 17; 44, Alexander 21.

21. On the date of the revolt, Chapter II. For exegeses of the edict based on the erroneous premise that it was issued after the revolt, A. E. R. Boak and H. C. Youtie, *The Archive of Aurelius Isidorus* (Ann Arbor, 1960), 23. For interpretations based on the correct chronology, see A. C. Johnson, *CP* 45 (1950), 17; Vandersleyen, *Chronologie* 58.

two appended documents, namely, an imperial edict and an attached schedule. The prefect describes the emperors' intent as being to stop the inequitable distribution of taxes by issuing a salutary rule, and he asserts that it is now "possible for all to know the amount imposed on each aroura in accordance with the character of the land, and the amount imposed on each head of the rural population, and the minimum and maximum ages of liability."[22]

What is the innovation? It may be suggested that the lost imperial edict did two things. First, it ordained that taxes in Egypt for the period 297–302 be based on a census to be taken between 16 March 297 and the beginning of the fiscal year 297–298.[23] Second, it supplied a schedule for calculating the tax liability, perhaps expressed in uniform, theoretical units, on the area of land (expressed in arourae) and number of persons which each taxpayer reported in the census returns. The Syro-Roman lawbook attributes to Diocletian the introduction of the *iugum* as a theoretical unit equivalent to different amounts of different types of land (121, translated by C. Ferrini and J. Furlani, *FIRA*[2] 2.795–796), and a schedule which seems to be designed for such a purpose, the *Gallicani census communis formula,* is known to have existed outside the diocese of Oriens as early as 306 (*Pan. Lat.* 5(8).5.5). The edict of Aristius Optatus, therefore, seems indirectly to confirm the attribution of the fifth-century source. However, neither the prefect's edict nor the lost imperial edict of 297 can constitute the reform itself. For, if there were empire-wide censuses in 296, 291, and 286, then the schedule was presumably introduced and applied for the first time in one of those, perhaps in 291. Equally important, the taking of a census in Egypt in 297 proves that its tax system still differed from the rest of the Roman Empire.

(b) Diocletian's Currency Reform

In 301 Diocletian issued an edict which doubled the value of at least some imperial coins, including the *argenteus,* from 1 September 301, and decreed that from this date the revalued currency be used both for paying debts to the *fiscus* and in private contracts (*AE* 1973.526, from *JRS* 61 (1971), 172–174). This edict has recently been argued, on internal grounds, to be exactly contemporaneous with the edict on maximum prices, although the latter is firmly dated by its heading to November/December 301 (Chapter III, no. 2).[24] Since the

---

22. In Lines 7–8, πόσα ἐπεβλήθη could be translated as either "the amount assessed" or "the amount levied," see F. Preisigke, *Wörterbuch der griechischen Papyrusurkunden* 1 (Berlin, 1925), 543.

23. For the quinquennial tax cycles 287–292, 292–297, and 297–302, see L. Amundsen, on *O. Osl.* 22; J. D. Thomas, *ZPE* 22 (1976), 271 ff.; R. S. Bagnall and J. D. Thomas, *BASP* 15 (1978), 185 ff.

The beginning of the tax year is argued to fall in late May or June (not on 29 August) by J. D. Thomas, *Proceedings of the Fourteenth International Congress of Papyrologists* (London, 1975), 66; *BASP* 15 (1978), 133 ff.

24. M. H. Crawford, *CR,* n.s. 15 (1975), 277.

Currency Edict refers forward to 1 September, it was issued in or before August 301. The date of 1 September 301 derives its significance from the census of 301: on that day the new assessments began to be used as the basis for taxation.[25]

(c) A Law of Maximinus

The Theodosian Code preserves the following extract of a letter addressed to the *praeses* of Lycia et Pamphylia, which, in the manuscript, bears the date 1 June 313: "plebs urbana, sicut in Orientalibus quoque provinciis observatur, minime in censibus pro capitatione sua conveniatur, sed iuxta hanc iussionem nostram immunis habeatur, sicuti etiam sub domino et parente nostro Diocletiano seniore A(ugusto) eadem plebs urbana immunis fuerat" (*CTh* 13.10.2). Seeck perceived the correct date and attribution (though not all have been swayed by his arguments) — Maximinus on 1 June 311, as part of a policy which included canceling the census at Nicomedia (Lactantius, *Mort. Pers.* 36.1).[26] In 306 Maximinus had followed the instructions of Galerius by including city dwellers on the tax rolls (Eusebius, *Mart. Pal.* 4.8).[27] In 311 he exempted them again from taxation, first in the provinces of Oriens which he had ruled since 305, then in Asia Minor, which he acquired in early summer. Hence the references to the *Orientales provinciae* and to Diocletian: Maximinus is reintroducing a state of affairs which already prevailed in Oriens on 1 June 311, and which had prevailed in Asia Minor throughout the reign of Diocletian, until Galerius introduced a change in 306. In Palestine in 312, Eusebius implies that the census registers contained the names of the rural population, but not of city dwellers (*HE* 9.8.5). Fifty years later city dwellers in Asia Minor were still exempt from taxation on their persons (Sozomenus, *HE* 5.4.5).

(d) The Brigetio Table

An inscription discovered in 1930 preserves a letter of Licinius written only a few days after the preceding document (*AE* 1937.232 = *FIRA*² 1.93): it was issued at Serdica on 9 June 311 and is addressed to *Dalmati carissime nobis,* whose post is neither stated not identifiable with certainty.[28] The historical con-

---

25. For the relevance of the tax year, K. T. Erim, J. Reynolds, and M. H. Crawford, *JRS* 61 (1971), 173.

26. O. Seeck, *Zeitschrift für Social- und Wirtschaftsgeschichte* 4 (1896), 290 ff.; *Regesten* 52 f., cf. Stein, *Bas-Empire* 1².89 f.; Jones, *LRE* 1.63; H. Castritius, *Studien zu Maximinus Daia (Frankfurter Althistorische Studien* 2, 1969), 9 ff.; T. D. Barnes, *JRS* 63 (1973), 35 n. 60. The transmitted date is retained by H. Grégoire, *Byzantion* 13 (1938), 551 ff.; Seston, *Dioclétien* 44 f.; J. Moreau, *Lactance* 398 ff.; R. Andreotti, *Diz. ep.* 4 (1958), 998; W. A. Goffart, *Caput and Colonate* (1974), 46. The dates of 1 July 312 and 1 January 313 are canvassed by A. Demandt, *Gnomon* 44 (1972), 693.

27. Also Lactantius, *Mort. Pers.* 23.2: "in civitatibus urbanae ac rusticae plebes adunatae."

28. *PLRE* 1.240, Dalmatius 2, asserts confidently that he was a military commander; he could be *vicarius* of the diocese of Pannoniae or Licinius' praetorian prefect.

text is crucial to understanding the document.[29] To put the matter crudely, it sets out to bribe the soldiers of the Danubian armies to support Licinius and his ally Constantine against Maximinus — who is pointedly (and irregularly) omitted from the imperial college in whose name Licinius issued the letter.[30] Soldiers in service (Licinius ordains) may exempt five *capita* "from the register and from the normal obligations to make payments to the *annona*" (*ex censu adque a praestationibus sollemnibus annonariae pensitationis*), and these same five *capita* shall remain exempt from tax after the completion of the statutory term of service and an honorable discharge (lines 12–15). Soldiers already retired after twenty years of service, or discharged because of wounds before completing twenty years of service, by contrast, may exempt only two *capita,* which are defined as those of the individual and his wife (lines 15–20).

What is the innovation here? The Brigetio Table, like a law of 325 (*CTh* 7.20.4), assumes that soldiers were not totally exempt from taxation, but were merely allowed to deduct a standard amount, expressed in *capita,* from their assessment.[31] It may be suggested, therefore, that in June 311 Licinius raised the exemption for soldiers serving under his command from two *capita* to five, and that two *capita* had previously been the standard exemption. Whatever *caput* may mean elsewhere,[32] in the Brigetio Table of 311 it seems to denote both the tax assessment for a single individual exclusive of his property and its equivalent. Licinius writes as if the tax assessment of a soldier serving under him is to be obtained by subtracting five *capita* from what would be the normal assessment of a civilian with the same family and property. By implication, therefore, total tax assessments were normally expressed in numbers of *capita.*

(e) The Panegyric of 311

The speech which thanks Constantine for alleviating the tax burdens of Autun (*Pan. Lat.* 5(8)) can only be understood when it is correctly dated: it was not delivered on 31 March 312 (as has often been assumed),[33] but in 311, probably on 25 July,[34] and it alludes to the empire-wide censuses of 306 and 311.

On the unknown orator's presentation, the city of Autun was reduced to penury and despair by the *novi census acerbitas* (5.4).[35] Yet he has to concede

---

29. D. van Berchem, *L'armée de Dioclétien et la réforme constantinienne* (Paris, 1952), 75 ff.

30. R. Egger, *Römische Antike und frühes Christentum* 2 (Klagenfurt, 1963), 51 ff.

31. In the definition of the contemporary jurist Charisius, soldiers and veterans were exempt from *munera personalia* and *munera mixta,* but liable to *munera patrimoniorum,* levied on their property, but not on their persons (*Dig.* 50.4.18.21 ff.).

32. Passages where *caput* appears to be equivalent to *iugum* are collected in *TLL* 3.407.

33. As in the lengthy studies by E. Faure, *Byzantion* 31 (1961), 1 ff.; *Varia: Études de droit romain* 4 (Paris, 1961), 1 ff. For a more recent exegesis, though with an imprecise chronology ("about 312"), see R. MacMullen, *Roman Government's Response to Crisis A.D. 235–337* (New Haven and London, 1976), 137 ff.

34. Chapter V, n. 107.

35. Mynors prints Cuspinianus' unnecessary emendation *enormitas* (p. 178).

that Autun had the land which was registered and, like other cities, was bound by "the common schedule of the Gallic census" (5.5: *Gallicani census communi formula*), or, as he expresses it a few lines later, "we have both the number of men who were entered and the quantity of farmland" (6.1). The "new census" should be that of 306: on the preceding arguments, the "harshness" will have consisted of adding the urban population of Autun to the land and rural population to produce a higher total assessment.

To remedy the situation, Constantine did two quite separate things (10.5 ff.). He reduced the assessment of Autun from 32,000 *capita* to 25,000 (11–12), and he remitted the arrears of taxation which the city owed for the last five years (13–14). That is, he remitted the arrears owing since the census of 306, and he reduced by 7,000 *capita* the city's assessment in the census of 311. The orator makes it clear that 32,000 *capita* represents the city's assessment in 306 still in force at the time of the speech: "nescit taxare indulgentiam tuam qui te putat septem milia capitum sola donasse: donasti omnia quae stare fecisti. quamquam enim adhuc sub pristina sarcina vacillemus, tamen levior videtur quia vicino ⟨fine⟩ perfertur; exonerandi praesumptio dat patientiam sustinendi" (12.1/2). In other words, Autun is still suffering from the "burden" of the assessment of 306, but it will soon be replaced by a lighter burden, when the new assessment takes effect on 1 September 311. How did Constantine hit on a reduction of precisely 7,000 *capita*? Comparison with Maximinus' actions in 311 suggests that the figure of 7,000 represents the *plebs urbana* of Autun, assessed for the first time in 306, but exempted again five years later.[36]

(f) An Edict of Constantine

In 1908 B. P. Grenfell and A. S. Hunt published a fragmentary papyrus from Oxyrhynchus under the title "Edict of Diocletian and Petition" (*P. Oxy.* 889), Their statement of the date of the document remained unchallenged until J. D. Thomas and I independently realized that it must be an edict which Constantine issued in autumn 324. Thomas published a photograph of the papyrus and proposed revisions to Grenfell and Hunt's text of the first thirteen lines, while I attempted to deduce from the document some details of the fiscal policy of Licinius and the identity of the Proculus who was consul in 325.[37] But we had worked in complete independence of each other, and neither of us proposed a full restoration of the imperial titles. Accordingly, I print below a text which results from my subsequent discussion of the document with Dr. Thomas and consultation of a photograph of the papyrus.[38] The readings and supplements are those of Grenfell and Hunt unless otherwise stated.

36. Hence a valuable addition to the meager evidence for the size of city populations assembled and discussed by R. Duncan Jones, *The Economy of the Roman Empire: Quantitative Studies* (Cambridge, 1974), 259 ff.

37. J. D. Thomas, *Ancient Society* 7 (1976), 301 ff.; T. D. Barnes, *ZPE* 21 (1976), 279 ff.

38. Kindly supplied by Dr. J. R. Rea in advance of the publication of *Ancient Society* 7 (1976), Plate VI.

[Αὐτοκράτωρ Καῖσαρ Φλαούιος Οὐαλέριος Κωνσταντῖνος
Σαρματικὸς
    μέγιστος Γε]ρμανικὸς μέγιστος Γουνθικ[ὸς
2 [μέγιστος Περσικὸς μέγιστος...c. 33 letters
    ...Εὐσεβὴς Ε]ὐτυχὴς Νικητὴς Σεβαστὸς κ[αὶ
[c. 13 letters... Φλαούιος Ἰούλιος Κρῖσπος καὶ Φλαούιος
Κλαύδιος
    Κωνσταντῖνο]ς Σαρματικοὶ μέγιστοι Γερμαν[ικοὶ
4 [μέγιστοι...c. 29 letters... καὶ Φλαούιος Ἰούλιος
    Κωνστάντιο]ς οἱ ἐπιφανέστατοι Καίσαρε[ς
    φιλ]ανθρωπίᾳ κεκελεύκαμεν [
6   ]ου χρόνου τῆς πολυαιτίας α . [
        ] καταλαμβανόντων διὰ τ[
8   ἐ]ξάκτορες καὶ ἐπίσταθμοι κο[
        ]οις ἑξηκονταετῖς ὡς εἰ ελα[
10   ] ιᾳ τῇ α΄ εἰδῶν Δεκεμβρίω[ν
[c. 41 letters... τοῖς ἐπιφανεστάτοις
    Καίσαρ]σιν τὸ γ΄ ὑπάτοις. ὑπατίας Οὐ[αλερίου
12 [Πρόκλου καὶ...c. 33 letters... Ἀνικίου Παυλίνου
    τῶν λαμ]προτάτων Παχὼν κθ . [
      πό]λεως διὰ τοῦ ἐνάρχου πρυτάν[εως
14   τῆς] αὐτῆς πόλεως
    παρὰ τῆς] αὐτῆς πόλεως. τοῦ προτεταγ[μένου
16   ἑξηκο]στὸν ἐνιαυτὸν ὑπερβεβηκοτ[
      ἑβδο]μηκοστὸν καὶ τρίτον ἐνιαυ[τὸν
18   π]ερὶ ἐμὲ γῆρας καὶ τὴν τοῦ σώ[ματος ἀσθένειαν
    γηροβ]οσκίαν μήτε κτῆσιν [
20   ]ν ἐπιρωσθῆναι κἀμοὶ τον .[
    ]αι ἐπὶ τῶν ὁμοίων μου φθασαντ . [

1   Αὐτοκράτωρ...μέγιστος[1] supp. Thomas
2   μέγιστος Περσικὸς μέγιστος Barnes, cetera GH
3   Γερμαν[ικοὶ Thomas, cetera Barnes
4   μέγιστοι[1] Thomas
     καὶ Φλαούιος Ἰούλιος Κωνστάντιο[ς οἱ Barnes
     Μαξιμιανὸ]ς οἱ GH   μέγισ]τοι Thomas
8   ἐ]ξάκτορες Thomas   πρ]άκτορες GH
10 προετέθη ἐν Ἀλεξανδ]ρίᾳ GH
     ἐν Νικομη]δίᾳ Thomas dubitanter
11 τοῖς ἐπιφανεστάτοις supp. Thomas
     Οὐ[αλερίου Barnes   Οὐ[Thomas   Ὀκ[GH
12 supp. Barnes
18 τὴν corr. e τῆς

235

Commentary

1. For Constantine's first three victory titles in this order, *ILS* 695 (Sitifis, 315); *CIL* 2.481 (Emerita). Since Constantine became *Germanicus maximus* for the first time in 307, the preceding *Sarmaticus maximus* must derive in the first instance from a victory won by another emperor, presumably Galerius, late 306 or early 307 (Tables 7, 8). It follows that the victory titles observe the principle of collegiality — which is very relevant to the conjectural restoration of lines 2–4.

2. The division between lines is uncertain. I have placed the μέγιστος which must follow Γουνθικός in line 2 and supplied Περσικὸς μέγιστος from Table 7. There still remains a gap of c. 33 letters, which may be supplemented from comparison with *ILS* 8942 (Semta, 315) and *ILS* 696 (near Sitifis, 318), where Constantine seems to have the titles *Adiab(enicus) max(imus), Med(icus) max(imus)* (*ILS* 696 adds *Armen(icus) max(imus)*) in virtue (it appears) of victories won by Licinius in 313–315 (Chapter V, n. 145)). Presumably, therefore, supply here Ἀδιαβηνικὸς μέγιστος Μηδικὸς μέγιστος.

3–4. Although in line 4 tau seems palaeographically preferable to sigma, it is historically impossible: appointed Caesar on 8 November 324, Constantius cannot have acquired any victory titles by 12 December 324 (line 10). Hence [Κωνστάντιο]ς should be restored: the space of c. 29 letters preceding his name will have been occupied by two titles reflecting victories won between 318 and 324 either by Constantine or by Crispus or by Licinius. Further, in order to respect the principle of collegiality, the Caesars Crispus and Constantinus cannot possess victory titles which Constantine lacks. Perhaps, therefore, either Γουνθικοὶ μέγιστοι or Περσικοὶ μέγιστοι should be supplied together with Ἀρμενικοὶ μέγιστοι (a total of 33 letters) — which will imply victories of Licinius for which no explicit evidence appears to exist. The title Σαρματικοὶ μέγιστοι in first place must reflect an imperial victory won between 1 March 317 and Crispus' German victory c. 319 — i.e. a victory won by Licinius c. 318 (Chapter V, nn. 147, 151). The space of c. 13 letters at the beginning of line 3 will presumably have been occupied by some phrase such as οἱ υἱοὶ αὐτοῦ (see F. Preisigke, *Wörterbuch der griechischen Papyrusurkunden* 3 (Berlin, 1931), 67; Supp. 1 (Amsterdam, 1971), 349).

5–9. See below, on lines 15–21.

10. The date of 12 December represents either the day on which Constantine issued the edict in Nicomedia (Thomas) or the day of its publication in Alexandria (Grenfell and Hunt). Since the traces before the iota are most uncertain, I suspend judgment.

10–11. The large space can easily be filled by supplying the names of the Caesars Crispus and Constantinus in full again.

11. Although Grenfell and Hunt printed Ὀκ[they also stated that "Οὐ[may be read for Ὀκ[": hence the consular date may be 325 and the first con-

sul's name Valerius Proculus. This identification was proposed in *ZPE* 21 (1976), 280 f., and is adopted above in Chapter VI.

12. The size of the space implies that the Sextus Anicius Paulinus who was consul in 325 possessed several names in addition to the three attested. It is tempting to supply Σέξτου Ἰουνίου Καισωνίου Νικομάχου (31 letters).

13-15. On the destination of the petition of lines 15 ff., see J. D. Thomas, *Ancient Society* 7 (1976), 308.

15-21. The edict (5-9) and the petition which appeals to it (15-21) need to be considered together. Although the exact content of the edict appears to be irretrievably lost, enough survives to discern its main purport. It spoke of imperial generosity (5), of old age (6), of officials who collected taxes (8), and of persons aged sixty or more (9). Accordingly, in *ZPE* 21 (1976), 280, I adduced Eusebius, *HE* 10.8.12; *VC* 1.55 (translated above, section 1), and argued that Constantine is here reducing to sixty the age of exemption from the poll tax, which Licinius had raised in the census of 321. It follows from this interpretation of the edict that the petitioner is applying to have his name removed from the tax rolls forthwith (15-21). His age is now seventy-two: if the petition belongs to 325 (as seems probable), he was under seventy in 321, and the tax registers still contained his name among those liable to poll tax. A caveat must be entered. The papyrus has normally been taken to refer to exemption from liturgies (N. Lewis, *Atti dell' XI Congresso Internazionale di Papirologia* (Milan, 1966), 519; A. K. Bowman, *The Town Councils of Roman Egypt* (American Studies in Papyrology 11, 1971), 167). If that is correct, then it may be inferred that in 321 Licinius raised the age of exemption from liturgy *pari passu* with the maximum age of liability to poll tax, and that Constantine reduced both in 324.

CHAPTER XV

CONSTANTINE AND THE DONATISTS

The early history of the Donatist schism is known almost exclusively from documents quoted by Eusebius of Caesarea, and from documents which Optatus of Milevis and Augustine of Hippo used in their polemical works against the Donatists. The single most important source of such documents is the collection which Optatus appended to his work.[1] But a large part of this appendix has been lost in transmission,[2] and it seems that in the early fifth century Augustine was still able to procure authentic documents of the Constantinian period not in Optatus' collection.[3] Hence the reports of both Optatus and Augustine must sometimes serve in lieu of lost documents.

Many of the documents, extant and reported alike, have been claimed as bogus or interpolated at one time or another.[4] But none of the arguments yet

---

1. L. Duchesne, *MEFR* 10 (1890), 589 ff. On the use of this dossier at the Conference of Carthage in 411, see S. Lancel, *Actes de la Conférence en 411* 1 (*SC* 194, 1972), 91 ff.

2. As extant, Optatus' appendix comprises the following documents: App. 1, *Gesta apud Zenophilum* of 13 December 320, incomplete at the end; App. 2, *Acta purgationis Felicis* of 15 February 315, of which only the end survives; App. 3-10, various documents registered below as nos. 9, 11 a, 12, 15, 18, 14, 25, and 30.

3. G. Roethe, *Zur Geschichte der römischen Synoden im 3. und 4. Jahrhundert* (Stuttgart, 1937), 119 ff.

4. O. Seeck, *ZKG* 10 (1889), 505 ff.; 30 (1909), 181 ff.; E. Batiffol, *BALAC* 4 (1914), 284 ff. (each claiming several documents as forgeries); G. Roethe, *Synoden* 55 f., 123 (no. 5); W. H. C. Frend, *The Donatist Church* (Oxford, 1952), 152 f. (no. 12); H. Kraft, *Kaiser Konstantins religiöse Entwicklung* (*Beiträge zur historischen Theologie* 20, 1955), 38 ff., 172 ff., 185 ff. (nos. 9, 11 a, 12); K. Girardet, *Kaisergericht und Bischofsgericht: Studien zu den Anfängen des*

advanced has been compelling, and the integral authenticity of all the documents is here assumed.[5] There are real and serious problems on at least three levels. A genuine document is not necessarily a truthful one;[6] Optatus' appendix survives only in a single manuscript of the eleventh century, which presents a corrupt text in several passages;[7] and most of the documents lack a full and formal protocol and subscription, so that they must be dated from their contents and from general historical considerations.

A correct chronology for the crucial years between 314 and 317 was until recently precluded. For, if Constantine fought Licinius in 314 and was in the Balkans from September 314 to June 315, then he cannot have been in Gaul during these months—and the chronology of the Donatist dispute was deduced from this assumption.[8] But if Constantine was in Gaul throughout 314 and 315, except for a journey to Rome in summer 315, and went to war with Licinius in autumn 316,[9] then the chronology of his dealings with the Donatists must be constructed afresh on this basis.[10] This chapter accordingly lists and attempts to date Constantine's recorded pronouncements which are relevant to Donatism. Although the dates in standard accounts need wholesale revision only for the years from 312 to 317, all the items of Constantinian date (i.e., between autumn 312 and summer 337) which H. von Soden included in his collection of documents relating to Donatism are for convenience listed and dated.

Donatistenstreites (313–315) und zum Prozess Athanasius von Alexandrien (328–346) (*Antiquitas* 1.21, 1975), 6 ff. (no. 5).

Some of these scholars blur a crucial distinction: if Constantine incorporated the suggestions of an ecclesiastical adviser into a document which he promulgated, that cannot be called an interpolation—a term which must be reserved strictly for insertions made after the document left the emperor (S. Calderone, *Costantino e il Cattolicesimo* 1 (Florence, 1962), 265 n. 2).

5. The conclusions of Seeck and Batiffol never won wide assent; in refutation of Frend and Kraft, see respectively H. Chadwick, *JEH* 5 (1954), 104; H. U. Instinsky, *Gnomon* 30 (1958), 132 f. Girardet argues that Donatists cannot have called bishops of the opposing party *episcopi*, and that a request for plural *iudices* is impossible (*Kaisergericht* 21). Refutation of such a priori reasoning is not necessary—despite the apparent acquiescence of reviewers.

6. *JTS*, n.s. 26 (1975), 14 ff. (on the proceedings of the Council at Cirta quoted by Augustine, *Contra Cresconium* 3.27.30 = Soden, *Urkunde* 5).

7. See, e.g., H. Schrörs, *ZSS*, Kanon. Abt. 11 (1921), 421 ff.; C. H. Turner, *JTS* 27 (1926), 283 ff. (also commenting on defects on Ziwsa's edition); E. Caspar, *ZKG* 46 (1927), 335 ff.; N. H. Baynes, *Constantine the Great and the Christian Church* (London, 1931), 76 ff.

8. Seeck, *Regesten* 142 f.; 162 ff.; N. H. Baynes, *Constantine* 11 ff. The latter's chronology was taken over (with minor deviations) in W. H. C. Frend, *The Donatist Church* (Oxford, 1952), 141 ff.—a book which a sober reviewer characterized as "a mass of half-truths" (S. L. Greenslade, *CR*, n.s. 4 (1954), 155).

9. Chapter V: Constantine.

10. C. Habicht, *Hermes* 86 (1958), 372 f.; S. Calderone, *Costantino* 1. 287 ff.; E. L. Grasmück, *Coercitio: Staat und Kirche im Donatistenstreit* (*Bonner Historische Forschungen* 22, 1964), 26 ff. Girardet unfortunately reasserts the disproved chronology of 314–317 (*Kaisergericht* 39 n. 192), with appeal to H. Feld, *Der Kaiser Licinius* (Diss. Saarbrücken, 1960), 95 ff.

1. Eusebius, *HE* 10.5.15–17 = Soden, *Urkunde* 7
   312/3, winter
   Letter of Constantine to Anullinus

2. Eusebius, *HE* 10.6.1–5 = Soden, *Urkunde* 8
   312/3, winter
   Letter of Constantine to Caecilianus, bishop of Carthage

3. Eusebius, *HE* 10.7.1/2 = Soden, *Urkunde* 9
   313, February
   Letter of Constantine to Anullinus

4. Augustine, *Epp.* 88.2 = Soden, *Urkunde* 10
   313, April 15
   Report of Anullinus to Constantine

5. Optatus 1.22 = Soden, *Urkunde* 11
   313, April
   Petition of the Donatists to Constantine, attached to the preceding

These five documents must be considered together. The report of Anullinus quotes the preceding letter:[11]

> διόπερ ἐκείνους τοὺς εἴσω τῆς ἐπαρχίας τῆς σοι πεπιστευμένης
> ἐν τῇ καθολικῇ ἐκκλησίᾳ, ᾗ Καικιλιανὸς ἐφέστηκεν, τὴν ἐξ αὐτῶν
> ὑπηρεσίαν τῇ ἁγίᾳ ταύτῃ θρησκείᾳ παρέχοντας, οὕσπερ κληρι-
> κοὺς ἐπονομάζειν εἰώθασιν, ἀπὸ πάντων ἅπαξ ἁπλῶς τῶν λει-
> τουργιῶν βούλομαι ἀλειτουργήτους διαφυλαχθῆναι, ὅπως μὴ διά
> τινος πλάνης ἢ ἐξολισθήσεως ἱεροσύλου ἀπὸ τῆς θεραπείας τῆς
> τῇ θειότητι ὀφειλομένης ἀφέλκωνται, ἀλλὰ μᾶλλον ἄνευ τινὸς
> ἐνοχλήσεως τῷ ἰδίῳ νόμῳ ἐξυπηρετῶνται, ὥνπερ μεγίστην περὶ
> τὸ θεῖον λατρείαν ποιουμένων πλεῖστον ὅσον τοῖς κοινοῖς πράγ-
> μασι συνοίσειν δοκεῖ.   (Eusebius, *HE* 10.7.2)

> scripta caelestia maiestatis vestrae accepta atque adorata Caeciliano
> et his, qui sub eodem agunt quique clerici appellantur, devotio mea
> apud acta parvitatis meae insinuare curavit eosdemque hortata est,
> ut unitate consensu omnium facta, cum omni omnino munere in-
> dulgentia maiestatis vestrae liberati esse videantur, catholicae cus-
> todita sanctitate legis debita reverentia ac divinis rebus inserviant.
> (Augustine, *Epp.* 88.2)

11. As noted by H. J. Lawlor and J. E. L. Oulton, *Eusebius: Ecclesiastical History* 2 (London, 1928), 315 f.; N. H. Baynes, *Constantine* 68 f.

Moreover, the first two letters are clearly earlier than the third.[12] The exact date of Anullinus' report is subject to a slight uncertainty. As transmitted and printed by von Soden,[13] the text gives 15 April 315 as the date of the petition rather than of the report: "transmissi libelli duo, unus in aluta suprascriptus ita: libellus ecclesiae catholicae criminum Caeciliani traditus a parte Maiorini, item alius sine sigillo cohaerens eidem alutae, datus die XVII Kalendas Maias Carthagine domino nostro Constantino Augusto III." Since Anullinus addresses three Augusti (*Auggg. nnn.* in the heading), the original consular date has clearly been altered by the deletion of the name Maximinus. In addition, the proconsul ought to date his letter—a matter of far more moment than the date of the Donatist petition handed to him. The original letter, therefore, probably read: ". . . alutae. Datum die XVII Kalendas Maias Carthagine dominis nostris Constantino et Maximino Augustis ter consulibus."[14]

6. Optatus 1.23 (not included by von Soden)
   313, June
   Constantine's reply to the Donatists

Optatus quotes only a brief clause or sentence (p. 26.7–9 Ziwsa) which closely resembles a sentence in Constantine's letter to the Council of Arles (App. 5, p. 209.22–23 Ziwsa).[15]

7. Eusebius, *HE* 10.5.18–20 = Soden, *Urkunde* 12
   313, June
   Letter of Constantine to Miltiades, bishop of Rome, and Marcus

Constantine instructs the bishop of Rome to hear the Donatist appeal with three Gallic bishops, presumably as soon as he received Anullinus' report of 15 April (cf. Optatus 1.23).

8. Soden, *Urkunde* 13 = Optatus 1.23/24 + Augustine, *Contra partem Donati post gesta* 33.56 + *Brev. Coll.* 3.12.24, 3.17.31 + *Epp.* 43.5.16
   313, probably September 30–October 2[16]
   Synod at Rome under Militiades

12. No. 1 orders the speedy restoration of property to "the Catholic church," while no. 2 refers to instructions which Constantine gave to Anullinus in person (*HE* 10.6.4), i.e. at Rome very shortly after 28 October 312.

13. From A. Goldbacher, *CSEL* 34.2 (1898), 408.

14. The Maurist editors printed *datum* and punctuated accordingly (whence *PL* 33.303). Observe also that in *Epp.* 88.2 the Maurist editors correctly print "indulgentia maiestatis vestrae" where Goldbacher and von Soden read "indulgentiae."

15. E. L. Grasmück, *Coercitio* 254 f., assumes that Optatus is quoting (and altering) Optatus, App. 5.

16. G. Roethe, *Synoden* 65 n. 44, arguing that the date of 2 October (Optatus 1.23) should refer to the last, not the first day of the hearing, which lasted three days (*Cap. Coll. Carth.* 3.323).

9. Optatus, App. 3 = Soden, *Urkunde* 14
   314, spring
   Letter of Constantine to ?Aelafius, *vicarius* of Africa

10. Eusebius, *HE* 10.5.21–24 = Soden, *Urkunde* 15
    314, spring
    Letter of Constantine to Chrestus, bishop of Syracuse

Both these letters are concerned with transport to the Council of Arles, which met in August 314.

11. Soden, *Urkunden* 16, 17, 17a, comprising:
    a. Optatus, App. 4: letter of the bishops at Arles to Silvester, bishop of Rome
    b. Canons and subscriptions of the Council of Arles. (Von Soden gives only extracts: for the full texts from collections of canon law, see *Concilia Galliae A. 314–A. 506*, ed. C. Munier (*CCL* 148, 1963), 9–24.)
    314, August 1
    Council of Arles

For the date, see Optatus, App. 3, p. 206.5 Ziwsa; Eusebius, *HE* 10.5.23; headings to the subscriptions, *CCL* 148.14–22.

12. Optatus, App. 5 = Soden, *Urkunde* 18
    314, August/September
    Letter of Constantine to the *episcopi catholici* at Arles

The date of this letter is deduced from four facts:
a. The council began on 1 August 314.
b. Appended to the letter of the bishops (no. 11a) is the sentence: "tunc taedians iussit omnes ad sedes suas redire," where the subject of the verb appears to be Constantine.[17]
c. The letter orders the bishops to depart: "proficiscimini et redite ad proprias sedes" (p. 210.7/8 Ziwsa).
d. The Donatists have appealed from the Council of Arles to the emperor (p. 209.13 ff. Ziwsa, cf. Augustine, *Epp.* 43.7.20).

13. Soden, *Urkunde* 19 = Optatus, App. 2
    315, February 15
    Acta purgationis Felicis

---

17. L. Duchesne, *MEFR* 10 (1890), 594, cf. Millar, *Emperor* 596 n. 33.

Augustine states the date as "Volusiano et Anniano consulibus XV Kal. Mart.," i.e. 15 February 314 (*Contra partem Donati post gesta* 33.56). But it has long been recognized that the year must be an error for *post consulatum Volusiani et Anniani:*[18] the *acta* contain the reading of a document dated 18 August 314 (p. 198.19 Ziwsa).

14. Optatus, App. 8 = Soden, *Urkunde* 22
    315, April 28
    Letter of Petronius Annianus and Julius Julianus to Domitius Celsus, *vicarius* of Africa

15. Optatus, App. 6 = Soden, *Urkunde* 21
    315, c. May 1
    Letter of Constantine to the Donatist bishops

16. Augustine, *Epp.* 88.4 = *Contra Cresconium* 3.70.81 = Soden, *Urkunde* 20
    315, c. May 1
    Letter in the name of both Constantine and Licinius to Probianus, proconsul of Africa

These three documents cohere very closely. The first is a travel pass issued at Trier on 28 April (p. 212 Ziwsa: "Hilarius princeps obtulit IIII Kal. Maias Triberis"): if the diurnal date is correct, then the year can only be 315.[19] In the second document, Constantine informs the Donatist bishops that a few days earlier he had decided to allow them to return to Africa as they desired, but that now he wishes to keep them at court: the effect of the letter, therefore, is to cancel the travel pass of 28 April 315.[20] The reason for Contantine's change of mind can be inferred from the third document, which is his response to receiving a report from the proconsul Aelianus that Felix had been vindicated at the hearing on 15 February 315. Both the letter to the bishops and that to the new proconsul Probianus refer to Constantine' desire to settle the dispute himself:

> placuit mihi, sicut dixi, ut Caecilianus iuxta prius tractatum huc potius veniat, quem credo iuxta litteras meas mox adfuturum. polliceor autem vobis, quod si praesente ipso de uno tantum crimine vel facinore eius per vosmet ipsos aliquid probaveritis, id apud me sit, ac si universa, quae ei intenditis, probata esse videantur. (Optatus, App. 6, pp. 210.31–211.1 Ziwsa)

18. O. Seeck, *ZKG* 10 (1889) 516; *Regesten* 162 f.
19. Chapter IX.1. Hilarius was presumably the *princeps officii* of the praetorian prefect at Trier (so *PLRE* 1.434); hence 28 April will be the day on which the Donatist bishops received the pass to return to Africa.
20. L. Duchesne, *MEFR* 10 (1890), 619 f.

unde volumus, ut eundem ipsum Ingentium sub idonea prosecutio-
ne ad comitatum meum Constantini Augusti mittas, ut illis, qui in
praesentiarum agunt atque diurnis diebus interpellare non desi-
nunt, audientibus et coram adsistentibus apparere et intimare possit
frustra eos Caeciliano episcopo invidiam comparare atque adversus
eum violenter insurgere voluisse. ita enim fiet, ut omissis, sicuti
oportet, eiusmodi contentionibus populus sine dissensione aliqua
religioni propriae cum debita veneratione deserviat.   (Augustine,
Epp. 88.4)

The most natural deduction from their contents appears to be that the second
and third documents were written no more than a few days after 28 April 315.[21]

17. Soden, *Urkunde* 24 = Optatus 1.26
    315, summer
    Mission of Eunomius and Olympius

The mission of Eunomius and Olympius to Carthage is normally dated
no earlier than winter 315/6.[22] However, in his letter to the Donatists of early
May 315 (no. 15), Constantine refers to a mission which either never occurred
or is otherwise unknown or was that of the two bishops: "hoc mihi placuerat,
ut ad Africam reverteremini, ut illic omnis causa, quae vobis adversus Caecilianum competere videtur, ab amicis meis quos elegissem cognosceretur atque
finem debitum reciperet" (Optatus, App. 6, p. 210.20–23 Ziwsa). Moreover,
during the forty days which Eunomius and Olympius spent in Carthage, the
Donatists rioted (Optatus 1.26), and Constantine alludes to Donatist riots in a
letter to the *vicarius* Celsus: "Perseverare Menalium eum, quem iam dudum
susceperat insania, ⟨et⟩ ceteros qui a veritate dei digressi errori se pravissimo
dederunt, proxima etiam gravitatis tuae scripta testata sunt, quibus inhaeren-
tem te iussioni nostrae de merito seditionis ipsorum eoque tumultu, quem ap-
parabant, inhibitum esse memorasti, frater carissime" (Optatus, App. 7, p.
211.5–10 Ziwsa). The most economical hypothesis is to identify the two sets of
riots: hence, since the letter to Celsus can be no later than winter 315/6, the
mission of the two bishops should belong to the summer of 315.

18. Optatus, App. 7 = Soden, *Urkunde* 23
    ?315, autumn
    Letter of Constantine to Celsus, *vicarius* of Africa

21. C. Habicht, *Hermes* 86 (1958), 373 n. 1.
22. Thus N. H. Baynes, *Constantine* 15, accepting Seeck's date of 27 February 316 for Optatus, App. 8 (no. 14).

Constantine refers to the flight of the Donatists from the imperial court at Milan c. October 315 (Augustine, *Epp.* 43.7.20) as if it were recent (p. 211. 10–13 Ziwsa). The date, therefore, is probably late in 315 (though it could be very early in 316).[23]

19. Augustine, *Contra Cresconium* 3.71.82 = Soden, *Urkunde* 25 (A)
316, November 10
Letter of Constantine to Eumelius, *vicarius Africae*

The date is stated in Augustine, *Contra partem Donati post gesta* 33.56 = Soden, *Urkunde* 25 (B).

20. Augustine, *Epp.* 88.3 = Soden, *Urkunde* 26
?316, November
Law of Constantine *ut loca congregationum vestrarum fisco vindicarentur.*

Presumably to be dated shortly after Constantine's letter to Eumelius.

21. Soden, *Urkunde* 27
317
Repression of Donatists by Leontius and Ursacius[24]

22. Soden, *Urkunde* 29 = Augustine, *Brev. Coll.* 3.21.39
?317
Donatist petition to Constantine

The reported content of the petition implies a date between the repressive measures of 316–317 and the recall of Donatist bishops in 321:[25] "ibi dicunt nullo modo se communicaturos antistiti ipsius nebuloni paratosque esse perpeti quidquid eis facere voluisset; quem Constantini antistitem nebulonem utique Caecilianum intellegi volebant."

23. Soden, *Urkunde* 28 = Optatus, App. 1
320, December 13
Gesta apud Zenophilum

---

23. L. Duchesne, *MEFR* 10 (1890), 620 f.

24. Soden prints no text, but merely refers to the *Sermo de passione Donati* (*PL* 8.752–758, discussed in Chapter X). P. Monceaux, *Histoire littéraire de l'Afrique chrétienne* 5 (Paris, 1920), 61, argued that Donatus was executed on precisely 12 March 317.

25. E. L. Grasmück, *Coercitio* 88. The order of documents adopted by Soden implies a date between December 320 and May 321.

24. Augustine, *Contra partem Donati post gesta* 31.54, 33.56 = Soden, *Urkunde* 30
321, May 5
Letter of Constantine to Verinus, *vicarius Africae*

25. Optatus, App. 9 = Soden, *Urkunde* 31
321, ?May 5
Letter of Constantine to all the bishops throughout Africa and the laity of the *ecclesia catholica*

The letter represents Constantine's justification to Catholic bishops for the reversal of policy announced in the letter to Verinus, which allowed banished Donatist bishops to return from exile; it should, therefore, belong to the same date.[26]

26. Soden, *Urkunde* 32 = Eusebius, *VC* 2.66
324, October
Mission of eastern clerics to Africa[27]

27. *CTh* 16.5.1 = Soden, *Urkunde* 33
326, September 1
Excerpt from a constitution addressed to Dracilianus (*vicarius* of Oriens), restricting clerical immunity to Catholics alone[28]

28. Soden, *Urkunde* 34 = *CIL* 8.21517
Inscription from Mauretania (found near Oran) honoring martyrs who died on 21 October: although the inscription is explicitly dated to 329, the year may be that of the construction of the *memoria* rather than that of the martyrdoms.[29] Moreover, the martyrs are not certainly Donatist.[30]

29. *CTh* 16.2.7 = Soden, *Urkunde* 35
330, February 5
Letter of Constantine to Valentinus, *consularis* of Numidia

---

26. L. Duchesne, *MEFR* 10 (1890), 611.

27. H.-G. Opitz, in a note on his *Urkunde* 17.4, interprets the passage as a reference to events a decade earlier. That is impossible: "the common foe of the whole world, who set his own unlawful opinion against your holy councils" must be Licinius (H. Dörries, *Das Selbstzeugnis Kaiser Konstantins* (*Abh. Göttingen,* Phil.-hist. Klasse³ 34, 1954), 56), and later in the same letter Constantine alludes to the Donatist schism as continuing (*VC* 2.68.1).

28. For Dracilianus' office, Eusebius, *VC* 3.31.2.

29. L. Duchesne, *MEFR* 5 (1885), 148.

30. A possibility exists that one or more of the martyrs has gained admittance to the *Martyrologium Hieronymianum,* see H. Delehaye, *Acta Sanctorum,* Nov. 2.2 (Brussels, 1931), 565.

30. Optatus, App. 10 = Soden, *Urkunde* 36
    330, February 5
    Letter of Constantine to eleven catholic bishops of Numidia

Constantine replies to a letter informing him that the Donatists had seized the basilica at Cirta (30) and issues instructions to officials in the light of this information (29).[31]

31. Soden, *Urkunde* 37 = Optatus 3.3
    336/7
    Letters of Donatus to Gregorius, who was then praetorian prefect in Africa

32. Soden, *Urkunde* 38 = Augustine, *Epp.* 93.10.43
    ?
    Donatist council held at Carthage some years before 347, in which 270 bishops took part

---

31. The law is dated by day, month, and year, the letter to the bishops by day and month alone, both being issued at Serdica. *PLRE* 1.1020, Anonymus 95, deduces from no. 30 the existence of an otherwise unknown *consularis Numidiae* in 320 or 321.

TABLES

STEMMATA

BIBLIOGRAPHY

INDEXES

TABLES

TABLE 1. IMPERIAL CONSULATES, 285–337

	cos.	cos. II	cos. III	cos. IV	cos. V	cos. VI	cos. VII	cos. VIII	cos. IX	cos. X
Diocletian	284	285	287	290	293	296	299	303	304	308
Maximian	287	288	290	293	297	299	303	304	307	–
Constantius	294	296	300	302	305	306	–	–	–	–
Galerius	294	297	300	302	305	306	308/307	311	–	–
Severus	307	–	–	–	–	–	–	–	–	–
Maximinus	307	311	313	–	–	–	–	–	–	–
Constantine	307/309	312	313	315	319	320	326	329	–	–
Licinius	309	312	313	315	318	321	–	–	–	–
Crispus	318	321	324	–	–	–	–	–	–	–
Licinius Caesar	319	321	–	–	–	–	–	–	–	–
Constantinus Caesar	320	321	324	329	–	–	–	–	–	–
Constantius	326	–	–	–	–	–	–	–	–	–
Constans	–	–	–	–	–	–	–	–	–	–
Dalmatius	–	–	–	–	–	–	–	–	–	–

TABLE 2. *Tribunicia Potestas* and *Imperator*

	trib. pot. imp.	trib. pot. ii imp.	Irregularities
Diocletian	20.11.284– 9.12.284	10.12.284– 19.11.285	none
Maximian	1.4.286– 9.12.286	10.12.286– 31.3.287	trib. pot. viii imp. vii, 10.12.292–28.2.293 trib. pot. ix imp. viii, 1.3.293–31.3.293
Constantius	1.3.293– 9.12.293*	10.12.293– 28.2.294*	*imperator* apparently computed from 1 May 305, but no addi- tional renewal of *tribunicia po- testas* on that day
Galerius	1.3.293– 9.12.293*	10.12.293– 28.2.294*	trib. pot. xiii imp. xiii, 1.3.305–30.4.305 trib. pot. xiv imp. xiv, 1.5.305–9.12.305
Severus	1.5.305– 9.12.305*	10.12.305– 30.4.306*	
Maximinus	1.5.305– 9.12.305*	10.12.305– 30.4.306*	
Constantine	25.7.306– 9.12.306*	10.12.306– 24.7.307*	trib. pot. ii imp. ii, 25.7.307–c. Sept. 307 trib. pot. iii imp. iii, c. Sept. 307–9.12.307
Licinius	8.11.308– 9.12.308	10.12.308– 7.11.309	none
Constantinus	1.3.317– 9.12.317*	10.12.317– 28.2.318*	
Constantius	8.11.324– 9.12.324*	10.12.324– 7.11.325*	
Constans	25.12.333– 9.12.334*	10.12.334– 24.12.334*	

*Title *imperator* not used at the time, though its possession then is assumed in later computations, when the Caesar became an Augustus.

Evidence for irregularities: Maximian — *ILS* 640; Chapter III, no. 2.
Constantius — *ILS* 651; *AE* 1895.80 = Kolbe, *Statthalter* 55 nos. 1, 2.
Galerius — Chapter III, no. 7.
Constantine — Table 3, Computation A.

TABLE 3. THE FOUR COMPUTATIONS OF CONSTANTINE'S
TRIBUNICIA POTESTAS AND IMPERATORIAL ACCLAMATIONS

	A: actual	B: no additional renewals	C: Galerius	D: *imp.* reckoned from promotion to Augustus
trib. pot. imp.	25.7.306–9.12.306*	25.7.306–9.12.306*	c. Sept. 306–9.12.306*	trib. pot.: 25.7.306–9.12.306
trib. pot. ii imp.	10.12.306–24.7.307*	10.12.306–24.7.307*	10.12.306–c. Sept. 307*	trib. pot. ii: 10.12.306–c. Sept. 307
trib. pot. ii imp. ii	25.7.307–c. Sept. 307*	25.7.307–9.12.307	c. Sept. 307–9.12.307*	trib. pot. ii imp.: c. Sept. 307–9.12.307
trib. pot. iii imp.				10.12.307–c. Sept. 308
trib. pot. iii imp. ii		10.12.307–24.7.308	10.12.307–c. Sept. 308*	c. Sept. 308–9.12.308
trib. pot. iii imp. iii	c. Sept. 307–9.12.307	25.7.308–9.12.308	c. Sept. 308–9.12.308*	
trib. pot. iv imp. iii	10.12.307–24.7.308	10.12.308–24.7.309	10.12.308–c. Sept. 309*	c. Sept. 309–9.12.309
trib. pot. iv imp. iv	25.7.308–9.12.308	25.7.309–9.12.309	c. Sept. 309–9.12.309*	

* Title *imperator* not used at the time, though its possession then is assumed in later computations after Constantine was acknowledged as an Augustus.

Evidence used: A: *FIRA*² 1.93; *CIL* 8.8412 = *ILS* 696: Chapter III, no. 8.
B: *CIL* 8.8477 = *ILS* 695; *CIL* 8.22017; 23116 = *ILS* 8942
C: Chapter III, no. 7.
D: *CIL* 8.18905; 23897 = *ILS* 8941.

Evidence rejected: *CIL* 5.8059 (*trib. pot. XXIII imp. XXII cos. VIII:* contrast *ILS* 697, etc. with *cos. VII*); 8.8476 (*trib. pot. X imp. VI cons. IIII:* the second numeral is probably incomplete, see H. Dessau, *EE* 7 (1892), 431).

TABLE 4. IMPERIAL VICTORY TITLES IN 301

	Number of times title taken by			
	Diocletian	Maximian	Constantius	Galerius
Germanicus maximus	6	5	2	2
Sarmaticus maximus	4	3	2	[2]
Persicus maximus	2	[2]	2	[2]
Brittanicus maximus	1	[1]	1	[1]
Carpicus maximus	1	[1]	1	[1]
Armenicus maximus	1	[1]	1	[1]
Medicus maximus	1	[1]	1	[1]
Adiabenicus maximus	1	[1]	1	[1]

Evidence: Chapter III, nos. 1 and 2.

TABLE 5. THE DATES OF THE VICTORY TITLES ATTESTED IN 301

	Diocletian	Maximian	Constantius and Galerius
285	Germanicus maximus	–	–
285	Sarmaticus maximus	–	–
287	Germanicus maximus II	Germanicus maximus	–
287	Germanicus maximus III	Germanicus maximus II	–
288	Germanicus maximus IV	Germanicus maximus III	–
289	Sarmaticus maximus II	Sarmaticus maximus	–
293	Germanicus maximus V	Germanicus maximus IV	Germanici maximi
294	Sarmaticus maximus III	Sarmaticus maximus II	Sarmatici maximi
?295	Persicus maximus	Persicus maximus	Persici maximi
296	Brittanicus maximus	Brittanicus maximus	Brittanici maximi
296	Carpicus maximus	Carpicus maximus	Carpici maximi
298	Armenicus maximus	Armenicus maximus	Medici maximi
298	Medicus maximus	Medicus maximus	Medici maximi
298	Adiabenicus maximus	Adiabenicus maximus	Adiabenici maximi
298	Persicus maximus II	Persicus maximus II	Persici maximi II
299 or 300	Sarmaticus maximus IV	Sarmaticus maximus III	Sarmatici maximi II
300 or 301	Germanicus maximus VI	Germanicus maximus V	Germanici maximi II

Taken from *Phoenix* 30 (1976), 188, with three modifications:

1. The first three German victories are here identified as (i) Maximian's defeat of the Chaibones and Heruli, (ii) his repulse of a German raid on 1 January 287, and (iii) his expedition across the Rhine during 287. *Pan. Lat.* 10(2) speaks of a *triumphus* and *victoria* on 1 January 287 (6.4).

2. I no longer regard *ILS* 640 as sufficient proof that all four emperors had officially taken the title of *Persicus maximus* between 1 March 293 and the end of 294 (cf. *ILS* 618, with *Persici maximi* for Diocletian and Maximian in 290).

3. I no longer regard *Chr. Min.* 1.230 as sufficient for dating the fourth Sarmatian victory to 299, even tentatively: (i) the date is not certain, (ii) Diocletian may have celebrated the defeat of the Marcomanni by taking the title *Germanicus maximus VI,* not *Sarmaticus maximus IV* (P. Brennan, *Chiron* 10 (1980), 564 n. 36).

TABLE 6. THE VICTORY TITLES OF GALERIUS

Title	Number of times title taken before:		
	20 Nov./9 Dec. 301	7 Jan. 306	April 311
Germanicus maximus	2	5	[7]
Aegyptiacus maximus	omitted	omitted	1
Thebaicus maximus	omitted	omitted	1
Sarmaticus maximus	2	3	5
Persicus maximus	2	2	3
Brittanicus maximus	1	2	2
Carpicus maximus	1	5	6
Armenicus maximus	1	1	1
Medicus maximus	1	1	1
Adiabenicus maximus	1	1	1

Evidence: Chapter III, nos. 1, 2 (301), 4 (306), and 6–8 (311).

Table 7. The Dates of Galerius' Victory Titles

293	Germanicus maximus	
293/4	Aegyptiacus maximus	
293/4	Thebaicus maximus	
294	Sarmaticus maximus	
?295	Persicus maximus	
296	Brittanicus maximus	
296	Carpicus maximus	
298	Armenicus maximus	
298	Medicus maximus	
298	Adiabenicus maximus	
298	Persicus maximus	II
299 or 300	Sarmaticus maximus	II
300 or 301	Germanicus maximus	II
302, 303, 304	Germanicus maximus	III, IV, V
301, 302, 303, 304	Carpicus maximus	II, III, IV, V
?302	Sarmaticus maximus	III
305	Brittanicus maximus	II
306/7	Sarmaticus maximus	IV
307, 308	Germanicus maximus	VI, VII
308/309	Carpicus maximus	VI
310	Sarmaticus maximus	V
310	Persicus maximus	III

Taken from *Phoenix* 30 (1976), 193, with minor modifications.

TABLE 8. VICTORIES OF CONSTANTINE REFLECTED IN HIS OFFICIAL TITULATURE C. FEBRUARY 337

307	Germanicus maximus	
308	Germanicus maximus	II
c. 314	Germanicus maximus	III
323	Sarmaticus maximus	
328 or 329	Gothicus maximus	
328/9	Germanicus maximus	IV
332	Gothicus maximus	II
334	Sarmaticus maximus	II
336	Dacicus maximus	

Evidence: *AE* 1934.158 = Chapter III, no. 8, cf. *ZPE* 20 (1976), 150–153.

TABLE 9. THE DATES OF APPOINTMENT OF *PRAEFECTI URBIS*, 302–338

	Jan.	Feb.	March	April	May	June	July	Aug.	Sept.	Oct.	Nov.	Dec.
302	–	19	–	–	–	–	–	–	–	–	–	–
303	–	–	–	–	–	–	–	–	12	–	–	–
304	4	–	–	–	–	–	–	–	–	–	–	–
305	–	12	–	–	–	–	–	–	–	–	–	–
306	–	–	19	–	–	–	–	–	–	–	–	–
307	–	–	–	–	–	–	–	27	–	–	–	–
308	–	–	–	13	–	–	–	–	–	–	–	–
309	–	–	–	–	–	–	–	–	–	30	–	–
310	–	–	–	–	–	–	–	–	–	28	–	–
311	–	–	–	–	–	–	–	–	–	28	–	–
312	–	9	–	–	–	–	–	–	–	27	29	–
313	–	–	–	–	–	–	–	–	–	–	–	8
314	–	–	–	–	–	–	–	–	–	–	–	–
315	–	–	–	–	–	–	–	20	–	–	–	–
316	–	–	–	–	–	–	–	4	–	–	–	–
317	–	–	–	–	15	–	–	–	–	–	–	–
318	–	–	–	–	–	–	–	–	–	–	–	–
319	–	–	–	–	–	–	–	–	1	–	–	–
320	–	–	–	–	–	–	–	–	–	–	–	–
321	–	–	–	–	–	–	–	–	–	–	–	–
322	–	–	–	–	–	–	–	–	–	–	–	–
323	–	–	–	–	–	–	–	–	13	–	–	–
324	–	–	–	–	–	–	–	–	–	–	–	–
325	4	–	–	–	–	–	–	–	–	–	–	–
326	–	–	–	–	–	–	–	–	–	–	13	–
327	–	–	–	–	–	–	–	–	–	–	–	–
328	–	–	–	–	–	–	–	–	–	–	–	–
329	–	–	–	–	–	–	–	–	7	8	–	–
330	–	–	–	–	–	–	–	–	–	–	–	–
331	–	–	–	12	–	–	–	–	–	–	–	–
332	–	–	–	–	–	–	–	–	–	–	–	–
333	–	–	–	7	10	–	–	–	–	–	–	–
334	–	–	–	27	–	–	–	–	–	–	–	–
335	–	–	–	–	–	–	–	–	–	–	–	30
336	–	–	–	–	–	–	–	–	–	–	–	–
337	–	–	10	–	–	–	–	–	–	–	–	–
338	13	–	–	–	–	–	–	–	–	–	–	–

Evidence: *Chr. Min.* 1.67–68 (Chapter VII.1).

TABLE 10. PROVINCES OF ORIENS, PONTICA, AND ASIANA
IN THE NICENE SUBSCRIPTIONS

Province	See of the first bishop listed	Province	See of the first bishop listed
ORIENS		PONTICA	
Aegyptus	Alexandria	Cappadocia	Caesarea
Thebais	Schedia	Armenia Minor	Sebasteia
Libya Superior	Berenice	Diospontus	Amasia
Libya Inferior	Paraetonium	Pontus Polemoniacus	Neocaesarea
Palaestina	Jerusalem	Paphlagonia	Pompeiopolis
Phoenice	Tyre	Galatia	Ancyra
Syria Coele	Antioch	Bithynia	Nicomedia
Arabia	Bostra		
Mesopotamia	Edessa	ASIANA	
Cilicia	Tarsus	Asia	Cyzicus
Cyprus	Paphos	Lydia	Sardis
Isauria	Barata	Phrygia	Laodicea
		Pisidia	Iconium
		Lycia	Patara
		Pamphylia	Perge
		Insulae	Rhodes
		Caria	Antiochia

Taken from H. Gelzer, H. Hilgenfeld, and O. Cuntz, *Patrum Nicaenorum nomina* (Leipzig, 1898), lx–lxiv ("Index patrum Nicaenorum restitutus").

TABLE 11. EUROPEAN PROVINCES AND SEES IN THE NICENE SUBSCRIPTIONS

Province	Sees
Achaea	Athens, Euboea, Hephaesteia
Africa	Carthage
Calabria	Calabria
Dacia	Serdica
Dardania	Macedonia
Europe	Heraclea
Galliae	Divia
Macedonia	Thessalonica, Stobi
Moesia	Marcianopolis
Pannonia	Pannonia
Thessalia	Thessalia, Thebes

Based on H. Gelzer, H. Hilgenfeld, and O. Cuntz, *Patrum Nicaenorum nomina* (Leipzig, 1898), lxiv, and *EOMIA* 1.83–91. This section is very confused in the Latin versions; for Euboea and Thessalia, the index of Theodore Lector has Boeotia and Larissa (Gelzer, Hilgenfeld, and Cuntz, p. 70).

TABLE 12. PROVINCES AND SEES IN THE ANTI-ARIAN ("WESTERN")
CONCILIAR LIST OF SERDICA (343/4)

Province	Sees
Achaea	Thebes, Elatea, Macaria, Megara, Patrae, Asopus, Scyros, Naupactus, Elis, Ciparissia, Mothone, Corone
Apulia	Canusium
Asia	Tenedos
Campania	Capua, Beneventum, Naples
Dacia	Serdica, Naissus
Dacia Ripensis	Aquae, Castra Martis, Oescus
Dardania	Scupi, Ulpiana
Galatia	Ancyra
Gallia	Lugdunum
Italia	Verona, Aquileia, Ravenna, Brixia, Milan
Macedonia	Diocletianopolis, Philippi, Heraclea Lyncestis, Lychnidus, Thessalonica, Parthicopolis, Dium, Beroea
Palaestina	Gaza
Savia	Siscia
Spania(e)	Corduba, Castalona, Emerita, Asturica, Caesaraugusta, Barcelona
Thessalia	Thebes, Hypata, Larissa
Thracia	Gannos, Hadrianople
Tuscia	Luca

Evidence: *CSEL* 65 (1916), 132–139, cf. A. Feder, *Sb. Wien,* Phil.-hist. Klasse 166 (1910), Abh. 5.

The following entries are not incorporated in the table:

17 *Dioscorus de Terasia*
31 *Athanasius ab Alexandria*
39 *Eliodorus a Nicopoli*
40 *Euterius a Pannoniis*
41 *Arius a Palestina*
42 *Asterius ab Arabia*

TABLE 13. A LIST OF EASTERN PROVINCES IN 343/4

The seventy-three subscriptions of the Arian bishops at Serdica are preserved (edited by A. Feder, *CSEL* 65 (1916), 74–78), but virtually none record the province in addition to the see. The provinces are specified in general terms at the beginning of their synodical letter (*CSEL* 65.49.1–6):

Thebais	Cappadocia	Pisidia
Palaestina	Galatia	Insulae Cycladon
Arabia	Pontus	Lydia
Phoenice	Bithynia	Asia
Syria (74: Syria Coele)	Pamphylia	Europa
Mesopotamia	Paphlagonia	Hellespontus
Cilicia	Caria	Thracia
Isauria	Phrygia	Haemimontus

This list appears to be both incomplete and slightly inaccurate:
1. The version of the letter quoted by Hilary of Poitiers, *De Synodis* 33 (*PL* 10. 506–7) (a) omits Isauria, but (b) adds Aegyptus, Moesia and the two Pannonias, and (c) has *Phrygiis duabus* instead of *Frygia*.
2. Theodoretus, *HE* 2.8.1, preserves a similar list of provinces from which the anti-Arian bishops came in 343/4: it includes both Φρυγία and Φρυγία ἄλλη.

STEMMATA

The following stemmata are based
on the discussion of emperors and
their families in Chapter IV.

STEMMA 1. DIOCLETIAN, GALERIUS, AND MAXIMINUS

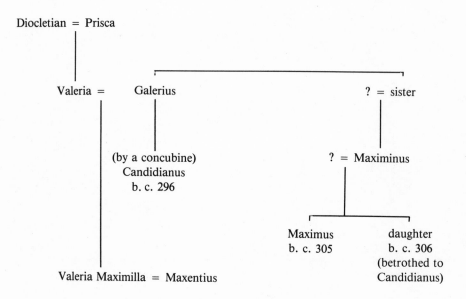

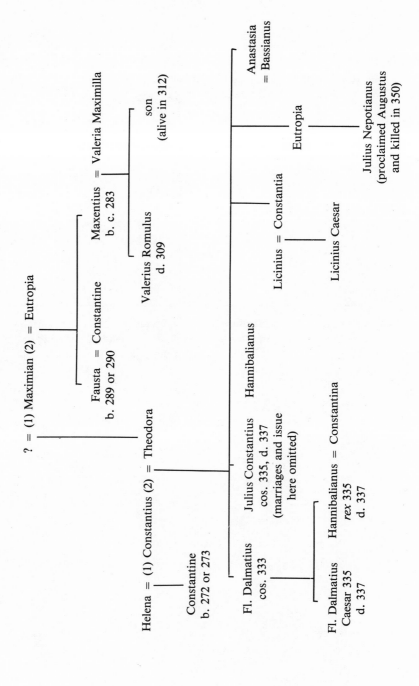

STEMMA 2. MAXIMIAN AND CONSTANTIUS

? = (1) Maximian (2) = Eutropia

Helena = (1) Constantius (2) = Theodora

Constantine
b. 272 or 273

Fausta = Constantine
b. 289 or 290

Maxentius = Valeria Maximilla
b. c. 283

Valerius Romulus
d. 309

son
(alive in 312)

Julius Constantius
cos. 335, d. 337
(marriages and issue
here omitted)

Hannibalianus

Fl. Dalmatius
cos. 333

Hannibalianus = Constantina
rex 335
d. 337

Fl. Dalmatius
Caesar 335
d. 337

Licinius = Constantia

Licinius Caesar

Eutropia

Anastasia
= Bassianus

Julius Nepotianus
(proclaimed Augustus
and killed in 350)

265

STEMMA 3. THE FAMILY OF CONSTANTINE

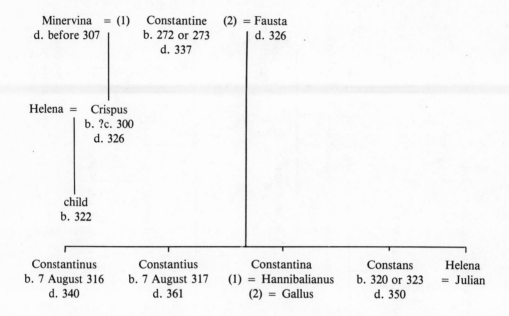

Minervina   = (1)   Constantine   (2)   = Fausta
d. before 307   b. 272 or 273   d. 326
                d. 337

Helena =   Crispus
       b. ?c. 300
       d. 326

     child
    b. 322

Constantinus	Constantius	Constantina	Constans	Helena
b. 7 August 316	b. 7 August 317	(1) = Hannibalianus	b. 320 or 323	= Julian
d. 340	d. 361	(2) = Gallus	d. 350	

BIBLIOGRAPHY

The following is not intended to be a full bibliography of modern work on the Roman Empire under Diocletian and Constantine. It includes only works cited in the present book, and within this category I have set out to list only (1) all articles and reviews published in periodicals and *Festschriften,* whatever their subject; (2) books and monographs published in the proceedings of learned academies and similar series; (3) books, monographs, and even some encyclopedia articles which deal exclusively or mainly with the history of the period 284–337. In principle, books and monographs on different or wider subjects are excluded, and I have not deemed it necessary to include the "modern works most frequently cited," whose abbreviations are listed at the front of the book. Also omitted are unpublished articles for which I cannot yet give a precise reference.

"Acta Sancti Julii veterani martyris." *Analecta Bollandiana* 10 (1891), 50–52.
Alačević, X. "La via romana da Sirmio a Salona." *Bullettino di archeologia e storia dalmata* 4 (1881), 5–8; 20–23; 52–53; 66–68; 100–102; 132–134; 148–149; 5 (1882), 69–70; 83–87; 115–118; 133–140.
Alföldi, A. "Epigraphica, IV." *Archaeológiai Értesítö* 2³ (1941), 30–59.
Alföldi, M. R. "Die constantinische Goldprägung in Trier." *Jahrbuch für Numismatik und Geldgeschichte* 9 (1958), 99–139.
Alt, A. "Augusta Libanensis." *Zeitschrift des deutschen Palästina-Vereins* 71 (1955), 173–186.
Amore, A. *I martiri di Roma. Spicilegium Pontificii Athenaei Antoniani* 18. Rome, 1975.

Anastos, M. V. "The Edict of Milan (313). A Defence of its Traditional Authorship and Designation." *Revue des Études Byzantines* 25 (1967), 13–41.

Anderson, J. G. C. "The Genesis of Diocletian's Provincial Re-organisation." *Journal of Roman Studies* 22 (1932), 24–32.

Andreotti, R. "Problemi di epigrafia constantiniana I: La presunta alleanza con l'usurpatore Lucio Domizio Alessandro." *Epigraphica* 31 (1969), 144–180.

———— "Licinius (Valerius Licinianus)." *Dizionario epigrafico di antichità romane* 4, 979–1040. Rome, 1958–1960.

Arnaldi, A. "La successione dei *cognomina devictarum gentium* e le loro iterazione nella titolatura dei primi tetrarchi." *Rendiconti dell'Istituto Lombardo,* Classe di Lettere, Scienze Morali e Storiche 106 (1972), 28–50.

———— "Osservazioni sul convegno di Carnuntum." *Memorie dell'Istituto Lombardo,* Classe di Lettere, Scienze Morali e Storiche 35 (1975), 217–238.

———— "La successione dei *cognomina devictarum gentium* e le loro iterazioni nella titolatura di Costantino il Grande." *Contributi di storia antica in onore di A. Garzetti. Pubblicazioni dell'Istituto di Storia antica e Scienze ausiliarie dell'Università di Genova* 14, 175–202. Genoa, 1976.

Babelon, E. "Un nouveau médaillon en or de Constantine le Grand." *Mélanges Boissier,* 49–55. Paris, 1903.

Bagnall R. S., and Thomas, J. D. "Dekaprotoi and epigraphai." *Bulletin of the American Society of Papyrologists* 15 (1978), 185–189.

Bagnall, R. S., and Worp, K. A. *Chronological Systems of Byzantine Egypt. Studia Amstelodamensia* 8. Zutphen, 1978.

———— "Chronological Notes on Byzantine Documents." *Bulletin of the American Society of Papyrologists* 15 (1978), 233–246; 16 (1979), 221–237; 17 (1980), 5–36.

———— *Regnal Formulas in Byzantine Egypt. Bulletin of the American Society of Papyrologists,* Supplement 2. Missoula, 1979.

Balil, A. "Hispania en los años 260 a 300 d. d. J. C." *Emerita* 27 (1959), 269–295.

———— "De Marco Aurelio a Constantino. Una introducción a la España del bajo imperio." *Hispania* 27 (1967), 245–341.

Ballu, A. "Rapport sur les travaux de fouilles exécutés en 1906 par le Service des monuments historiques en Algérie." *Bulletin Archéologique du Comité des Travaux Historiques et Scientifiques* 1907. 231–301.

Barbieri, G. "Nuove iscrizioni campane." *Akte des IV. Internationalen Kongresses für griechische und lateinische Epigraphik,* 40–50. Vienna, 1964.

Barnes, T. D. "Pre-Decian *Acta Martyrum.*" *Journal of Theological Studies,* n.s. 19 (1968), 509–531.

———— "The lost *Kaisergeschichte* and the Latin historical tradition." *Bonner Historia-Augusta-Colloquium 1968/69* (1970), 13–43.

———— "Some Persons in the Historia Augusta." *Phoenix* 26 (1972), 140–182.

———— "More Missing Names (A.D. 260-395)." *Phoenix* 27 (1973), 135-155.

———— "Lactantius and Constantine." *Journal of Roman Studies* 63 (1973), 29-46.

———— "Another Forty Missing Persons (A.D. 260-395)." *Phoenix* 28 (1974), 224-233.

———— "The Unity of the Verona List." *Zeitschrift für Papyrologie und Epigraphik* 16 (1975), 275-278.

———— "The Beginnings of Donatism." *Journal of Theological Studies,* n.s. 26 13-22.

———— "The Composition of Eusebius' *Onomasticon.*" *Journal of Theological Studies,* n.s. 26 (1975), 412-415.

———— "Publilius Optatianus Porfyrius." *American Journal of Philology* 96 (1975), 173-186.

———— "Two Senators under Constantine." *Journal of Roman Studies* 65 (1975), 40-49.

———— "The Chronology of Plotinus' Life." *Greek, Roman and Byzantine Studies* 17 (1976), 65-70.

———— "The Emperor Constantine's Good Friday Sermon." *Journal of Theological Studies,* n.s. 27 (1976), 414-423.

———— "Imperial Campaigns, A.D. 285-311." *Phoenix* 30 (1976), 174-193.

———— "The Victories of Constantine." *Zeitschrift für Papyrologie und Epigraphik* 20 (1976), 149-155.

———— "Sossianus Hierocles and the Antecedents of the 'Great Persecution'." *Harvard Studies in Classical Philology* 80 (1976), 239-252.

———— "Three Imperial Edicts." *Zeitschrift für Papyrologie und Epigraphik* 21 (1976), 275-281.

———— "The *Epitome de Caesaribus* and Its Sources." *Classical Philology* 71 (1976), 258-268.

———— "Two Speeches by Eusebius." *Greek, Roman and Byzantine Studies* 18 (1977), 341-345.

———— "A Correspondent of Iamblichus." *Greek, Roman and Byzantine Studies* 19 (1978), 99-106.

———— *The Sources of the Historia Augusta. Collection Latomus* 155. Brussels, 1978.

———— "Claudian and the Notitia Dignitatum." *Phoenix* 32 (1978), 81-82.

———— "Emperor and Bishops, A.D. 324-344: Some Problems." *American Journal of Ancient History* 3 (1978), 53-75.

———— "Imperial Chronology, A.D. 337-350." *Phoenix* 34 (1980), 160-166.

Bastianini, G. "Lista dei prefetti d'Egitto dal 30ª al 299ᵖ." *Zeitschrift für Papyrologie und Epigraphik* 17 (1975), 263-328.

Bastien, P. *Le monnayage de l'atelier de Lyon: Dioclétien et ses corégents avant la réforme monétaire (285-294). Numismatique Romaine* 7. Paris, 1972.

—— "Le pseudo-atelier monétaire de Tarragone au Bas-Empire et le gouvernement de l'Espagne du 1ᵉʳ mars 293 à 312." *Latomus* 38 (1979), 90–109.

Batiffol, P. "Un historiographe anonyme arien du IVᵉ siècle." *Römische Quartalschrift* 9 (1895), 57–97.

—— Review of H. von Soden, *Urkunden zur Enstehungsgeschichte des Donatismus* (Bonn, 1913). *Bulletin d'Ancienne Littérature et d'Archéologie Chrétiennes* 4 (1914), 284–287.

Baynes, N. H. "Two Notes on the Great Persecution." *Classical Quarterly* 18 (1924), 189–194.

—— "The Chronology of Eusebius. Rejoinder." *Classical Quarterly* 19 (1925), 95–96.

—— "Three Notes on the Reforms of Diocletian and Constantine." *Journal of Roman Studies* 15 (1925), 195–208. Reprinted in his *Byzantine Studies and Other Essays,* 173–185. London, 1955.

—— "Athanasiana." *Journal of Egyptian Archaeology* 11 (1925), 58–69. Pages 61–65 are reprinted in his *Byzantine Studies and Other Essays,* 282–287. London, 1955.

—— *Constantine the Great and the Christian Church.* London, 1931. Reprinted from *Proceedings of the British Academy* 15 (1929), 341–442. Second edition, with preface by H. Chadwick: Oxford, 1972.

Bean, G. E., and Harrison, R. M. "Choma in Lycia." *Journal of Roman Studies* 57 (1967), 40–44.

Berchem, D. van. *L'armée de Dioclétien et la réforme constantinienne.* Institut Français d'Archéologie de Béyrouth, *Bibliothèque Archéologique et Historique* 56. Paris, 1952.

Bersanetti, G. M. "Iscrizione leptitana in onore di Massenzio." *Epigraphica* 5–6 (1943–44), 27–39.

—— "Un governatore equestre della Licia-Panfilia." *Aevum* 19 (1945), 384–390.

Bickermann, E. "Die römische Kaiserapotheose." *Archiv für Religionswissenschaft* 27 (1929), 1–31. Reprinted in A. Wlosok, ed., *Römische Kaiserkult. Wege der Forschung* 372, 82–121. Darmstadt, 1978.

—— "Diva Augusta Marciana." *American Journal of Philology* 94 (1973), 362–376.

Bidez, J. "Notes sur quelques passages des écrits de l'empereur Julien." *Mélanges P. Thomas,* 54–65. Bruges, 1930.

Bizzarri, M., and Forni, G. "Campagnatico (Grosseto) — Ritrovamenti archeologici a Poggio Rotigli." *Notizie degli Scavi di Antichità*[8] 13 (1959), 56–65.

—— "Diploma militare dell 306 D.C. rilasciato a un pretoriano di origine italiana." *Athenaeum,* n.s. 38 (1960), 3–25.

Boak, A. E. R., and Youtie, H. C. *The Archive of Aurelius Isidorus in the Egyptian Museum, Cairo, and the University of Michigan (P. Cair. Isidor.).* Ann Arbor, 1960.

Bodnar, E. W., and Mitchell, C. *Cyriacus of Ancona's Journeys in the Propontis and Northen Aegean 1444–1445. Memoirs of the American Philosophical Society* 112. Philadelphia, 1976.

Bonfioli, M. "Soggiorni imperiali a Milano e ad Aquileia da Diocleziano a Valentiniano III." *Aquileia e Milano. Antichità Altoadriatiche* 4, 125–149. Udine, 1973.

Bosković, D., Duval, N., Gros, P., and Popović, V. "Recherches archéologiques à Sirmium. Campagne franco-yougoslave de 1973." *Mélanges de l'École Française de Rome: Antiquité* 86 (1974), 597–656.

Bosworth, A. B. "Vespasian and the Provinces: Some Problems of the Early 70's A.D." *Athenaeum,* n.s. 51 (1973), 49–78.

Bowersock, G. W. "A Report on Arabia Provincia." *Journal of Roman Studies* 61 (1971), 219–242.

Bowman, A. K. "Aurelius Mercurius — a 'ghost' prefect?" *Bulletin of the American Society of Papyrologists* 6 (1969), 35–40.

—— "Papyri and Roman Imperial History, 1960–75." *Journal of Roman Studies* 66 (1976), 153–173.

—— "The Military Occupation of Upper Egypt in the Reign of Diocletian." *Bulletin of the American Society of Papyrologists* 15 (1978), 25–38.

Braunert, H. "Der römische Provinzialzensus und der Schätzungsbericht des Lukas-Evangeliums." *Historia* 6 (1957), 192–214.

Brennan, P. "Combined legionary detachments as artillery units in late Roman Danubian bridgehead dispositions." *Chiron* 10 (1980), 553–567.

Bresslau, H. "Ein lateinischer Empfehlungsbrief (*Pap. lat. Argent.* 1)." *Archiv für Papyrusforschung* 3 (1906), 168–172.

Bruun, P. *The Constantinian Coinage of Arelate. Finska Fornminnesföreningens Tidskrift* 52.2. Helsinki, 1953.

—— *Studies in Constantinian Chronology. Numismatic Notes and Monographs* 146. New York, 1961.

—— *Roman Imperial Coinage* 7: *Constantine and Licinius* A.D 313–337. London, 1966.

—— "Constantine's *Dies Imperii* and *Quinquennalia* in the Light of the Early Solidi of Trier." *Numismatic Chronicle*[7] 10 (1969), 177–205.

—— "Notes on the Transmission of Imperial Images in Late Antiquity." *Studia Romana in honorem P. Krarup,* 122–131. Copenhagen, 1975.

—— "Constantine's Change of Dies Imperii." *Arctos* 9 (1975), 11–29.

—— "The Negotiations of the Conference of Carnuntum." *Numismatica e Antichità Classiche* 8 (1979), 255–278.

Bulić, F. *L'imperatore Diocleziano. Nome, patria e luogo della sua nascità; anno, giorno, luogo e genere della sua morte.* Estratto dal *Bullettino di archeologia e storia dalmata.* Split, 1916.

Burckhardt, J. *Die Zeit Constantin's des Grossen.* Basel, 1853: second, revised edition, Leipzig, 1880 (frequently reprinted).

Bury, J. B. "The Provincial List of Verona." *Journal of Roman Studies* 13 (1923), 127-151.

Cagnat, R. "Les limites de l'Afrique Proconsulaire et de la Byzacène." *Klio* 2 (1902), 73-79.

———— "La réorganisation de l'Afrique romaine sous Dioclétien." *Philologie et Linguistique: Mélanges offerts à L. Havet,* 65-75. Paris, 1909.

Calder, W. M. Review of A.Wilhelm, "Griechische Grabinschriften aus Kleinasien." *Sb. Berlin,* Phil.-hist. Klasse 1927. 792-865. *Gnomon* 10 (1934), 502-504.

Calderone, S. *Costantino e il Cattolicesimo* 1. Florence, 1962.

Cameron, A. "The Roman Friends of Ammianus." *Journal of Roman Studies* 54 (1964), 15-28.

Camodeca, G. "Iscrizioni inedite di Pozzuoli." *Atti dell'Accademia di Scienze Morali e Politiche, Napoli* 82 (1971), 24-48.

Cantarelli, L. "La diocesi italiciana da Diocleziano alla fine dell'impero occidentale." *Studi e Documenti di Storia e Diritto* 22 (1901), 83-148; 23 (1902), 49-100, 259-283; 24 (1903), 143-173, 273-311.

———— "La serie dei Prefetti di Egitto. II. Da Diocleziano all morte di Teodosio I (a. D. 284-395)." *Memorie della reale Accademia dei Lincei,* Classe di Scienze Morali, Storiche e Filologiche[5] 14 (1909, publ. 1911), 313-358.

———— "Notizie di recenti trovamenti di antichità in Roma e nel suburbio." *Bullettino della Commissione Archeologica Comunale di Roma* 45 (1917), 220-242.

———— "Per la storia dell'Imperatore Costanzo Cloro," *Memorie della Pontificia Accademia Romana di Archeologia*[3] 1.1 (1923), 31-35.

Caputo, G., and Goodchild, R. G. "Diocletian's Price-Edict at Ptolemais (Cyrenaica)." *Journal of Roman Studies* 45 (1955), 106-115.

Carson, R. A. G. "The Geneva Forgeries." *Numismatic Chronicle*[6] 18 (1958), 47-58.

———— "The Mints and Coinage of Carausius and Allectus." *Journal of the British Archaeological Association*[3] 22 (1959), 33-40.

Carton, L. "Les fouilles de Bulla Regia en 1916." *Comptes Rendus de l'Académie des Inscriptions et Belles Lettres* 1917. 149-154.

Casey, P. J. "Carausius and Allectus – Rulers in Gaul?" *Britannia* 8 (1977), 283-301.

Caspar, E. "Kleine Beiträge zur älteren Papstgeschichte," *Zeitschrift für Kirchengeschichte* 46 (1927), 321-355; 47 (1928), 162-202.

Castritius, H. "Der Armenienkrieg des Maximinus Daia." *Jahrbuch für Antike und Christentum* 11/12 (1968/9), 94-103.

———— *Studien zu Maximinus Daia. Frankfurter Althistorische Studien* 2. Kallmünz, 1969.

Chadwick, H. Review of W.H.C. Frend, *The Donatist Church* (Oxford, 1952). *Journal of Ecclesiastical History* 5 (1954), 103-105.

———— "The Relativity of Moral Codes: Rome and Persia in Late Antiquity." *Early Christian Literature and the Classical Intellectual Tradition. In honorem R. M. Grant. Théologie Historique* 53, 135–153. Paris, 1979.

Chastagnol, A. "Observations sur le consulat suffect et la préture du Bas-Empire." *Revue Historique* 219 (1958), 221–253.

———— "La carrière du proconsul d'Afrique M. Aurelius Consus Quartus." *Libyca* 7 (1959, publ. 1962), 191–203.

———— "L'administration du Diocèse Italien au Bas-Empire." *Historia* 12 (1963), 348–379.

———— "Un gouverneur constantinien de Tripolitaine: Laenatius Romulus, *Praeses* en 324–326." *Latomus* 25 (1966), 539–552.

———— "Les consulaires de Numidie." *Mélanges d'archéologie, d'épigraphie et d'histoire offerts à J. Carcopino,* 215–228. Paris, 1966.

———— "Les années régnales de Maximien Hercule en Égypte et les fêtes vicennales du 20 Novembre 303." *Revue Numismatique*[6] 9 (1967), 54–81.

———— "Les préfets du prétoire de Constantin." *Revue des Études Anciennes* 70 (1968), 321–352.

———— "Le diocèse civil d'Aquitaine au Bas-Empire." *Bulletin de la Société nationale des Antiquaires de France* (1970), 272–290.

———— "Deux chevaliers de l'époque de la Tétrarchie," *Ancient Society* 3 (1972), 223–231.

———— Review of *PLRE* 1 (1971). *Revue des Études Latines* 50 (1972), 382–384.

———— Review of W. Goffart, *Caput and Colonate* (Toronto, 1974). *Revue des Études Anciennes* 77 (1975), 390–393.

———— "La datation par années régnales égyptiennes à l'époque constantinienne." *Aiôn: Le Temps chez les Romains. Caesarodunum* 10bis, 221–238. Paris, 1976.

———— "Les inscriptions constantiniennes du cirque de Mérida." *Mélanges de l'École Française de Rome: Antiquité* 88 (1976), 259–276.

———— "Corrector regionum duarum." *Latomus* 36 (1977), 801–804.

———— "L'impôt payé par les soldats au IVe siècle." *Armées et fiscalité dans le monde antique. Colloques Internationaux du Centre National de la Recherche Scientifique* 936 (Paris, 1979), 279–301.

Christensen, T. *C. Galerius Valerius Maximinus: Studier over Politik og Religion i Romerriget 305–313. Festskrift udgivet af Københavns Universitet i anledning af Hendes Majestaet Dronningens Fødselsdag 16. April 1974.* Copenhagen, 1974.

Christol, M. "À propos d'inscriptions de Césarée de Palestine: compléments aux fastes de Syrie Palestine." *Zeitschrift für Papyrologie und Epigraphik* 22 (1976), 169–176.

Corsaro, F. "Studi sui documenti agiografici intorno al martirio di S. Euplo." *Orpheus* 4 (1957), 33–62.

Costa, G. "Diocletianus." *Dizionario epigrafico di antichità romane* 2, 1792–1908. Rome, 1912.

Crawford, M. H. Review of S. Lauffer, *Diokletians Preisedikt* (Berlin, 1971). *Classical Review,* n.s. 15 (1975), 276–279.

Crawford, M. H., and Reynolds, J. "The Publication of the Prices Edict: A New Inscription from Aezani." *Journal of Roman Studies* 65 (1975), 160–163.

Cumont, F. "Les Actes de Dasius." *Analecta Bollandiana* 16 (1897), 5–16.

Curle, J. "An Inventory of Objects of Roman and Provincial Roman Origin found on Sites in Scotland not definitely associated with Roman Constructions." *Proceedings of the Society of Antiquaries of Scotland* 66 (1931/32), 277–400.

Czwalina, C. *Über das Verzeichnis der römischen Provinzen vom Jahre 297.* Prog. Wesel, 1881.

Decker, D. de. "La politique religieuse de Maxence." *Byzantion* 38 (1968), 472–562.

Delehaye, H. "Eusebii Caesariensis *de Martyribus Palaestinae* longioris libelii fragmenta." *Analecta Bollandiana* 16 (1897), 113–139.

——— "La Passion de S. Théodote d'Ancyre." *Analecta Bollandiana* 22 (1903), 320–328.

——— "Saints de Thrace et de Mésie," *Analecta Bollandiana* 31 (1912), 161–300.

——— "La Passion de S. Félix de Thibiuca." *Analecta Bollandiana* 39 (1921), 241–276.

——— "Les martyrs d'Égypte." *Analecta Bollandiana* 40 (1922), 5–154; 299–364.

——— "Les Actes de S. Marcel de Centurion." *Analecta Bollandiana* 41 (1923), 257–287.

Demandt, A. Review of H. Castritius, *Studien zu Maximinus Daia* (Kallmünz, 1969). *Gnomon* 43 (1971), 692–697.

Demougeot, É. "La *Notitia dignitatum* et l'histoire de l'Empire d'Occident au début du Vᵉ siècle." *Latomus* 34 (1975), 1079–1134.

Desanges, J. "Étendue et importance du Byzacium avant la création, sous Dioclétien, de la province de Byzacène." *Cahiers de Tunisie* 11 (1963), 7–22.

Dessau, H. "De acclamationibus quae dicuntur imperatoriis saeculo p. Chr. IV." *Ephemeris Epigraphica* 7 (1892), 429–435.

Devos, P. "La liste martyrologique des Actes de Guriā et Shamōnā." *Analecta Bollandiana* 90 (1972), 15–26.

——— Review of J. B. Segal, *Edessa 'The Blessed City'* (Oxford, 1970). *Analecta Bollandiana* 90 (1972), 430–433.

Devreker, J. "Une inscription inédite de Caracalla à Pessinonte." *Latomus* 30 (1971), 352–362.

Dörries, H. *Das Selbstzeugnis Kaiser Konstantins. Abhandlungen der Akademie der Wissenschaften in Göttingen,* Philologisch-historische Klasse[3] 34. Göttingen, 1954.

Dolbeau, F. Review of G. Lanata, *Gli atti dei martiri come documenti processuali* (Milan, 1973). *Revue des Études Latines* 52 (1974), 570–573.

Domaszewski, A. von. "Titulus Divitiensis vindicatus." *Rheinisches Museum,* n.f. 59 (1904), 479–480.

Drake, H. A. "When Was the *De Laudibus Constantini* Delivered?" *Historia* 24 (1975), 345–356.

——— *In Praise of Constantine. A Historical Study and New Translation of Eusebius' Tricennial Orations. University of California Publications:* Classical Studies 15. Berkeley, 1976.

Duchesne, L. Review of E. Revillout, *Le Concile de Nicée d'après les textes coptes et les diverses collections* (Paris, 1881). *Bulletin Critique* 1 (1881), 330–335.

——— "Les documents ecclésiastiques sur les divisions de l'Empire romain au quatrième siècle." *Mélanges Graux,* 133–141. Paris, 1884.

——— "Les sources du Martyrologe Hieronymien." *Mélanges d'Archéologie et d'Histoire de l'École Française de Rome* 5 (1885), 120–160.

——— "Le dossier du Donatisme." *Mélanges d'Archéologie et d'Histoire de l'École Française de Rome* 10 (1890), 589–650.

Duncan-Jones, R. P. "Praefectus Mesopotamiae et Osrhoenae." *Classical Philology* 64 (1969), 229–233.

——— "Praefectus Mesopotamiae et Osrhoenae: A Postscript." *Classical Philology* 65 (1970), 107.

——— "An African Saint and his Interrogator." *Journal of Theological Studies,* n.s. 25 (1974), 106–110.

——— Review of W. Goffart, *Caput and Colonate* (Toronto, 1974). *Journal of Roman Studies* 67 (1977), 202–204.

Dupont, C. "Constantin et la préfecture d'Afrique." *Studi in onore di G. Grosso* 2, 517–535. Turin, 1968.

——— "Constantin et la préfecture d'Italie." *Études offertes à J. Macqueron,* 251–267. Aix-en-Provence, 1970.

——— "Constantin et la préfecture d'Orient." *Studi in onore di G. Scherillo* 2, 819–848. Milan, 1972.

Durry, M. "Vocabulaire militaire. Praepositus." *Mélanges de philologie, de littérature et d'histoire anciennes offerts à A. Ernout,* 129–133. Paris, 1940.

Duval, N. "Les palais impériaux de Milan et d'Aquilée: Réalité et mythe." *Aquileia e Milano. Antichità Altoadriatiche* 4, 151–158. Udine, 1973.

Egger, R. "Aus dem Leben der donauländischen Wehrbauern." *Anzeiger der Österreichischen Akademie der Wissenschaften,* Philosophisch-historische Klasse 86 (1949), 1–26. Reprinted in his *Römische Antike und frühes Christentum* 2, 51–68. Klagenfurt, 1963.

Ehrhardt, A. A. T. "Some Aspects of Constantine's Legislation," *Studia Patristica* 2. *Texte und Untersuchungen* 64, 114–121. Berlin, 1957.

Elia, S. d'. "Richerche sui panegirici di Mamertino a Massimiano." *Annali della Facoltà di Lettere e Filosofia dell'Università di Napoli* 9 (1960–61, publ. 1962), 121–391.

Enmann, A. "Eine verlorene Geschichte der römischen Kaiser und das Buch *De viris illustribus urbis Romae:* Quellenstudien." *Philologus,* Supplementband 4 (1884), 335–501.

Ensslin, W. "Dalmatius censor, der Halbbruder Konstantins I." *Rheinisches Museum,* n.f. 78 (1929), 199–212.

——— "Maximianus (Herculius)." Pauly-Wissowa, *Realencyclopädie der classischen Altertumswissenschaft* 14 (1930), 2486–2516.

——— "Maximianus (Galerius)." Pauly-Wissowa, *Realencyclopädie der classischen Altertumswissenschaft* 14 (1930), 2516–2528.

——— "Valerius (Diocletianus)." Pauly-Wissowa, *Realencyclopädie der classischen Altertumswissenschaft* 7A (1948), 2419–2495.

Erim, K. T., and Reynolds, J. "The Copy of Diocletian's Edict on Maximum Prices from Aphrodisias in Caria." *Journal of Roman Studies* 60 (1970), 120–141.

——— "The Aphrodisias Copy of Diocletian's Edict on Maximum Prices." *Journal of Roman Studies* 63 (1973), 99–110.

Erim, K., Reynolds, J., and Crawford, M. "Diocletian's Currency Reform: A New Inscription." *Journal of Roman Studies* 61 (1971), 171–177.

Évrard, G. "Une inscription inédite d'*Aqua Viva* et la carrière des Iunii Bassi." *Mélanges d'Archéologie et d'Histoire de l'École Française de Rome* 74 (1962), 607–647.

Faure, E. "Notes sur le Panégyrique VIII." *Byzantion* 31 (1961), 1–41.

——— "Étude de la capitation de Dioclétien d'après le Panégyrique VIII." *Varia. Études de droit romain* 4, 1–153. Paris, 1961.

Feder, A. L. *Studien zu Hilarius von Poitiers* II. *Bischofsnamen und Bischofssitze bei Hilarius: Kritische Untersuchungen zur kirchlichen Prosopographie und Topographie des 4. Jahrhunderts. Sitzungsberichte der kaiserlichen Adakemie der Wissenschaften in Wien,* Philosophisch-historische Klasse 166, Abhandlung 5. Vienna, 1910.

Feld, H. *Der Kaiser Licinius.* Diss. Saarbrücken, 1960.

Filow, B. "Die Teilung des Aurelianischen Dakiens." *Klio* 12 (1912), 234–239.

Fornari, F. "Roma. Scoperte di antichità a Piazza Colonna." *Notizie degli Scavi di Antichità*[5] 16 (1917), 9–26.

Forni, G. "Il diploma militare frammentario *CIL* XVI 157 della prima tetrarchia." *Bulletino dell'Istituto di Diritto Romano*[3] 1 (1959), 247–266.

Foss, C. "Late Antique and Byzantine Ankara." *Dumbarton Oaks Papers* 31 (1977), 27–87.

Franchi de' Cavalieri, P. *Note agiografiche* 1–9. *Studi e Testi* 8, 9, 22, 24, 27, 33, 49, 65, 175. Vatican, 1902–1953.

—— "Osservazioni sopra alcuni atti dei martiri da Settimio Severo a Massimo Daza." *Nuovo Bullettino di Archeologia Cristiana* 10 (1904), 5–39. Reprinted in his *Scritti agiografichi* 2. *Studi e Testi* 222, 77–103. Vatican, 1962.

—— *Constantiniana. Studi e Testi* 171. Vatican, 1953.

Franciscis, A. de. "Recupero di un diploma militare." *Rendiconti dell'Accademia di Archeologia, Lettere e Belle Arti, Napoli*, n.s. 32 (1957), 181–182.

Frank, R. I. *Scholae Palatinae: The Palace Guards of the Later Roman Empire. Papers of the American Academy in Rome* 23. Rome, 1969.

Gaiffier, B. de. "S. Marcel de Tanger ou de Léon? Évolution d'une légende." *Analecta Bollandiana* 61 (1943), 116–139.

—— "*Sub Daciano praeside:* Étude de quelques passions espagnoles." *Analecta Bollandiana* 72 (1954), 378–396.

—— "Palatins et eunuques dans quelques documents hagiographiques." *Analecta Bollandiana* 75 (1957), 17–46.

Gascou, J. "Le rescrit d'Hispellum." *Mélanges d'Archéologie et d'Histoire de l'École Française de Rome* 79 (1967), 609–659.

Gaudemet, J. "Constantin et les curies municipales." *Iura* 2 (1951), 44–75.

Gelzer, H. "Geographische Bemerkungen zu dem Verzeichniss der Väter von Nikaea." *Beiträge zur alten Geschichte und Geographie. Festschrift für H. Keipert,* 45–62. Berlin, 1898.

Gelzer, H., Hilgenfeld, H., and Cuntz, O. *Patrum Nicaenorum Nomina.* Leipzig, 1898.

Giacchero, M. *Edictum Diocletiani et Collegarum de pretiis rerum venalium in integrum fere restitutum e Latinis Graecisque fragmentis.* 1: *Edictum;* 2. *Imagines. Pubblicazioni dell'Istituto di Storia Antica dell'Università di Genova* 8. Genoa, 1974.

Giardina, A. "L'epigrafe di Iunius Bassus ad Aqua Viva e i criteri metodici di Godefroy." *Helikon* 11/12 (1971/2), 253–278.

Giessen, A. "Numismatische Bemerkung zu dem Aufstand des L. Domitius Domitianus." *Zeitschrift für Papyrologie und Epigraphik* 22 (1976), 280–286.

Gilliam, J. F. "The Governors of Syria Coele from Severus to Diocletian." *American Journal of Philology* 79 (1958), 225–242.

—— "Caesonius Bassus: Cos. Ord. A.D. 317." *Historia* 16 (1967), 252–254.

Girardet, K. M. *Kaisergericht und Bischofsgericht: Studien zu den Anfängen des Donatistenstreites (313–315) und zum Prozess des Athanasius von Alexandrien (328–346).* Antiquitas 1.21. Bonn, 1975.

Goffart, W. *Caput and Colonate: Towards a History of Late Roman Taxation. Phoenix,* Supplementary Volume 12. Toronto, 1974.

Goodchild, R. G. "The Coast Road of Phoenicia and Its Roman Milestones." *Berytus* 9 (1948–49), 91–127.

Graetz, H. "Zur römischen Kaisergeschichte aus talmudischen Quellen." *Monatschrift für Geschichte und Wissenschaft des Judentums* 28 (1878), 1–16.

Grant, R. M. "The Case against Eusebius or, Did the Father of Church History write history?" *Studia Patristica* 12. *Texte und Untersuchungen* 115, 413–421. Berlin, 1975.

——— "The Religion of Maximin Daia." *Christianity, Judaism and Other Greco-Roman Cults. Studies for M. Smith* 4. *Studies in Judaism in Late Antiquity* 12, 143–166. Leiden, 1975.

Grasmück, E. L. *Coercitio: Staat und Kirche im Donatistenstreit. Bonner Historische Forschungen* 22. Bonn, 1964.

Grasso, S. "Martyrorum? Intorno all'epigrafe di Iulia Florentina." *Epigraphica* 15 (1953), 151–153.

Greenslade, S. L. Review of W. H. C. Frend, *The Donatist Church* (Oxford, 1952). *Classical Review,* n.s. 4 (1954), 154–156.

Grégoire, H. "Rapport sur un voyage d'exploration dans le Pont et en Cappadoce." *Bulletin de Correspondance Hellénique* 33 (1909), 1–169.

——— "About Licinius' Fiscal and Religious Policy." *Byzantion* 13 (1938), 551–560.

——— "Deux champs de bataille: 'Campus Ergenus' et 'Campus Ardiensis'." *Byzantion* 13 (1938), 585–586.

Grégoire, H., and Orgels, P. "La passion de S. Théodote, oeuvre du Pseudo-Nil, et son noyau montaniste." *Byzantinische Zeitschrift* 44 (1951), 165–184.

——— "S. Gallicanus, Consul et Martyr dans la Passion des SS. Jean et Paul, et sa vision 'constantinienne' du Crucifié." *Bulletin de l'Académie royale de Belgique,* Classe des Lettres[5] 42 (1956), 125–146.

Groag, E. "Notizen zur Geschichte kleinasiatischer Familien." *Jahreshefte der Österreichischen Archäologischen Instituts* 10 (1907), 282–299.

——— "Der Dichter Porfyrius in einer stadtrömischen Inschrift." *Wiener Studien* 45 (1926/7), 102–109.

——— "Maxentius." Pauly-Wissowa, *Realencyclopädie der classischen Altertumswissenschaft* 14 (1930), 2417–2484.

——— *Die Reichsbeamten von Achaia in spätrömischer Zeit. Dissertationes Pannonicae* 1.14. Budapest, 1946.

Guadagno, E., and Panciera, S. "Nuove testimonianze sul governo della Campania in età constantiniana." *Rendiconti della Accademia Nazionale dei Lincei,*[8] Classe di Scienze Morali, Storiche e Filologiche 25 (1970), 111–129.

Guthrie, P. "The Execution of Crispus." *Phoenix* 20 (1966), 325–331.

Guyon, J. "Les Quatres Couronnés et l'histoire de leur culte des origines au milieu du IXᵉ siècle." *Mélanges de l'École Française de Rome: Antiquité* 87 (1975), 505–561.

Habicht, C. "Zur Geschichte des Kaisers Konstantin." *Hermes* 86 (1958), 360–378.

Hagedorn, D. "Papyri aus Panopolis in der Kölner Sammlung." *Proceedings of the Twelfth International Congress of Papyrology. American Studies in Papyrology* 7, 207–211. Toronto and Amsterdam, 1970.

Halkin, F. "L'Apologie du martyr Philéas de Thmuis (Papyrus Bodmer XX) et les Actes latins de Philéas et Philoromus." *Analecta Bollandiana* 81 (1963), 5–30.

Harper, R. P. "Roman Senators in Cappadocia." *Anatolian Studies* 14 (1964), 163–168.

Hassall, M. W. C. "Britain in the Notitia." *Aspects of the Notitia Dignitatum. British Archaeological Reports,* Supplementary Series 15, 103–117. Oxford, 1976.

Haupt, M. "Varia. LIV." *Hermes* 5 (1871), 23–25. Reprinted in his *Opuscula* 3, 491–494. Leipzig, 1876.

Heitsch, E. *Die griechischen Dichterfragmente der römischen Kaiserzeit* 1². *Abhandlungen der Akademie der Wissenschaften in Göttingen,* Philologisch-historische Klasse³ 49. Göttingen, 1963.

Hendy, M. "Mint and Fiscal Administration under Diocletian, His Colleagues and His Successors, A.D. 305–24." *Journal of Roman Studies* 62 (1972), 75–82.

Heuberger, R. "Raetia prima und Raetia secunda." *Klio* 24 (1931), 348–366.

Higgins, M. J. "Reliability of Titles and Dates in Codex Theodosianus." *Byzantion* 10 (1935), 621–640.

Hoffmann, D. *Das spätrömische Bewegungsheer und die Notitia Dignitatum. Epigraphische Studien* 7. Bonn, 1969/70.

Hombert, M., and Préaux, C. *Recherches sur le recensement dans l'Égypte romaine (P. Bruxelles Inv. E. 7616). Papyrologica Lugduno-Batava* 5. Leiden, 1952.

Honoré, A. M. " 'Imperial' Rescripts A.D. 193–305: Authorship and Authenticity." *Journal of Roman Studies* 69 (1979), 51–64.

Hooff, G. van. "Acta Sancti Agathonici martyris et sociorum nunc primum edita e codice Leidensi." *Analecta Bollandiana* 2 (1883), 99–115.

Ihm, M. "Additamenta ad corporis vol. IX et X." *Ephemeris Epigraphica* 8 1899), 1–221.

Illuminati, A. "Appunti di epigrafia africana." *Rendiconti della Accademia Nazionale dei Lincei,*⁸ Classe di Scienze Morali, Storiche and Filologiche 27 (1972), 467–481.

Instinsky, H. U. Review of H. Dörries, *Das Selbstzeugnis Kaiser Konstantins* (Göttingen, 1954) and H. Kraft, *Kaiser Konstantins religiöse Entwicklung* (Tübingen, 1955). *Gnomon* 30 (1958), 125–133.

Jacquetton, M. Report of inscriptions on Roman milestones (presented by S. Gsell). *Bulletin Archéologique du Comité des Travaux Historiques et Scientifiques* 1901. ccvi–ccix.

Jehasse, J. "Les fouilles d'Aléria." *Comptes Rendus de l'Académie des Inscriptions et Belles Lettres* 1961. 363–378.

Jeločnik, A. *Čenturska zakladna najdba: Folisow Maksencija in Tetrahije / The Čentur Hoard: Folles of Maxentius and of the Tetrarchy. Situla* 12. Ljubljana, 1973.

Jobst, W. *11. Juni 172 n. Chr. Der Tag des Blitz- und Regenwunders im Quadenlande. Sitzungsberichte der Österreichischen Akademie der Wissenschaften,* Philosophisch-historische Klasse 335. Vienna, 1978.

Johnson, A. C. "Lucius Domitius Domitianus Augustus." *Classical Philology* 45 (1950), 13–21.

Jones, A. H. M. "The Roman Civil Service (Clerical and Sub-clerical Grades)." *Journal of Roman Studies* 39 (1949), 38–55. Reprinted in his *Studies in Roman Government and Law,* 151–175, 201–216. Oxford, 1960.

———— "Census Records of the Later Roman Empire." *Journal of Roman Studies* 43 (1953), 49–64. Reprinted in his *The Roman Economy: Studies in Ancient Economic and Administrative History,* 228–256. Oxford, 1974.

———— "The Date and Value of the Verona List." *Journal of Roman Studies* 44 (1954), 21–29. Reprinted in *Roman Economy,* 263–279.

———— "Notes on the Genuineness of the Constantinian Documents in Eusebius' Life of Constantine." *Journal of Ecclesiastical History* 5 (1954), 196–200. Reprinted in *Roman Economy,* 257–262.

———— "*Capitatio* and *Iugatio.*" *Journal of Roman Studies* 47 (1957), 88–94. Reprinted in *Roman Economy,* 280–292.

———— "Collegiate Prefectures." *Journal of Roman Studies* 54 (1964), 78–89. Reprinted in *Roman Economy,* 375–395.

Jullian, C. "Corrections à la liste de Vérone (Provinces africaines)," *Mélanges d'Archéologie et d'Histoire de l'École Française de Rome* 2 (1882), 84–93.

———— "Notes gallo-romaines. C. Questions hagiographiques—le cycle de Rictovar." *Revue des Études Anciennes* 25 (1923), 367–378.

Keenan, J. G. "The Names Flavius and Aurelius as Status Designations in Later Roman Egypt." *Zeitschrift für Papyrologie und Epigraphik* 11 (1973), 33–63; 13 (1974), 283–304.

Keyes, C. W. "The Date of the Laterculus Veronensis." *Classical Philology* 11 (1916), 196–201.

Kienast, D. "Die Rückeroberung Britanniens im Jahre 297 und die frühe Trierer Follesprägung." *Jahrbuch für Numismatik und Geldgeschichte* 10 (1959–60), 71–78.

Klein, R. "Der *nomos teleotatos* Konstantins für die Christen im Jahre 312." *Römische Quartalschrift* 67 (1972), 1–28.

König, I. "Die Berufung des Constantius Chlorus und des Galerius zu Caesaren: Gedanken zur Entstehung der Ersten Tetrarchie." *Chiron* 4 (1974), 567–576.

Kraft, H. *Kaiser Konstantins religiöse Entwicklung. Beiträge zur historischen Theologie* 20. Tübingen, 1955.

Krüger, P. "Beiträge zum Codex Theodosianus. X. Zur Zeitbestimmung der Konstitutionen." *Zeitschrift der Savigny-Stiftung,* Romanistische Abteilung 42 (1921), 58–67.

Krusch, B. "Der heilige Florian und sein Stift." *Neues Archiv* 28 (1903), 339–392.

Kuhn, E. "Über das Verzeichnis der römischen Provinzen aufgesetz um 297." *Neue Jahrbücher* 115 (1877), 697–719.

Lacau, P. "Inscriptions latines du temple de Louxor." *Annales du Service des Antiquités de l'Égypte* 34 (1934), 17–46.

Lackner, W. "Zwei griechische Inedita über die Märtyrer Klaudios, Asterios, Neon und Theonilla." *Analecta Bollandiana* 87 (1969), 115–132.

—— "Eine uneditierte griechische Passion der kilikischen Märtyrin Domnina." *Analecta Bollandiana* 90 (1972), 241–259.

—— "Ein epigraphisches Zeugnis für den Praeses Ciliciae Marcianus in der Passion des Iulianos von Anazarbos." *Vigiliae Christianae* 27 (1973), 53–55.

Lafaurie, J. "Remarques sur les dates de quelques inscriptions du début du IVᵉ siècle." *Comptes Rendus de l'Académie des Inscriptions et Belles Lettres* 1965. 192–210.

—— "Dies Imperii Constantini Augusti: 25 Decembre 307. Essai sur quelques problèmes de chronologie constantinienne." *Mélanges d'archéologie et d'histoire offerts à A. Piganiol* 2, 795–806. Paris, 1966.

Laffranchi, L. "L'usurpazione di Domizio Alessandro nei documenti numismatici di Aquileia e delle altre zecche massenziane." *Numismatica* 13 (1947), 17–20. Reprinted with additions from *Aquileia Nostra* 9 (1938), 123–125.

Lallemand, J. "Le monnayage de Domitius Domitianus." *Revue Belge de Numismatique* 97 (1951), 89–103.

Lanata, G. "Gli atti del processo contro il centurione Marcello." *Byzantion* 41 (1972), 509–522.

—— "Note al Papiro Bodmer XX." *Museum Philologum Londiniense* 2 (1977), 207–226.

Lanzoni, F. "La 'Passio s. Sabini' o 'Savini'." *Römische Quartalschrift* 17 (1903), 1–26.

Laubscher, H. P. *Der Reliefschmuck des Galeriusbogens in Thessaloniki. Archäologische Forschungen* 1. Berlin, 1975.

Lauffer, S. *Diokletians Preisedikt. Texte und Kommentare* 5. Berlin, 1971.

Lawlor, H. J. *Eusebiana: Essays on the Ecclesiastical History of Eusebius, Bishop of Caesarea.* Oxford, 1912.

—— "The Chronology of Eusebius: Reply." *Classical Quarterly* 19 (1925), 94–95.

Leschi, L. "Le 'centenarium' d'Aqua Viva près de M'Doukal (commune mixte de Barika)." *Revue Africaine* 87 (1943), 5–22. Reprinted in his *Études d'épigraphie, d'archéologie et d'histoire africaines*, 47–57. Paris, 1957.

Lewis, N. "Exemption from Liturgy in Roman Egypt." *Atti dell' XI Congresso Internazionale di Papirologia*, 508–543. Milan, 1966.

Liebs, D. *Hermogenians Iuris Epitomae: Zum Stand der römischen Jurisprudenz im Zeitalter Diokletians. Abhandlungen der Akademie der Wissenschaften in Göttingen*, Philologisch-historische Klasse[3] 57. Göttingen, 1964.

Lietzmann, H. "Die älteste Gestalt der Passio SS. Carpi, Papylae et Agathonices." *Festgabe für K. Müller*, 46–57. Tübingen, 1922. Reprinted in his *Kleine Schriften* 1. *Texte und Untersuchungen* 67, 239–250. Berlin, 1958.

—— "Ein Blatt aus einer Weltchronik." *Quantulacumque: Studies presented to K. Lake*, 339–348. London, 1937. Reprinted in his *Kleine Schriften* 1, 420–429. Berlin, 1958.

Lifshitz, B. "Légions romaines en Palestine." *Hommages à M. Renard* 2. *Collection Latomus* 102, 458–469. Brussels, 1969.

Lucien-Brun, X. "Minervine, épouse ou concubine?" *Bulletin de l'Association Guillaume Budé* 1970. 391–406.

MacMullen, R. *Constantine*. New York, 1969.

—— "Two Notes on Imperial Properties." *Athenaeum*, n.s. 54 (1976), 19–36.

Maehler, H. "Zur Amtszeit des Präfekten Sossianus Hierocles." *Collectanea Papyrologica: Texts Published in Honor of H. C. Youtie* 2. *Papyrologische Texte und Abhandlungen* 20, 527–533. Bonn, 1976.

Malcus, B. "Die Prokonsuln von Asien von Diokletian bis Theodosius II." *Opuscula Atheniensia* 7 (1967), 91–160.

Manganaro, G. "Iscrizioni latine e greche di Catania tardo-imperiale." *Archivio storico per la Sicilia orientale*[4] 11–12 (1958–59), 5–30.

Marec, E. "Nouvelles bornes milliaires d'Hippone." *Bulletin Archéologique du Comité des Travaux Historiques et Scientifiques 1955–56* (1958), 101–111.

Marmorstein, A. "Dioclétien à la lumière de la littérature rabbinique." *Revue des Études Juives* 98 (1934), 19–43.

Masai, F. "Mélectures d'abbréviations romaines dans les Actes du centurion Marcel." *Scriptorium* 20 (1966), 11–30.

Maslev, S. "Die staatsrechtliche Stellung der byzantinischen Kaiserinnen." *Byzantinoslavica* 27 (1966), 308–343.

Matthews, J. F. Review of *PLRE* 1 (1971). *Classical Review*, n.s. 24 (1974), 97–106.

Maurice, J. "Mémoire sur la révolte d'Alexandre en Afrique." *Mémoires de la Société Nationale des Antiquaires de France* 61 (1902), 1–22.

—— *Numismatique constantinienne*. Paris, 1908–12.

Mazzarino, S. "Sull'*otium* di Massimiano Erculio dopo l'abdicazione." *Rendi-*

conti della Accademia Nazionale dei Lincei,[8] Classe di Scienze Morali, Storiche e Filologiche 8 (1953), 417–421.

Michaelidou-Nicolaou, I. "Antistius Sabinus, an unknown *praeses* of Cyprus." *Acta of the Fifth International Congress of Greek and Latin Epigraphy,* 381–383. Oxford, 1971.

Michon, E. "Le 'modius' de Ponte Puñide (Espagne)." *Mémoires de la Société Nationale des Antiquaires de France* 74 (1914), 215–312.

Miltner, F. "XXII. Vorläufiger Bericht über die Ausgrabungen in Ephesos." *Jahreshefte des Österreichischen Archäologischen Institutes in Wien* 44 (1959), Beiblatt 243–314.

Mispoulet, J.-B. "Diocèses et ateliers monétaires de l'Empire romaine sous le règne de Dioclétien." *Comptes Rendus de l'Académie des Inscriptions et Belles Lettres* 1908. 254–266.

—— "Chronologie de Maximien Hercule." *Comptes Rendus de l'Académie des Inscriptions et Belles Lettres* 1908. 455–465.

Mommsen, T. "Über die Zeitfolge der Verordnungen Diocletians und seiner Mitregenten." *Abhandlungen der königlichen preussischen Akademie der Wissenschaften* 1860. 349–447. Reprinted in his *Gesammelte Schriften* 2, 195–291. Berlin, 1905.

—— "Verzeichniss der römischen Provinzen aufgesetzt um 297." *Abhandlungen der königlichen preussischen Akademie der Wissenschaften* 1862. 489–518. Reprinted in his *Gesammelte Schriften* 5, 561–588. Berlin, 1908.

—— "De C. Caelii Saturnini titulo." *Memorie dell'Istituto di Corrispondenza Archeologica* 2 (Leipzig, 1865), 298–332.

—— "Additamenta secunda ad corporis vol. III." *Ephemeris Epigraphica* 4 (1881), 25–191.

—— "Consularia." *Hermes* 32 (1897), 538–553. Reprinted in his *Gesammelte Schriften* 6, 324–342. Berlin, 1910.

—— "Das Theodosische Gesetzbuch." *Zeitschrift der Savigny-Stiftung,* Romanistische Abteilung 21 (1900), 149–190. Reprinted in his *Gesammelte Schriften* 2, 371–405. Berlin, 1905.

—— "Die diocletianische Reichspraefectur." *Hermes* 36 (1901), 201–217. Reprinted in his *Gesammelte Schriften* 6, 284–299. Berlin, 1910.

—— "Consularia: Nachtrag zu Bd. 32 S. 538." *Hermes* 36 (1901), 602–605.

—— "Erwiderung." *Hermes* 37 (1902), 156–157.

Monceaux, P. "Les 'actes' de Sainte Crispine, martyre à Théveste." *Mélanges Boissier,* 383–389. Paris, 1903.

Moreau, J. "Fragment, découvert à Sinope, de l'édit de Constantin *de accusationibus.*" *Historia* 5 (1956), 254–256.

—— "Constantius I." *Jahrbuch für Antike und Christentum* 2 (1959), 158–160.

Morin, G. "La patrie de Saint Jérôme; le missorium d'Exsupérius: deux retractations nécessaires." *Revue Bénédictine* 38 (1926), 217–220.

Morris, J. "Prosopography of the Later Roman Empire." *Klio* 46 (1965), 361–365.

Mowat, R. "Milliaire de Carausius trouvé à Carlisle." *Bulletin de la Société Nationale des Antiquaires de France* 1895. 145–148, 351.

—— "Les noms de l'empereur Carausius." *Revue Numismatique*[3] 13 (1895), 129–133.

Müller, K. *Beiträge zur Geschichte der Verfassung der alten Kirche. Abhandlungen der preussischen Akademie der Wissenschaften,* Philosophisch-historische Klasse 1922, Abhandlung 3. Berlin, 1922.

Munro, J. A. R. "Some Pontic Milestones." *Journal of Hellenic Studies* 20 (1900), 159–166.

Nesselhauf, H. *Die spätrömische Verwaltung der gallisch-germanischen Länder. Abhandlungen der preussischen Akademie der Wissenschaften,* Philosophisch-historische Klasse 1938, Nr. 2. Berlin, 1938.

Nöldeke, T. "Die römischen Provinzen Palaestina Salutaris und Arabia." *Hermes* 10 (1876), 163–170.

Noll, R. "Eine goldene 'Kaiserfibel' aus Niederemmel vom Jahre 316." *Bonner Jahrbücher* 174 (1974), 221–244.

Novak, D. M. "Constantine and the Roman Senate: An Early Phase of the Christianization of the Roman Aristocracy." *Ancient Society* 10 (1979), 271–310.

Ochsenschlager, E. L., and Popović, V. "Excavations at Sirmium, Yugoslavia." *Archaeology* 26 (1973), 85–93.

Ohnesorge, W. *Die römische Provinzliste von 297. 1. Ein Beitrag zur Geschichte der römischen Provinzteilungen.* Duisburg, 1889.

Olivetti, A. "Sulle Stragi di Constantinopoli succedute alla Morte di Costantino il Grande." *Rivista di Filologia* 43 (1915), 67–79.

Opitz, H.-G. "Die Zeitfolge des arianischen Streites von den Anfängen bis zum Jahre 328." *Zeitschrift für die neutestamentliche Wissenschaft* 33 (1934), 131–159.

Orbeliani, R. d'. "Inscriptions and Monuments from Galatia." *Journal of Hellenic Studies* 44 (1924), 24–44.

Palanque, J.-R. "Chronologie constantinienne." *Revue des Études Anciennes* 40 (1938), 241–250.

—— "Les préfets du prétoire de Constantin." *Mélanges H. Grégoire* 2. *Annuaire de l'Institut de Philologie et d'Histoire Orientales et Slaves* 10, 483–491. Brussels, 1950.

—— "La préfecture du prétoire de Junius Bassus." *Mélanges d'archéologie et d'histoire offerts à A. Piganiol* 2, 837–842. Paris, 1966.

Paribeni, R. "Roma: Iscrizioni dei Fori Imperiali." *Notizie degli Scavi di Antichità*[6] 9 (1933), 431–523.

Passerini, A. "Osservazioni su alcuni punti della storia di Diocleziano e Massimiano." *Acme* 1 (1948), 131–194.

"Passiones tres martyrum Africanorum: SS. Maximae, Donatillae et Secundae, S. Typasii veterani, et S. Fabii vexilliferi." *Analecta Bollandiana* 9 (1890), 107–134.

Peeters, P. "Comment S. Athanase s'enfuit de Tyr en 335." *Bulletin de l'Académie Royale de Belgique,* Classe des Lettres⁵ 30 (1944), 131–177. Reprinted in his *Recherches d'Histoire et de Philologie Orientales* 2. *Subsidia Hagiographica* 27, 53–90. Brussels, 1951.

Petersen, H. "A Roman Prefect in Osrhoene."*Transactions of the American Philological Association* 107 (1977), 265–282.

Peyras, J. "L. Junius Junillus, *comes divini lateris.*" *Bulletin de la Société Nationale des Antiquaires de France* 1973. 24–27.

Pflaum, H.-G. "Les gouverneurs de la province romaine d'Arabie de 193 à 305." *Syria* 34 (1957), 128–144.

——— "Émission au nom des trois empereurs frappée par Carausius." *Revue Numismatique⁶* 2 (1959–60), 53–73.

——— "L'alliance entre Constantin et L. Domitius Alexander." *Bulletin d'Archéologie Algérienne* 1 (1962–65, publ. 1967), 159–161. Reprinted in his *Afrique romaine. Scripta Varia* 1, 226–228. Paris, 1978.

Picard, G. C. *Civitas Mactaritana. Karthago* 8. Tunis, 1957.

Picozzi, V. "Una campagna di Licinio contro Massenzio nel 310 non attestata dalle fonti letterarie." *Numismatica e Antichità Classiche* 5 (1976), 267–275.

Piganiol, A. "Notes épigraphiques." *Revue des Études Anciennes* 31 (1929), 139–150. Reprinted in his *Scripta Varia* 3. *Collection Latomus* 133, 245–257. Brussels, 1973.

——— *L'empereur Constantin.* Paris, 1932.

Poinssot, L. "La carrière de trois proconsuls d'Afrique contemporains de Dioclétien." *Mémoires de la Société Nationale des Antiquaires de France* 76 (1919–23), 264–341.

Poinssot, L., and Lantier, R. "Quatre préfets du prétoire contemporains de Constantin." *Comptes Rendus de l'Académie des Inscriptions et Belles Lettres* 1924. 229–233.

Polara, G. "Il nonno di Simmaco." *La Parola del Passato* 29 (1974), 261–266.

Poulle, A. "De l'ère Mauritanienne et de l'époque de la division de la Mauritanie Césarienne en deux provinces." *Annuaire de la Société Archéologique de la Province de Constantine* 6 (1862), 161–183.

——— "Inscriptions de la Mauritanie Sétifienne et de la Numidie." *Recueil des Notices et Mémoires de la Société Archéologique du Département de Constantine* 18 (1876/7), 463–633.

——— "Le Centenarium d'Aqua-Frigida et le Praeses T. Aurelius Litua." *Recueil des Notices et Mémoires de la Société Archéologique du Département de Constantine* 20 (1879/80), 255–265.

Premerstein, A. von. "Zu den Inschriften der Ostgermanen." *Zeitschrift für deutsches Altertum und deutsche Literatur* 60 (1923), 71–80.

Radet, G., and Paris, P. "Inscriptions de Pisidie, de Lycaonie et d'Isaurie," *Bulletin de Correspondance Hellénique* 10 (1886), 500–514; 11 (1887), 63–70.

Rahmani, I. E., Tisserant, E., Power, E., and Devreesse, R. "L'Onomasticon d'Eusèbe dans une ancienne traduction syriaque." *Revue de l'Orient Syrien* 23 (1922–23), 225–270.

Ramsay, W. M. "Unedited Inscriptions of Asia Minor." *Bulletin de Correspondance Hellénique* 7 (1886), 258–278, 297–328.

——— "Studies in the Roman Province Galatia. VI. Some Inscriptions of Colonia Caesarea Antiochia." *Journal of Roman Studies* 14 (1924), 172–205.

Rea, J. R. "Notes on Some III^d and IVth Century Documents." *Chronique d'Égypte* 46 (1971), 142–157.

——— Review of E. M. Husselman, *Michigan Papyri* 9 (Ann Arbor, 1971). *Journal of Egyptian Archeology* 60 (1974), 292–294.

Rees, B. R. "Theophanes of Hermopolis Magna." *Bulletin of the John Rylands Library* 52 (1968/9), 164–183.

Reinach, T. "Un nouveau proconsul d'Achaie." *Bulletin de Correspondance Hellénique* 24 (1900), 324–328.

Richardson, G. W. "The Chronology of Eusebius: Addendum." *Classical Quarterly* 19 (1925), 96–100.

Rist, J. M. "Basil's 'Neoplatonism': Its Background and Nature." In *Basil of Caesarea: Christian, Humanist, Ascetic,* ed. P. J. Fedwick, 139–222. Toronto, 1981.

Robert, J., and Robert, L. "Bulletin épigraphique." *Revue des Études Grecques* 69 (1956), 104–191.

——— "Bulletin épigraphique." *Revue des Études Grecques* 77 (1964), 127–259.

Roberts, C. H. "A Footnote to the Civil War of A.D. 324." *Journal of Egyptian Archaeology* 31 (1945), 113.

Robinson, D. M. "Greek and Latin Inscriptions from Sinope and Environs." *American Journal of Archaeology*^{2} 9 (1905), 294–333.

——— "Mr. Van Buren's Notes on Inscriptions from Sinope." *American Journal of Archaeology*^{2} 10 (1906), 429–433.

——— "New Inscriptions from Sinope." *American Journal of Philology* 27 (1906), 447–450.

Roethe, G. *Zur Geschichte der römischen Synoden im 3. und 4. Jahrhundert. Forschungen zur Kirchen- und Geistesgeschichte* 11: *Geistige Grundlagen römischer Kirchenpolitik,* Heft 2. Stuttgart, 1937.

Roueché, C. "Rome, Asia and Aphrodisias in the Third Century." *Journal of Roman Studies* 71 (1981), 103–120.

Rougé, J. "La pseudo-bigamie de Valentinien Ier." *Cahiers d'Histoire* 3 (1958), 5–15.

——— "Justine, la belle Sicilienne." *Latomus* 33 (1974), 676–679.

Rouquette, J.-M. "Trois nouveaux sarcophages chrétiens de Trinquetaille (Arles)." *Comptes Rendus de l'Académie des Inscriptions et Belles Lettres* 1974. 254–273.

Rousselle, A. "La chronologie de Maximien Hercule et le mythe de la Tétrarchie." *Dialogues d'Histoire Ancienne* 2 (1976), 445–466.

Roxan, M. M. *Roman Military Diplomas 1954–1977.* University of London: Institute of Archaeology, *Occasional Publication* No. 2. London, 1978.

Ste Croix, G. E. M. de. "Aspects of the 'Great' Persecution." *Harvard Theological Review* 47 (1954), 75–109.

Salama, P. "Les bornes milliaires de Djemila-Cuicul et leur intérêt pour l'histoire de la ville." *Revue Africaine* 95 (1951), 213–272.

―――― "À propos de l'usurpateur africain L. Domitius Alexander." *Bulletin van de Vereeniging tot Bevordering der Kennis van de Antieke Beschaving* 29 (1954), 67–74.

―――― "Un follis d'Alexandre tyran conservé à Madrid." *Numario Hispánico* 9 (1960), 171–177.

―――― "Les trésors maxentiens de Tripolitaine: rapport préliminaire." *Libya Antiqua* 3/4 (1966/7), 21–27.

Salvo, L. de. "La data d'istituzione delle provincie d'Aegyptus Iovia e d'Aegyptus Herculia." *Aegyptus* 44 (1964), 34–46.

Saumagne, C. "Un tarif fiscal au quatrième siècle de notre ère." *Karthago* 1 (1950), 105–200.

Savigny, F. K. von. "Römische Steuerverfassung unter den Kaisern." *Vermischte Schriften* 2, 67–215. Berlin, 1850. The greater part of the essay was originally published in *Abhandlungen der Akademie der Wissenschaften zu Berlin* 1822–23. 27–71.

Schäfer, O. *Die beiden Panegyrici des Mamertinus und die Geschichte des Kaisers Maximianus Herculius.* Diss. Strassburg, 1914.

Schoenebeck, H. von. *Beiträge zur Religionspolitik des Maxentius und Constantin. Klio,* Beiheft 43. Berlin, 1939.

Schrörs, H. "Die Aktenstücke in betreff des Konzils von Arles (314). Textverbesserungen und Erläuterungen." *Zeitschrift der Savigny-Stiftung,* Kanonische Abteilung 11 (1921), 429–439.

Schulthess, A. *Die syrischen Kanones der Synoden von Nicaea bis Chalcedon nebst einigen zugehörigen Dokumenten herausgegeben. Abhandlungen der königlichen Gesellschaft der Wissenschaften zu Göttingen,* Philologisch-historische Klasse, n.f. 10.2. Göttingen, 1908.

Schulze, W. *Zur Geschichte der lateinischen Eigennamen. Abhandlungen der königlichen Gesellschaft der Wissenschaften zu Göttingen,* Philologisch-historische Klasse, n.f. 5.5. Göttingen, 1904.

Schwartz, E. "Zur Geschichte des Athanasius." *Nachrichten von der königlichen Gesellschaft der Wissenschaften zu Göttingen,* Philologisch-historische Klasse 1904. 333–401, 518–547; 1905. 164–187, 257–299, 305–374; 1911.

367–426, 469–522. Largely reprinted in his *Gesammelte Schriften* 3 (Berlin, 1959), except for 1904. 518–547 which is reprinted as "Der Aufstieg Konstantins zur Alleinherrschaft," in H. Kraft, ed., *Konstantin der Grosse. Wege der Forschung* 131, 109–144, Darmstadt, 1974.

—— "Constantin." *Meister der Politik* 1², 275–324. Stuttgart and Berlin, 1923. Reprinted in his *Charakterköpfe aus der Antike²*, 223–280. Leipzig, 1943.

—— *Über die Bischofslisten der Synoden von Chalkedon, Nicaea und Konstantinopel. Abhandlungen der Bayerischen Akademie der Wissenschaften*, Philosophisch-historische Abteilung, n.f. 13. Munich, 1937.

Schwartz, J. *L. Domitius Domitianus: Étude numismatique et papyrologique. Papyrologica Bruxellensia* 12. Brussels, 1975.

—— "L. Domitius Domitianus." *Zeitschrift für Papyrologie und Epigraphik* 25 (1977), 217–220.

Seeck, O. "Die Zeitfolge der Gesetze Constantins." *Zeitschrift der Savigny-Stiftung*, Romanistische Abteilung 10 (1889), 1–44, 177–251.

—— "Zur Entstehungsgeschichte des Donatismus." *Zeitschrift für Kirchengeschichte* 10 (1889), 505–568.

—— "Die imperatorischen Acclamationen im vierten Jahrhundert." *Rheinisches Museum*, n.f. 48 (1893), 196–207.

—— "Zur Entstehung des Indictionencyclus." *Deutsche Zeitschrift für Geschichtswissenschaft* 12 (1894), 279–296.

—— "Die Schätzungsordnung Diocletians." *Zeitschrift für Social- und Wirtschaftsgeschichte* 4 (1896), 275–342.

—— "Zu den Festmünzen Konstantins und seiner Familie." *Zeitschrift für Numismatik* 21 (1898), 17–65.

—— "Zur Chronologie des Kaisers Licinius." *Hermes* 36 (1901), 28–35.

—— "Zur Chronologie Constantins." *Hermes* 37 (1902), 155–156.

—— "Zur Chronologie und Quellenkritik der Ammianus Marcellinus." *Hermes* 41 (1906), 481–539.

—— "Neue und alte Daten zur Geschichte Diocletians und Constantins." *Rheinisches Museum*, n.f. 62 (1907), 489–535.

—— "Urkundenfälschungen des 4. Jahrhunderts." *Zeitschrift für Kirchengeschichte* 30 (1909), 181–227, 399–433.

—— "Die Reichspraefektur des vierten Jahrhunderts." *Rheinisches Museum*, n.f. 69 (1914), 1–39.

Seston, W. "Recherches sur la chronologie du règne de Constantin le Grand." *Revue des Études Anciennes* 39 (1937), 197–218.

—— "De l'authenticité et de la date de l'édit de Dioclétien contre les Manichéens." *Mélanges de philologie, de littérature et d'histoire anciennes offerts à A. Ernout*, 345–354. Paris, 1940.

—— "Jovius et Herculius ou l'"épiphanie' des Tétrarques." *Historia* 1 (1950), 257–266.

——— "À propos de la *Passio Marcelli centurionis:* Remarques sur les origines de la persécution de Dioclétien." *Aux Sources de la Tradition chrétienne: Mélanges offerts à M. Goguel,* 239–246. Neuchâtel and Paris, 1950.

——— "La Conférence de Carnuntum et le 'dies imperii' de Licinius." *Carnuntina: Ergebnisse der Forschungen über die Grenzprovinzen des römischen Reiches: Vorträge beim Internationalen Kongress der Altertumsforscher Carnuntum 1955. Römische Forschungen in Niederösterreich* 3, 175–186. Graz and Cologne, 1956.

Shackleton Bailey, D. "Ausoniana." *American Journal of Philology* 97 (1976), 248–261.

Smith, R. E. "The Regnal and Tribunician Dates of Maximianus Herculius." *Latomus* 31 (1972), 1058–1071.

Sölch, J. "Bithynische Städte im Altertum." *Klio* 19 (1925), 140–188.

Sotgiu, G. "Un miliario sardo di L. Domitius Alexander e l'ampiezza della sua rivolta." *Archivio Storico Sardo* 29 (1964), 149–158.

Srejović, J. "An Imperial Roman Palace in Serbia." *Illustrated London News* 263 (October 1975), 97–99.

Stein, E. "Kleine Beiträge zur römischen Geschichte." *Hermes* 52 (1917), 558–593.

——— "À propos d'un livre récent sur la liste des préfets du prétoire." *Byzantion* 9 (1934), 327–353.

Steinwenter, A. "Eine vergessene Kaiserkonstitution." *Studi in onore di E. Betti* 4, 137–144. Milan, 1962.

Strauss, R. "Les monnaies divisionnaires de Trèves après la réforme de Dioclétien." *Revue Numismatique*⁵ 16 (1954), 19–69.

Sutherland, C. H. V. *Roman Imperial Coinage* 6: *From Diocletian's Reform (A.D. 294) to the Death of Maximinus (A.D. 313).* London, 1967.

Sydenham, E. A. "The Vicissitudes of Maximian after his Abdication." *Numismatic Chronicle*⁵ 14 (1934), 141–165.

Syme, R. "The Ancestry of Constantine." *Bonner Historia-Augusta-Colloquium 1971* (1974), 237–253.

Thomas, J. D. Review of Vandersleyen, *Chronologie* (1962). *Journal of Hellenic Studies* 84 (1964), 207.

———– "Chronological Notes on Documentary Papyri." *Zeitschrift für Papyrologie und Epigraphik* 6 (1970), 175–182.

——— "On Dating by Regnal Years of Diocletian, Maximian and the Caesars." *Chronique d'Égypte* 46 (1971), 173–179.

——— "The Disappearance of the Dekaprotoi in Egypt." *Proceedings of the Fourteenth International Congress of Papyrologists,* 66. London, 1975.

——— "The Date of the Revolt of L. Domitius Domitianus." *Zeitschrift für Papyrologie und Epigraphik* 22 (1976), 253–279.

——— "An Unrecognized Edict of Constantine (*P. Oxy.* 889)." *Ancient Society* 7 (1976), 301–308.

―――― "Epigraphai and Indictions in the Reign of Diocletian." *Bulletin of the American Society of Papyrologists* 15 (1978), 133-145.

Tomassetti, G. "Note sui Prefetti di Roma." *Museo Italiano di Antichità Classica* 3 (1890), 41-68, 479-550.

Tomlin, R. "The Date of the 'Barbarian Conspiracy'." *Britannia* 5 (1974), 303-309.

Tschantz, G., Schwartz, J., Collomp, P., and Karst, R. "Papyrus grecs de la Bibliothèque nationale et universitaire de Strasbourg." *Bulletin de la Faculté des Lettres de Strasbourg* 15 (1937), 173-176, 229-323.

Turner, C. H. "Canons Attributed to the Council of Constantinople A.D. 381, Together with the Names of the Bishops, from Two Patmos Mss." *Journal of Theological Studies* 15 (1914), 161-178.

―――― "Adversaria Critica: Notes on the Anti-Donatist Dossier and on Optatus, Books I, II." *Journal of Theological Studies* 27 (1926), 283-296.

Unger, J. "De censibus provinciarum Romanarum." *Leipziger Studien zur Classischen Philologie* 10 (1887), 1-76.

Vandersleyen, C. "Le préfet d'Égypte de la colonne de Pompée à Alexandrie." *Chronique d'Égypte* 33 (1958), 113-134.

Velkov, V. "Zu den Fragmenta Vaticana 315 (Durocortorum oder Durostorum?)" *Charisteria F. Novotný octogenario oblata,* 151-153. Prague, 1962.

Vetters, H. *Dacia Ripensis.* Österreichische Akademie der Wissenschaften: *Schriften der Balkankommission,* Antiquarische Abteilung 11.1. Vienna, 1950.

Vickers, M. "The Hippodrome at Thessaloniki." *Journal of Roman Studies* 62 (1972), 25-32.

―――― "Observations on the Octagon at Thessaloniki." *Journal of Roman Studies* 63 (1973), 111-120.

Violet, B. *Die palaestinischen Märtyrer des Eusebius von Caesarea. Texte und Untersuchungen* 14.4. Leipzig, 1896.

Vogt, J. "Streitfragen um Konstantin den Grossen." *Römische Mitteilungen* 58 (1943), 190-203.

―――― *Konstantin der Grosse und sein Jahrhundert.* Munich, 1949; second edition, 1960.

―――― "Pagans and Christians in the Family of Constantine the Great." *The Conflict between Paganism and Christianity in the Fourth Century,* ed. A. Momigliano, 38-55. Oxford, 1963. Originally published as "Heiden und Christen in der Familie Constantins der Grossen." *Eranion: Festschrift für H. Hommel,* 149-168. Tubingen, 1961.

―――― "Helena Augusta, das Kreuz und die Juden: Fragen um die Mutter Constantins des Grossen." *Saeculum* 27 (1976), 211-222. An English version of this article is printed in *Classical Folia* 31 (1977), 135-151.

Volterra, E. "Remarques sur les *Inscriptiones* de quelques Constitutions de Dioclétien." *Mélanges d'histoire ancienne offerts à W. Seston,* 489–508. Paris, 1974.

Vulić, N. "Les deux Dacies." *Le Musée Belge* 27 (1923), 253–259.

Webb, P. H. "The Reign and Coinage of Carausius." *Numismatic Chronicle*[4] 7 (1907), 1–88.

———— "The Linchmere Hoard." *Numismatic Chronicle*[5] 5 (1925), 173–235.

Weinstock, S. "Saturnalien und Neujahrsfest in den Märtyreracten." *Mullus: Festschrift T. Klauser. Jahrbuch für Antike und Christentum,* Ergänzungsband 1, 391–400. Münster, 1964.

Westerhuis, D. J. A. *Origo Constantini Imperatoris sive Anonymi Valesiani Pars Prior.* Diss. Groningen, 1906.

Wilhelm, A. "Griechische Grabinschriften aus Kleinasien." *Sitzungsberichte der preussischen Akademie der Wissenschaften,* Philosophisch-historische Klasse 1932. 792–865.

Winkler, G. *Die Reichsbeamten von Noricum und ihre Personal bis zum Ende der römischen Herrschaft. Sitzungsberichte der Österreichischen Akademie der Wissenschaften,* Philosophisch-historische Klasse 261.2. Vienna, 1969.

Wistrand, E. "A Note on the *geminus natalis* of the Emperor Maximian," *Eranos* 62 (1964), 131–145.

Wolff, H. J. "Vorgregorianische Reskriptensammlungen." *Zeitschrift der Savigny-Stiftung,* Romanistische Abteilung 69 (1952), 128–153.

Youtie, L. C., Hagedorn, D., and Youtie, H. C. "Urkunden aus Panopolis." *Zeitschrift für Papyrologie und Epigraphik* 7 (1971), 1–40; 8 (1971), 209–234; 10 (1973), 101–170.

INDEX OF TEXTS DISCUSSED

INDEX OF PERSONS

295

FRAGMENTARY NAMES